FOOTSTEPS IN THE SKY

An Informal Review of U.S. Airlines Inflight Service 1920s to the Present

by

Helen E. McLaughlin

Best Wishes
Helen Elizabeth McLaughlin

Footsteps In The Sky

by Helen E. McLaughlin

First Printing 1994

ISBN: 0-930161-02-5

Published by:
State of the Art, Ltd.
4942 Morrison Road
Denver, Colorado 80219
(303) 936-1978

Distributed by:
Aviation Book Company
25133 Anza Drive
Santa Clarita, California 91355
(800) 423-2708

Helen E. (Betty Bailey) McLaughlin, author of *Walking On Air* and *Footsteps In The Sky*. She was a Hostess for Continental Air Lines 1943-1945 and a Stewardess for United Air Lines 1946-1947.

This book is dedicated to the skilled men and women who have left their footprints in the sky.

Perhaps Robert F. Six, former President and Chairman of the Board Emeritus of Continental Airlines worded it best when he said that flight attendants are:

. . . there to comfort the apprehensive, cheer the saddened, guide and assist the aged, handicapped and bewildered, divert and watch over the minor traveling alone, the guardian of the sound sleeper and the friendly ear of the first flier. [You] had confidence, charm and authority, yet you could be gentle with the innocent and stern with fools. Your wings were your badge, your manner, your medals.

From a speech given at the 43rd reunion of Continental's inflight service

TABLE OF CONTENTS

Note: In the early era of commercial aviation, some airlines used the words *Air Lines* (example: *United Air Lines*). As logos changed for jet aircraft, the name changed to *Airlines* (example: *United Airlines*). *Delta Air Lines* has remained the same. American has always been *American Airlines*. Other name changes have taken place for other airlines.

Author "Betty" Bailey McLaughlin.
Continental Air Line Hostess, 1943-1945.

Preface

As a young girl, weekly Sunday drives in the family car were a pastime our family enjoyed. My father always drove to the Denver Stapleton Airport when the United Air Lines' flight was due to land. We joined the crowds of people who were there to see the big plane land and take off. This was always thrilling for me. I always watched the stewardess. I dreamed of becoming one myself. . . .

I learned that being a registered nurse was a requirement to become a stewardess. Chemistry was my *Waterloo!* I was not able to pass this requirement for nursing school. Instead, I entered college and set my sights on a B.A. degree in Sociology and also to get qualified to teach in Elementary Education.

While I was in college the U.S. was attacked by Japanese fighters at Pearl Harbor on December 7, 1941 and the U.S. entered World War II. The nurses on the airlines were needed in the war effort and the airlines now wanted college graduates. As fate would have it, the nursing requirement was dropped. I got the opportunity to become an air hostess for Continental Air Lines in war time conditions and a stewardess for United Air Lines in the post war build up of commercial aviation.

I have always had a keen interest in aviation and kept informed of the vast changes in inflight service in each decade since the 1940's. I have also kept in close contact with the special bonding of airline friends, both with Continental and United Airlines. I am a member of their inflight organizations: Continental's Golden Penguins and United's Clipped Wings.

At the time of United's 50th Anniversary of stewardess service in May 1980, I attended United's Clipped Wings celebration in New York City at the Plaza Hotel. Some of my Denver United Airline friends had flown to New York for the festivities. It was at this time I decided to write a book about the history of inflight service and how the job became a career of professionals.

Walking On Air was published in December 1986. The wonderful people I had known and met with the airlines made this possible. A book of individuals' experiences they laced with humor.

My Denver publisher had a disastrous fire in September of 1992 and all my remaining books were destroyed. I have since undertaken the revising, updating and expanding for *Footsteps In The Sky: An Informal Review Of U.S. Airlines' Inflight Service.*

I am indebted to so many in inflight service who have given me information, stories and photographs.

An Eastern Air Transport Curtiss Condor, 1931. (Eastern Airlines Photo)

50th Anniversary
Flight Attendant Service
1930-1980
50 Years of Flight Attendant Service
On May 15, 1930 eight young women took to the air as flight attendants for
a United Airlines predecessor. They were the world's first stewardesses, and they pioneered
a profession for women and men with airlines around the globe.

Acknowledgements

I wish to thank the following airlines for their information on inflight service and photographs:

Aloha Airlines - Inflight Service

American Airlines, Inc. - *Corporate Communications*, Martha McFarland-Goetz

Continental Airlines - Rick Webb, Bert Astrup, and Debbie Terrago of Inflight Training and their staff; Sherrill Dickey and Captain James Minor

Capital Airlines Retired Association - James McLendon and Portland Mainliner Club President

Delta Air Lines - *Corporate Communications* Manager, Jackie B. Pate

Eastern Airlines - Silverliners International; Trudy Von Hoven Pracny; Elinor Lykins; Willie Podesta Young; Jean Suluta Brown; Lynn Grubb

Mesaba Northwest Airlink - V.P. Patrick Thompson; Ann Moreno; Inflight Service

Northwest Airlines Inc. - V.P. Inflight Service, Hector Adler; Carol J. Grewing, Director Customer Service Training

TWA - Inflight Service; Jerrlea Costello Currigan, President of TWA's Clipped Wings International; Uli Derickson; Floyd D. Hall

Trump Shuttle - Becky Barnes Hobart

United Airlines - *Corporate Communications*; Inflight Training; Jackie Pryor; John Corpening; Doug Tulp

USAir - *Corporate Communications*; Inflight Service; Sharon Hendry, and Sandy Mixon of Charlotte, NC

I am also indebted to the stewardesses, hostesses and flight attendants whose stories and photographs made it possible to tell this informal history of U.S. airlines' inflight service. Special thanks to the following for their assistance and the use of their scrapbooks:

American Airlines - Izola Readle Tanner; Helen Vaubel Boyd and Grace Humbert Benge

Capital Airlines - Margaret Jo Humbert; Shanna Madden Nicholson; June Porter Rittenhouse; Florence Wiese Espy;

Continental Airlines - Mildred "Tommie" Heck Carlisle; Clara Lou Casey Bascom; Sherrill Dickey

TWA - Ruth Ensley McFarland; Teresa Ensley Terrell; Pauline Ensley Marshall; Ona Gieschen, Annie Gilmore Schmitt, Marion Korenchan Wozniak, Mildred Drews Gesell.

United Airlines - Margaret Jo Humbert; Marie Hess Conway; Mary O'Connor; Nan Cavanagh; Virginia Riley; ***Vicy Morris Young, Clipped Wings Historian.***

Continental Airlines 60th Anniversary Commemorative Flight July 15, 1994: photo courtesy of the *Albequerque Journal.*

My thanks to Ron Chappell, the manager and owner of Photographic Arts in Moline, Illinois, for copying photos and the colorization of the cover photos; Paul Arbor, *Time/Life* Picture Sales; Dale Cavanagh, former United Captain and Management in Pilot Training for his advice and editing; John T. Corpening, United flight attendant and aviation historian for his assistance and as author of *First Steps*, about early couriers and stewards; and Dr. Charles C. Quarles, aviation historian, for his encouragement and input to develop *Footsteps In The Sky*: with contacts, information on inflight service, photos, wings, and logos from his aviation archives; Ruth Bailey for editing; Allyson Townend for layout.

Wings for the cachet for Jo Humbert; photographer, David Crosby. The cachet was developed by James McLendon, formerly of Capital Airlines and manager of the United Portland Station. I appreciate his assistance to me on my project.

Alexander C. Morton: Information
from: *Commemorative Edition,*
The 50th Anniversary Of The
Flight Attendants 1930 - 1980

Pan American Airways System Pacific Division stewards, 1930.

Dr. Charles C. Quarles, D.D.S, P.A.
Aviation Historian

The history of commercial aviation and inflight service is being recorded by Aviation Historians. Dr. Charles C. Quarles, D.D.S. by profession and an Aviation Historian by avocation is well known in this field. I am indebted to him for his assistance in the writing of Footsteps In The Sky.

Dr. Charles Quarles, Aviation Historian, as weekend flight attendant for Sentimental Journey's charter DC-3 flights, 1985.

Dr. Charles Quarles, a North Carolina dentist, has shown an avid interest in commercial airlines for as long as he can remember. His father used to take him to the Kanawaha Airport outside Charleston, West Virginia to watch propeller driven airliners take off and land. "That was when a chain-link fence allowed a kid to look at the airplanes," he related. "Douglas DC-3s were flying, there was adventure in air travel and to me, it was exciting! I grew up with these DC-3s, Convairs, Martins, DC-7s and the Constellations."

Charles has kept his enthusiasm and interest in aviation. He pursued a professional career as a graduate with honors from West Virginia University Medical Center's School of Dentistry and an avocation as an aviation collector and historian in his spare time. He has gathered one of the largest private collections of airline memorabilia in the world. He has amassed a collection of over 3,000 wing and cap insignias of pilots, inflight pursers, stewardesses, hostesses and flight attendants. His collection includes: uniforms; manuals; books; tapes; slides; photographs; airline logos; post cards; timetables; baggage tags; and airline china and silverware of the 1940s and 1950s when first class airline passengers received elegant dining service to compare with cruise ship luxury. His collection includes models of aircraft made specifically for the airlines by Boeing and McDonnell Aircraft. These were used for display purposes in executive offices and at tour agencies. Many other airline items are collected and on display in a large finished basement at his home in Spindale, North Carolina. Special heating and air flow protects uniform fibers.

Charles became a flight attendant in a 1940 uniform on weekends for Sentimental Journey's charter DC-3 flights in 1985. He drove 4 hours to Bluefield, West Virginia to work these flights. He says, "That was my living part of airline history before liability insurance rates rose and grounded the company."

Charles corresponds constantly with contacts to follow through on leads for collectibles. He attends trade shows, airline hobby clubs and conventions and is associate historian for the Capital Airline Association. He is consulted by aviation enthusiasts and authors for his knowledge and expertise.

I became acquainted with Charles after my first book, *Walking on Air*, was published. I have also been actively involved in helping to add items to his collection. He has helped me in innumerable ways in my own quest for information for *Footsteps in the Sky*. He continues his contribution to aviation helping preserve airline history. His story follows . . . .

A DREAM TAKES FLIGHT

"Children tend to be fascinated by airports and the airliners that land and take off at them. Their emotions about the experience are generally one of two: either that of general interest or total captivation. Something magical happens to those that are captivated, most likely a life long love of airplanes and flying. That is just what happened to me when I saw the Capital, Piedmont, American, and Eastern airliners that served the Charleston, West Virginia Airport in the 1950's when I was a child. A need arises that says *I have to be part of this; I need to participate in this industry of adventure.* People who feel this way avidly pursue careers with the airlines, be it as a pilot, flight attendant, mechanic, dispatcher, or other avenue that lets them be close to it. They have a dream.

"Most of us have a special emotional compartment that lets us store our dream until it can be acted upon, while at the same time keeping the captivation alive. People are shocked when they hear "I was an attorney, but now I'm a flight attendant." Not strange at all, just the desire for something finally becoming reality. A career in dentistry has certainly been a challenging and rewarding profession, yet nothing can compare when I took to the sky as a flight attendant a few years ago for a DC-3 luxury charter airline. A beautifully preserved vintage airliner let my dream take flight while flying in the past at the same time. The combination is one that I will always cherish. Being part of an airline crew is something special indeed. It is the essence of being part of a team, a team to which very few people will ever belong. I think that's what people miss the most when they stop flying, that instant kinship that crew members have with each other.

"Although no longer flying, the captivation continues with an ever growing collection of airline memorabilia. It has literally taken over the lower level of my home, yet I'll always find room for more things from people and places that tell the story of the airlines. Looking at a uniform wing from the 1930's evokes memories of long days inside an unpressurized airplane filled with people who were on an adventure to be sure. Did that wing venture to Paris or Peoria? Sunshine or a dangerous storm? Sad to be put away in a box when the stewardess married and had to resign? The stories it could tell!! Meanwhile my dream is alive and well."

INTRODUCTION

Life was never the same after the invention of the airplane at the turn of the century. The network of U.S. airways was determined in the 1920s and 1930s by Postmaster Generals Brown and Farley who were given the power by Congress to consolidate air mail routes in the best interest of the American public. Thus, the *Big Four* major airlines' emerged: United Air Lines, Eastern Air Lines, American Airlines, and Transcontinental and Western Airlines. Some airlines were left out of this first network.

At first only mail was flown, but gradually passenger travel started to build. Flying was done in daylight hours, because night flying was still considered to be hazardous. The first few early passengers were given helmets, goggles and parachutes, and sometimes had to sit on mail bags, which were given first priority. At mealtimes the copilot served apples, sandwiches and coffee from a thermos. If a passenger became airsick he had to fend for himself. Something better had to follow - inflight service. *Footsteps In The Sky* tells the story of the vast changes in inflight service from the 1920s to the present. Individual, often humorous, vignettes of early stewards, hostesses, and stewardesses documented by photographs chronicle these changes through each decade to today's professional flight attendants.

The *First Steps* of early couriers and stewards in the 1920s is written by John T. Corpening (United Airlines' Inflight Training Instructor and aviation historian). The story is told of the combined idea of Steve Stimpson and Ellen Church's "Original Eight" stewardesses for Boeing Air Transport, the predecessor of United Air Lines, on May 15, 1930. As one of the Original Eight, Harriet Fry Iden tells in her own words about her hiring, training, and experiences. This was given to me by her husband Howard Iden from Harriet's speaking notes. Other airlines followed with their first hostesses and stewardesses. In 1931 Eastern Air Lines hired its first seven young women on a year's probation to be hostesses on their 18-passenger Curtiss Condors. By 1933 American Airways had trained four registered nurses as their first stewardesses. In 1935 TWA trained its first hostess class. Inflight service was now well established and highly accepted not only in America, but in Europe as well.

The onset of World War II ushered in a new era during the 1940's. The requirement that all stewardesses be registered nurses was dropped because nurses were needed in the war effort. However, the requirements for single women of a certain age, dimensions of height and weight, and 20/20 vision were still strictly enforced. Instead of registered nurses, college graduates or young women with previous experience working with the public were now preferred, opening up new horizons. The job took on a glamorous image and even though salaries were low and job security nonexistent, many young women wanted to become airline stewardesses and only a few were chosen. The average stewardess at that time stayed two years, or until she married.

In the late 1940s stewardesses were required to sign a contract agreeing to quit by age 32. They were beginning to think the hiring practices the airlines used were discriminatory. A United stewardess, Ada Brown, in 1946 began organizing stewardesses into a bargaining force, with the help of the Air Line Pilots Association. Within two months a majority of United's stewardesses were organized into the first airline association and soon other airlines' stewardesses also organized unions. As a result, under the unions, wages and working conditions started to improve.

Other changes were also taking place in the flight attendant profession. For the first time since the early stewards, male flight attendants were being hired by the airlines for particular flights. United Air Lines, for example, hired eight Hawaiian men to serve on their route to Hawaii. The union had protested the hiring of an *island girl* and United hired the Hawaiian men instead, claiming that particular flights required heavy lifting. The men could marry and have families, whereas the stewardesses had to remain single. There were now separate seniority lists for men and for women. This practice was not changed until July 1976.

The Civil Rights Act of 1964 prohibited discrimination on the basis of age, sex, race and marital status. The act also brought about a revision of job training and requirements. The new name flight attendant was adopted to include men and women.

The issue of flight attendants returning to work after giving birth first affected TWA in 1983, and then other airlines as well. Previously, flight attendants were required to give up their positions when they became mothers. Individual cases were determined in court for flight attendants wanting to return to their jobs lost because of the *no children* requirement at the time they were hired. Maternity uniforms and new work rules for maternity leaves and nursing mothers were adopted by airlines.

Commercial air travel is constantly changing through legislation that governs the airways and by new and better equipment. Today's flight attendants are safety conscious, highly trained, skilled and organized professionals in a career serving masses of people. They are men and women of all ages and races, married with families, single parents, or unmarried. They have their own input into their profession of inflight service through total involvement with the company they work for.

For more than sixty years flight attendants have served the public and the airlines well. In the past few years several of the airlines have celebrated fifty and sixty years of inflight service and have honored their flight attendants past and present. If there is a phrase which describes flight attendants as a whole, and commercial airlines in general, it is *Professional People-Pleasers* and *Today's Safety Specialists*. This is their story. . . .

Emblem for United Airlines' celebration of 50 years of inflight service: 1930-1980. (United Airlines Photo)

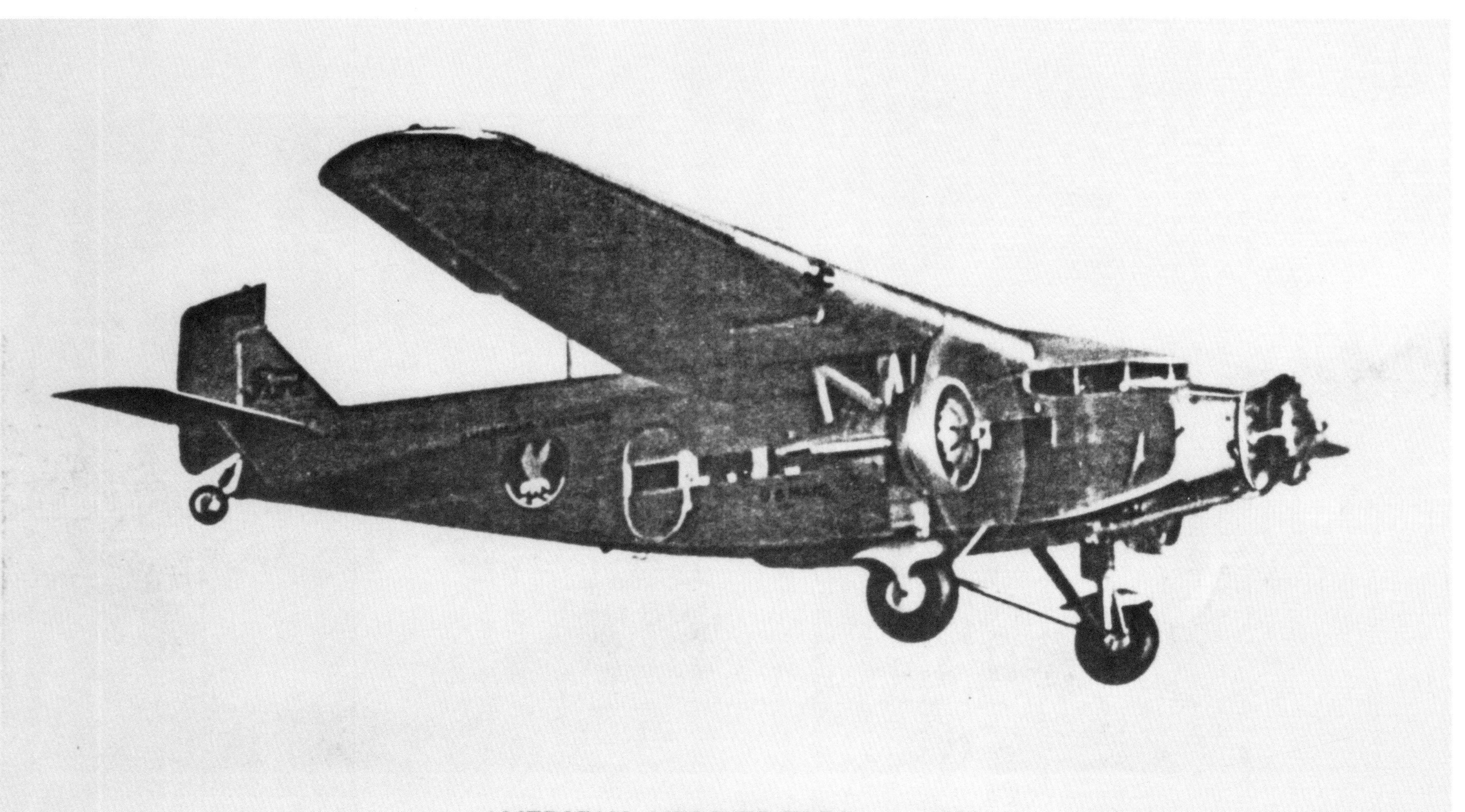

AMERICAN AIRLINES FORD 1928

The Ford Tri-Motor "Tin Goose", built by Stout Metal Airplane Co., a division of the Ford Motor Co., carried 10 to 14 passengers. The all-metal plane had corrugated skin and a two-man cockpit. Some models of this plane are still in use in various parts of the world.

THE EARLY ERA

1920 - 1930:

THE FIRST STEPS of early couriers and stewards in the 1920s.

THE "ORIGINAL EIGHT," the world's first stewardesses who, in 1930, pioneered a new age that followed for women in the sky.

1930 - 1940:

Other airlines followed with their first hostesses and stewardesses:

Eastern Air Transport (Eastern Air Lines) - 1931
American Airways (American Airlines) - 1933
Transcontinental and Western Airlines (TWA) - 1935
Northwest Airlines - 1939

FIRST STEPS
John Corpening
Aviation Historian and Author

John T. Corpening, Aviation Historian. United Airlines' inflight training photo, 1993.

During the early 1920s when the commercial airlines of the world were struggling to get aloft, little if any thought, or for that matter attention, was given to inflight service. Airliners of the era were small, cramped, and didn't have the cabin space to accommodate an attendant. Passengers were literally left to fend for themselves as the early airlines assumed that they would survive the flight! However, in 1922 Daimler Airways of Britain did something remarkable; it hired the world's first flight stewards. They were undoubtedly hired because of their small stature and weight. The *cabin boys* reportedly didn't serve any refreshments, but offered passengers general assistance and reassurance, a good dose of which was needed in the early days of *flying contraptions*. With these first footsteps in the sky, the career of the flight attendant was launched.

A Stout Air Services courier sightsees along with passengers between Grand Rapids and Detroit, about 1926.

Jack Sanderson was one of the world's first three flight attendants. He flew for Britain's Daimler Airways and later died in a crash, about 1922.

The first attendants in the United States began flying in 1926 when Stout Air Services of Detroit hired male aerial couriers to serve aboard their Ford Trimotors between Detroit and Grand Rapids, Michigan. How long they served is unknown. Stout became part of the United conglomerate in 1929.

1928 also was a banner year for inflight service when several airlines around the world introduced flight attendants on their aircraft. Western Air Express, a forerunner of Western Airlines, began using stewards on the *model airway* between Los Angeles and San Francisco. The concept was to demonstrate to the public just how safe, reliable, and comfortable airline travel could be. Box lunches were catered by the *Pig 'n' Whistle* restaurant in Los Angeles. Miles Davis was the first steward on the run. Although a success, the experiment was terminated about 1931.

Following the new trend, Lufthansa of Germany hired waiter Arthur Hofe to serve lunch aboard their Junkers aircraft between Berlin and Vienna. Mexicana, established to safely transport cash payrolls around rugged Mexico, employed stewards on their Ford Trimotors. Air Union, a forerunner of Air France, hired stewards for their luxury *Golden Ray* service between London and Paris.

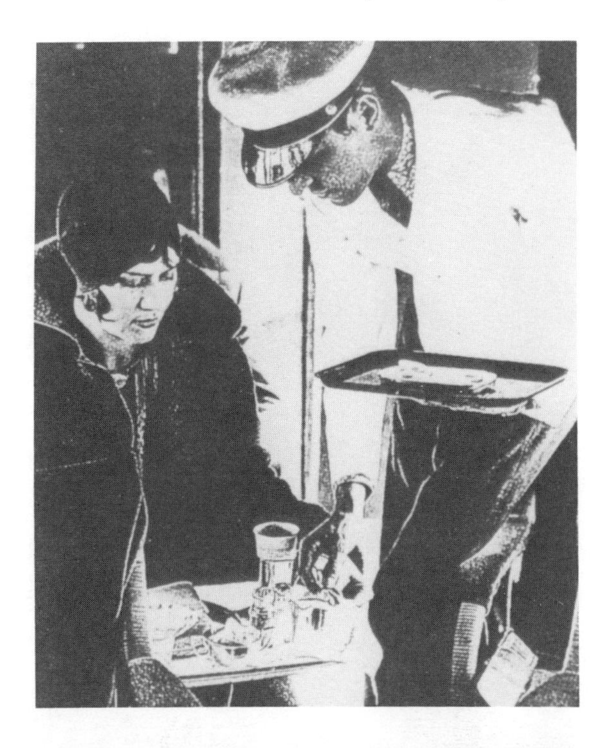

Steward serving lunch aboard Western Air Express between San Francisco and Los Angeles, about 1928.

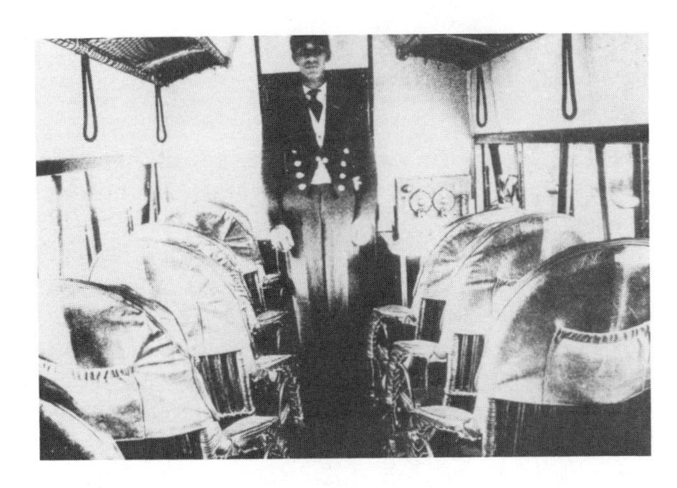

A Mexican steward awaits passengers, about 1928.

The flight attendant's role as a safety expert was evident early on. Imperial Airways (now British Airways), issued very implicit ditching instructions to their stewards in case their craft went down in the English Channel. These included assisting passengers into their life belts and handing out a brochure to each passenger that implored them to listen to the steward's instructions, because no public address system was on board.

Transcontinental Air Transport (now TWA), employed several male couriers on their trimotor aircraft as well. Prior to their introductions, TAT first officers (or first mates as they were referred to then) were required to serve passengers their meals. No doubt they were now happy to focus their full attention in the cockpit.

In 1929 Pan American Airways introduced the cabin-boy type of attendant insisting on *alert and good looking youngsters,* as an early article pointed out. The Pan American stewards served on board Sikorsky flying boats and Fokker aircraft between Miami and points in the

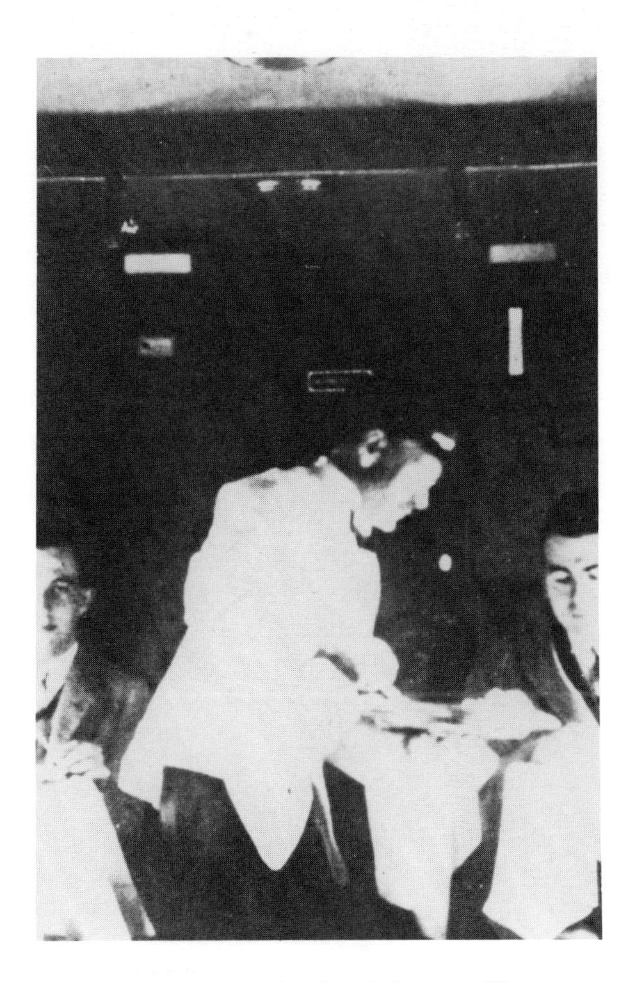

Lufthansa steward serving lunch between Vienna ar Berlin, about 1928.

Two couriers for Transcontinental Air Transport model the summer and winter uniforms, about 1928.

An Air Union steward has the tables set for lunch, about 1928. Notice the retaining rails to prevent sliding.

Caribbean and South America. Inflight service equipment consisted of a thermos of water and paper cups along with the prerequisite cotton wool for the passengers' ears and chewing gum. Joey Carrera, an early Pan American steward, recalls how the crew would lug along several days worth of food *as nothing edible could be found at their stopover points.* In the early flying boats, the so-called galley was in the tail and could only be reached by crawling on hands and knees through a low narrow passageway. Returning to the passenger cabin balancing food and drink took skill.

Unpressurized cabins, poor or non-existent soundproofing, no air conditioning, and lavatories referred to as *slop boxes* made each flight an adventure to be sure. Fly swatters and a wrench to tighten the seats to the cabin floor were standard issue to the early attendants. The compact and efficient aircraft galley had not yet been designed. Food and beverages were boarded in either tin or wicker hampers. Regardless of the hardships, the cornerstones of inflight service had been laid: safety and service.

It would be an oversight not to mention the stewards who served aboard the giant airships. DELAG and HAPAG, the German airship transport lines employed a

One of Pan Am's first stewards (left) poses with pilots and mail in Miami, about 1929.

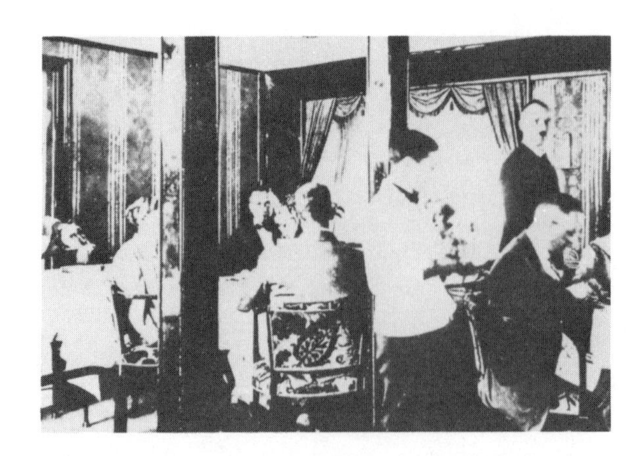

DELAG Airship's steward (foreground) serving lunch in the dining room of the *Graf Zeppelin*, about 1928.

number of stewards to serve passengers in the dining rooms and private compartments of these quiet giants. Although the Hindenburg disaster comes immediately to mind, the airship lines transported tens of thousands of passengers safely and in sheer luxury between 1910 and 1937.

In May of 1930, little New England & Western Airways hired the world's first black crew members. It enticed black pullman porters away from the railroads to serve on their flights between New York, Albany, Springfield, Hartford, and Boston. The porters, once they overcame their nervousness about flying, were tremendously proud of their jobs and, of course, had the necessary training and background to render the right sort of service. This significant historical event was overshadowed however, when on May 15, 1930, Boeing Air Transport rocked the commercial aviation world by hiring eight female crew members to serve as the world's first airlines stewardesses. Their story, of course, has been well told.

The first cabin boys, couriers, aerial attendants, stewards, and stewardesses were pioneers in every sense of the word. Their courage, daring, dedication, and caring forged the pathway over which footsteps in the sky will continue to be walked.

TWA'S COURIERS, PURSERS, CABIN ATTENDANTS[1] 1928

In 1926 Western Air Express and Transcontinental Air Transport (TAT), both TWA predecessors, began the first scheduled commercial flights.

TAT couriers, the very first flight attendants in TWA history, were the young sons of the railroad, steamship and industrial magnates who financed the airline. TAT management had promised these magnates that their sons would have long and successful careers in aviation launched by serving passengers. Their duties were extensive and began long before take-off. They collected their passengers at a downtown location and drove them to the airport. Along the way they stopped by the caterers to pick up the meals. They weighed and loaded baggage and mail after helping their passengers to board. In flight, they were responsible for attending to the passengers' needs by adjusting seats, safety belts, ventilators and heaters, as well as serving meals.

From February 1930 until the latter part of 1935, First Mates served as cabin attendants in place of couriers as well as performing the duties of copilot. They were taught the basics of how to pour liquid from a thermos bottle and how to kneel in the aisle rather than leaning over. They were instructed to gargle with Listerine before serving box lunches to passengers. The short cabin-duty career of First Mates was brought to an end with the July 1935 meeting of TWA's Board of Directors. Jack Frye, who had become TWA's president in 1934, presented the idea of female *hostesses.*

That proposal ended the TWA male *flight attendant* career until January of 1942 when TWA hired *pursers.* Pursers were hired solely because the U.S. War Department adamantly refused to let *hostesses* work the ICD (Inter Continental Division) flights and TWA had committed to providing the crews and materials necessary for this wartime activity.

For the next 20 years men were restricted to the purser position on international flights and later, to Flight Service Manager on domestic. It wasn't until May of 1972 that the tides of social reform resulted in the hiring of the first male cabin attendants. November 11, 1945, TWA's first international training class graduated 22 pursers and 25 air hostesses.

PAN AM'S EARLY STEWARDS PURSERS 1928 - 1929 - 1930

Steward in Pan American Airlines' vocabulary meant "Service, Tact, Efficiency, Wisdom, Ability, Responsibility, Dependability." Being a male American citizen was the prime requirement for becoming a Pan Am steward. He was required to speak three languages fluently, including French and English; be a high school graduate; have experience preparing and serving food in first class restaurants, hotels or steamships; and have a good personality and an aptitude for handling people. In addition, he had to be between 23 and 32 years of age, and, because of a desired uniformity in size and weight, he had to be between 5 feet 5 inches and 5 feet 9 inches in height and weigh no more than 150 pounds.

After a prospective steward met these requirements, he underwent two months of training. In training he was required to work a week in the equipment shop to know all the Clipper aircraft. He also spent two to three weeks working with the port steward helping equip all departing Clippers for passenger service. At least one week was

[1] *St. Louis Weekly*, TWA Publications, May 15, 1992.

First Pan Am Flight Steward Uniform 1929

spent with a beaching crew to get necessary training in seamanship, including throwing ropes, tying knots, rowing, swimming, and the operation of life rafts.

The steward trainee was required to complete a five-week course in first aid. After meeting this requirement, he went on to take a course in advanced first aid given by the head of Pan Am's medical department. A week in the traffic department followed. Then the new steward was required to apprentice with a senior steward in the duties of making up berths, using the galley, and practicing emergency skills.

Pan American realized that celebrities boarding a clipper flight could distract a steward from his duties which included checking luggage, making up passenger lists, checking in mail and express, and making out weight reports, plus the usual duties greeting passengers and making them comfortable. Management then created a theatrical celebrity course for all stewards and called it the *Gable Routine*.

Practice handling a film star such as Clark Gable and his luggage, was a part of Pan Am's traffic training course. "To make them feel the problem was real, the stewards juggled dummy packages and mail sacks," explained traffic instructor Charles Schafer. "This was done in addition to boarding 'Gable' and was special help when several celebrities would be on the same flight."

At the end of a 60-day probation period, the new steward was allowed to go on a flight to Bermuda as a working crew member. After he attained efficiency on the job, he was then placed on transatlantic runs as a full-fledged Pan American steward.

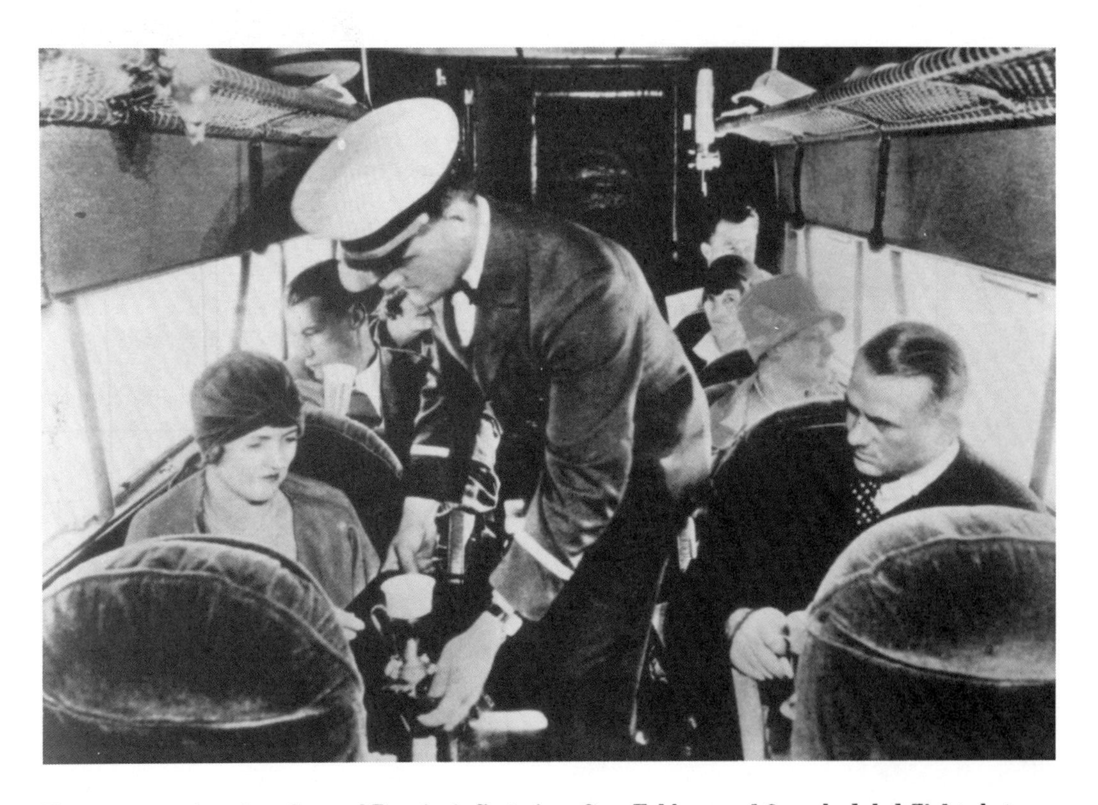

Ten-passenger interior of one of Pan Am's first aircraft, a Fokker used for scheduled flights between Key West and Havana. Pan Am later used Fokker F-7 and F-10 aircraft to extend its service throughout the Caribbean. (Photo courtesy of Pan Am)

Pan Am's Inter-American stewards of the 1930s. (Photo, Pan Am)

THEY CALLED HIM BILL MORENO

Ovilio "Bill" Moreno

Everyone called him Bill because no one with Pan Am could pronounce his name, Ovilio Moreno. His home was Key West, Florida, which by coincidence was the site

Pan Am stewards Joey Carrera and Nil Borges, 1941.

of Pan American's inaugural flight to Havana, Cuba on October 28, 1927.

On May 17, 1930, Moreno left his home in Key West and headed for New York intending to work for the Big Apple Hotel. "I never got there," said Moreno. "I stopped over in Miami. There I had dinner and met a friend, Rafael Vega, who was a steward for Pan American. He convinced me that I should apply for a steward position, which was a new and growing profession at the time.

"Adventure flows in my blood," Moreno says. "I had a bad case of wanderlust and a job as a steward on an airplane was the answer to a dream."

The lure of traveling changed Ovilio's mind about a hotel job. His friend Rafael escorted him to Pan American's ticket office at the Columbus Hotel in Miami. The Manager, J. Addison Thomas, liked Moreno's enthusiasm and hired him the same day. Neither Thomas nor his secretary, Inez Stawe, could pronounce Ovilio properly, so Moreno agreed to the nickname "Bill," the name he was called for the following forty-six years.

"Those early days were marvelous!" Moreno remembers. "One thing I especially liked was the purser's responsibility to type up the inflight menus for the Miami - Buenos Aires hop and to give one to each passenger."

Moreno flew as a purser until 1938, when he transferred to the clearance department as a supervisor. He helped in Pan American World Airways' growth. "I retired from Pan American the youngest man with the longest length of service (46 years) on New Year's Day 1976," he recalls. "It was like belonging to a prestigious fraternity or sorority."

UNITED'S MAIN LINE: THE OVERLAND TRAIL[2]

A rich history of exploration is the legacy of the Overland Trail. It was the main line for over a century of coast-to-coast transportation in America.

The route was first used by Indians, fur traders and explorers. In 1830 it took six months for ox-drawn covered wagons to travel from Missouri to the Pacific coast. By 1850, the route required twenty-four days by stagecoach and rail. The time by Pony Express and rail was twelve and a half days. The trip made via the first transcontinental railroad in 1869 took seven days. The first cross-continent telegraph line followed the tracks leading west, and the Overland Trail was later paved and became the first east-west transcontinental highway across the United States, Route 30.

The U.S. Post Office Department originated the idea of coast-to-coast air mail service. The 2,600 mile mid-continent route between New York, Chicago and San Francisco, which had been the route of the pioneers, became *U.S. Air Mail Route No.1* on September 8, 1920.

The first mail was flown only in daylight hours. Trains carried the mail by night. The mail took seventy hours coast-to-coast.

The Post Office Department proved air mail service was financially possible. It began turning over the service

[2]*The Mainline, The Story Of United Air Lines*, (United States), a 1946-1947 seat pocket booklet in DC-3, DC-4 aircraft.

United Air Lines' Mainline route of the 1930s and early 1940s. The aircraft flown by United were known as the Mainliners.

to private contractors in 1926. The first two of United Airlines' predecessor companies were born through competitive bidding. Boeing Air Transport first flew the route between San Francisco and Chicago on July 1, 1927. National Air Transport flew the route from Dallas to Chicago to New York City. From these beginnings, United Air Lines began to emerge.

The first revenue passengers paid $400 for a coast-to-coast flight which took 32 hours and required fourteen refueling stops en route. Conditions for the air traveler had begun to improve by 1930, when Boeing Air Transport hired the world's first stewardess to provide inflight service for passengers. By 1931, United Air Lines was formed out of its various predecessor divisions: Varney Air Lines, Pacific Air Transport, Boeing Air Transport and National Air Transport. United was now known as the Mainline which through the decades has become the *Friendly Sky* Airline, the first airline to fly to all fifty states. International routes added, today United is a global airline.

HISTORIC FOOTSTEPS IN THE SKY

United Air Transport / United Air Lines
Stephen A. Stimpson
1929 - 1962

It was Steve Stimpson who first developed the idea of the airline stewardess.

Steve Stimpson, the father of stewardess service, arm in arm with stewardesses wearing (left) a 1930 uniform and (right) a 1959 uniform.

In 1929, Stephen Stimpson was the District Traffic Manager for Boeing Air Transport at San Francisco, (the predecessor of United Air Lines). In the first pioneering days of aviation, air mail was the main factor in airline operation. Very few passengers were carried and were left to fend for themselves on the long flights. The copilot did pass out a box lunch and pour hot coffee from a thermos. This had no set schedule; it was when he thought about it or became hungry.

The San Francisco office handled all of Boeing Air Transports' business. This included airmail, freight and passengers. A big sign in the window read: *Chicago In 20 Hours"* Steve said about the sign, "That operation was pretty fantastic in 1929."[3]

In 1930, Steve was a passenger on a mid-winter west bound flight on a Boeing Air Transport plane. The B-80A carried ten passengers plus a crew of two pilots. The aircraft was delayed in its' flight time due to strong head winds. Steve observed the passengers frequently looking at their watches and obviously nervous. There was no one to reassure them or to answer any questions. It was then that Steve informed the passengers about the head winds causing the delay and answered other questions. He also adjusted the heat to make the cabin more comfortable.[4]

This experience also prompted Steve to thinking that passengers now needed care on the long flights. He thought about stewards on airplanes like the steamship lines used to assist passengers.[5]

In the meantime, Steve had been noticing a young woman pass by his office each day. She would often pause and look at the sign in the window. One day she entered his office and asked if she could get a job on an airplane. Her name was Ellen Church, a Registered Nurse, and she worked at a nearby hospital. Ellen also told Steve that she was very interested in aviation. This friendly, likeable, nurse impressed Steve. However, he had no authority to

[3] *United Mainliner Magazine*, July 1974 (Excerpts from *The Grand Rapids Press*, 1973), edited by Del Ten Dyke.

[4] Ibid.

[5] Ibid.

A Boeing Air Transport B-80A in 1930. (United Airlines Photo)

hire her for a job on an airplane, so he could not give her any encouragement.[6]

After this first introduction, Ellen would often stop by to chat with Steve about aviation. The two became good friends. Steve related to Ellen his idea of stewards on airplanes to give care to passengers on the long flights. Ellen suggested, why not women, they could do the job as well as men. Also nurses would be reassuring to encourage people to fly...if women were on airplanes and nurses to take care of them.[7]

Steve wrote a letter to the Traffic Manager at Cheyenne with his suggestions and he included Ellen Church's idea to use nurses in this capacity. The prompt answer was *"No"*! Steve, however, pursued this idea and took it to the Assistant to the President, W.A. Patterson. Patterson was convinced that stewardesses would be a great improvement for passenger service that was starting to grow. Patterson talked with the President and permission was given to hire Ellen Church as Chief Stewardess to hire seven more nurses to become the world's "Original Eight" stewardesses. Stewardesses were aboard Boeing Air Transport flights on May 15, 1930.[8]

Steve and Ellen had set some rigid requirements for the first stewardesses and developed a manual of *Do's and Don't's.* Some of the first requirements are listed as follows:

Remember at all times when on duty to retain the respectful reserve of the well-trained servant. A ready smile is essential, but never permit yourself the intimate attitude of a travelling companion.

Punch each ticket at each point passed, even though some flight segments involve 13 or more stops. Tag all passenger baggage and check it on board the aircraft.

Remember to carry on board picnic hampers containing cold fried chicken, apples, rolls, cake and vacuum flasks with hot coffee for passenger meals.

Captains and cockpit crew will be treated with strict formality while in uniform. A rigid military salute will be rendered the captain and copilot as they go aboard and deplane before the passengers. Check with the pilots regarding their personal luggage and place it on board promptly.

Wind the clocks and altimeters mounted in some cabins; dust window sills and straighten lamp shades. Use a small broom on the floor prior to every flight. Check the floor bolts on the wicker seats in the Ford Trimotor to make sure they are securely fastened down.

[6] *United Mainliner Magazine*, July 1974, (Excerpted from an interview with Stephen A. Stimpson, *The Grand Rapids Press*, 1973, Edited by Del Ten Dyke).

[7] Ibid.

[8] Ibid.

In 1930, the world's first stewardesses modeled their smart-looking uniforms: dark green double-breasted suits with matching capes and hats. The "Original Eight" were Ellen Church (upper left), Alva Johnson (upper right), Margaret Arnatt (left), Inez Keller, Cornelia Peterman, Harriet Fry, Jessie Carter and Ellis Crawford. (United Airlines Photo)

A propeller in motion can be fatal to anyone who walks into it.

Swat flies in cabin after take-off.

Warn passengers against throwing lighted smoking butts or other objects out the windows, particularly over populated areas.

Face the rear of the cabin when talking with passengers or serving lunch. Bending over while facing toward the front of the plane tends to place the seat of your pants in the passenger's face. Tuck your skirt in carefully and assume a lady-like squatting position beside the passenger when carrying on a conversation.

Carry a railroad timetable in event the plane is grounded somewhere. Stewardesses are expected to accompany stranded passengers to the railroad station.

When slippers are available on long night flights you will advise persons desiring to sleep as follows, "I have slippers available, sir, if you would care to remove your shoes and rest your feet." Assist the passenger to remove his shoes, if he so desires. Clean the shoes thoroughly before returning them to him. So as not to startle a passenger when awakening him, touch him gently on the shoulder and if this does not work, tweak his elbow sharply...that is guaranteed to waken him.[9]

[9]Vicy Morris Young, United Clipped Wings Archivist, excerpted from *The 1930 stewardess Manual.*

THE WORLD'S FIRST STEWARDESS

Ellen Church and the "Original Eight" 1930

May 1930 marked a new era in aviation history. It was then that Boeing Air Transport inaugurated the world's first inflight service. And it was all started by a young lady from Cresco, Iowa. Her name was Ellen Church.

Ellen was interested in aviation from her early years. She was born on a farm north of Cresco, Iowa in 1904. Ellen loved to watch the barnstormers and daredevils who performed stunts over the Cresco fairgrounds. She especially liked the acrobats whose wing-walking thrilled her in the 1920's.

After graduating from nurse's training at the University of Minnesota in 1926, Ellen took a job as a nurse caring for the wife of an army pilot. To show his deep appreciation for Ellen's skill and compassion, he asked Ellen what he could to repay her.

"I'd like to go on a ride in an airplane," Ellen replied. She got the ride. In fact, it changed the course of her life, because it was after that ride that Ellen realized how much she would like to fly.

Ellen left Iowa to pursue her nursing career in San Francisco. On her way to work every day at French Hospital, Ellen passed the district manager's office of Boeing Air Transport. One day in February 1930, Ellen took a detour into the office and introduced herself to the district manager, Steve Stimpson, and asked him if she could get some kind of job flying, possible as a co-pilot.

Native Of Cresco Was First Air Steward-ess

ELLEN E. CHURCH

As histories on aviation are being written, the name of Ellen E. Church, native of Cresco, finds itself included amidst the important data for the Iowa farm girl was the world's first airline stewardess. The date of the history-making event was May 15, 1930 . . . a time when flying was considered primarily a man's game and airline pilots viewed intrusion with suspicion.

Stimpson could not give her any encouragement, although he did realize that the passengers needed more care that they were receiving from the overburdened co-pilots who did double duty in the cockpit and looking after passengers. He had been thinking of putting men as pursers on flights. Besides, traffic was increasing, and he knew that Boeing Air Transport would be hiring soon. In the back of his mind, Steve thought that a woman's personal care might appeal to passengers.

As if she could read his mind, Ellen suggested that nurses could do a good job caring for passengers. She suggested that it would be good psychology to have women on board the aircraft, to show that flying was a safe and a reliable form of transportation.

Steve Stimpson could hardly deny that Ellen had a good idea. In a letter to Cheyenne headquarters, Steve reiterated Ellen's suggestion. He was convinced that hiring Ellen and other women as regular crew members would be good for the airline. The publicity it would stir up would be great advertising.

The reply from headquarters was a one-word telegram: "No." Undaunted, Steve contacted the assistant to the company's president, W.A. Patterson. Patterson talked it over with his wife and then the president. They were dubious about the proposition, but the president gave Stimpson permission to hire eight stewardesses for a three-month trial period.

Ellen was hired along with seven other nurses, whom Ellen had helped to select. They were all hired on the basis of their intelligence, personality and single marital status. Weight and height were other important considerations because the first ten-passenger Boeing Air Transport B-80s had narrow aisles and low ceilings. The maximum weight could not exceed 115 pounds, and the maximum height could be no more than five feet, four inches. Enthusiasm was important, so the age limit was set at twenty-five. The salary would by $125 per month for 100 hours of flying.[10]

Ellen wrote the stewardess manual, outlining the qualifications and duties of the position. She also helped design the uniforms that she and her seven air stewardesses were to wear aboard the B-80 aircraft. The uniform featured a long, dark green wool cape lined with gray, a double-breasted jacket with

[10]United Airlines, *The Friendly Skies*, (U.S. 1980)

silver buttons, a plain green wool skirt, and a shower-cap type hat that was to be worn at all times. The cape had large pockets to hold a wrench, screwdriver and railroad timetable, all of which the stewardess would need to use frequently.

The air stewardesses were responsible for a number of duties which included sweeping and dusting the aircraft; checking that the wicker seats were securely bolted to the floor; keeping passengers from throwing cigarette and cigar butts and other trash out of the windows; passing out lunches of cold chicken, sandwiches, relishes, soup, apples, cake and hot coffee; checking heat and ventilation in the cabin; checking, tagging, and carrying luggage for passengers; and at times helping to refuel the aircraft. They also were responsible for carrying a railroad timetable at all times to arrange ongoing transportation for passengers in the event of flight cancellations due to bad weather. The most important task of the air hostess was to watch out for passengers who wanted to use the lavatory to be sure they didn't use the exit door instead. In case of a forced landing the stewardesses were expected to help cut down fences in wheat fields. At the airport they were needed to help push the aircraft into its hangar.

The first eight air stewardesses were divided into two groups for the twenty-hour flight between Chicago and San Francisco. Four flew between San Francisco and Cheyenne and four flew between Cheyenne and Chicago. The roster looked like this:

OAKLAND TO CHEYENNE	CHICAGO TO CHEYENNE
Jesse Carter	Margaret Arnatt
Ellen Church	Harriet Fry
Ellis Crawford	Alva Johnson
Inez Keller	Cornelia Peterman

There were thirteen stops between San Francisco and Chicago, and the stewardesses punched tickets at every stop.

At the end of the three-month trial, Boeing Air Transport's passenger traffic had greatly improved. Businessmen were booking a particular flight in order to fly with a certain stewardess. Women and families also started flying because of increasing confidence in air transportation and greater comfort during the flights. To accommodate the increase in passenger travel, Boeing hired twenty more stewardesses and planned additional training classes.[11]

Other airlines followed suit and hired women to become stewardesses as regular crew members: Eastern Air Transport in 1931; American Airways in 1933; Trans World Airlines in 1935; Northwest in 1939; and other airlines all over the world started hiring stewardesses very soon after.

In 1975, United Airlines honored its "Original Eight" air stewardesses by naming a Boeing 747 "The Original Eight" and inscribed their names under the cockpit window.

A bronze plaque was mounted in the cabin showing the eight air hostesses in the flowing green capes and *shower caps* they wore fifty years ago beside a Boeing 80A.[12]

For the 50th Anniversary of stewardess service May 15, 1980, United celebrated with a *High Flying Fashion* show. The fashion show was a nationwide salute to all of the world's 125,000 flight attendants and the thousands of former flight attendants, stewardesses and air hostesses who have walked the skies. The fashion shows were presented in various cities across the nation: New York City's Plaza Hotel, May 14; the U.S. House of Representatives' Sam Rayburn Building in Washington, DC, May 15; the Bonaventure Hotel in Los Angeles, May 17; the Continental Plaza Hotel in Chicago, May 19; and the Olympic Hotel in Seattle, May 23. Proceeds from the six fashion shows were donated to Clipped Wings, the association of current and former United Airlines flight attendants, whose members have worked for handicapped children since 1954.

And for the lady from Cresco, Iowa who helped Steve Stimpson make it all possible, there is a sign on the edge of town pointing to the Cresco airport which reads, *Ellen Church Field.* The sign was erected in 1975 when the Cresco airport was rededicated after a major expansion, in honor of the free-spirited woman who brought inflight stewardess service to the world, and who put Cresco, Iowa on the map and Ellen Church and the "Original Eight" in the pages of aviation history.

[11]Ken Becker, "Honored Here: Ellen Church Started It All 50 Years Ago," *Times Plain Dealer*, Cresco, Iowa, 28 May 1980, Section B.

[12]Ken Becker, "Honored Here: Ellen Church Started It All 50 Years Ago," *Times Plain Dealer*, Cresco, Iowa, 28 May 12980, Section B.

PLAQUE AT ELLEN CHURCH FIELD
Cresco, Iowa

WORLD'S FIRST AIRLINE STEWARDESS
ELLEN CHURCH MARSHALL 1904-1965

Humanitarian, War Heroine and Aviation Pioneer.
Ellen Church dedicated her indomitable spirit to the service of mankind.

As the world's first airline stewardess, she created a new and exciting profession for young girls of the twentieth century.

As a much-decorated Air Corps nurse in World War II, she brought comfort and relief to thousands of American soldiers who were wounded on the battlefields of Europe.

And as a peacetime Nursing Instructor and Hospital Administrator, she guided vast numbers of young women along the path once trod by another humanitarian, Florence Nightingale.

Born September 22, 1904 on a farm near Cresco, Iowa, Ellen Church Marshall combined imagination, persistence and her own personal warmth to meet life's challenges along the way, and with her death on August 24, 1965, the world lost a truly great and dedicated woman.

Her name will serve forever as a symbol of the selfless devotion that rests in the hearts of nurses and stewardesses all over the world.

Inflight service is indebted to the world's first stewardess, Ellen Church, RN. This photo was taken not long before her death in 1965.

THE FIRST STEWARDESSES
Boeing Air Transport
Harriet Fry Iden
1930

Harriet had often charmed audiences relating her experiences as one of the first stewardesses for Boeing Air Transport, the predecessor of United Air Lines. She wrote a detailed account of these experiences before her death at the age of 72 years in December 1979. Her husband, Howard Iden has graciously given me this story which is related in her own words:

"On May 1, 1930 the Chicago girls, and Ellen Church, were flown to Cheyenne. Ellen had explained to us we weren't popular, to expect company personnel to be curious about us and we were not to get out of the plane until we landed in Cheyenne. Should there be any passengers on the plane we were not to talk to them. We were supposed to just sit quietly and not move back and forth in the aisle. That trip should have warned us what to expect in the future. We were supposed to leave Chicago at 8 a.m., however one of the motors was not working correctly so we were three hours late taking off. Neither the pilot nor copilot ever spoke with us.

"The first stop was Iowa City to refuel and pick up mail, but no passengers. After takeoff we ate our box lunch. Just before reaching Des Moines, Iowa, we ran into rain and continued to fly to Omaha. The pilots changed there and as they came through the cabin they did not speak, they just glared at us.

"We continued to have stormy weather all the way to Cheyenne and the entire trip was a good twelve hours plus. We had come prepared to stay over the weekend to meet the San Francisco girls and Steve Stimpson, but, because of bad weather and fog, the West Coast plane could not get through to Cheyenne for ten days.

"During that time, we were given several lectures by Colonel Coffin, a flight surgeon from nearby Fort Francis E. Warren. He said we would have to see what happened to the passengers, perhaps we would have more than air sickness. He suggested giving Amytal, a light sedation, to air sick passengers after they had used the *burp cup*, recline their chair and, in winter, cover them with a blanket. In the summer we could put a cold cloth over the upper part of their face.

"The rest of the time we spent learning how to put on seat covers, set up tables and how to serve the food. The only instructions we had about a crackup was to get the passengers out of the aircraft. If the pilot was unconscious, we were to run to the cockpit and turn off the magneto and try to avoid a fire.

"When the west coast stewardesses arrived they brought our uniforms with them. Everyone's fitted perfectly except mine, they had sent a size forty-two instead of a ten! We were to get into our uniforms, meet Steve at the airport and have our pictures taken. They pinned the back of my jacket and skirt with safety pins to make it look like it fit me. We were lined up along the plane and they also sat us down, etc. All the while we were facing the sun which was shining on a tin roof and we could not see. We were told to close our eyes and to open

The "Original Eight" stewardesses: (left to right)Jessie Carter, Cornelia Peterman, Ellen Church, Inez Keller, Alva Johnson, Margaret Arnatt, Ellis Crawford and Harriet Fry. Harriet is in her over-sized uniform, pinned in the back for the photo. (United Photos)

them when they said ready. Not one of us thought we would see those awful pictures again, but they were part of history and we have lived with them. A tailor in Cheyenne stayed up all night to fit my uniform as I was to leave the following morning.

"The planes in which we flew were Boeing 80-A Trimotors which carried ten passengers at a cruising speed of a hundred twenty-five miles per hour. The plane consisted of a cockpit, mail pit, cabin, and baggage compartment in the tail. The size of the cabin was nineteen feet long, six and three quarters feet in height and five and a third feet wide. We had to walk down the aisle sideways as there was a double row of seats on one side and a row of single seats on the other. Serving was difficult because of the vibration of the plane and we had many line squalls and much turbulence flying at two to three thousand feet. The interior of the plane was made to look like the interior of a train coach to reassure passengers by putting them in a familiar setting. The seats were upholstered in a gray fabric and the seat could be reclined. We also had pillows and blankets for the comfort of our passengers. On the back of each seat was a pouch which contained a map, cards and burp cup. Our lavatory was very nice with hot and cold water, but the toilet was a can set in a ring and a hole cut in the floor, so when one opened the toilet seat, behold, open air toilet! Soon chemical toilets made their debut. The only thing wrong with them was in rough weather and turbulence, I would often see the contents of the toilet running out into the cabin from under the door, which meant a quick mop up, that I didn't like!

A 1930 stewardess is shown in the galley of a B-80A. Fried chicken is the entree.

"When we first started there was no radio on the plane, the weather teletype report was picked up at each airport we landed at. They were working on radio and before too many months each plane had this equipment installed. Later they had the beam which was useful to the pilot to keep on course during no visibility.

"Some of our duties were: to arrive at the airport one hour before take off, put covers on seat backs and arms, wind and set the clock, set the altimeter, change the altimeter during flight to correct sea level, and change time as necessary. See that the cabin was clean, towels and tissue in toilet, see that food was aboard and one gallon of coffee and one gallon of hot water, plus tea bags and bouillon cubes. Check for current magazines, blankets and pillows, packets of gum and cotton for the passengers' ears because of the noise. Gum was to chew to ease the pressure on the ear drums. Be sure each seat had an air sick container. Also test each seat to assure it was bolted firmly to the floor.

"At takeoff, we would welcome passengers aboard (except those that were intoxicated, we did not take them). See that baggage was put in the compartment in the tail section of the plane. At Des Moines and Lincoln the

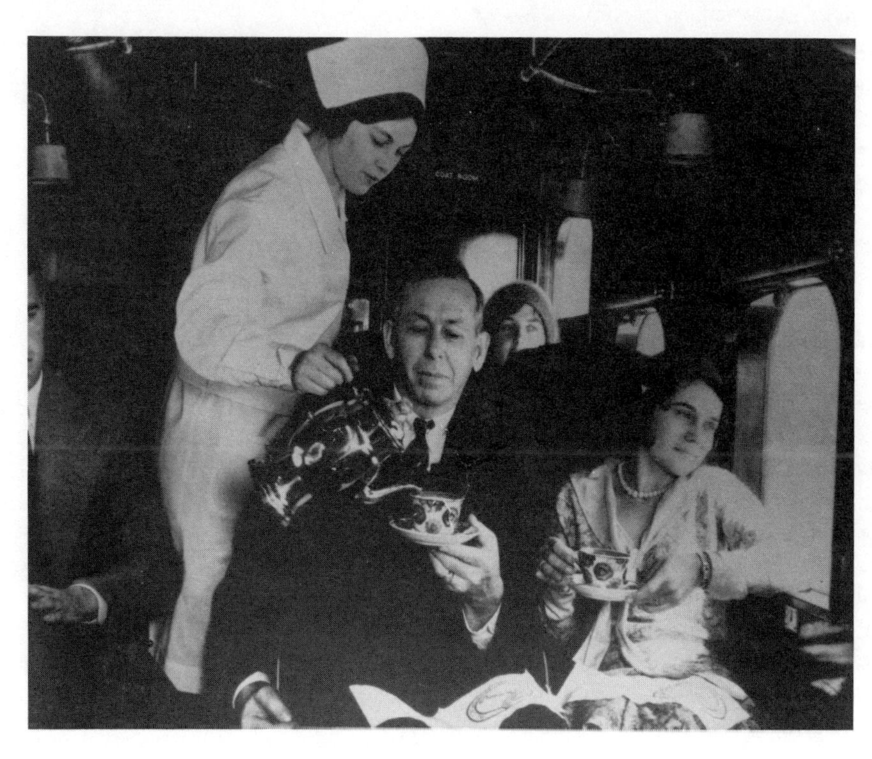

A 1930 stewardess in her gray nurse's uniform used while serving on a Boeing 80-A.

stewardess did the loading and unloading of the baggage. Check that all seat belts were fastened and take tickets and punch them to our destination. If the flight was terminated, we punched the town nearest to our cow pasture or emergency landing field, or if we were lucky, an airport.

"West bound we served food between Des Moines and Omaha. We had one-legged tables, the leg fit into a hole in the floor, and two clips on the table fastened into the side of the cabin. However the vibration and rough weather made this arrangement practically impossible. So we used an old hospital trick: we put a pillow in the passenger's lap and served the plate on that and I do believe this method was used for quite a few years. Our menu, from the Palmer House in Chicago, was as follows: fried chicken, bread and butter sandwiches, potato chips, pickle and olive, brandied fruit cocktail, tea, coffee or bouillon. Our table service was china with a modernistic design, glasses, cups and saucers, linen napkins at first and then paper napkins. Because the china and glasses were broken so often because of rough weather and the landings, we did get around to using paper plates. Our serving table was the top of a metal cabinet in which our supplies were kept. The thermos jugs fitted into a special rack alongside the cabinet. Each thermos had a spigot. We gave out ash trays that fastened to the side of the cabin. Cigarette smoking was allowed, but no pipes or cigars. And of course, take care of the unhappy passengers that became sick. Just do whatever was necessary to keep passengers happy and comfortable as possible, pass out blankets and pillows, etc.

"Away from home port, we were allowed $6.00 per day expenses, $4.00 for hotel and $2.00 for meals. We could not get a decent hotel for that price, nor three meals per day for that allowance; if we spent more it came out of our own pockets. Also we were not allowed to have dinner, or dates, with a passenger or to go out with the pilots or copilots — just like hospital rules. However all rules were made to be broken on occasion. After the pilots and copilots did finally accept us and found us to be useful, we would be invited to the cockpit when there were no passengers aboard; a sack of mail was put between them which made a good seat. Sometimes the pilots would do hedge-hopping about 500 feet from the ground. We would frighten the pigs and the farmers did not like that. Also out of North Platte we would see herds of antelopes and give them a little chase too. In the beginning, many times we would have no passengers.

"We were issued large brief cases, almost as large as a suit case; in this we carried our supplies: gray smock and cap (which we wore only a few trips and gradually discarded) ash trays, ticket punch, and magazines. We were supposed to buy new magazines and papers and collect for them on our expense accounts. We made reports after each trip, received bulletins almost every day which we kept in a note book; most of them were not much use to us. We were each insured for $5,000 in case of an accidental death.

"We sat out storms in cow pastures and emergency fields, sometimes an hour and maybe three or four. Often times east-bound we would find Chicago socked in so we would land at an emergency field at Sterling, Waterman or Aurora, Illinois and sit it out until the fog lifted. It was important to sit out a storm or fog, as flying had to be kept safe.

"There were times we had to set down in the nearest emergency field because of lack of visibility and we could not get above the dust and heat layer because of head winds. The heat, the dust, the vibration of the trimotor, and the wool suit made a clean white uniform and cool hospital look mighty inviting.

"I flew almost eighteen months. I did not like the heat during the summer and in the winter the cabin was supposed to be heated but only the front got the heat and the stewardess' seat was in the rear. I did like the passengers; some were well known people: Jay Gould, Will Rogers, Amelia Earhart, J.H. Kraft, and Peter B. Kyne (the novelist).

"It was a great experience and I am glad I was one of the 'Original Eight'!"

I DIDN'T HAVE ENOUGH SENSE TO BE SCARED

One of the "Original Eight" Jesse Carter Bronson 1930

Jesse Carter Bronson was 72 years old and one of United's four living stewardesses of the Original Eight of 1930, when United celebrated its 50th Anniversary of inflight service in 1980. Today only Margaret Arnatt survives.

"We were all registered nurses and hired at $125 a month, and got $5 extra pay if we were stuck because of a storm or other delay," said Jesse. "All of us were young and the hours of delay didn't bother us. The mail bags were the main payload, and we always had piles of them in the back of the airplane. If the plane was overweight, out went the stewardess, and the passengers if it was necessary. The mail must go through.[13]

"It was rough work because there was no airport in San Francisco and I commuted across the San Francisco Bay to Oakland on a coast guard cutter that had once been

[13]Murray Olderman, "The Friendly Skies Weren't Always So Friendly," *Rocky Mountain News*, 23 September 1974.

a rum runner," Jesse remembers. "Four of us flew from Oakland to Cheyenne. You left in the evening and you flew all night and got to Cheyenne in the morning. There were stops in such places as Reno and Salt Lake City to drop off the mail. In Reno people would hang over fences to watch us land, as it was big event. The most passengers I had were five - either people on emergency trips or businessmen."

According to Jesse, the stewardesses were not allowed to have anything to do with the pilots, copilots or passengers. "We were all young; it was a different era. I was a naive, innocent girl. We stayed in a hotel room for a day or two of rest before we took our flight back to San Francisco."

Jesse didn't consider her job dangerous. "I didn't have enough sense to be scared," she says. One time her plane had to land in a pasture outside of Sacramento. "A bonfire was lit by the passengers while the pilot walked three miles to the nearest telephone," Jesse says, recalling the incident.

"I was tired all the time," said Jesse. "My ears hurt all the time and at the end of three months I quit my job as an air stewardess and returned to nursing." In reflection she said, "If I had it to do over, I would have stayed with the airlines."[14]

THE SKY ANGEL

One of the "Original Eight" Inez Keller Fuite

Flight attendants of today's jet age sometimes complain about being "flying waitresses" serving hundreds of people nonstop every day. Inez Keller Fuite thinks of the "good old days," when being one of the "Original Eight" meant one hundred hours of flying each month for $125 a month.

The 1930s stewardess not only provided comfort for her passengers in the air, but spent time in pre-flight duties helping service the aircraft. In case of delays or forced landings she assisted the crew and saw to her passengers' needs as well. Extra hours of duty on the ground were not compensated by pay. They were part of her job.

In 1930 Inez Keller, a 24-year-old RN, lived in San Francisco. She flew on Boeing's Trimotor 80-A, a ten-passenger aircraft, between Oakland and Cheyenne. The 950-mile flight made five stops en route.

"It was supposed to take eighteen hours," Mrs. Fuite said, "but it was usually more like twenty-four hours. If the weather got bad, we would land in a field for awhile, and wait for the storm to clear up."

If all the seats were full, the stewardess sat on the mail sacks or on a suitcase in the rear of the airplane. The Trimotors were not pressurized and they were cold and drafty.

On the ground, the stewardesses wore their forest green wool twill suits with dashing capes and berets. "While serving food to passengers, we wore light gray nurse's uniforms and caps," said Mrs. Fuite. "Regardless of the time of day, we served the same menu of coffee or tea, fruit cocktail, fried chicken and rolls."

Mrs. Fuite recalled that passengers liked the new stewardesses, but pilots and their wives had a much different opinion of the flying nurses.

"The pilots didn't want us at all and were not enthusiastic about women as crew members. They were rugged and temperamental characters who wore guns to protect the mail. They wouldn't even speak to us during the first couple of trips. The wives of the pilots began a letter-writing campaign to Boeing, saying the stewardesses were trying to steal their husbands and requesting their removal," said Mrs. Fuite. "One pilot's wife always met her husband at the plane in Salt Lake City. She was really jealous."

Regarding her interesting but short career as a stewardess, Mrs. Fuite remembered an incident when a stabilizer broke, making the plane "quiver like a bird" and forcing a landing on the shores of Salt Lake. Another time, the plane ran out of gas and made an emergency landing in a wheat field near Cherokee, Wyoming.

"People from the surrounding area came in wagons and on horseback to see the plane," she said. "They'd never seen an aircraft before, and they wanted to touch it and to touch me. One of them called me 'The angel from the sky." Mrs. Fuite recalls that her funniest experience happened when the pilot couldn't get enough altitude to get over the mountain outside of Salt Lake City.

"He flew back to the airport and dropped me off," she said. "I only weighed 115 pounds, but the plane did make it over the mountain."

Another humorous incident occurred when she was on board the plane equipped with the first two-way radio.

"The pilot thought the radio wasn't working," she said. "He started to sing 'Springtime in the Rockies' during the flight, and when we landed there were officials waiting for him. They grounded him for ninety days."

After she had flown for four months she lost the hearing in her left ear when the plane hit extreme turbulence near Reno and suddenly dropped five hundred feet.

"I quit a few days later because I didn't want to go deaf in my other ear, too," said Mrs. Fuite. "My husband and I now fly on most of our trips. It's a lot safer than the freeways, even though I've had some hair-raising experiences in my days as one of the first stewardesses."[15]

[14]Murray Olderman, "The Friendly Skies Weren't Always So Friendly." *Rocky Mountain News*, 23 September 1974.

[15]Judy Klemesrush, "stewardess, 1930 Style," *New York Times*, 14 May 1970, Section C, page 41.

PIONEER IN AVIATION
Boeing Air Transport United Air Lines, American Airways American Airlines Harriett Heffron Gleeson 1931 - 1934

This pioneer in aviation flew for two airlines as an early stewardess.

Dubuque, Iowa hosts an aviation pioneer for not only one airline,, but two in their days of early stewardess service. Harriett Heffron Gleeson, 84 years of age has been a resident of the Sunnycrest Nursing Home for over twelve years. She wrote me letters between my visits. Her letters in her own words expanded on her experiences as an early stewardess.

Harriett was born December 29, 1908 in East Dubuque, Iowa. After high school she completed nurses training at Oak Park Hospital in Chicago in 1930. After a short time in private duty nursing Harriett became interested in the new occupation afforded nurses: that of a stewardess for Boeing Air Transport to fly as third crew member cabin attendants on Boeing B-80A, ten passenger aircraft. Requirements were: intelligent, petite RN's no taller than 5 foot 4 inches; weight no more than 115 pounds; attractive; single; good health; enthusiastic and no older than 25 years of age. Salary $125 for 100 hours of flying.

Harriett was hired April 25, 1931 to fly between Chicago and Cheyenne. She was in the second group of stewardesses hired by Boeing Air Transport to fly the airline's route between Chicago, Cheyenne and San Francisco. The "Original Eight" stewardesses had first taken to the sky May 1, 1930 to launch a new career for women. Ellen Church had convinced skeptical Boeing Air Transport's officials, with the help of Steve Stimpson, a District Manager for Boeing, that nurses on board aircraft to care for passengers' needs was good psychology. The Original Eight stewardesses passed their three month probationary period and air travel started to build. Soon passengers booked a particular flight to fly with a certain RN stewardess. Boeing officials realized that they had a good idea. Harriett was one of those chosen to follow in airline history of the early occupation as stewardess and relates her experiences flying for two lines.

BOEING AIR TRANSPORT

"The Boeing B-80A was slow and flew at low altitudes. Air was often turbulent and air-sickness was common among passengers. The wires between the wings would often twang in the wind; it was unnerving. Ventilation was crude and often exhaust fumes would enter the fuselage. We would turn off the heat and passengers wore their coats, and wrapped in blankets.

"Early stewardesses did have time to talk to passengers, to point out interesting points of interest and often joined in a card game. No drinks were served, as this was during Prohibition. In fact, we had to watch passengers for flasks and cough syrup bottles containing alcohol.

"Our food service consisted of cold chicken, sandwiches, relishes and fruit cocktail. Hot bullion and coffee were served from thermos containers.

"Aircraft were sometimes forced to make emergency landings in open fields. I helped crew members take down

Harriett Heffron Gleeson (second from left), a stewardess for Boeing Air Transport (United Airlines) in 1931.

Will Rogers, an aviation enthusiast, frequently flew on flights with 1930s stewardesses. (United Airlines Photo)

fences when we made an unscheduled landing in a farmer's field so the airplane could take off after it was repaired. We did everything except fly the airplane. We did it because we knew we could be replaced by men.

"Work was exciting, but not without danger. My roommate, Mary Carter, was killed in a crash. Later, another friend, Ada Huckelby was also killed. It's something you don't forget. It was terrible to hear of the crash and then realize Mary and Ada were on those flights.

"Dangers also came from passengers. I had a frightening experience in 1931. After taking off from Chicago, as I was walking down the aisle greeting passengers, I noted a man bleeding profusely from a chest wound. The man became very nervous and quite rude when I questioned him about the blood. I convinced him I was a nurse and knew what needed to be done. I applied a pressure dressing. He then confessed it was a bullet wound. After taking care of him I went back to our small galley and wrote a note to the pilot:

> *Passenger has bullet wound, profuse bleeding, needs ambulance, MD and police at next landing.*

I folded the note and placed it under a coffee cup on a tray. I took the two cups of coffee to the pilot and copilot in the cockpit. The passenger questioned me on my return as he was very suspicious. I told him it was customary to serve coffee to the crew. When we landed, the M.D., police and the ambulance were waiting. It was an anxious time as I didn't know if the passenger was carrying a gun."

CHANGE OF TERRAIN
American Airways
(1933 - 1934)

Harriett became bored with the flat, uninteresting terrain between Chicago and Cheyenne and weary of the constant turbulence and airsickness of passengers. She learned American Airways had started stewardess service May 3, 1933 with four Registered Nurses. American was flying East out of Chicago to Newark, with stops at Detroit and Buffalo. Harriett applied to American and was accepted. She enjoyed the change of scenery. She was on several inaugural flights, including opening service to Boston's Logan Airport.

Her experiences as a pioneer stewardess was rewarding one for Harriett. After being grounded in 1934 by marriage to William Gleeson (stewardesses had to be single), she became the mother of Patricia. This marriage ended in divorce five years later, Harriett then returned to her former home of Dubuque. She did private duty at Finley and Mercy Hospitals. Other positions in nursing included serving as resident nurse of the Conrad Hilton Hotel in Chicago, and at Sunnycrest Sanatorium for Tuberculosis, little knowing that Sunnycrest would later become a nursing home and become her home.

Because of a bone disease, Harriett had been confined to Sunnycrest twelve years and for the past years used a wheelchair instead of a walker.

United Airlines stewardess alumni association, Clipped Wings, made Harriett Heffron Gleeson an honorary member. She is also one of the early stewardesses featured in *Walking on Air.* In May 1990, I took a former RN friend of Harriett's from Oak Park Hospital's 1930 nursing school training (Mildred Lasner of Bettendorf, Iowa) to visit her. The two former nurses had not seen each other

Harriett Heffron Gleeson with crew members at American Airways' opening of service to Boston, 1933.

for 60 years. I also brought another surprise, the 1930 first uniform for Boeing Air Transport like the one Harriett had worn. The uniform was loaned from the United's Training Center in Chicago for the special occasion to honor a pioneer in aviation history and the 60th anniversary year of this new career Harriett had helped launch. Her hometown newspaper featured the story of their pioneer in aviation. Harriett Heffron Gleeson passed away on September 12, 1993.

UNITED'S LEGEND[16]

Mary O'Connor 1933 - 1960

An aircraft was named after this great lady representing United Air Lines in her own time in inflight service.

She was known as the "most flyingest woman in the world." Mary O'Connor retired in December 1960 after twenty-two years as a United Airlines stewardess, having logged over seven million miles in the air. She returned to nursing at St. Francis Hospital in Evanston, Illinois, where she had graduated from nursing school in 1932.

The year after her graduation from St. Francis Hospital in Evanston, Illinois, she applied for a job as stewardess for United when she heard the airline was recruiting nurses. Mary joined United May 18, 1933.

Mary O'Connor by a Convair, the second aircraft to be named the *Mainliner O'Connor*. Mary was also the first stewardess instructor. (United Airlines Photo)

Gregory Peck, Mary, John Houston and Frank Ledebur on the steps of the *Mainliner O'Connor*. (United Airlines Photo)

There was no formal training for stewardesses as there is today. In the early 1930s the co-pilots informed the stewardesses of many of their duties. Mary took her first flight as a stewardess in May, 1933. She did not realize that she would make this her career for nearly the next three decades.

"We flew ten-passenger trimotor Fords that were supposed to cruise at 100 miles an hour, but if they made 80 miles an hour, it was because we had a tail-wind," Mary said and added, "It wasn't coffee, tea and milk in those days, just coffee. We served fruit cocktail and three kinds of sandwiches: chicken, Canadian bacon and cheese. The first passengers offered the tray always got the chicken and the last, the cheese."

Mary also thought that the service was more personalized in the early days. She said, "For instance, if we were ready to take off and a passenger called and said he'd be an hour late, we'd hold the plane for him."

By 1940, Mary had become United's Chief stewardess. In 1943, she took a leave of absence to enlist as a Navy nurse during World War II. She attained the

[16]"Mary O'Connor," *United Clipped Wings Quarterly*, October 1955, Convention Issue.

Mary in the galley of a DC-3 as a promotion for Borden milk in 1937. Advertisements were also on buses and billboards. (United Airlines Photo)

Mary O'Connor, Executive Stewardess for the Convair *Mainliner O'Connor* with some of the celebrities she served in more than 3 decades with United. Left to right: Pilar Wayne, John Wayne, Mrs. Bond, Mary and Ward Bond. (United Airlines Photo)

rank of First Lieutenant, and as a chief nurse she organized the Navy's school for air evacuation at Alameda, California.

After the war, in 1946, Mary returned to United as Chief stewardess and wrote the first complete stewardess manual. She was selected to serve on United's executive aircraft. The plane was named the "Mainliner O'Connor" in honor of her dedicated service. By 1955, Mary had logged 4,500,000 miles in her flight log.

The Mainliner O'Connor was used by United's President Patterson as well as other United officials, as a

Mary with Jimmy Stewart on the steps of the *Mainliner O'Connor.* (United Airlines Photo)

flying office. It was also used for special chartered flights for movie tours and political campaigns. The DC-3 was later replaced by a twin-engine Convair, which kept the name "Mainliner O'Connor."

Mary was many things to many, people. She met many celebrities on her flights, including movie stars and Presidents of the United States. She has served Presidents Herbert Hoover, Dwight D. Eisenhower, John Kennedy, and Richard Nixon who was then Vice President. Celebrities included Will Rogers, Jack Webb, James Stewart, Amelia

Mary (President W.A. Patterson's Executive Stewardess) aboard the DC-3 *Mainliner O'Connor*, 1946. (United Airlines Photo)

Earhart, Arthur Godfrey, Gregory Peck, Jack Benny, Joan Crawford, Jerry Lewis, Tony Bennett, Mitch Miller and John Wayne.

In 1956 Mary accompanied West German Chancellor Konrad Adenauer on a tour of several cities in the United States. He was so charmed by her that he asked her to come to Germany as his guest. Mary accepted on the spot, with no time to pack a bag, and she was airborne for Germany in two hours.

All totaled, it has been estimated that Mary had three-and-a-half years of constant flying time on Ford Trimotors, Boeing- 247s, DC-3s, DC-4s, DC-6s and DC-7 aircraft.

Former President Patterson said of Mary, "She was always answering a fire alarm for others. When one of the employee's children were very ill, she flew to their aid. She was the Fiorence Nightingale of the air."She says of her flying experience, "Up there the views are gorgeous, never the same any two days or any two hours. I never stayed long enough in one place to get married. My first love was flying, and I'm still in love."

Mary O'Connor, like Ellen Church of the Original Eight, has a special place in the history of United Airlines. Clipped Wings made Mary an honorary member, honoring United's legend in her own time. I for one, feel honored to have known this lovely woman who has given so much to so many.

Mary O'Connor passed away on April 12, 1994 at the age of 87 years.

Left to right: United captain, Dale Cavanaugh; Mildred "Sugar" Kane Connell, United stewardess in 1937; Dr. John Connell; Captain W.J. "Dub" Smith pictured at the 1986 United Clipped Wings conference at Keystone, Colorado.

AN ANGEL ON HER SHOULDER

United Air Lines
Marie Hess Conway
1933 - 1940

The following story relates the career of another prominent stewardess who attained a unique position with United Air Lines.

A pretty, petite nurse became a legend for United, like her friend, Mary O'Connor. She hired and trained hundreds of stewardesses (all registered nurses like herself) as Chief stewardess for the Chicago Division 1934 through 1940.

Marie was born to Anthony and Christina Hess. Her father had immigrated from Stuttgart, Germany and had located in Kansas. At age one Marie moved with her parents to the small town of Reno, Kansas. Her father was known for his love of people as a grocery merchant and Justice of the Peace. His love of people rubbed off on Marie.

Marie, ready for a flight on a Ford Trimotor, 1933.

A one room school room educated Marie through eighth grade and then she attended Toganoxie Kansas High School. She entered nurses' training at St. Joseph's Hospital in Kansas City and was capped in 1930.

Marie used her nursing skills for two years. It was in the years of the great depression and she was fortunate to have employment. While attending the wife of the County Assessor of Kansas City, he suggested that she apply for a new job opened up to women - that of flying as a stewardess for United Air Transport. The salary was $125 for 100 hours of flying; this sounded good to Marie. She had never seen an airplane, and didn't know anything about them, but she was curious about the job and decided to interview. Besides, the pay sounded good.

The prerequisites for the job were: to be a Registered Nurse, good health, under 25 years of age, single, between 5 feet 2 inches and 5 feet 4 inches in height, weigh no more than 115 pounds, and 20/20 vision. Marie was interviewed by Mr. E.P. Lot and two pilots were also present. Marie says, "three of us went. One was too short, one was too heavy and I was just right and got the job."

A trip trade proved to be fortunate for her. She had been supposed to take a one day flight from Kansas City to Chicago to Kansas City, while another stewardess was assigned a trip Kansas City to Dallas with an overnight layover. She, however, wanted to be back in Kansas City for a date, so asked Marie for a trade. This was most agreeable as Marie thought it would be great to have the layover in Dallas. However, the following day, she was called to report to the airport early ahead of her crew. The United manager informed her the flight she had traded had crashed at LaSalle-Peru out of Chicago en route back to Kansas City. He wanted to tell her first, before she heard it on the radio. She felt sickened by the news, but knew she'd had an angel on her shoulder.

Another time Marie had a "biffy ride" holding on for dear life! She had gone on the aircraft early to check on supplies and see that the lavatory was clean. While in there, the test pilots that had been working on the airplane suddenly took off for a test run. Marie yelled...but no one heard her above the roar of the engines. After this, an order was issued to always check in the cabin and lavatory before take off.

In October of 1934, Marie was first selected to become the Chief Hostess of the Chicago Cheyenne Division and later the Eastern Division. Her duties were to select and train new stewardesses. She also represented United in many areas of publicity and became the most photographed stewardess. Mary O'Connor hired one day ahead of Marie became the personal stewardess of the President of United, W.A. Patterson and worked on his executive DC-3.

Often Marie traveled coast to coast speaking on behalf of stewardesses. She also attended the National Air Races. Three stewardesses represented the airlines, Marie as Miss United Air Lines, and also a Miss TWA and a Miss American Airlines. She was on radio talk shows, including Amos and Andy shows, as well as a *Wheaties* and a *Pepsodent* toothpaste commercial. She was also invited by the members of the Poor Richard's Club, an exclusive men's club in Philadelphia, to speak about stewardesses. She had combed her hair just before going to the podium. While speaking she felt something catching on her collar. Her poise was shown by removing the comb and continuing with her speech. She was presented a medallion that had been given only twice before — to Charles Lindbergh and Amelia Earhart.

Boeing 247 shows interior and nose compartment where a fire started with mail bags during a check ride in 1933.

Marie related other experiences, "On a check flight as Chief stewardess on a night flight, we were refueled at Iowa City. A cloth was left near the heating unit in the nose baggage compartment where many mail bags were stowed. An odor smelled like something burning. I called the stewardess to get the pilot to come into the cabin. The pilot did not smell anything in the rear of the cabin. Walking to the cockpit he suddenly smelled smoke - the draft of his opening the cockpit door had caused a suction to flame a fire. An emergency landing was made and a fire truck and an ambulance met our plane. It was discovered 25 mail sacks were smoldering. They were packed so tightly they had saved an all out fire. This made newspaper news.

Chief Stewardess Marie Hess Conway sits on the tail of a B-247. She was the most photographed stewardess for publicity. (United Airlines Photo)

"On just one of my many charter flights, Bloomingdale's held a special fashion show over New York City, promoting 'Barbara Lee Shoes' with sanitized linings. I served lunch on the DC-3 while the fashion show went on. They gave me six pair of their spectator navy and white tie oxford shoes. These shoes were a part of our summer uniform, the lining provided comfort for the many steps walked by stewardesses," stated Marie. "Another charter was the Courtesy DC-4 flight by Boeing Aircraft. I was the only stewardess to work this particular aircraft. Rosalie Gimple, also a chief stewardess, and I spent two weeks at Santa Monica where the DC-4 was being worked up on a draft board. The engineers wanted to know what they needed for passenger comfort and valued our input.

"It took two years to build and, when ready, made its maiden voyage to New York City. United had only leased the aircraft. It was on display at each of the major cities - this portion was flown by United crews. On June 6, 1939 it was flown from New York to Washington, DC by Bendix race pilots, Jacklaine Cockrand and Benny Howard. Courtesy hops for dignitaries and the press were flown all day in Washington, DC. Our last load of passengers were Japanese. Some weeks later I had a letter from Japan from a Douglas crew member who said the Japanese had bought the DC-4. The crew had helped dismantle it and the plane had been taken to Japan to assemble. They said the Japanese were poor mechanics, but natural born pilots. Then, later, we learned Japan was buying our scrap iron and equipment. They returned that visit with their bombing of Pearl Harbor on December 7, 1941.

"The original DC-4 had the tail assembly redesigned and became a four-mile-a-minute commercial plane that brought new luxury to forty four passengers."

THE DOCTOR MEETS THE NURSE

Marie did not know she was being observed by a handsome young doctor, Martin Conway. He had accompanied his friend, also a doctor, to a farewell party being given for a United stewardess who was getting married. His friend was dating a stewardess and had wanted Martin to drive with him to Chicago to also attend the party being held at the hotel where Marie lived. Cocktails were being served frequently. Marie had sipped hers, and refilled the glass with Coca Cola. Everyone was

On a flight in 1937, Eleanor Roosevelt was one of Marie's passengers. When the other passengers wanted to meet her, she obliged them by walking down the aisle in the DC-3 to meet every one.

smoking cigarettes and Marie had been offered a cigarette several times, which she had politely refused.

Martin was noticing this petite, pretty young girl and he liked what he saw. He managed to introduce himself and asked if he could take her home, Marie replied, "I am home, I live here at the hotel." He did persuade Marie to go to dinner with him; he knew he liked this young lady!

After the party Martin told his friend, "There is a young woman who is different! She doesn't drink and she doesn't smoke." He tried to get in touch with Marie the following day and found her to be out of town. Undaunted, he had a florist send two orchids to her hotel. It had been Marie's day off and she had flown to Kansas City to see a former patient. On her return she found the orchids and a note from Martin asking for a date. The romance blossomed and Marie and Dr. Martin Conway made plans

United played host to Bloomingdale's department store and fashion writers on a luncheon flight over the New York World's Fair on July 20, 1939. Marie is wearing the 1939 summer uniform and sanitized shoes. (United Airlines Photo)

to wed.

In the meantime, Marie told her student stewardesses, "Always be yourself. I didn't know I was being observed, I was doing what I believed for myself. I found the man of my dreams and he said he found me." Martin and Marie were wed February 3, 1940. They moved to Aledo, Illinois where Martin had his practice. Stewardesses were grounded at the time of their marriage. *Marie had flown over 200,000 miles in her career.* She sums up her time as a United stewardess and Chief stewardess, "I loved every minute of my job. People made every day interesting and

On February 1, 1936, each of the following stewardesses had flown one and a half million miles: Marie Hess (middle left), Vi Hart (top left), Jerry Kees (top right), Rosalie Gemple (middle right), Ruth Flekke (bottom right) and Catherine Muse (left). (United Airlines Photo)

my life has always continued to be people."

Marie is 84 years old and still involved in her Aledo community today and loved by all. She has two sons. Martin, Jr. makes his home in Aledo and is a Circuit Judge. Son, Michael, is in business in Chicago. She is the proud grandmother of five and always a lady and proud legacy of United Air Lines.

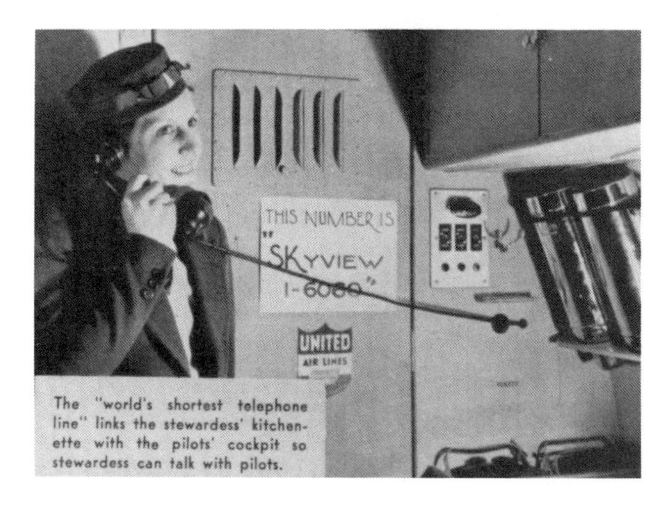

The "world's shortest telephone line" links the stewardess' kitchenette with the pilots' cockpit so stewardess can talk with pilots.

Mary O'Connor was on the maiden flight of the first sleeper plane. She is shown at the galley phone. (United Airlines Photo)

LADY OF THE AIR

United Air Lines
Mildred J. (Sugar) Kane Connell
1937 - 1938

"I was born at home on my parents' farm near Fairmont, IA, on August 19, 1914. When I was six, I joined my older brother and sister in the mile and a half walk through the fields to our school, Rabbit Ridge. This was the same little one-room country school that my father had attended years before. The education was excellent. It was at Rabbit Ridge School when I learned about Wilbur and Orville Wright. I found their interest in flying fascinating.

"When I was nine years old, a young pilot thrilled our entire rural community by landing his small plane in a neighbor's pasture. He spent the afternoon taking farmers up for their first airplane rides. I wish I could remember how they looked when they got off of that ride. My father and I just stood there with our mouths open the whole time.

"As the years went by, United Air Lines began having flights that passed over our farm. They flew quite low in those days, and they were noisy. We found it exciting every time.

"I remember, too, when Charles Lindbergh flew across the Atlantic and landed near Paris. The newspapers were full of excitement that he should be able to fly clear across the ocean, and all alone in such a small plane.

"After high school, I decided to go for nurse's training. I graduated from Iowa Lutheran Hospital in Des Moines in October, 1935. After some private duty nursing, I took a position as Assistant Surgical Supervisor at Iowa Methodist Hospital. I was happy in that position, so oddly enough, I can't recall just what it was that turned my interest toward working for the airline. I would go in to the United offices now and then, and speak with Eddy Butler, then Manager of Operations for United in Des Moines. I was accepted to work as a stewardess for United on July 10, 1937. The operating room nurses gave me a nice going away breakfast and a compact make-up kit, and one of the doctors gave me a rabbit's foot for good luck. I was outfitted with custom-made shoes and hand-tailored uniforms and spent three weeks training in Chicago for my stewardess duties. I was based in Chicago and flew on the B-247s and then the DC-2, United's Mainliner Sleeper, a 14 passenger deluxe aircraft that by night made up into sleeping berths similar to a pullman car on a train. My route was Chicago, Denver and Salt Lake City."

Mildred "Sugar" Kane Connell, United stewardess in front of a Boeing 247 in 1937.

Mildred was nicknamed *Sugar* for Kane. Her passengers liked her as much as she enjoyed the opportunity to meet them. One passenger committed his thoughts to poetry:

To An Air Hostess

by
Hugh R. Porter, Chicago

Little Lady of the Air,
Flitting here and flying there,
Over mountain tops and lakes,
Courage real is what it takes
To go on from day to day,
On your highly dangerous way;
Yet you smile and carry on,
Through the night and at the dawn,
Though you know if ship should break,
You will sleep to never wake;
Still because it is your work,
You in no way seem to shirk
Tasks that they assign to you,
But with purpose firm and true,
Through the sunshine or the rain,
Every day you "Play the Game."

Little Lady of the Air,
God is always everywhere,
O'er the mountain tops and dales,
In the valleys and the vales;
O'er the desert so forlorn,
In the tempest and the storm;
Everywhere that you may go,
Through the rain and sleet and snow.
And your mother's fervent prayers,
Her devotion and her tears,
To the Throne of Grace shall rise,
For your safety in the skies.
So with God and mother too,
Caring for and guarding you,
E'en though dangers may appall,
He will never let you fall.

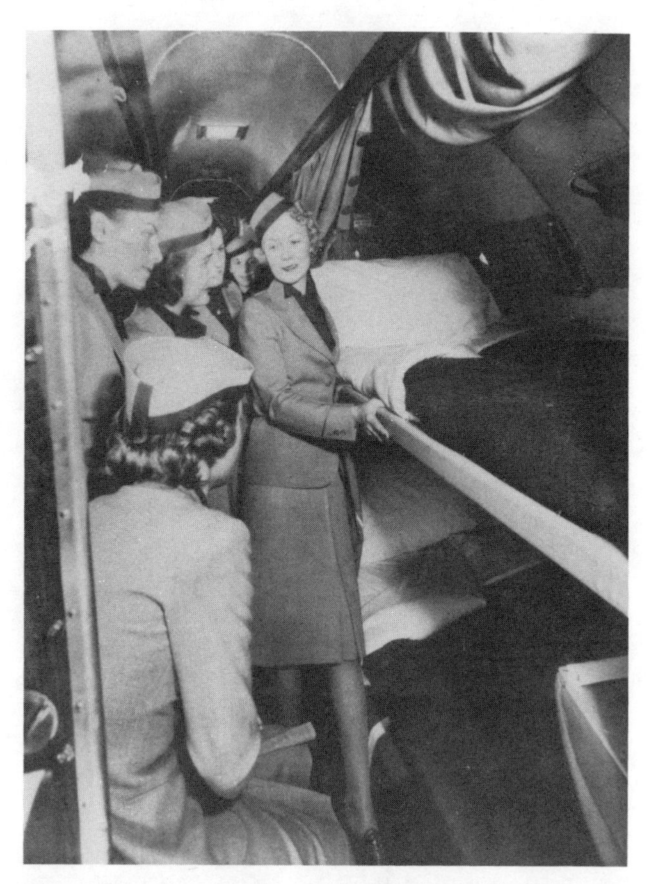

Florence Pond instructing stewardesses how to make up a berth aboard the DST sleeper aircraft, 1936. (United Airlines Photo)

The young intern *Sugar* had met before becoming a United stewardess proposed marriage. After ten months of flying she married Dr. John Connell, Jr. in 1938 in Denver, Colorado. Today they make their home in Denver. Mildred participates as an active member of United's Clipped Wings Association of current and former flight attendants. She says of her days flying. "It gave me the opportunity to meet so many fine people. I surrendered my wings for marriage but I've always kept my interest in flying to this day."

Sugar Kane, United Air Lines stewardess, greeting a passenger in the doorway of a DC-2 on the ramp at Chicago's Midway Airport in 1937. (United Airlines Photo)

Passengers on United Air Lines' overnight DC-3 sleeper planes traveled in style. Stewardesses served breakfast in bed, then passengers changed clothes in a luxurious lounge while their berths were made up. Upper berths folded into the ceiling and lower berths converted into two facing seats. By day, meals were served on fine china and linen, with bouquets of fresh flowers at each table. (United Airlines Photo)

1936 DC-3 14-passenger deluxe model with upholstered chairs and meals served on Haviland china with sterling silver and damask linens. (United Airlines Photo)

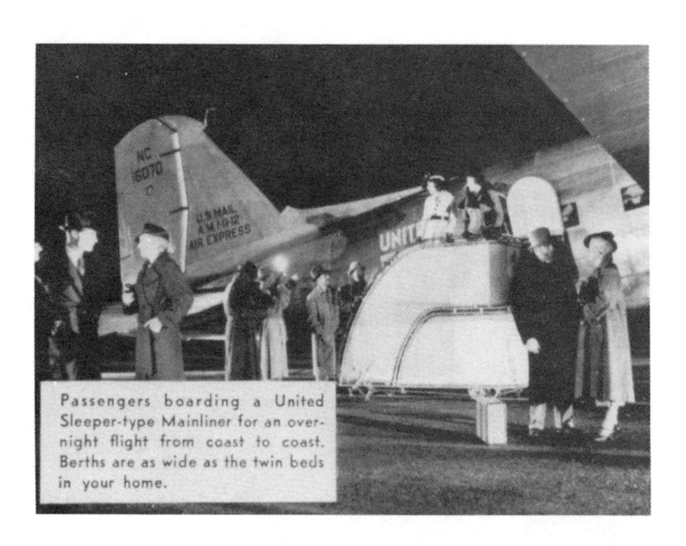

NC 16070
Passengers boarding a United Sleeper-type Mainliner for an over-night flight from coast to coast. Berths are as wide as the twin beds in your home.

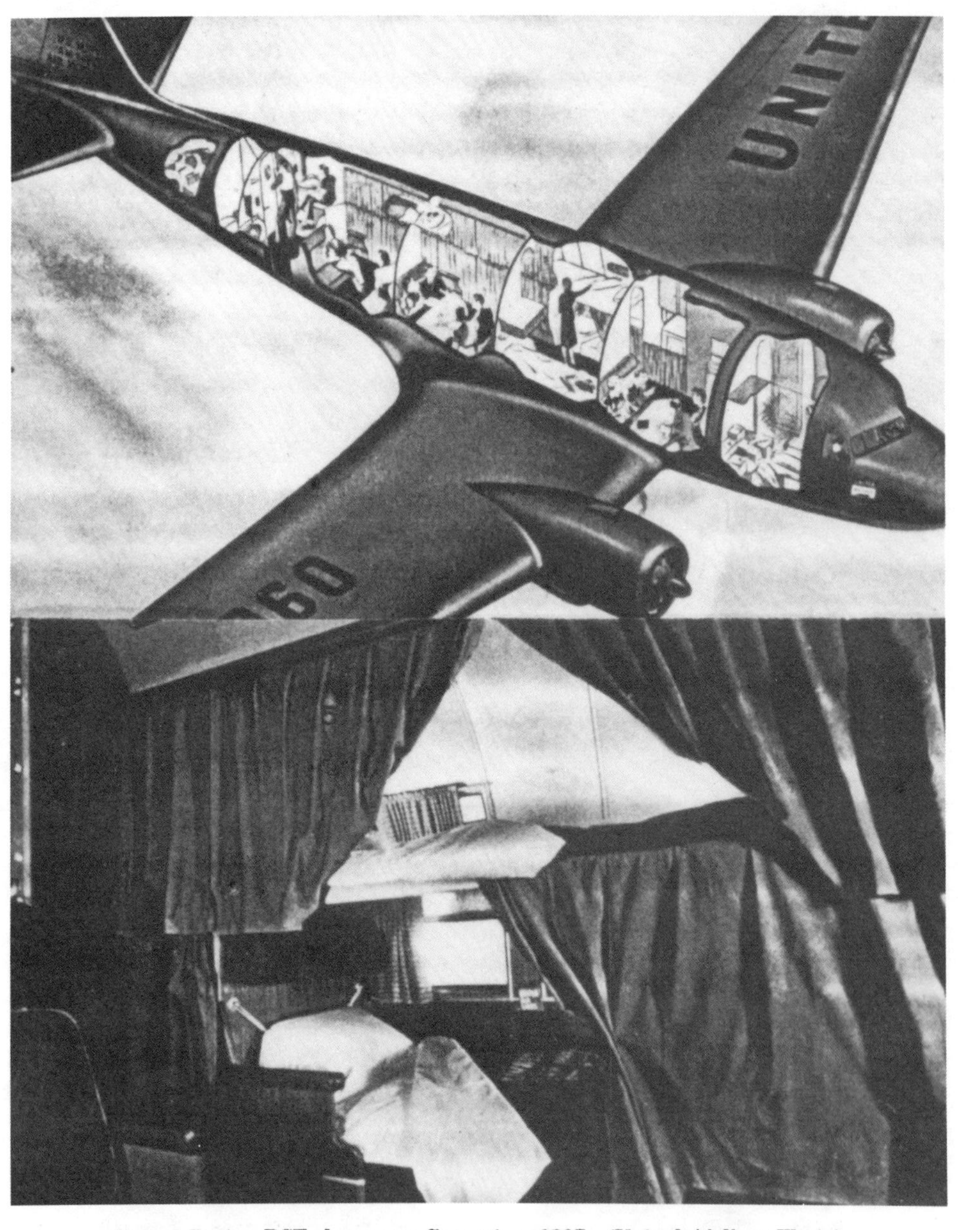

United Boeing DST sleeper configuration, 1937. (United Airlines Photo)

Trudy Von Hoven Pracny, one of seven hostesses for Boeing Air Transport in 1931. She is shown in the doorway of a Curtiss Condor. (Eastern Airlines Photo)

EASTERN AIR TRANSPORT

Eastern Air Transport hired seven air hostesses in 1931 to fly on their 18 passenger Curtiss Condors to follow Boeing Air Transport's example of women as stewardesses.

TRUDY'S WINGS

Eastern Air Transport
Trudy Von Hoven Pracny
1931

Eastern Air Transport hired Trudy before she knew it as one of their first seven air hostesses in 1931.

Trudy Von Hoven Pracny has an enthusiastic approach to life. "Being an air hostess when a woman in aviation was a novelty is by far the greatest thing that ever happened to me," says Trudy. It was 1931 when she became one of the seven first air hostesses for Eastern Air Transport. Today she is an active member of Eastern Silverliners and Eastern Airline's Retirement Association. Trying to get in touch with her at her home in Florida is a feat in itself. One is fortunate if you can find her there between travels coast to coast and to far away places. She is always on the go!

When Trudy flies, the cockpit crew always asks her to visit them, even on a recent flight on the Concorde. She is witty and vivacious and interesting as a pioneer in aviation and a world traveler. At 85 years of age this bouncy woman enjoys people, travel, bridge, golf and life in general.

Trudy asked to write her own story of her experiences as an air hostess. The following is her story in her own words:

"In 1931, among others, I was dating Bob Reichert, a copilot for Colonial Airways. He'd phoned from Boston to say he could not keep our date to go to a party on Long Island at a local *Speakeasy*. When I assured him the weather was beautiful in Hempstead Gardens, he reiterated that weather was *socked in* and he could do nothing about it. I commented that he'd soon be *socked out* with a flimsy excuse like that.

"Several days later Bob called to say he was going to Colonial's hangar in Newark and would like me to drive over with him. He added, 'My friend, Ralph Lockwood, is

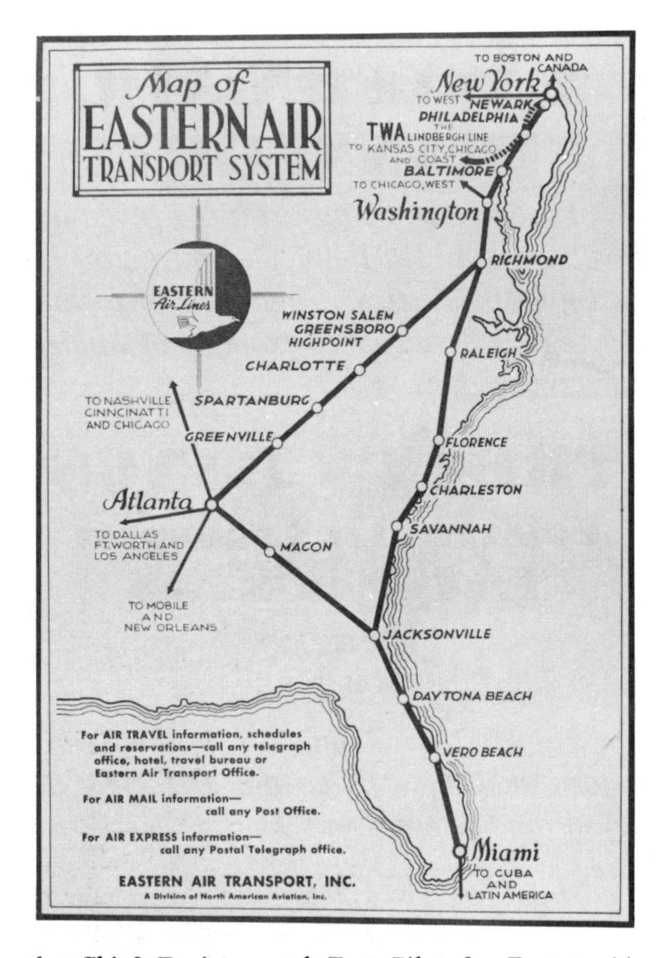

the Chief Engineer and Test Pilot for Eastern Air Transport, and I'll introduce you to him. If he is testing EAT's two 625 Curtiss Condors, he may take you with him.' That, I was all for! Bob also mentioned that EAT was experimenting with flying hostesses and Ralph would tell me about it. I thought he'd really flipped at that as I hadn't ever heard or read about it. I agreed to go.

"Ralph invited me to sit in the copilot's seat and off we went to North Beach (now LaGuardia Airport) and then he landed on one motor and then the other at Floyd Bennett Field in Brooklyn and Teaneck, NJ. Having been born in Hempstead Gardens and surrounded by Mitchell Field, Curtiss Field, and Roosevelt Field, I had flown in two-place open-seat jobs which were fun and exciting! This huge commercial Curtiss Condor was pretty interesting too.

"After a few hours we returned to Newark. Ralph took me up to the second floor at EAT's offices to meet Mrs. Cullum, the Chief Hostess. She told me they already had several girls flying from Newark to Atlanta and Newark to Jacksonville, and also the Frost sisters flying the Ford *Tin Goose* between Washington, DC and Newark with stops at Baltimore and Philadelphia.

"Bob returned and said he was ready to leave. Mrs. Cullum and I exchanged pleasantries, and she asked for my phone number. Bob and I went back to Long Island.

"That evening about 9:00, Mrs. Cullum phoned and asked if I could be at the Newark Airport about 5:45 in the morning. I emphatically said no, because it required a two mile taxi ride to the Hempstead Rail Road Station and the Long Island Rail Road. In those days it took over an hour to get to the Penn Station where I'd have to find a subway to Newark and then another taxi to the airport. It was too long and too expensive. She replied for me to get there as soon as I could. I got to Newark's airport vowing to never, ever again get involved in that trek.

"Mrs. Cullum asked what size dress I wore and since I was a size 12 and she had one, I donned a three-piece knit suit. It was navy blue with a navy tam-o-shanter (beret) on which I pinned a two-inch oval EAT. A one-inch pin with the word Hostess went on the lapel. Mrs. Cullum then announced we would go *down the line* to Richmond in a huge biplane which was then licensed to fly the largest number of passengers in the U.S.A. It carried eighteen passengers, plus a crew of three.

"We had very few passengers that morning. Mrs. Cullum passed out the gum and the cigarettes after Camden, Baltimore and Washington, and then we alighted at Byrd Field in Richmond. There we enthusiastically trooped into the hangar where the Ground Hostess supervised the serving of a delicious southern luncheon to passengers who were all seated at a picnic table."

Trudy Von Hoven Pracny, 1931.

A hostess for Eastern Air Transport, 1931.

UP THE LINE . . .

"After lunch, Mrs. Cullum suggested I take the 1:00 plane from Jacksonville *up the line* and she would take the 2:00 one from Atlanta. She said for me to be sure and secure the latch on the closing door before taking off, and if anyone of note boarded the plane, write a little *blurb* and hand it in at Newark, so it could be written up in the house organ *Wings*. I asked how you could be sure if anyone was important. (My idea was movie stars: Wallace Berry, Theda Bara or Mary Pickford.) Mrs. Cullum said, 'For instance, I've just heard that Mr. Hoover may get on at Washington and if he does, write it down and hand it in at Newark.'

"So off again we go. We flew at 1200 feet, and only short distances between hops - there was a lot of turbulence. For the first time I offered gum and cigarettes. The cigarettes first. The tin boxes of Lucky Strikes and Chesterfields containing 50 cigarettes each were popular with passengers. By then most civilized people didn't even frown on women indulging.

"I sat next to the most pleasant gentleman, a Mr. Du Pont, who asked if I had been with EAT very long. I replied that I wasn't sure I was with them yet, that I had just been asked to fly *down the line* for the first time in my life, and I was delighted to be doing so. He proceeded to educate me regarding our whereabouts. He told me names of the rivers and towns of Virginia, Mount Vernon, and pointed out a few manufacturing plants belonging to his family. This was the way my training started.

"After landing and departing from Washington (and latching the door) I sat next to a man who again asked if I was new - etc., etc. I told him I was glad that only he and two other passengers had gotten on the airplane and that the President hadn't. He said, 'What President?' I said I guessed of the United States. He replied that he had never heard of the President flying, and I agreed I hadn't either. I explained Mrs. Cullum's instructions. He said, 'Maybe she meant the other Mr. Hoover,' and added, 'in fact, my

"Putting Travel On A Higher Plane"

EASTERN AIR TRANSPORT SYSTEM

A DIVISION OF NORTH AMERICAN AVIATION, INC.

PASSENGERS

U. S. AIR MAIL

GENERAL OFFICES—SPERRY BUILDING, MANHATTAN BRIDGE PLAZA, BROOKLYN, N. Y.
Telephone: CUmberland 6-0442

Pass.-Mail

NEW YORK — WASHINGTON

Southbound Read Down				Eastern Standard Time	Northbound Read Up			
Trip 17*	Trip 7*	Trip 33b	Trip 11*		Trip 12*	Trip 34b	Trip 8*	Trip 18*
am 7.15	am 8.15	am 11.15	pm 4.15	lv N. Y. City ar Hotel Pennsylvania	am 11.50	pm 6.00	pm 6.50	pm 7.50
8.00	9.00	pm z12.00	†5.00	lv Newark Airp. ar	§11.05	¶5.15	‖6.05	‖7.05
8.50	9.50	....	....	lv Philadelphia lv	....	....	5.20	6.20
9.45	10.45	1.30	6.45	lv Baltimore lv	9.25	....	4.25	5.25
10.10	11.10	1.45	7.10	ar Washington lv	8.55	3.30	3.55	4.55

* Daily. b Daily except Sunday and Monday.

CONNECTIONS

z From Boston and Hartford, via American Airways (daily except Sunday and Monday).
† From Boston and Hartford, and from Montreal and Albany, via American Airways (daily except Sunday); from Chicago and Cleveland via United Air Lines (daily).
§ To Boston and Hartford, via American Airways (daily except Sunday); to Chicago and Cleveland, via United Air Lines (daily).
¶ To Boston, via American Airways (daily except Sunday).
‖ To Boston, via American Airways (daily).

Pass.-Mail

NEW YORK — RICHMOND — ATLANTA

Southbound Read Down			Eastern Standard Time—Daily	Northbound Read Up		
		No. 7		No. 8		
....	....	8.15 am	lv N. Y. City ar Hotel Pennsylvania	6.50 pm	....	....
....	....	9.00 am	lv Newark Airp. ar	¶6.05 pm	....	....
....	....	9.50 am	lv Philadelphia lv	5.20 pm	....	....
....	....	10.45 am	lv Baltimore lv	4.25 pm	....	....
....	....	11.10 am	ar Washington lv	3.55 pm	....	....
....	....	†11.20 am	lv Washington ar	†3.45 pm	....	....
....	....	‡§12.15 pm	ar Richmond lv	§2.50 pm	....	....
....	....	§12.45 pm	lv Richmond ar	§2.40 pm	....	....
....	....	2.25 pm	ar *Greensboro lv	1.00 pm	....	....
....	....	2.35 pm	lv *Greensboro ar	‡12.30 pm	....	....
....	....	3.30 pm	lv Charlotte lv	11.45 am	....	....
....	....	4.20 pm	lv Spartanburg lv	10.55 am	....	....
....	....	4.45 pm	lv Greenville lv	10.30 am	....	....
....	....	‖5.05 pm	ar Atlanta (CST) lv	‖8.00 am	....	....

(CST) Central Standard Time.
‡ Luncheon Stop.
* Greensboro stop also serves High Point and Winston-Salem; direct bus connection.

CONNECTIONS

¶ Boston via American Airways.
† Pittsburgh, Akron and Cleveland via Pennsylvania Airlines.
§ Norfolk and Hopewell via Eastern Air Transport.
‖ New Orleans, Dallas and Los Angeles via American Airways; Augusta, Jacksonville and Miami via Eastern Air Transport (overnight stop).

Pass.-Mail

NEW YORK — RICHMOND — JACKSONVILLE

Southbound Read Down			Eastern Standard Time—Daily	Northbound Read Up		
		No. 17		No. 18		
....	....	7.15 am	lv N. Y. City ar Hotel Pennsylvania	7.50 pm	....	....
....	....	8.00 am	lv Newark Airp. ar	¶7.05 pm	....	....
....	....	8.50 am	lv Philadelphia lv	6.20 pm	....	....
....	....	9.45 am	lv Baltimore lv	5.25 pm	....	....
....	....	10.10 am	ar Washington lv	4.55 pm	....	....
....	....	10.20 am	lv Washington ar	†4.45 pm	....	....
....	....	‡11.15 am	ar Richmond lv	3.50 pm	....	....
....	....	§11.40 am	lv Richmond ar	§3.40 pm	....	....
....	....	*12.55 pm	ar Raleigh lv	*2.25 pm	....	....
....	....	*1.05 pm	lv Raleigh ar	‡*1.55 pm	....	....
....	....	2.30 pm	lv Florence lv	12.40 pm	....	....
....	....	‖3.20 pm	ar Charleston lv	‖11.40 am	....	....
....	....	3.30 pm	lv Charleston ar	11.30 am	....	....
....	....	4.20 pm	ar Savannah lv	10.40 am	....	....
....	....	‖4.30 pm	lv Savannah ar	‖10.30 am	....	....
....	....	z5.40 pm	ar Jacksonville lv	z9.20 am	....	....

‡ Luncheon stop.

CONNECTIONS

¶ Boston via American Airways.
† Pittsburgh, Akron, Cleveland via Pennsylvania Airlines.
§ Norfolk and Hopewell via Eastern Air Transport.
* Pinehurst via Knollwood Airport, Inc.
‖ Augusta and Atlanta via Eastern Air Transport.
z Daytona Beach, St. Petersburg, Miami via Eastern Air Transport (overnight stop); rail to Miami ("Havana Special"), for Pan-American to Havana, Nassau, Central and South America.

Pass.-Mail

NEW YORK — ATLANTIC CITY

Southbound Read Down			Eastern Standard Time—Daily	Northbound Read Up		
		Trip 23		Trip 24		
....	....	2.45 pm	lv N. Y. City ar Hotel Pennsylvania	9.55 am	....	....
....	....	z3.30 pm	lv Newark Airp. ar	¶9.10 am	....	....
....	....	4.25 pm	ar *Atlantic City lv	8.15 am	....	....

* Atlantic City also serves Ocean City; direct bus connection.

CONNECTIONS

¶ To Hartford, Boston and Albany, Buffalo, via American Airways; to Cleveland, Chicago, San Francisco via United Air Lines.
z From Boston and Hartford via American Airways.

Pass.

RICHMOND — NORFOLK

Southbound Read Down			Eastern Standard Time—Daily	Northbound Read Up		
No. 31	No. 9	No. 29		No. 10	No. 30	No. 32
9.00 am	§12.25 pm	†3.50 pm	lv Richmond ar	†11.15 am	§2.40 pm	5.30 pm
f	f	f	. Hopewell	f	f	f
9.45 am	1.10 pm	4.35 pm	ar *Norfolk lv	10.30 am	1.55 pm	4.45 pm

f Flag stop; reservations through Richmond office; does not stop for Richmond passengers except for transfer for points on main line.
* Norfolk also serves Virginia Beach; direct bus connection.

CONNECTIONS

§ Washington, Baltimore, Philadelphia and New York via Eastern Air Transport.
† Atlanta and Jacksonville via Eastern Air Transport.

Pass.-Mail

ATLANTA — JACKSONVILLE — ST. PETERSBURG — MIAMI

Southbound Read Down			Eastern Standard Time—Daily	Northbound Read Up		
	Trip 21	Trip 15		Trip 16	Trip 22	
....	....	¶9.15 am	lv Atlanta (CST) ar	¶4.40 pm	....	....
....	....	11.10 am	lv Macon lv	4.55 pm	....	....
....	....	‡1.00 pm	ar Jacksonville lv	3.00 pm	....	....
....	....	†1.25 pm	lv Jacksonville ar	†2.50 pm	....	....
....	....	2.15 pm	ar Daytona Bch. lv	2.00 pm	....	....
....	2.30 pm	2.25 pm	lv Daytona Bch. ar	1.50 pm	1.45 pm	....
....	3.05 pm	....	lv Orlando lv	....	1.15 pm	....
....	3.55 pm	....	lv Tampa lv	....	12.25 pm	....
....	4.05 pm	....	ar St. Petersburg lv	....	12.10 pm	....
....	....	§4.45 pm	ar Miami lv	§11.30 am	....	....

(CST) Central Standard Time.
‡ Luncheon stop.

CONNECTIONS

¶ Augusta, Richmond, Washington, and New York via Eastern Air Transport; New Orleans and Los Angeles, Louisville and Cleveland via American Airways (overnight stop).
† Augusta, Richmond, Washington, New York via Eastern Air Transport (overnight stop).
§ Havana, Nassau, Central and South America via Pan-American Airways (overnight stop).

Pass.

ATLANTA — AUGUSTA — CHARLESTON — SAVANNAH

Eastbound Read Down			Eastern Standard Time—Daily	Westbound Read Up		
	No. 25	No. 27		No. 26	No. 28	
....	¶7.55 am	z12.45 pm	lv Atlanta (CST) ar	z12.15 pm	¶5.10 pm	....
....	10.15 am	3.05 pm	ar *Augusta lv	11.55 am	4.50 pm	....
....	10.25 am	3.15 pm	lv *Augusta ar	11.45 am	4.40 pm	....
....	§11.30 am	....	ar Charleston lv	....	§3.30 pm	....
....	....	†4.20 pm	ar Savannah lv	†10.40 am	....	....

(CST) Central Standard Time.
* Augusta stop also serves Aiken and Columbia; direct bus connection.

CONNECTIONS

¶ Richmond, Washington and New York, Jacksonville and Miami via Eastern Air Transport (overnight stop).
z Cleveland, Cincinnati and Nashville via American Airways.
§ Richmond, Washington and New York via Eastern Air Transport.
† Jacksonville, St. Petersburg and Miami via Eastern Air Transport.

name is Hoover.' I asked if he'd ever done anything important, and he said he wasn't sure. I told him that was fine and I wouldn't have to write anything and didn't. Of course, time would tell, and he was indeed J. Edgar Hoover, the head of the FBI. Neither of us ever told EAT about that.

"When we arrived in New York, we had a bus that transported all New York passengers to the Pennsylvania Hotel. I was able to go there and cross the street to the Penn Station and return to Long Island without that horrible trip I'd had at dawn.

"The next day Mrs. Cullum called to ask how I'd gotten along. I skipped the details, as she was telling me *I was hired.* I asked her about the salary. She told me $27.50 a week, plus $4 a night for layovers for hotel accommodations, except when in Atlanta (Candler Field), where the Ground Hostess had twin beds, and I stayed there. The schedule was one day to Jacksonville and back, the next to Newark with the following day off. Then to Atlanta, and return to Newark the following day, with the next day off unless something interfered, like weather or forest fires. (We were not permitted to fly over them.)"

FLYING AS A HOSTESS FOR EASTERN AIR TRANSPORT

"Out of the nine stops on the schedule at least five or six of the airways were not lighted. At dusk or dark we had to cancel and take our passengers to a bus, train, or hotel, then the schedule was rescheduled. This was before the time the company, or the employees, seemed interested in how many hours a week you worked.

"We were given a navy leather jacket to wear, we wore navy shoes and carried a navy purse. (Whatever you could afford.) In the spring we were given a light blue one-piece dress with a matching jacket, a cloche style hat, and a red and white scarf. My name plate was hung below the pilot's and copilot's in the cabin behind the cockpit, along with the altimeter and speedometer where the passengers could see them. But they always asked, *How high? How fast?* It was an easy way to start a conversation. They always wanted to know where we were and I answered that many times, *by guess and by God* – sometimes they corrected me.

"Prohibition was supposed to be enforced, so that at least we didn't have liquor to serve. Keeping an alert eye on the flask owners was often a chore, and being sure they *stayed put* after the pilot had signaled that he was leveling off for a landing, as pilots frowned on any movement at that point.

"We had many edicts that came from the second floor offices regarding Hostesses. A $1 fine if you forgot your nameplate; $2 to delay a ship's departure; $5 the second delay, and *three strikes you're out!* Also, a hostess with a missing badge in the middle of her cap was to be fined $1 for each offense. I wondered if the *Fly Boys* received the same instructions? I know they laugh heartily when I tell

them about it today.

1931
arding 18 Passenger E.A.T. Airliner, Washington–New Yor

"Only the Ground Hostess in Newark put a picnic hamper aboard the 6:00 am and 7:00 am flights. The hamper contained Coca Cola, tea biscuits, coffee cake, George Washington Instant Coffee, bouillon, tea bags, and a gallon jug of boiling water. There was no galley, and fixing coffee on a lounge was often the dangerous part of

the job. Turbulence and scalding hot water kept my mouth closed very often, and I did not advertise the goodies on board.

"Occasionally, you were trapped by an *old timer* who might suggest a cup of something. After he jiggled and spilled and wiped, no one bothered to join him in refreshments. I always seemed to have a bruised scalp,

elbow or knee. Frequently, I bounced off the ceiling of the Condors!

"On Christmas Day, 1931, the Ground Hostess had the day off at Atlanta. I was sitting in the airport twiddling my thumbs, as we had been grounded there for over a week with some motor trouble, then weather. Along came an *old* man of *35*, a pilot from my hometown, Hempstead, Long Island, who was a salesman for Champion Spark Plugs. He asked if I liked baseball. I said I did. He took me for a ride in his Pitcairn Autogyro, and we *hung* over the Atlanta Penitentiary watching the convicts' Christmas ball game. The convicts waved and gestured for us to *come on down*. As soon as we flew out of range, we'd circle back and watch some more. Today you might get forcibly evicted from such a lovely grandstand seat. He said later that it probably wasn't my best Christmas ever, and it wasn't, but when I was a nice old lady telling about it, he wagered no one else would have spent a whole day that way. Guess he was right!

"Many of our passengers were politicians, celebrities, show people and police officers taking their charges to their new home at the Atlanta Pen. Many of the *con men* the police escorted had great imaginations and were interesting. Mostly, I think our job was to dispel anxiety and probably my passengers thought as my mother had, *If Trudy can do it, it can't be difficult*.

"Occasionally, an actress with a Pomeranian (I was a *big dog* fan) would hand me her ugly little gem and tell me she was personally acquainted with Mr. Doe, EAT's President, and he'd given his permission for *Flopsy Mopsie* to fly with us. She hoped I'd be good enough to *walk the dog* at various fields where we landed. I wasn't thrilled to death about it. When the actress had *Flopsy Mopsie* kiss me goodbye, along with a $50.00 tip, I rearranged my priorities. Another part of our job was to get the pilot and copilot to pose with me, as the passenger wanted proof he had flown.

Madeline Moon, air hostess for Boeing Air Transport wearing her 1931 summer uniform in the doorway of an 18-passenger Curtiss Condor.

"Dear Will Rogers was a favorite passenger, also the German World War I flying ace, Count von Luckner. He gave me an autographed picture and he also invited me to visit him and the Countess on the yacht on which they lived on the Hudson River, but EAT said no fraternizing with passengers and EAT personnel. I often wondered how many gals married pilots and businessmen they met on their flights?

"In 1932, over 10,000 women applied for flying as hostesses with EAT. I was lucky to have been one of the very few to be selected. After I left Eastern, my social life improved, as once more I could make a date and keep it. I never saw Bob Reichert again, as I was in Newark when he was in Boston, so that was that. There were no New York airports then, and commuting was horrendous. The novelty of being a flying hostess was fun!"

MARRIAGE AND CELEBRITY STATUS

"I married George Chapman Butler, a lawyer, in 1936. In 1942, I joined the W.A.A.C. (later Women's Army Corps) when he went into the service. I was a member of the Fighting (joke) Quartermasters Corps. Six months later I was stationed at Ft. Francis E. Warren in Cheyenne, Wyoming. I was transferred to Buna Buna in New Guinea for a year. I then went to Lae, Hallaudia Biak, Maratai and the Philippines. I returned to the U.S. in 1946.

"Soon after, George and I went our separate ways. I went to California and proceeded to see all of the West. I've since seen all of the 50 states with my trip to Alaska in July, 1984

"In 1951, I married Anthony John Pracny, a banker. We lived in Bellmore, Wautagh and Ridge, Long Island for 30 years. He died the Christmas of 1981. It was shortly after this that the Eastern Silverliners entered my life. I have traveled a great deal since Tony's death. In 1982, I entertained Bob and Dorothy Kullman in Zurich, Switzerland. Dorothy was the Treasurer of Eastern's International Silverliners at that time. I stayed in Switzerland with one of my many cousins who live there. The Kullmans were returning from a Safari in Africa.

"After 50 years of silence I was rediscovered by the Eastern Silverliners in 1981. This outstanding group of young women have been the joy of my life. I was invited to attend the Tampa convention of the International Silverliners (all were former or present flight attendants of Eastern Airlines at the time). I was given an award along with several others and they gave me a standing ovation that warmed my heart. They still make a fuss over me and it feels pretty good.

"I have flown extensively throughout the country and half of the world. In the spring of 1992 a friend asked me to go to England on the Concord, so off I went! The travel agent had forewarned British Airways that I was going and they rolled out the Red Carpet. I was invited to the cockpit and I sat on the jump seat from Ireland to Heathrow. I was strapped in and had huge earphones. The trip took three hours and 16 minutes and we flew at 57,000 feet at 1,350 mph. The pilot added a lot of kisses, *xxx*, on my flight report saying, 'a pioneer and still breathing.' He also delivered kisses in person with a *bit* of enthusiasm! We returned a week later on the QE2 from Southampton to Ft. Lauderdale. An elegant flight and trip and all too short. You could learn to like the plush service, food and drink — no problem! Try it, you'll like it! The foreign pilots are great on *kissing* and our American pilots are hand-shakers, but so warm and friendly that I have had a great life and in many ways much to do with my job with EAT (Eastern Air Transport)..

"While in Nashville visiting Bob and Elinor Lykins (former Eastern stewardess) they took me to their old airport where B-17 and B-24 aircraft were on display. Some of the crews photographed us and asked me to join them on a flight when they come to Florida in January '94. I believe the B-24 is the *last of the lot* and the only one still flying . . . there are more places I can't fit now that I am pleasingly plump?!? And at 85 years October 1, 1993, I don't bend so easily either.

"In September, Audrey Feller, former President of International Silverliners drove from Tampa to get me, and we went to Williamsburg, Virginia to the REPA Convention (Retired Eastern Pilot's Association). I am a Pioneer Celebrity - however a block in my alleged mind, I always have to ask someone what I am supposed to be. This was the first time no one except me was present from the early 30's with whom I had flown with. Plenty my age, but they had flown for dear old Eastern later - what a great group! We heard true tales that were hard to believe and begged for more. They remind you of your experiences so you join forces with the *Tall Tailers!* I plan to go to the convention next year.

"At 85 years of age I am fortunate to be healthy, so I can swim, play golf and travel and enjoy life. I also am still involved in Silverliners that still meet, although membership has dropped since the demise of 60-year-old Eastern Airlines in January 1991. I also take part in EARA (Eastern Airlines Retirees Association) of former Eastern Airline employees. The Golden Era of Eastern Airlines remains in the hearts and memories of this wonderful group of people."

Trudy Von Hoven Pracny represents this era as one of their first pioneer hostesses in 1931. She is enthusiastic, vivacious, humorous and the lady has *pizazz* and a wonderful appreciation of people and life!

AMERICAN AIRLINES

Pistons to Jets[17]

1933

American Airways, the predecessor of American Airlines, inaugurated stewardess service in 1933. By 1935, the ranks had grown from four to seventeen stewardesses, all nurses. In 1936, American began its first formal stewardess training at Chicago's Hyde Park Hotel. The uniforms had a military look, with an overseas cap. For the first time the stewardesses were allowed to wear nail polish...Revlon's "Windsor Rose." By 1940, the nursing requirement was dropped. Training was changed with the addition of new aircraft, DC-3s, DC-2s and DC-4s.

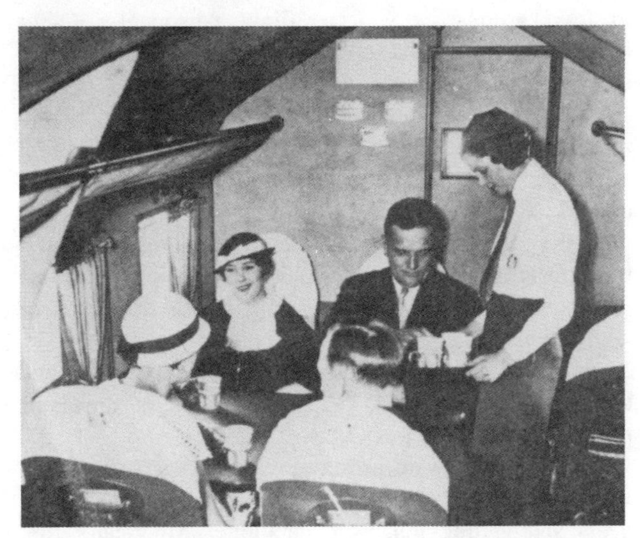

Serving coffee aboard an American Airways flight in 1933

Stewardess training during the period 1936-1949 was held at: Chicago; New York; Tulsa; and Ardmore, Oklahoma. It was moved to Chicago's Midway Airport in 1949 and continued there until 1957.

On November 21, 1957, American dedicated its new stewardess College. The campus on forty acres of land south of the passenger terminals of today's Dallas/Ft. Worth airport took over all the training for American's stewardesses. An intensive six week course included: familiarization in all types of aircraft flown on American's route system; food service; safety instructions and medical emergencies. Millie Alford was selected as the center's director and said, "Our curriculum has changed through the

[17]*Corporate Communications*, American Airlines, Dallas/Ft. Worth Airport, Texas.

years with equipment changes from pistons to jets. We are always ahead of the game in terms of our training methods and with our *esprit de corps*!

"The girls in 1957 were less sophisticated. American was very strict with rules and curfews at that time. Eleven pm was the curfew on weekdays and one am on weekends. Changes came about with the 'why' generation of the 60's. They were very independent, their independence was displayed in their appearance. Mini-skirts were very popular back then.

"By 1970, the curriculum had again changed to include more sophisticated trainees, most of whom had already had two or more years of college. Men were now in the program and the name 'stewardess' was changed to the non-sexist 'flight attendant.' The curriculum was modified to include subjects to accommodate male interests."

The stewardess College was also renamed the Flight Service College and later the American Airlines Learning Center. The center is used for meetings, conferences and to train ground as well as flight personnel. Other companies and organizations are encouraged to schedule the use of the facility.

From the beginning of American's inflight service to the present American has looked for quality in its flight attendants. Poise and the ability to present themselves well overall is desired, not just in appearance or personal warmth. Good listeners, sensitive, intelligent and alert individuals are chosen and the ratio of those selected is one hired out of twenty-five applicants of the thousands of applications each year.

The average age of flight attendants is 33.1 years and the average seniority 6.2 years. 80% of flight attendants plan to retire on the job.

The first stewardesses averaged two years on the job and 85% left to marry. Today tenure is well over nine years and getting longer in duration. American's first training in 1933 was three days. Today it has become five and a half week training course with on hand emergency training and computers, and American's equipment has gone from pistons to jets. What hasn't changed is the high quality of individuals in inflight service representing American Airlines today.

Velma Maul, American Airways' first stewardess, hired May 3, 1933.

AMERICAN AIRWAYS' FIRST FOUR LADIES IN THE AIR

1933

Velma Maul Tanger was the first hired of the first four American Airways stewardesses. She was a registered nurse and her home was Burlington, Iowa. On May 3, 1933, Velma worked the first flight to inaugurate stewardess service on a Curtiss Condor 18-passenger aircraft. She left Chicago's Midway Airport on a flight to Newark, New Jersey with stops at Detroit and Buffalo.

Velma served a meal of salted nuts, hot consomme, sandwiches, pickles, and a tossed green salad with a special American Airways dressing. Pistachio ice cream, cake and coffee were served for dessert. No liquor was served either before or after the meal, because in 1933 prohibition forbade selling or serving alcohol.

The luxurious Curtiss Condor cruised at 120 miles per hour with one class service for all passengers on board. A radio was in the cabin to provide news and music, and newspapers were furnished for each passenger. Velma made history as American's first stewardess.

Agnes Nohava Hinks was also a Registered Nurse and met American's requirements for the first class of four stewardesses. Her home was Lonsdale, Minnesota. She worked the return westbound flight from Newark to Chicago.

Agnes remarked about her experiences, "We were a novelty. We had more fun than flight attendants have today, because we got to know our passengers much better and we gave them a lot of personal attention. Because no liquor was served, some passengers smuggled liquor on board the aircraft in cough syrup bottles to 'spike' their coffee or milk. We had to watch for this."

Agnes married in 1937 and left American because early stewardesses were required to be single. She returned to a nursing career. She has always cherished the part she played as a pioneer of stewardess service for American. Today she and Marie Allen survive of the first four to take to the sky.

Mae Bobeck was also one of American's first four who made history on May 2, 1931. Like the others, she was a registered nurse. Her home was Chicago. She later became American's Chief Nurse after leaving her job as a stewardess. She remained as Chief Nurse at Chicago until her retirement December 31, 1965, at the age of sixty-five. In July, 1972, Miss Bobeck died. She left a legend of service as a nurse and as one of the first four stewardesses for American Airlines.

Marie Allen Sullivan was a Registered Nurse from Cincinnati. She, too, was selected to make history as one of American's first four stewardesses. Their training was very brief and took place at Chicago's Midway Airport.

The Curtiss Condors were configured with sleeping compartments for the passengers, as the transcontinental flights were 24 hours long with the transfers and stopovers.[18] Marie was often airsick in the turbulence on the low-flying Condors. She was the first of the four to leave to marry. Marie was used for many publicity photographs.

TWICE BEING FIRST
Marie Allen Sullivan

In late March, 1984 American Airlines celebrated a special first in its inflight service. Lisa M. Warren followed in her grandmother's footsteps as a flight attendant for American. What made the occasion so special was that her grandmother, Marie Allen Sullivan, was one of the airline's first four stewardesses hired in 1933.

Marie's daughter, Jane Sullivan Warren followed in her footsteps and became an American Airlines stewardess. Marie was present at Jane's graduation in 1949 and pinned on her daughter's wings. Like her mother, Jane had trained at American's stewardess center at Midway Airport, Chicago.

Jane's flights from Chicago to California on 40-passenger Convairs took eight hours, compared to her mother's 24-hour trips. Jane remembers flying all night and being very tired when the long flights ended. Unlike her mother, Jane had not been a nurse, as that requirement was dropped during World War II. Jane left her stewardess job when she married Joseph Warren in 1950.

Lisa Warren had always wanted to be an airline stewardess like her mother and grandmother. After graduation from Torrey Pines High School in Del Mar, California in 1980, she was old enough to apply for a job with the airlines. It was not until 1983, however, that her wish came true. She was hired in June by Imperial Airlines, a regional carrier operating out of San Diego.

Lisa took her flight attendant training in Moline, Illinois at Mississippi Valley Airline headquarters in June of 1983. (MVA trained flight attendants for other commuter airlines under contract.) There were 24 in her class: twelve trainees for MVA, three for Fischer Airlines and nine for Imperial Airlines. Lisa earned her wings on July 11, 1983 and immediately left Moline for California.

For the ensuing nine months she flew as a flight attendant for Imperial out of San Diego to Santa Barbara and Bakersfield. This experience proved to be a stepping stone for Lisa to join American Airlines, which had been her dream all along.

Lisa trained with American at their new Learning Center at the Dallas/Ft. Worth airport in Texas. The center resembles a college campus in contrast to the makeshift stewardess center attended by her grandmother and mother in the thirties and forties.

Lisa's mother and grandmother were flown to Dallas for her graduation in late March 1984. This was a first for American to have three generations in the same job. At the graduation ceremonies both Marie and Jane reflected on their experiences and were presented red roses. For Lisa, this was her dream, to be the third generation to join American. National as well as local news featured this special three-generation tradition.

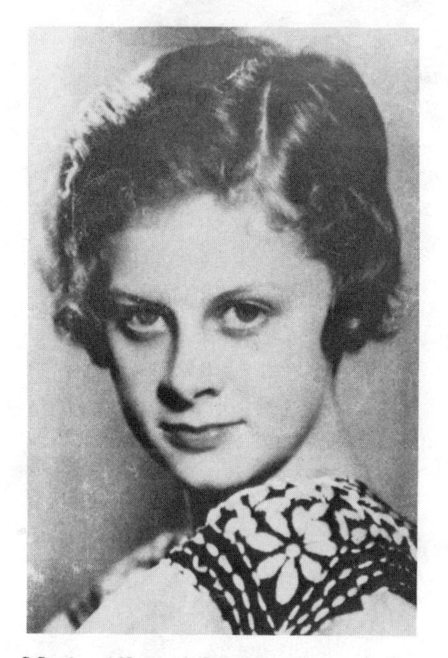

Marie Allen's photo was used for many publicity shots.

American Airways stewardesses getting weighed in at a hangar at Chicago's Midway Airport in 1933.

[18]Ibid.

American Airways' first four registered nurse stewardesses, May 3, 1933. Top to bottom on the steps of a Curtiss Condor: Mae Bobeck, Agnes Nohava, Marie Allen and Velma Maul. (American Airlines Photo)

ADVENTURE SHE FOUND

American Airways
Agnes Nohava Hinks
1933

A letter to the author from Agnes Nohava who was one of the four registered nurses chosen to be American Airways first stewardesses

Agnes Nohava, May 3, 1933.

"I came from a small town in Minnesota and after finishing high school I was looking for adventure. I always wanted to be a nurse. I could have gone in training closer to home, but Chicago sounded more exciting, so I chose Mercy Hospital and went in training there.

"Unfortunately it was during the depression and work was not plentiful, also there were not many openings for nurses in those days. So when I heard AA was hiring nurses, (from a patient) I didn't waste any time. I applied and I was lucky. I am proud to have been one of the first four and now after 60 years I'm proud to have been part of that history.

"Those days were adventurous and fun. Being a stewardess in the Curtiss Condor was sophisticated, but what I really enjoyed was flying in the old *Tin Goose,* the Ford Trimotor over West Virginia. That flight was established impromptu to obtain a mail route. The Ford was used because there were no radio ranges and we landed in Indianapolis, Cincinnati and Charleston. (The Condor could not have landed there.) We didn't fly very high, 12,000 to 14,000 feet, seemed low over the mountains but high over the valley. The hills were beautiful any time of year, but especially in spring.

"You could see spirals of smoke which a passenger said were *moonshiners* stills. You could see the bears and deer running scared by the overhead noise.

"Liquor was not served, but a few passengers that were probably a little squeamish about flying managed to have their drink. One passenger informed me he had ulcers and needed milk and cream. It was spiked by the time we reached Washington — and he was *happy.* Another passenger called his bottle cough medicine. When it got a little turbulent he took a swig of his medicine. He informed me about it and I told him, yes, I could smell it.

"It wasn't too long before the old Ford was replaced by the Curtiss Condor. Then we stopped in Indianapolis, Cincinnati and on to Washington and that trip went on to Newark.

"We occasionally made interesting side trips. American sent two planes to meet the Hindenburg transporting passengers to Newark. I had the first 23 passengers. One passenger gave me a pin that I treasure. By the time we got to Newark we heard the Hindenburg had blown up.

"I also have a pin from the Normandy ocean liner. I was asked to accompany one of their salesmen whose job was to arrange transportation to travel to the U.S. I was then taken on a tour of the ship and invited to have dinner

Agnes Nohava Hinks by an American Airways Ford Trimotor, 1933.

with the sales agent. My pictures of this and other memorabilia were destroyed in a fire.

Readle (or Tanner) and I have always kept track of each other — mostly by mail. I call her when traveling through Denver. She was the fifth hired.

"As for my husband - well, he was always there for me from the time I finished training. Eventually we got married in 1937 and had four great children. Now I have seven grandchildren, all pretty well on their own today...But you know they still like to hear about those days that I fondly remember.

"The progress in flying in 50 and 60 years is really something, but not so much fun as we had."

A FIRST LADY OF THE SKY

American Airways
Izola Readle Tanner
1933

During Prohibition, it was not only necessary for stewardesses to keep passengers from drinking out of flasks carried on board, it was routine on some flights to transport revenue officers looking for bootleggers.

I had the good fortune to meet one of American's first ladies of the sky at a Denver Interline luncheon I attended in the spring of 1984. I was then writing my first book on inflight service, *Walking on Air*. I attended this function as often as I could as a member of both Continental's Golden Penguins and United's Clipped Wings. It gave me the opportunity to see airline friends. Denver had been my home and I flew for both airlines with Denver as my domicile between 1943 and 1947.

Izola Readle Tanner was introduced by the American Kiwis. I arranged for an interview with this petite lovely lady. My friendship with "Tanner," as she prefers to be called, has become a big plus in my life as our friendship has grown. We correspond often and I often call her, Tanner gave me her account of being American Airway's 5th stewardess.

"We were all registered nurses I had worked as a surgical nurse at Woodlawn Hospital in Chicago since my graduate study at the University of Iowa.

"I was rooming with an anesthetist, Alice Mahoney, who worked at both Woodlawn and Garfield hospitals. At Garfield, Alice learned that American Airways was looking for RNs to hire as stewardesses. We both were ready for something else. I was twenty-seven years old.

"Alice was over the five feet four inch minimum height, but she encouraged me to inquire about the position. I called American Airways the following day, and was

Izola Readle Tanner, RN, the fifth stewardess hired by American Airways in 1933.

Izola Readle Tanner, number five stewardess for American Airways in 1933-1934, is shown by Ford Trimotor number 9683 at Denver's Stapleton Airport on Ocober 17, 1964, (the day it became an international airport). American Airlines presented the Ford Trimotor to the Air & Space Museum in Washington, DC later that same year.

asked to report immediately to their office at Chicago's airport for an interview. I was hired and put on the payroll that morning, May 11, 1933.

"Our training with American Airways was very brief. We were given a map of the cities we would fly over, with landmarks and a time schedule. My first airplane flight was the following day to the factory that made the Pratt-Whitney motors used in the Trimotor Ford Aircraft. These aircraft were made by a division of the Ford Motor Company. They were called *The Tin Goose* and *The Work Horse of the Air*. They had a metal fuselage with a corrugated skin and no upholstery. They were a safe airplane, but were noisy and drafty. American also flew 18 passenger Curtiss Condors. My first flight was from Chicago to Newark.

"We flew low, hedge-hopping over the landscape. We had a printed schedule that identified landmarks from point to point, by mileage and flying time. For instance, on the route between Chicago and Detroit, we could identify Ann Arbor, Michigan by the football field.

"At that time, there was no blind flying or instrument flying. We weren't allowed to fly over water, so flights flew on the edge of Lake Erie and on the Canadian side of Lake Michigan.

American Airways stewardesses in the doorway of a Curtiss Condor. Izola Readle Tanner (right) and Nina Bell (left).

Izola Readle Tanner (right) with Gracie Allen and radio program star "Baron Munchaven" Jack Pearl in 1933.

"On one flight the weather was so bad that our aircraft was forced to land in Canada. The Customs officers asked each crew member his name, and my captain said his name was Daniel Boone. The Canadian authorities were very upset, as they thought he was wisecracking, but his name actually was Daniel Boone!

"During this time I was based in Chicago and flew the route to Newark and Buffalo. My flights were mostly in 18-passenger Curtiss Condors, although I also had some flights in the Ford Trimotors that were known as the *Tin Goose*. When we flew in the Ford Trimotor aircraft, we wore our coats, and the pilots did too, because the heating was poor and the planes were drafty and cold.

"I was chosen to go with the first three crews sent to Cincinnati on October 11, 1993, to familiarize themselves with American's new route. Revenue officers flew frequently on later flights on this route.

"Since it was Prohibition, the government officers would check the landscape as we flew over, watching for curls of smoke that would identify whiskey stills. Sometimes we could see a man with a gun fire into the air as the aircraft passed overhead.

"Marie Allen, hired May 3, 1933, one of the first four original stewardesses, was the most photogenic and her photographs were used most frequently for publicity. One time my own photograph was used, taken with a radio on board the Curtiss Condor and showing the passengers all attentive as I pointed to the radio. The idea was to show that the passengers could hear the radio in the quiet Curtiss Condor cabin. A passenger was holding the radio on his legs for the photo.

"I also remember the merit and demerit system. My scrapbook holds many letters from satisfied passengers, and those qualified me for merits. At one time, a letter went to all crew members written by the general superintendent, Earl Ward. The letter said 'All behavior would be monitored on and off duty.' It required that while crew members were off duty, they were not to wear their uniforms. On all layovers and cancellation points for flights there would be separate hotel accommodations for the stewardess and male crew members.

"My own performance as a stewardess didn't go unnoticed. Chief Pilot Ed Weatherton selected me to be the stewardess on a week-long political junket out of Washington, DC. We took Postmaster Farley and other dignitaries to Vice President Garner's ranch in Uvalde, Texas in October 1933. Among the officials on board were the Honorable Jessie Jones and his secretary, John Tanner, who was also the Reconstruction Finance Officer.

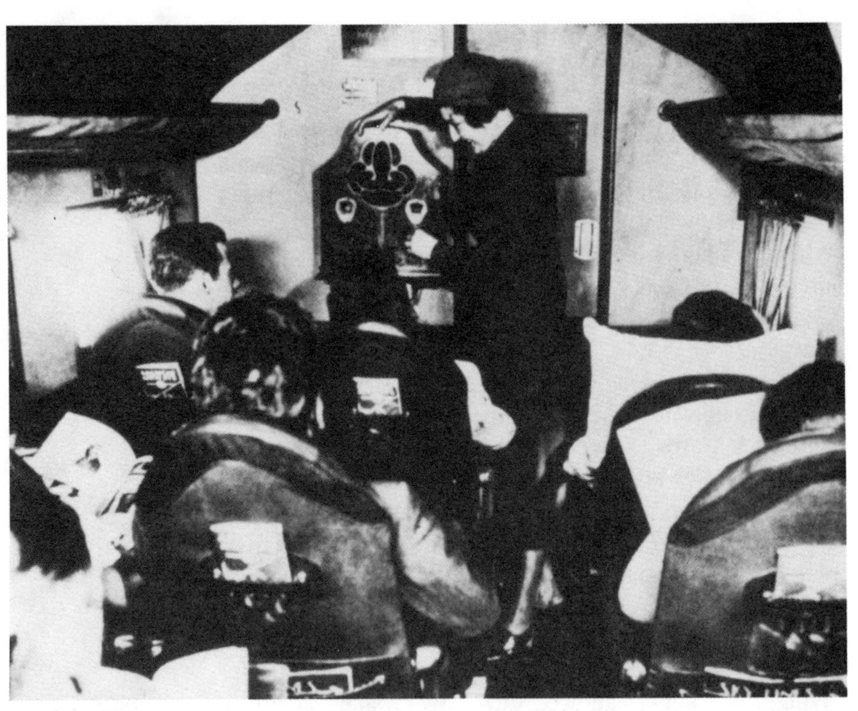

Izola Readle Tanner, shown by a radio in the cabin of a Curtiss Condor in 1933. This was a promotion to show that the aircraft had such a quiet cabin, a radio could be heard when the plane was in flight. (American Airlines Photo)

American Airways stewardess Izola Readle Tanner with Walt Disney and Mickey Mouse on the steps of a Curtiss Condor, 1933.

"John Tanner engaged me in a conversation at Washington, DC while waiting for the next flight on the Cincinnati itinerary. Weather delayed the flight and we became better acquainted. John learned that I would be flying into Washington, the new American route. The rest is history. We met on layovers and fell in love, and were married August 13, 1934."

Tanner and John made their home in Denver. They have two children and celebrated fifty years of marriage in 1984. Since John's death in July 28, 1988 Tanner has kept her home. She gives her time to hospital bazaars.

American's Kiwi club honored Izola on October 17, 1964 during a duel celebration of Stapleton Airport's 35th anniversary and its designation as an international airport. Her photograph was taken with Ford Trimotor, number 9683, in which she had flown in 1933 and 1934. The plane was donated that same year to the Aero Space Museum in Washington, DC. Today, Izola Readle Tanner is still active in the annual interline conventions, and is a member at large of the American Kiwi Club. She was honored again as one of the first ladies of the sky at American's 17th Denver annual Kiwi luncheon in 1992. Tanner says of their experience as an early stewardess, "Noisy they may have been, and premature in appearance, but the aircraft of the 1930s had their charm. American had the greatest personnel I have ever had the privilege to work with."

American Airways' Garner-Farley political junket from Washington DC to Uvalde, Texas, 1933. Izola Readle is in the door of the Curtiss Condor.

AN AMERICAN BEAUTY

American Airlines
Helen Vaubel Boyd
1937 - 1941

Inflight romances often ended in marriage and marriage ended the fledgling careers of many of the early stewardesses.

She is so tiny, he thought to himself. She must be under five feet tall and must weight less than a hundred pounds dripping wet. Tom Boyd, a Captain for American Airlines, was appraising a petite brunette stewardess who had just been hired by American. She was checking in to work his inaugural flight of the Douglas DC-2 between Buffalo and Newark. It was April 25, 1937.

Captain Boyd knew that the young lady was a nurse and no older than twenty-three, because those were two of American's requirements. She was well under the 118 pound limit and certainly didn't exceed the height limit of five feet, four inches. He also knew that she had just finished a week of training in Chicago.

"I don't know what her personality is like, but that little brunette surely has to have a good one. American really knows how to pick stewardesses," Tom Boyd thought to himself. Secretly, he was glad that this new stewardess was based in Buffalo, his own domicile. He wanted to get to know her.

Helen Vaubel checked into dispatch and headed out to board the DC-2 with her roommate and co-stewardess, Lil Kroll. They were scheduled for two stops at Rochester and Syracuse on the route between Buffalo and Newark. A senior stewardess, Nellie Nelson, was going along to give the two a check ride on their first flight. Helen and Lil were to take turns working the flight: Helen would work the flight to Newark and Lil would work the return.

Helen was very excited. She decided that she should check in with the crew in the cockpit, Captain Tom Boyd and copilot Lloyd Bedwell.

"Hello, I'm Helen Vaubel, a new stewardess," Helen said, looking Captain Boyd directly in the eyes. She was flustered by his direct gaze. Captain Boyd grinned and said, "I know you're new. Welcome aboard and welcome to American. If I can help you young ladies in any way, don't hesitate to ask. By the way, you may have some trouble reaching the overhead rack. How tall are you, anyway?"

"I'm four feet, eleven inches tall, sir," Helen replied, turning to leave the cockpit.

Helen Vaubel Boyd, American Airlines stewardess, 1937.

Helen boarding a New York bus to the airport.

Helen's crew on her first flight in 1937. Bottom row, left to right: Lloyd Bedwell and Tom Boyd. Upper row: Nellie Nelson (in doorway), Lil Kroll and Helen. (*Post Standard* Photo, Syracuse, NY)

"Lil, you'd better meet the crew too. They're very nice, especially Captain Boyd," Helen advised her friend, who was busy with pre-flight preparation.

This was an exciting day for Helen, starting a new job. She was ready to greet her twelve passengers and the flight ahead. Helen sat savoring the thrill of it all as she, Lil, and Miss Nelson strapped themselves into their seats for takeoff.

"I was based in Buffalo, Chicago and Cleveland," Helen says, recalling her four years, 1937 to 1941, with American. "I had so many interesting experiences, including opening the airport at Erie, Pennsylvania on June 15, 1938.

"Aviation was really just taking hold on the American public...," Helen says with a laugh, "...That's a play on words. American Airlines was becoming a competitor for transcontinental traffic with United and TWA.

"I liked the jaunty overseas cap we used to wear. It gave our otherwise drab blue wool men's-cut uniforms a snappy look. We were allowed to use nail polish, but we were otherwise limited to powder, rouge and lipstick."

Helen wore several uniforms during her four years with American. The cost of each new uniform was deducted from her paycheck. Helen wished this expense could have been footed by the airline, like it is today. "I didn't like it taken out of my $100 monthly paycheck," she says frankly.

The Peter Pan collar was adopted in 1937 for the summer uniform which replaced the heavy wool uniform American stewardesses wore year round.

"I liked this uniform," says Helen. "It was a reversal of the mannish-look uniform accented with a man's tie that we had worn previously. However, it didn't last long - only for the summer. By the fall we had oyster white uniforms with brown accents, which we all liked a lot. This lasted until 1940 when we started wearing the American Airlines blue uniform which featured a tight jacket and shorter flared skirt. Our caps were modeled after infantry caps, which gave us a quasi-military look.

"I had been dating the Captain I had met on my first flight, Tom Boyd. During my years with American we had really begun flying high. In 1941, Tom asked me to marry him." Helen reflected, "since I couldn't be married and still fly, I decided I'd like to be grounded."

UP-TO-THE-MINUTE FLIGHT INFORMATION ★ Suggest you check your position on route map in the seat pocket.

Our position at 8:33 A.M. (EAST *standard time) over* UTICA. *This information was given by radiotelephone to our ground radio station at* SYRACUSE. *Our next position report will be given to* SAME *at approximately* 8:42 A.M. *over* CITY OF SYRACUSE

Our air speed is 170 MPH. *Ground speed* 176 MPH. *Temperature outside* 15 ° *Altitude above sea level* ~~[illegible]~~ *ft.* *Above ground* 3000 *ft.* *We will arrive* SYRACUSE *at approximately* 8:52 A.M.

The weather there is AS HERE *Temperature* 60 °F.

REMARKS: DURING THE WEEK ENDING SEPT. 28TH OUR COMPANY CARRIED OVER 7000 PASSENGERS ON OUR NEWARK-BOSTON ROUTE, 115,000 LBS. OF RAILWAY MAIL AND 86,000 LBS. EXPRESS, EMERGENCY MATERIAL, SERUMS AND RED CROSS SUPPLIES. THERE WERE NO UNTOWARD INCIDENTS AND NO SUCH VOLUME OF BUSINESS HAS EVER BEEN EVEN APPROACHED BY ANY AIRLINE IN AVIATION'S HISTORY.

Your stewardess is anxious to answer any questions.

AMERICAN AIRLINES *Inc.* CAPTAIN CAPERTON FIRST OFFICER NEWHOUSE

National Air Races, Cleveland, Ohio, 1938. Left to right: Miss Ohio, Miss National Air Races, Miss Cleveland, "Wrong Way" Corrigan, Miss Hollywood, Dorothy Quackenbush (Miss TWA), Marie Hess (Miss United Air Lines), Helen Vaubel (Miss American Airlines).

20 The Detroit News Pictorial for May 15, 1938

Only One Girl in 55 Wins

It's a glamorous job, this being an airplane stewardess. The average length of service is two and a half to three years, the most common cause of leaving being marriage. —Acme

The class of prospective stewardesses gets a practical lesson on airplane motors. They must know enough about the planes they'll work on to answer passengers' questions.

The training course includes a lecture in the airport control tower. The passengers may want to know "Why?"

The stewardess of a sleeper plane answers a call for a glass of orange juice.

...practical instruction in methods of serving and packing foods in the ...commissary department.

Photo: *The Detroit Pictorial*, May 15, 1938.

Place in Airliner's Crew

This is all in the day's work. Earlier training as a nurse often comes in handy.

Hazel Brooks, senior stewardess of American Airlines, lectures on the philosophy of stewardess service. School lasts about a month.

SINCE aviation opened to young women the glamorous post of stewardess on giant liners, every major airline has been besieged by applicants. But only about one in 35 wins a job in the clouds, according to the personnel office of American Airlines, Inc.

The first question asked is: "Are you a registered nurse?" Second: "Do you weigh less than 120 pounds?" Third: "Are you less than five feet five inches tall?" If these basic physical requirements are met, the candidate must then show that she is neat, possesses a pleasing personality, and from her record in nursing must present absolute proof of her ability to handle people. A rigid physical examination follows and only then is she accepted as a student in the training school in Chicago.

Four weeks of intensive training follows, taking in every phase of airline and airplane operation, for the girls must be able to answer passengers' questions as well as perform their regular duties. Then there is an examination and those who pass receive uniforms and are sent on observation flights. Finally comes assignment to a specified schedule.

Capt. Bill Lester explains how a pilot flies by instruments. The stewardess will be able to reassure nervous passengers that their pilot knows where he's going.

Photo: *The Detroit Pictorial*, May 15, 1938.

TWA's inflight service began in 1935.

TWA'S IDA STAGGERS
1936 - 1972

TWA's legacy is Ida Staggers and her gifts of service to the airline she loved.

Ida was modest about her achievements. "People aren't interested in me personally. People who are first just get attention. Being number two doesn't count," says Ida Staggers, TWA's airline Hostess of 1936. Ida retired on July 24, 1972 at age sixty. She had logged 10 million miles aloft. During her time inflight she had chalked up three and a third years of constant flying as a hostess accumulating 29,000 flying hours.[19]

Her last flight was a Military Airlift Command, TWA flight T-272 from Honolulu to Travis Air Force Base, California. The flight carried 165 Vietnam servicemen and their families to Travis and continued as a ferry flight to San Francisco after military passengers had deplaned.

A large group of well-wishers greeted Ida's flight at San Francisco with flower leis and placards reading: "Good Luck Ida!" and "Ida, Sweet As Apple Cidah!" It was her 60th birthday and people were showing her their respect and love. To sum up her career as a TWA Hostess, Ida says, "I've had the good time of our profession."[20]

Ida grew up on a farm in Hill City, Kansas. In 1936, Ida was a registered nurse employed at Saint Luke's Hospital in Kansas City. She worked in the operating room and also did some private duty for two years after finishing nurses training. During this time she lived in the same apartment building with the secretary to TWA's Vice President, Paul Richter. The secretary, knowing Ida was an RN, which was a prime requirement for the airline hostesses TWA was starting to hire, suggested Ida apply for the job. Ida followed the secretary's suggestion and interviewed for a position as a TWA hostess. Her acceptance as a hostess trainee began a thirty-six year career that she loved.

Ida's training in Kansas City was brief. It included a twelve-hour familiarization flight to Los Angeles. She started her long hostess career with TWA in July, 1936. On September 15, 1937, she flew on the first DC-2 flight into San Francisco. She liked the Bay area so much that she transferred to the San Francisco base a year later. During this time TWA had noted the likeable, dependable Ida and chose her to train several classes of new hostesses.

Ida Staggers receiving a plaque from TWA's Charles Tillingast on the occasion of her retirement. (TWA Photo)

"I remember for one class of three hostess students, the training was for two weeks. The salary was $100 a month for over 100 hours of flight time," says Ida.

In 1940 Ida was designated Chief Hostess and sent to TWA's LaGuardia base in New York. In one year she was selected as the System Chief Hostess at TWA's Kansas City headquarters. "It was during this time that I found myself more in the office than in contact with hostesses," says Ida. "In 1946 I requested LaGuardia base once again. TWA had started to expand its international flights to Rome, London and the Middle East after World War II. I trained hostesses for the international flights."

After six weeks at LaGuardia, Ida was given a leave of absence from TWA to train Scandinavian Airline hostesses in Sweden. "I like to think I helped them get their flight service started," says Ida proudly. "I went back to LaGuardia but I wanted to return to my first love, flying the line, instead of training hostesses." She got her wish but TWA periodically used her to train, supervise and to line-check the hostesses and pursers in Paris and Cairo. When Ida left her job as Chief Hostess in December, 1945, TWA had 187 stewardesses.

Her favorite flight was an international route from New York to Paris, on an 18-passenger sleeper Constellation with one hostess and two pursers. Passengers paid an extra $25 for these flights. "We provided a personal touch that was so important for early hostesses. Today there are too many passengers for such a thing. Too bad!" reflected Ida.

[19]Daien, April. "Retired Stewardess Talks About 36 Years of Flying," *Arizona Republic*, 2 August 1972, Section D, p 1.

[20]Ibid.

A 1936 TWA hostess by a DC-3, a promotion for carrying a cargo of turkeys for Thanksgiving. (TWA Photo)

IDA'S MEMORIES

Ida had many celebrities and well-known passengers on board her many flights. "To me they were just regular folks," she says. "Some were nice and some were blown up with their own importance. I treated everyone the same."

One charter flight was especially interesting to Ida. In 1937 she was chosen to work a DC-2 two-week charter for the Honorable A.E. Guinness of England, who brought a party to the United States.

"We flew them across the U.S. and Canada to see important sights, and then left them in Chicago to board his yacht. In 1939 he returned for a similar trip, and we left them this time in Seattle to board his yacht. Those were the happy days. It is all vivid, and my memories are all good," says Ida.[21]

TWA's Charles Tillingast greets Ida after her last flight in 1972.

Regarding the many uniforms that Ida wore in the decades from 1936 to 1972, she didn't like the mini-skirt of the 60's, and thought the paper uniform of 1968 was a disgrace. The paper uniforms were a short-lived promotion to bring attention to TWA's international flights to France, England and Rome. The uniforms were worn on transcontinental flights and were made of high-fiber material. One size fit all, and the length was altered with scissors. There were four uniforms: a French gold lame cocktail dress, a British *pub wench* dress, a Roman toga, and New York penthouse black lounging pajamas. The uniforms were to give the international flavor of each country, and were supposed to compliment the culinary specialties of the country. However, it wasn't long before menus didn't match the uniform of the particular country because of uniform shortages. The new replacement fabric was of a higher fiber content and tore easily, as well as creating a fire hazard. Ida was disgusted and refused to wear the uniforms.

TWA realized that flight attendant's ideas in regard to their uniforms were important. Their next union contract included a provision giving hostesses a voice in uniform selection.

Ida says, "I was sorry to see the hat go. I think the uniform hat finished off a put-together look. It's the RN attitude, I guess."[22]

Ida's memories of the people she served are what is important to her. She was totally dedicated to excellence and to all that the word "hostess" implies: gracious personal consideration, as if the passengers on her flight were in her own home. She was always aware of her actions, wanting to represent TWA in the best manner. In a way, Ida had a love affair with TWA. It has been said, "She married TWA."

[21] Daien, April, "Retired Stewardess Talks About 36 Years of Flying," *Arizona Republic*, 2 August 1972, Section D, p 1.

[22] Ibid.

COURT OF EXCELLENCE[23]

Her long career of 36 years as a TWA hostess ended in a very unique way. TWA had fond memories of Ida Staggers. On June 21, 1972, TWA's board of directors honored their number one flight attendant. They prepared a retirement party in San Francisco with a guest list that included TWA people past and present who would honor Ida. Guests included: Chairman of the Board, Charles Tillingast, Jr.; Retired Captain, Lee Flanagen of Los Angeles, who helped Ida check in for her first flight; Mrs. Vivian McCanna, the 1972 President of TWA's Clipped Wings International; TWA's hostess, Barbara Maloney, who traced her birth to "Aunt Ida," who as a registered nurse had attended her mother when Barbara was born; Colonel Dan Jacobs, Inspector General of the 22nd Air Force, Military Airlift Command.

Colonel Jacobs commented on Ida's reputation of excellence in her care of military personnel and their families on TWA's MAC flights to Travis Air Force Base.

A letter was read from then-Governor of California, Ronald Reagan, in recognition of Ida's career of 36 years as a TWA hostess.

TWA's public relations manager, Jerry Cosley, prepared a tribute in the form of a trial. The charges brought to Ida being:

(A) "That at the sacrifice of many personal considerations you have devoted 36 years to the feeding and care of passengers."

(B) "While in the employ of TWA, you have sought to subvert Murphy's Law to achieve a standard of excellence in morale and performance as a TWA hostess with good humor. Physical evidence consists of mounds of newspaper clippings from around the world."

Ida was then asked how she pleaded. Over 240 people rose with a standing ovation to show their respect and love for Ida Staggers.

Ida was tearful and speechless as the jury announced the verdict: "Ida Staggers is guilty of endless love for people."

Ida trembled and whispered, "Thank you — one and all."

Officials and guests said, "Goodnight Ida. Thank you from the bottom of our hearts."

On Ida's return to her home she opened a letter from the White House written on behalf of President Nixon and signed by the Director of Communications, Herbert G. Klein, honoring her impressive achievements from the days of the DC-2's to the 747's, and her million miles in the air:

Ida (far right woth floral wreath) with her crew at the end of her last flight. (TWA photo)

THE WHITE HOUSE
Washington
July 28, 1972

Dear Miss Staggers:

On behalf of the President, I want to offer you belated congratulations on the event of your retirement as a stewardess for Trans World Airlines.

You have, during your career, compiled some impressive statistics - 36 years of flying, service to 100,000 servicemen on their flight to

[23]*TWA Skyliner*, March 26, 1993, p 4.

and from Vietnam, not to mention some 10 million miles in the air! I am sure that you must have some fascinating tales to tell from the DC-2s to 747s. I join the President in saluting these impressive achievements, and wishing you the very best in the years ahead.

Sincerely,
Herbert G. Klein
Director of Communications
for the Executive Branch

Ida moved to New York in 1980 after working for TWA's Service Canteen Corporation at the North Rim of the Grand Canyon after her retirement. She was always a good ambassador for TWA, the airline she had dedicated most of her life to serving - "Ambassador Service" all the way.[24] Ida Staggers died January 11, 1993 in New York City at the age of 81. Affection for Ida and her contributions to TWA will always be remembered and written in aviation's log book.[25]

The noted aviation author, Robert Serling wrote of Ida Staggers: "She wore her wings in two places: on her uniform and in her heart."[26]

NORTHWEST AIRLINES INFLIGHT SERVICE 1939

Carol J. Grewing,

Director Customer Service Training

Northwest Airways began operations in 1928. Northwest's first stewardesses were hired in 1939 after attending three weeks of training. Virginia Johnson and Dorothy Stump were hired by Camille Stein, assistant secretary and Treasurer for Northwest Orient Airlines. The first stewardess uniform of a suit in dark brown wool was purchased from a St. Paul department store. The uniform also featured a pointed cap of the same material.

In 1947, pursers were hired and in 1949, flight service attendants (FSAs). Both positions were held by men only. These positions were eliminated by 1972 and the new position, cabin attendant, was open to both men and women. Today male flight attendants make up 18% of the work force.

Today's flight attendants are among the top candidates applying for the position. An average of 15,000 applications a year are received, out of which one thousand may be selected. Northwest presently employs approximately 8,400 flight attendants with over 700 on layoff status.

An intense six week training program is provided to all flight attendant candidates which is held at the training center in Minneapolis/St. Paul, Minnesota. In contrast, the first stewardesses were responsible for handing out cold box lunches, serving coffee and assisting passengers.

Registered nurse, Helen Richardson, one of Northwest Airlines' first stewardesses, 1939. (Photo: *Minneapolis Star Tribune*, Kevel Milazaki)

Today's program incorporates a total submersion agenda where candidates begin with a complete review of the flight attendant's role, responsibilities and the impact to the organization. Orientation to the corporate structure, a

[24]*TWA Skyliner*, March 26, 1993, p 4.

[25]Ibid.

[26]Ibid.

Interior of Northwest Orient Airlines DC-6B's

Helen Richardson, one of Northwest Airlines' first stewardesses, 1939.

uniform fashion show, uniform fittings, make up and hair consultations are all incorporated into the first three days of training. Qualification on the Northwest fleet, emergency procedures and safety measures carry heavy emphasis for the next three weeks and concludes with a comprehensive oral exam.

The last three weeks candidates are submerged in learning about culture diversity, flight administration and the smallest of details to present effective beverage and meal services which range from domestic a la carte fare to the extensive international seven cart service. Proper service techniques, product merchandising and human interactions receive tremendous attention to ensure Northwest's newly hired flight attendants are prepared to provide the excellence in service our customers demand.

Overall the training takes six weeks during which all candidate are qualified on six aircraft types (747 200/400, 747, 727-200, DC-10, DC-9, A-320) over water operation, aircraft emergency, medical emergencies, fire fighting, food and beverage services, flight administration, customer skills and cultural awareness. Hands on operation of all equipment is provided on a series of 18 service, safety and evacuation trainers.

Standards of performance agreed to by the candidate requires a score of 85% (minimum) on all written exams. Retakes are allowed on three exams however further failure of a retake or failure of more than three exams results in disqualification.

Additional importance is place on interpersonal skills, personal grooming, organization, leadership, flexibility, human interaction, problem solving, honesty/integrity and a strong work ethic. A balance of all these skills is essential to ensure the success of the individual and ultimately the corporation.

Weekend training flights are concluded with a two day supervised training flight where each candidate must show proficiency in working as a flight attendant in each area of the aircraft.

Throughout the training program, training staff is available as mentors and guides; offering support and answering questions. Both management personnel and line flight attendants participate in the development of the new employees.

flight attendant domiciles are: Honolulu (HNL); Seattle (SEA); Los Angeles (LAX); San Francisco (SFO); Minneapolis (MSP); Chicago (CHI); Detroit (DTW); Memphis (MEM); New York City (NYC); and Boston (BOS).

More bilingual flight attendants are being hired for Northwest's Asian routes. Professionals speak Japanese, Chinese and Korean languages to make their passengers feel at home. All of Northwest's flight attendant candidates must have a permanent authorization to work in the United States, as well as the ability to have multiple exits and entries to the United States and all the countries Northwest serves.

For 45 years, Northwest Airlines has been a pioneer U.S. carrier to Asia.

THE BEST YEARS OF THEIR LIVES 50 YEARS AGO

Northwest Airlines 1939 - 1989

Early stewardesses for Northwest Airlines, Catherine Martinson and Helen Jacobson Richardson flew in the glory days for Northwest. They said standards were high, and only smart, stylish and energetic applicants were chosen. Besides stewardesses had to be Registered Nurses.[27]

Catherine and Helen reminisced over the good times when commercial flight in 1930 was novel and exciting. Passengers and curiosity-seekers at airports asked stewardesses for their autographs. stewardesses were taken by limousine to Wold Chamberlain Field. They had many publicity appearances on radio shows to plug their airline, at P.T.A. meetings and for civic organizations.[28]

Flights on the DC-3s flew low as cabins weren't pressurized, airsickness was frequent as the air below 10,000 feet was often turbulent. The stewardess had time to pamper passengers and get to know repeat passengers. Free playing cards were handed to passengers. Letters and post cards written to friends and relatives en route could be later stamped and mailed by the stewardess free of charge. This was good public relations for the airline.

Helen Jacobson Richardson was the third stewardess hired for Northwest Air Lines in 1939. She became a stewardess trainer and when she married she had to resign, as this was the rule. All stewardesses had to be single.

Reunions for stewardesses are special. In 1989, Northwest celebrated 50 years of Inflight Service. Sixteen of their first stewardesses met for a two day reunion organized by Helen. The group agreed that the time being a Northwest stewardess was the best of their lives.[29]

FROM "STEWARDESS" TO "FLIGHT ATTENDANT"

The title has changed since 1939, and so have many job requisites, though Northwest still emphasizes poise, tact, maturity, self-control, humor, good grooming and personal appearance. A comparison.

	1939	1989
Marital status	Single	No restrictions
Race/gender	White females	No restrictions
Age	21-25 to start; had to quit at 30	No upper limit; some are in their 60's
Work experience	Registered nurse	Posts involving public contact preferred
Height	5'2" to 5'5"	5'2" minimum
Weight	120 pounds maximum	Proportionate to height
Salary	$65/month in training; $110/month for first 6 months; maximum of $150 a month (equal to $1,640 today)	About $1,250 to $3,750 a month ($15,000 to $45,000 per year)
Total number	30	7,000

[27] *Star Tribune*, Minneapolis, MN, June 29, 1989, (excerpted from *They Civilized the Wild Blue Yonder*), Peg Meier

[28] Ibid.

[29] Ibid.

EL PASO
GATEWAY TO THE AMERICAS
We Salute You upon the Opening of Your
NEW MODERN AIR TERMINAL
El Paso del Norte . . . Pass of the North! It is historically fitting that you have become the gateway of the north-south air route from Alaska, across Canada, the United States, Mexico, Central America and South America to Cape Horn . . . the centuries have established the natural flow of traffic between the Americas through your city.
Complete expression of the fulfillment of your destiny is the new Air Terminal, which rises in majestic beauty from the storied plain. That the new era in commerce upon which you are now entering will be rich in reward is the sincere wish of Continental Air Lines. We are proud to salute you, El Paso . . . Gateway to the Americas!
CONTINENTAL AIR LINES
CONTINENTAL AIR LINES

THE GOLDEN ERA

1940s (World War II period)

The glamorous era for stewardesses and air hostesses. The American public was captivated by the aura of stewardesses and air hostesses.

Delta Air Lines began their first stewardess service — 1940
Continental Air Lines began their first hostess service — 1941
Pan American Airways first stewardesses — 1944

1950s - 1960s

The sex symbol was manifest: mini-skirts, hot pants and sexist slogan advertisements, stewards in the air and glamour in the skies. Everything was done to please the passengers.

1964

Civil Rights Act: new work rules for age, sex, race, and a new name *flight attendant.*

Military airlift flights for Viet Nam.

Laura Wizard, Delta's first stewardess, 1940. (Delta Air Lines Photo)

Delta Air Lines stewardess, La Juan Gilmore, aboard a 10-passenger Lockheed Electra. (Delta Air Lines Photo)

A Delta stewardess (in the 1942 summer uniform) with a passenger sampling a box lunch of fried chicken. (Delta Air Lines Photo)

1940: A NEW LOOK FOR DELTA

Delta Air Lines

Laura Wizard was hired to instruct Delta's first class of stewardesses. Stewardess service began for Delta Air Lines on March 15, 1940, with the inauguration of the new 14 passenger DC-2. Unlike the earlier ten passenger Lockheed Electra, the DC-2 was roomy enough for passengers to stand and walk through the aircraft in flight. No longer did the copilot double as the host, passing out lunches and pouring coffee from a thermos into paper cups for passengers.

Registered nurses were recruited for Delta's first class of stewardesses from the cities on Delta's system from Charleston, South Carolina to Fort Worth, Texas. Each applicant selected met the strict requirements: 21 to 28 years of age; five feet to five feet five inches in height; a maximum weight of 125 pounds; 20/20 vision; collar length hair; and unmarried status.[1]

The seven trainees met for two and a half weeks in a hangar at the Atlanta airport, to study Delta's route system, meteorology, ticketing, scheduling, food service and passenger service. In addition they had to pass a physical examination. Their instructor was Laura Wizard, a stewardess hired from American airlines, who taught the trainees the meaning of being a professional. Laura also taught them to treat passengers as if they were guests in their own home.

When the training ended, the first Delta stewardesses to earn their wings included Birdie Perkins, LaJuan Gilmore, Inez Jackson, Sybil Peacock and Eva Parrish. Each received a new two piece uniform featuring a navy blue blazer with gold Delta buttons, a tailored blouse and tie, and overseas style hat, spectator shoes and a purse. The outfits cost $110 each and had been purchased from Rich's department store in Atlanta. Neiman Marcus in Dallas supplied the beige summer uniforms.[2]

Once on board the DC-2, the newly trained stewardesses greeted boarding passengers much as they do today. However, ticketing was done on board by the

[1]"Inflight Service," *Delta Digest*, 8 March 1980, p. 16.

[2]Ibid.

Birdie Perkins Bomar of Delta's first stewardess class. (Delta Air Lines Photo)

Delta Air Lines stewardess Sybil Peacock in December, 1941. (Delta Air Lines Photo)

stewardesses, checking a manifest containing tickets with names, destinations baggage and its weight, and the passengers' weight. Carry-on baggage was not allowed, cameras had to be labeled and returned to a deplaning passenger. The only safety equipment was a fire extinguisher and a first aid kit. The stewardess pointed out the exits and checked seat belts before take off and landing and during turbulent air.[3]

Because planes were not pressurized, they cruised below 10,000 feet altitude, often encountering turbulent air. Passengers were frequently airsick and experienced ear discomfort during descents. Gum was dispensed before landing to ease air pressure on the passengers' ear drums. The first stewardesses had to put their training to work on every flight, to insure their passengers safety and comfort.

Training requirements have come a long way since its first class in 1940. No longer is it necessary to be a Registered Nurse. That changed when the United States entered World War II in December 1941, as the Registered Nurses were required for the war effort. Many more changes came after the war with the jet age.

The Federal Aviation Administration now requires flight attendants on all large scheduled aircraft. One flight attendant is required on any aircraft with a configuration for thirty passengers and two for each fifty passenger aircraft.

[3]"Inflight Service," *Delta Digest*, 8 March 1980, p. 16.

The glamorous era after World War II and the build up of commercial aviation in the 1940s. 1940: Delta Air Lines first stewardesses. 1941: Continental Air Lines first hostesses

CONTINENTAL'S EARLY YEARS
1934 - 1949

"America's Fastest" was to become the slogan of a small airline originally named Varney Speed Line. Varney operated Lockheed Vega aircraft - which traveled a mere 145 miles per hour - between Pueblo, Colorado and El Paso, Texas in 1934.

The purchase of a Denver route from Wyoming Air Transport in 1937 resulted in a new name for Varney. It was now Continental Air Lines, because the new route paralleled the Continental Divide.

Denver was chosen as the new headquarters for Continental. The former president of Varney Speed Line, Robert F. Six, became the President and Chief Executive Officer of Continental Air Lines in 1938.

Many changes occurred between 1939 and 1949. The Civil Aeronautics Authority awarded Continental Route 43 between Pueblo, Wichita, and Tulsa; Route 29 from Denver to El Paso and the *loop* or *horn* in the Rio Grande region, which included Roswell, Hobbs and Carlsbad, New Mexico.

Continental adopted the slogan *America's Fastest* after the purchase of six 14-passenger Lockheed Lodestars. Their Pratt and Whitney 1200-horsepower engines were the fastest and most powerful in U.S. commercial aviation at that time, earning it the slogan *America's Fastest.*

Continental's first hostess class began training in Denver on November 17, 1941. The first hostesses went on the line Christmas day, 1941.

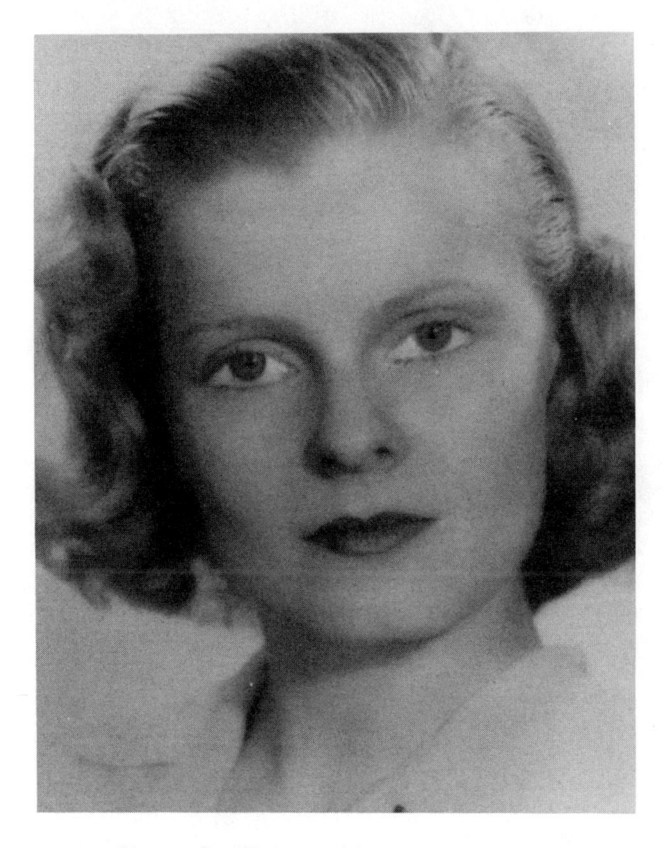

Jean Wahlberg Van Dyke, Continental's first Chief Hostess, 1941, hired from American Airlines by President Robert Six.

A new administrative building was constructed by the city of Denver. Offices, training facilities, shops and hangars were shared by Continental and United Air Lines. By 1949, Continental Airlines was America's fastest traveling and growing airline, as it started a long and steady growth building a major airline, that today has its headquarters in Houston, Texas.

A NEW ERA
Continental Air Lines
Jean Wahlberg
First Chief Hostess
1941

A new era of hostess service for Continental Air Lines and three ladies who held the office as Chief Hostess.

Continental Air Lines needed an extra plus. President Robert Six demanded perfection. With these requirements in mind, President Six hired Jean Wahlberg in October, 1941 from American Airlines to set up an air hostess qualifications, training and selection program.

Jean came to Continental well qualified for the job, as a graduate from the University of Minnesota's nursing school and as a stewardess with American Airlines. Jean had a great deal to accomplish in a very short time. Under the critical scrutiny of President Six, she immediately assembled a hostess Manual which listed job requirements and qualifications. The original job requirements listed in Continental's hostess Manual of 1941 were:

1. Applicants with previous hostess service work not to be considered.
2. Applicants must not be a member of the Red Cross Reserve.
3. Applicants should possess at least two years of accredited college work, or at least one year of business experience. High school graduates will be accepted if lack of college education can be supplemented by business experience.
4. Experience in handling the public is valuable and all applicants must possess poise, an excellent appearance, and careful grooming. It is also essential that the applicant's personality is one that will fit with this type of work.
5. Applicant's character must be above reproach and must stand careful investigation.
6. Married applicants will not be considered unless husbands are in the armed forces overseas.

7. All applicants must pass a physical examination prescribed by the company. The fee will be paid by Continental airlines.
8. Applicants should be between the ages of 21 and 26, inclusive. They should weigh between 100 and 120 pounds. Height should be between 5 feet and 5 feet 5 inches.
9. Applicants should be healthy and free from objectionable facial scars or blemishes; they must possess a good complexion and attractive teeth. Hands should be attractive and free from blemishes.
10. Applicants must indicate their willingness to accept any assignment made by the company, including availability and transfer at any time. Those who met the job requirements could obtain a preliminary interview from any of Continental airlines Station or District Traffic Managers and receive application forms from these offices, or they could arrange an interview with the Personnel Director in Denver. Applicants who chose to mail in their applications without a preliminary interview sent them directly to Denver. All applications were to be complete in every detail and include a recent photograph.

The conditions of continued employment stipulated that a physical examination was required every six months, or whenever circumstances dictated the need, for the best interest of the hostess as directed by the company.

CONTINENTAL'S FIRST HOSTESS CLASS

A whirl of activities started November 17, 1941 for Continental's twelve new hostess trainees. Perc Westmore was flown to Denver from Hollywood to teach grooming and help each hostess with makeup and hair styling. No starlet had more attention than did each of the carefully chosen prospective air hostesses.

The trainees were fitted with a stylish uniform, featuring a two-piece beige wool gabardine designer's jacket and A-line skirt; a beret-type cap trimmed in red grosgrain ribbon adorned with a Continental Thunderbird crest; a crisp white sharkskin V-neck blouse; and a double breasted wool top coat lined in red silk. Each hostess had a matching red leather shoulder bag and brown spectator pumps. Brown luggage with personalized name tags and brown leather boots were issued along with two name plates for the cabin of the aircraft. Each prospective hostess also received her own

Continental's first hostess class on the line Christmas Day, 1941. Left to right: Dorothy Wise, Jane Turner, Tommie Heck, Clara Lou Casey, Kate Black, Jean Wahlberg (Chief Hostess), Ruth Myers, Margaret Elkins, Marcelete Reid, Kate Haisley, Billie Smith and Jean Begley. (Continental Air Lines Photo)

Continental AirLines business cards.

The five-week training course included a history of the governing bodies of the airline: the Civil Aeronautics Board and the Civil Aeronautics Authority; a history of Continental Air Lines and its personnel structure; technical aspects of the Lockheed Lodestar; meteorology and causes of air turbulence; reservations, ticketing procedures and airline codes; food service aloft, as well as other inflight service to passengers; a Red Cross course to qualify each trainee to administer first aid; the points of interest on the routes Continental served, as well as a review of the geography of the United States and connecting airline routes.

During the hostess training in December 1941, the U.S. entered World War II. The federal government imposed war regulations upon all airlines and one half of each airline's fleet of aircraft went to the United States Ferry Command. Continental was left with three Lockheed Lodestars, #25635, #25636 and #25637.

Wartime regulations went into effect in the hostess training regarding passenger travel and special inflight procedures. The first class included: Clara Lou Casey, Mildred "Tommie" Heck, Jane Turner, Dorothy Wise, Jean Begley, Billie Smith, Kate Haisley, Marcelette Reid, Ruth Meyer, Margaret Elkin and Kate Black.

1942: WAR REGULATIONS

The U.S. government imposed wartime regulations on air travel in 1941. Air hostesses were required to look for signs of sabotage and to avoid discussion of political or military matters. The following list of regulations is taken from the 1942 Continental Air Lines Hostess Manual.

FBI REGULATIONS:

No foreigners - enemy aliens
- Nationalists
  - Italians
  - Germans
  - Japanese

1. Avoid political, religious, racial, and war discussions.
2. Baggage cannot be carried in same place as passenger and *must be inspected.*
3. Company reserves right to cancel en route for war priorities.
4. Aircraft Inflight Service
   a. Curtains drawn: Ramp, takeoff, landing, and troop movements, air bases. "Smoking" signs are signal.
   b. Lavatory door: Locked while on ground and 10 minutes after takeoff.
   c. Blankets: Carried in overhead rack. Wrapped or tied. They, as well as pillows, should be examined for concealment of sabotage.
   d. After passengers have left: Ash tray and surrounding vicinity should be inspected to see that passengers have left nothing that might damage aircraft or persons.
   e. Any extra baggage, parcels, brief cases not checked in baggage compartment must be checked, listed, tagged under passenger seat.
   f. Cameras: Tagged. Kept in locked compartment and returned to passenger deplaning.
   g. Conversation: Discreet. No military matters, war industries discussed.
   h. Failure of cooperation reported to Captain: A report of details, name, address, flight number, date.

The first class of hostesses for Continental Air Lines after WWII began, 1942. Left to right: Barbara Mason, Dora Midcap, La Dean Davis, Mary Hedrick and Eloise Seager. Standing is Jean Wahlberg, Chief Hostess. (Continental Air Lines Photo)

TO CATCH A SPY!

Continental Air Lines Clara Lou Casey Bascom 1941 - 1943

War time regulations for inflight service during World War II proved to be effective.

WAR PRIORITY SYSTEM FOR PASSENGERS

Priority One: Passengers traveling under Government orders of the Army, Navy or White House.
Priority Two: Ferry Command Pilots en route to ferry bases or military installations.
Priority Three: Military or civilians on war business.
Priority Four: Military on leave and military cargo.

When Continental inaugurated hostess service on Christmas Day 1941, these regulations were already in effect. They were part of the training program of the first air hostesses: Mildred "Tommie" Heck; Jean Begley; Clara Lou Casey; Katherine Black; Marge Booze; Margaret Elkin; Katherine Haisley; Ruth Meyers; Marcelete Reid; Billie Smith; Jane Turner and Dorothy Wise.

Clara Lou Casey Bascomb as a graduate of Continental's first hostess class, December 1941.

Continental hostess Clara Lou Casey in the 1942 summer uniform.

Clara Lou Casey grew up in Longmont, Colorado. She became a grade school teacher in Johnston, Colorado for one year after her graduation from college. At this time World War II was escalating in Europe. She wanted to be involved in the war effort; she loved airplanes and wanted to fly. She enrolled in the Woman's Air Force Service Pilot's Association in Denver. There were thirty women in the class studying navigation, and meteorology. The top ten percent would be chosen to go to Lowry Air Force Base to take the final exam before their flight training.

In the meantime Denver based Continental Air Lines advertised that they were interviewing young women that were 21 years of age, and preferably college graduates, to become their first air hostesses. Their aircraft were 14 passenger Lockheed Lodestars. Her friend, Gordon Olinger, a Station Agent for Continental, encouraged Clara Lou to apply. She did apply and was the first selected in Denver to join a class of twelve trainees starting November 17, 1941.

The twelve trainees were cloistered at the Olin Hotel in Denver. During their intensive four week training, a strict 8 pm curfew was imposed for studying every night. Each day they were driven in a bus to Denver Stapleton airport for their classes. Clara Lou learned she was chosen to take the final exam for the Women's Air Force Service Pilot's Association two weeks after hostess training had begun. She was required to go to President Robert Six to get permission to take the exam, as it would be after the 8 pm curfew.

The first class went on the line Christmas Day 1941. The U.S. had entered World War II December 7 with the attack by the Japanese on Pearl Harbor. Clara Lou had been flying as a hostess when she learned she had passed the exam and selected for pilot training. It was with mixed emotions that she'd decided to remain as an air hostess for Continental. Clara Lou relates her story:

"On all our flights curtains in the aircraft were pulled on all landings at the Army Air Force Bases where we landed. We had many other war time regulations and if a passenger asked questions about anything in these areas, we were to notify our Captain and note it on our irregularity report. We had all passengers names and addresses noted on tickets in our manifest and we called all passengers by name. We also had to unroll blankets and check seats and the overhead rack for any items of sabotage when passengers deplaned.

"I had a strange happening on a flight from Denver to El Paso, Texas. We had a stop at Santa Fe before Albuquerque. Curtains were pulled because we flew near a large military base at Los Alamos, New Mexico in this area. We did not know at the time that this was a proving area developing the atomic bomb.

"Flying into Santa Fe I noticed a little old lady leaning forward peeking out. I had to reprimand her three separate times. I wrote up this incident in every detail of her appearance, clothing, actions in my irregularity report, I also reported this to my Captain. On landing the Captain gave my report to the passenger agent at Santa Fe.

"On my return flight, after an overnight in El Paso, I was asked to deplane on landing in Santa Fe and report to the agent's office. There I met FBI agents who questioned me in regard to my report of yesterday's flight. They wanted to know in detail about the little old lady and my description of her. They then took me in another room with FBI agents who held a woman. She was the *same* person who had been on my other flight the other day, but not a little old lady now. I was told that my alertness had apprehended a *German spy*! She had used the disguise as an old woman, wig, glasses and used a microfilm pocket camera to take photos out the window of the top secret military installation at Los Alamos. They knew of the operation, but had to have evidence with the photos in her camera. I then felt, *to catch a spy*, I had really contributed to the war effort!

"Other experiences were not as thrilling. I was flying west out of Hutchinson, Kansas to Denver when we

Hostess Clara Lou Casey Bascomb (left), Rodeo star Homer Pettigrew and Pettigrew's manager (right) at the Denver airport, 1942. (Photo: *The Denver Post*)

encountered severe turbulence in a thunderstorm. I quickly picked up all the food trays. One man insisted he keep his coffee. I was strapping the extra food trays to the floor that wouldn't fit into the food compartment, when I was suddenly thrown to the ceiling and landed sitting up in the only vacant seat in the rear of the aircraft. Needless to say, the man wore his coffee. The airline always paid for cleaning so I put his name down on my report.

"Another time I was dead heading on an empty plane back to Denver from Tulsa, as the flight had been cancelled due to bad weather and they needed the aircraft in Denver. My captain knew of my interest in flying and invited me to stand at the open cockpit door while he explained different instruments to me. We were near landing at Denver when he yelled at me, 'Casey get back on the biffy seat and stay there!' I wondered what I had said to make him angry.

"On landing, the captain said, 'Casey you saved the day. I couldn't get the tail of the aircraft down and you were good ballast!' I became the joke all over Continental — *She may not be the best hostess, but she sure is the best ballast!*

"Another time I almost lost my job. It was on a flight into Denver with a professional rodeo star on board, Homer Pettigrew. His manager had literally carried him on board drunk at Colorado Springs. I had told the manager that he shouldn't fly in that condition. He told me that he had gotten Pettigrew drunk on purpose as he was afraid to fly and that he'd just go to sleep and be no trouble. This was true, he did go to sleep and did not become ill.

"On landing at Denver, *The Denver Post's* photographer was there to greet the flight and wanted publicity photos of Homer Pettigrew. At the door I tried to hold him up so he wouldn't fall. He suddenly weaved and grabbed me around the waist. I was reprimanded when the photo appeared on the front page of the newspaper. We had been strictly forbidden to pose for photographs without permission from management. I explained the situation, so it all ended up alright."

Clara Lou met and married Lt. Perry Bascom, a handsome Army dentist stationed at the Army Hospital in Denver. Four months after their marriage, Christmas 1943, she received a letter from Continental's Director of Operations, Paul Carmichael. He asked Clara Lou to come back on a temporary basis as they were short on hostesses due to wartime marriages and they had only one hostess on reserve to cover all flights. There would be no contract, but an agreement she would fly a trip for $19.95 prorated pay, plus per diem for expenses.

December 1941 inauguration of first hostess service. Tommie Carlisle (left) and Clara Lou Casey (right). Others in photo include Paul J. Carmichael, CAL Traffic Manager (far left) and Tom Hinman of the Denver ticket office (second from right). (Continental Air Lines Photo)

"I flew five flights," says Clara Lou. "After being weathered out several days at a time, I decided it was a priority to be with Perry. I grounded myself for my second career as a wife and mother of seven children."

Today Clara Lou has remained active with the Denver Golden Penguins and was honored with Tommie Heck, (also of Continental's first hostess class) at the fiftieth Anniversary of hostesses in Dallas, October 2, 1992. She says of her time as a Continental hostess. "I liked the challenges of variety each day, a different crew, new weather, new passengers - it all was exciting. Passengers were treated like guests in our home. They responded and many wrote letters thanking us for an enjoyable trip. I've also kept my Continental friends that are a great joy to me.

A GOLDEN ERA HOSTESS

Continental Air Lines Mildred Heck Carlisle Second Chief Hostess 1941 - 1946

Mildred "Tommie" Heck was involved in debate, drama, chorus, and was editor of her Kaw City, Oklahoma High School newspaper. In her senior year she was voted Arkalala Queen and was chosen valedictorian. She went on to attend Tonkawa Junior College to study home economics. While at

Continental Air Lines hostesses and American Airlines stewardesses celebrate the opening of the new terminal at El Paso, Texas in 1942. Tommie Heck is fourth from left.

Mildred "Tommie" Heck Carlisle was first chosen for her beauty and poise to represent Continental Airlines in publicity photos, 1942. (Continental Air Lines Photo)

Tonkawa, she was selected football queen.

To continue her studies in home economics, Tommie attended Oklahoma State University. Fashion became her primary interest. While attending OSU, she turned down a marriage proposal; marriage was not a consideration at this point in her life. Finishing her education and, later, travel and a career were her goals. She was driven to improve herself, to be the best and to make the most of her many talents. She graduated in 1940 with academic honors as a member of Phi Kappa Phi, the equivalent of the Phi Beta Kappa honor society. She also won special honors for her skills and talents in the field of fashion.

After graduation she worked for a short time in a dress shop in St. Louis. Better pay soon lured her to Wichita to work for Cessna Aircraft Company as part of the war effort in the spring of 1941.

In the fall, Tommie noted an advertisement in the newspaper. Continental airlines was holding interviews at the Wichita airport for the selection of the airline's first hostess class. The prestige of the job and the excitement of travel was of interest to her and she submitted her application

Tommie was one of twelve hostess trainees culled from over 500 applicants in November, 1941. The chosen few had survived intensive screening by Station Managers in major cities on Continental's route system: Wichita, Kansas; Tulsa, Oklahoma; Albuquerque, New Mexico; El Paso, Texas; and the personnel office at Continental's headquarters in Denver, Colorado. The Station Managers' choices met the qualifications Chief Hostess Jean Wahlberg had specified for Continental's first hostesses under the direction of President Robert Six.

The trainees were sent to Denver for individual scrutinizing and final approval in the office of Mr. Six. All of Continental's vice-presidents were present, as was Chief Hostess Wahlberg and Chief Pilot Al Shelley. Mr. Six wanted Continental's first hostesses to be outstanding. He also wanted them to be not only beautiful, but to have intelligence, poise, personality, and charm as well for the first hostess class to start November 17, 1941.

Tommie caught Six's eye. Tommie had all the attributes Six was looking for, so he selected her to participate in the pubic relations campaigns Continental would pursue in presenting the new hostess service. She was asked to sign a release for the use of her picture. She was also to be trained for publicity interviews which Continental was planning as a marketing ploy to advertise the hostess service. At the same time. Chief Hostess Jean Wahlberg saw Tommie as a helpmate and a confidante in the stressful days following the inauguration of hostess service on Christmas Day, 1941. The U.S. entered World War II on December 7, 1941. The class began in peacetime and graduated in wartime.

Hostesses Barbara Mason and Tommie Heck in the doorway of a Continental Lockheed Lodestar promoting the sale of WWII War Bonds, 1942. (Continental Air Lines Photo)

Thus the era began when Tommie Heck became a legend. Her picture represented Continental's hostess service in advertisements, on desk calendars, and on all of the posters and paraphernalia at the special events the airline scheduled for public relations. All of Continental's employees knew of her cool sophistication and beauty. She seemed to create an aura of glamour and in the airline industry for Continental in the years 1941 through 1946.

Jean Wahlberg recom mended Tommie to replace herself as Chief Hostess in November 1943. Jean planned to resign to become the bride of Navy Lt. Van Dyke. Chief Hostess Wahlberg's recommendation was approved and Tommie assumed the duties as the airline's second Chief Hostess.

Loneliness became part of being a supervisor. Continental suggested that Tommie move out of the apartment she was sharing with three other hostesses. The company wanted her to be objective. She now understood Jean's note regarding her appointment as Chief Hostess, for it had been more condolence than congratulations.

Chief Hostess Tommie Heck pictured at the opening of Continental's service to Kansas City in 1943. With her are (left to right) A. Smith of radio station WHB in Kansas City, Kansas City Chamber of Commerce President Robert L. Mehorney, WHB "Magic Carpet" engineer Lindsey Riddle and Kansas City Mayor John B. Gage.

To fill in the gap, Tommie decided to pursue her interest in fashion design by taking night courses at Denver University. Soon she was putting her knowledge of fashion to the test by designing a new winter uniform for Continental's hostesses: an entire ensemble of dark brown gabardine, complete with a swagger topcoat, brown gabardine shoulder bag, brown leather gloves, and brown lizard pumps. The traditional Continental overseas cap in brown and white gabardine, designed by Cornelius Kittredge, topped the outfit.

Tommie also designed the summer hostess uniform. It featured a pearl gray A-line skirt and fitted jacket, accented with navy and white spectator pumps, a red leather shoulder bag, and topped with the traditional overseas cap in gray and white.

In the meantime, Tommie had become the official model to represent Continental's hostess

Chief Hostess Tommie Heck shows food tray service to hostess trainees in the aft section of a Lockheed Lodestar, 1943. Left to right: Margery Dickman, Dixie Malphurs, Joy Williams and Rhea Creeley. (Continental Air Lines Photo)

Chief Hostess Tommie Heck shown pinning wings on her first hostess class, 1943. Left to right: Margery Dickman, Rhea Creeley, Jane Middlemist, Dixie Malphurs and Joy Williams. (Continental Air Lines Photo)

service during the years 1941 to 1943, and she established public relations programs in many cities to interview prospective hostesses.

In the summer of 1944, she developed health problems which required surgery. After returning from a leave of absence, she decided to extend the time and continue her education, pursuing a Master's degree at Colorado College. She was appointed dormitory head resident of Montgomery Hall which paid her tuition, room and board. Marguerite "Peg" Kellerman was named to fill the position as Continental's third Chief Hostess.

Tommie returned to Continental Air Lines for the second time as Chief Hostess in September of 1945, following Peggy Kellerman's resignation to be married. The timing couldn't have been better as she had just finished a year of study toward her Master's.

Many changes had taken place during her first stint as Chief Hostess, and they had multiplied two-fold during her leave of absence: new faces, new routes, and a new aircraft, the 21 passenger DC-3, to replace the 14 passenger Lodestar.

Number one on her list of priorities was to fly Continental's route system of all scheduled flights to reacquaint herself with hostesses, station personnel, and the new DC-3 equipment and service aloft. Continental had adopted a reserve system and for the first time hostesses were domiciled away from the Denver base. At the new base, San Antonio, all hostesses lived at a large rented estate. It was known as the "Country Club" for the many good times the crews had there, and for its grounds which included a pool and tennis court.

Tommie stayed with Continental as Chief Hostess until 1946 when she was offered a job in Los Angeles, a place she had always dreamed about. Her airline career as a hostess and as Chief Hostess had been an exciting one, and she knew that it would take a drastic change to wrench her from it. But she didn't want to stay in the job so long that her level of enthusiasm would start to wane. She never wanted her position of Chief Hostess to become just a job she had to do, so she resigned a second time with a heart full of memories and a lifetime of friends.

In Los Angeles, she met a former Lieutenant Commander of the Navy, a graduate of the University of California at Berkeley and noted All-American basketball player. (He was inducted into the Sports Hall of Fame at the University of California in 1988.) His six-foot-four-inches of blond, dynamic good looks, personality, and intelligence made this man very captivating to the independent Tommie. His name was Chet Carlisle. One day Chet blurted out, "Oh, Heck, let's get married!" As fate had it, Tommie agreed to this unique proposal.

She married Chester Carlisle in June, 1948. The couple made their home near San Francisco. Seven children later, Tommie is still as beautiful today as she was when she promoted Continental's hostess service. Continental Air Lines shares in the pride of the golden era of its first hostesses who represented the high quality of service that still exists today.

A SUMMER DREAM

Continental Air Lines Jean Begley Bluestein 1941

Jean Begley was the first hired in Albuquerque for Continental's first class of hostesses to inaugurate hostess service on December 24, 1941. This was Continental Air Lines' President, Robert Six's, gift to his airline.

Jean says of her challenge, this was a new endeavor when jobs for women consisted of working in department stores, being a social worker, secretary, school teacher or nurse. Working as a stewardess was thought to be daring and out-of-the ordinary.

"I think my parents wondered if everything would be alright about my decision to be an airline hostess. I was a second grade teacher in Albuquerque. I took my class to the Albuquerque Municipal Airport on a field trip. While the children were eagerly inspecting a Continental Lockheed Lodestar, I was inspecting a Continental official. We got into

Perk Westmore, Hollywood make-up artist, instructing Jean Begley of Continental's first hostess class, November 1941.

conversation and I told him how exciting I thought it would be to be an airline stewardess. His reply surprised me. He said Continental planned to hire its first hostesses and he suggested I should apply. I did and I was selected for the class beginning in November 1940.

One of the thrills of training was the famed motion picture make-up artist, Perk Westmore's beauty tips. President Six had him flown from Hollywood to do this for our class.

My first trip was one of the most exciting and thrilling experiences of my life. On flights we spent a lot of time with the passengers - you really need to like people. I did and I liked travel. After a year flying I was grounded by marriage."

Jean raised three children and is a grandmother. She is the Regional Director of the People to People High School Student Ambassador Program in Albuquerque, New Mexico. Working with young people has always been a prime interest to Jean.

Jean also did a 1976 summer dream experience. She returned to Continental airlines for the summer, not as a flight attendant, but as an inflight interviewer for the company. Jean says of her time being a hostess, "Even though I was in aviation for a short time in 1941, it was so much fun to be a part of those 'horse and buggy' days. I still get a tingly sensation when I fly and I love the big jets."

Jean Begley Bluestein's 1941 uniform was presented to the National Air and Space Museum at the Smithsonian Institute in November 1988.

CONTINENTAL'S IRISH COLLEEN

Continental Air Lines
Ligea McCracken Painter
1942

Stewardesses not only fly with celebrities, sometimes they become celebrities of sorts, themselves.

Bob Hope flew on Continental Air Lines with Ligea McCracken in the early forties. Later, on a show, he quipped, "I met a Continental hostess who had a ski nose like mine." Ligea had a pixie face with a decidedly turned up nose and a smile that melted many a heart. This Irish colleen captivated celebrities as well as all her passengers with her happy personality. She really cared for people.

Ligea was named "Mother Mac" after caring for the only woman, a young wife with a baby, on a flight with Ferry Command pilots. The mother was flying on Continental Air Lines' Lodestar to Wichita to join her husband before he went overseas in 1942. She became violently airsick on the up-and-down flight on a warm summer day. Ligea took care of the baby with the help of the bomber pilots. The same Ferry Command pilots flew frequently out of Wichita on Continental, and each time they saw Ligea again they called her "Mother Mac."

"Women were rarely on flights in wartime," says Ligea. "Most of our passengers were military or involved in the war effort and held priority space.

"On one of my flights to Tulsa, we landed at La Junta, Colorado at the Army air Force base. A young girl was flying there to marry her boyfriend before he shipped overseas. She held a wedding cake in her lap, and was going to be married with no family or friends present. She asked me to be her bridesmaid, but we only stopped there long enough to deplane or board passengers, so I couldn't." There were other poignant experiences connected with wartime. "I remember grown men in uniform crying as they waved goodbye to families on the ground." Ligea said.

Continental hostess Ligea McCracken Painter in the 1942 summer uniform.

"How different air accidents are today. I was in two, one a ground-loop at Santa Fe. No one was badly injured, but the plane was severely damaged. Another time we landed with the landing gear not locked. Fire trucks and ambulances followed us along the runway as we landed."

Ligea lived with three other Continental hostesses at 1080 Logan Street in Denver. "Our life on Logan Street was respected and glamorous. We received fan mail, gifts, even proposals of marriage. One passenger even offered to buy me my own plane! We sometimes received flowers with no cards. Some of the older crew members treated us like little sisters. Once a captain threatened to put a passenger off at the next stop if he made another "suggestive" remark to me. Nowadays, the same remark wouldn't even raise an eyebrow," she laughed.

"I married Jack Painter, a Denver co-pilot, after I'd flown for two years. He flew for Continental for 39 years, and retired at age sixty. He had been the number one senior captain for five years. We have three sons and two grandchildren, and make our home in Kailua-Kona, Hawaii.

"Jack and I saw Continental grow from a small airline to a big one. It was wonderful being a part of that growth, and the friends we made have been our life. Many of us have kept in touch through the years.

A TRAVEL CAREER
Continental Air Lines
Velma Brust Gay
1942

Flying gets in the blood. Many flight attendants continue to travel and many continue in travel related careers.

Velma Brust, a pretty, slim, brunette, was a grade school teacher after college, teaching in the small town of Johnstown, Colorado. Her friend and fellow teacher Clara Lou Casey had just left after a year's teaching to go to Denver. She had been interested in flying and wanted to become a pilot in the Women's Air Force Pilots volunteer training program. She had been side-tracked into becoming an air hostess for Continental Air Line's first hostess class in November 1991. This really interested Velma to also apply. It sounded exciting!

Velma was accepted for the second class starting training on February 1, 1942. She was on the line as an air hostess three weeks later. Her classmates were Phyllis Bergen from Denver; Ligea McCracken, Tulsa; and Cora Lindeberg, Albuquerque.

The pay was $110 while in training and a raise to $130 a month starting on the line. Flying time was to be 80 hours a month. Velma says of her experiences:

"Our routes had a great deal of turbulence. We flew out of Denver to Tulsa, and west out of Denver to Albuquerque and El Paso, when I just started flying. On an exceptionally turbulent flight over New Mexico one hot summer day, I had seen to it that all my passengers were firmly strapped in their seats, and I had picked up all the lunch trays except the two in front...as I walked up the aisle to get them, the bottom seemed to drop out . . . my head hit the ceiling and luckily a passenger caught me, as I fell across the seats in a horizontal position. Needless to say everything came out of the overhead racks, and the leftover luncheon trays in the back of the plane were scattered all over. As soon as I could, I went to the two passengers in the front of the plane. One, a bald headed man, had a slice of tomato right on the top of his head, and he was taking potato salad out of his eyes! I cleaned him up as best I could, and a bit later he called to me and said, 'Miss Brust, I'm going to suggest to your company that they serve all their meals in capsule form!' In spite of his disheveled appearance, he had kept his humor. We both had a good laugh.

"Another passenger I recall was a Naval Captain who boarded my flight at Santa Fe, New Mexico (near Los Alamos). As I checked his ticket off my manifest, I noted that he was to transfer to a United flight to San Francisco when we reached Denver. I asked if he was going further west than San Francisco, and he said *Yes, quite a way west.* I commented that I had a brother then stationed in China, and I hoped on his return that he would be able to bring some jade back to me. Captain Parsons then showed me two jade pieces he wore on a chain along with his dog tags. He said he had served in China and acquired these pieces there. The one I recall was a carving of white jade of two tigers fighting one another. It was exquisite. Then

Continental hostesses Velma Brust Gay (second from left) and Ligea McCracken Painter (far right).

Continental hostess Velma Brust Gay being greeted by the mayor of Topeka, Kansas at Continental's inaugural flight into Topeka, 1944.

imagine my surprise when about two weeks later, I read in the papers that the same Captain Parsons had been the official naval observer on the Enola Gay over Hiroshima!

"I was pulled off the line to train new hostesses during the interim between Chief Hostess Jean Wahlberg's resignation and the appointment of Tommie Heck to the position in November 1943. I trained two hostesses in just five days: Betty Bailey and Jo Anne Hastings. They were both known as the Five Day Wonders.

"I flew the inaugural flight in 1944 out of Denver to Topeka and Kansas City. I presented flowers to both the Mayor of Topeka and the Mayor of Kansas City. My life as a Continental hostess was a great training for the career I have had in travel since that time. I also made life-long friends while a hostess with Continental."

Velma calls San Francisco home. Life has been busy for her since leaving Continental. She became the first woman to be made an outside salesperson in the cruise industry. For twelve years she was District Manager of P&O Line, a British Company that owns Princess Cruises. She then worked for the Cruise Line Trade Association conducting workshops for travel agents. Then Velma says, "I got tired of living out of a suitcase, and then became assistant to the manager of the cruise conference until my retirement. I still travel as often as possible by air - my first love - or on cruises for leisurely travel to far away places."

CONTINENTAL'S THIRD CHIEF HOSTESS

Continental Air Lines
Marguerite Kellerman Paty
1942 - 1945

Marguerite (Peggy) Kellerman Paty, Continental Air Lines hostess, 1942.

Gifts came not only from admiring men, but from the ladies as well.

The Irish colleen not only had a heart of gold, she stole the heart of many a would-be suitor. Continental recognized the charm of Marguerite Kellerman when she was interviewed for hostess in 1942.

Peggy had learned about the job from friends at the University of Colorado. "I wanted to help the war effort," Peggy remembers, "and the job sounded exciting. I needed a career anyway, since my boyfriend had just gone off to war. I interviewed with Continental and got the job."

The regular five-week training course was shortened and intensified to accommodate a class of two trainees. Peggy and Frances Bradbury. "We were taught to give very personal service, to call each passenger by name, and to have something personal to say to each one as he deplaned. The milk run through Colorado, New Mexico and Texas gave us the opportunity to really take care of airsick passengers. We carried a number of service wives, some with tiny babies. The women needed our frequent reassurance and attention, many would be put off the route due to wartime priorities. When flights were cancelled due to bad weather we'd take our passengers to the train station, placating and reassuring them all the way. Sometimes we'd have to stay at a hotel overnight with them and Continental paid the bills.

"I really felt that we were friends, angels of mercy, nursemaids, confidantes, and public relations experts, always ready to serve," Peg adds. "We all did it because we liked being air hostesses and because it made us feel needed, respected and loved. Many of the hostesses were also good friends."

Peggy was the all-American girl, and her smile stole the heart of many Continental Air Lines' passengers. One elderly lady was so impressed with Peg's assistance that she pressed a tiny pillbox into Peggy's hand as she deplaned at Albuquerque. After all the passengers had left the aircraft, Peggy continued with her ground duties: straightening blankets and pillows before the next leg of the flight. When she finally opened the small tin box, she found a neatly folded fifty-dollar bill.

I can't keep this," she said with a gasp. Her crew, however, insisted that she keep the money. It was a gift from the heart to Peg.

Peggy Kellerman's name, like Tommie Heck's, was known by everyone in the airline business. As a line hostess, Peggy had flown over 160,000 miles in two years. When Chief Hostess Tommie Heck took a leave of absence to return to college in 1944, Peggy was appointed to the position. Peggy had many firsts including Continental's adding the DC-3 in service.

Her duties as Chief Hostess included hiring and training new hostesses, scheduling, and handling public relations, as well as settling any problems involving air hostesses. When Peggy's longtime boyfriend, William Paty, returned from active service, Peggy left Continental to marry him.

Peggy and Bill made their home in Hawaii, and are the parents of five children. Through the years Peggy has applied her love of people to community affairs and her church. She has been active as a legislative lobbyist. "I'm sure my career as a wife and mother has been enriched by my airline experience," Peggy says. "I gained satisfaction from my job which added yet another dimension to my life."

ENTHUSIASM PLUS

Continental Air Lines
Jo Anne Hastings Gray
1943 - 1945

Jo Anne Hastings Gray, Continental Air Lines hostess, 1943, later assistant to Chief Hostess, Peggy Kellerman.

Jo Anne Hastings and I were each trained in just five days in 1943. Continental was desperate for hostesses and couldn't wait to get us on the line.

"Good things come in small packages" and "the blonde bombshell" both describe petite, vivacious and spunky Jo Anne Hastings. She had personality spiked with a mind of her own. Her ideas and opinions packed plenty of punch, and occasionally touched off sparks. Wherever she happened to be, things got done with enthusiasm.

Jo Anne majored in psychology and sociology at the University of Colorado. She graduated in June 1943, fully intending to pursue a career as a psychiatric social worker.

"I was sidetracked by Peg Kellerman. Her enthusiasm for her job rubbed off on me, and a vacancy occurred just as I graduated from CU. I was hired and they needed me flying the line like yesterday," Jo Anne said with a laugh, remembering her crash training.

"Betts Bailey and I were each trained by a senior Continental Air Lines hostess, Velma Brust, in just five days. We were the only two ever given such a short, compact training course. Continental hadn't yet hired a new Chief Hostess, and several hostesses had suddenly quit to marry their servicemen home on leave, so Continental Air Lines needed us in a *hurry*.

"Betts and I became good friends. A lot of the same things seemed to happen to us. We were sent to cover different legs of the first flight on a new route to San Antonio, we were both in a ground-loop in a Lockheed Lodestar, and we both dated pilots named Gray. We played jokes on each other and on the crews, something a lot of hostesses did. Many of us had known each other in college and we were all good friends.

"I became Chief Hostess, Peg Kellerman's assistant in 1945. Betts left Continental to be a stewardess for United. In the meantime, my romance with co-pilot Dan Gray was getting serious. I liked my job training hostesses, making schedules and giving check rides. I had to fight for a hostess reserve system, but convinced President Six it was needed. In fact when Peg submitted her letter of resignation, Mr. Six offered me the Chief hostess position if I promised not to get married. But I chose to trade Hastings for Gray. After leaving Continental, I taught a stewardess training course at Denver University until I was expecting a baby.

Continental hostess Peggy Booker on the steps of a Lockheed Lodestar, 1943. Peggy later became a Chief Hostess.

"MOTHER SILLS" SAVED THE DAY

Continental Air Lines
Jane Middlemist Winterroth
1943 - 1945

Airsickness was a common hazard of early air travel that modern medications and pressurized aircraft have almost, but not quite, eliminated.

Hostess Jane Middlemist was so airsick on her first flight to El Paso that she wondered if it was because she was so excited. Captain Olson took pity on her and helped all he could. Sick as she was, though, Jane was thrilled to be an air hostess.

Jane was hired by Continental in the early spring of 1944. She had an extra modeling job assignment she had to finish. The training class had already started so she had to make up a week of studying and tests. Undaunted, Jane passed with flying colors.

"I had to have a sense of humor because airsickness seemed to be something I couldn't get over," Jane says. "At some point on every flight I'd become airsick, sometimes for most of the flight. In spite of this, I loved my job. Lucky for me, in the fall of 1944 a new motion sickness pill, *Mother Sills Airsickness Pills*, was put on the market. It really helped me a lot. Sometimes I took too many and got a little lightheaded, but those pills really saved the day. I'd forgotten what it was like to feel good on the job."

One day, Jane was due for a check ride. She was very worried about doing everything right, especially calling passengers by name, under the watchful and critical eye of Chief Hostess Tommie Heck.

"As the passengers deplaned, I called them by any name that popped into my head, and I had a name for every one of them," Jane says, recalling that particularly nerve-wracking ride. "After the last passenger deplaned, Tommie told me what a marvelous job I'd done and said that she was especially proud of my ability to recall every passenger's name. I just swallowed hard and grinned. She hadn't seen the blank stares some of those passengers had given me when I called them by some crazy name!"

Jane, a brunette with pixie features and an infectious grin, had left a job with the telephone company to join Continental. She'd done some modeling too, and attended the University of Colorado. Her friend and former roommate was Peggy Kellerman. It was Peggy's urging that prompted Jane to interview with Continental Air Lines.

Continental hostess Jane Middlemist Winterroth, 1943.

Continental hostesses in the doorway of a Lockheed Lodestar, 1944.

"All of the hostesses were friends we were like a family at Continental. Being an air hostess has always been an important part of my life," Jane says warmly. "My on-the-job training with the public helped me as a faculty wife at Chapman College. My experiences allowed me to relate well with students and to integrate myself into many activities. When I see a sunset or a sunrise, I think of those flights over southwestern Colorado, New Mexico and Texas, and of flying over all that beautiful scenery. It made me feel so good and appreciate the opportunity of flying. You know, the friends I made as an air hostess are still my friends. There have been so many beautiful people who have touched my life...it's the people, the wonderful people, who have added so much to my life."

Four Continental hostesses, the first to be based outside Denver, lived in a house known as "The Country Club" in San Antonio. Bottom to top: Betty Weimer, Julie Borgman, Mary Jean Stevenson and Marion Nixon.

THE COUNTRY CLUB "GIRLS' TOWN"
Continental Air Lines
Marion Nixon Braubach
1945

To share expenses as they come and go on flights, many flight attendants in the past and present have shared a house.

Continental first based air hostesses outside its Denver Headquarters base in 1945. Eight hostesses were sent to San Antonio, Texas. They decided to rent a house together as a cooperative project to save money. This house was called the "Country Club" by crew members, but was a hostess haven to them and they called the house "Girl's Town" located at 137 Park Drive.

Girl's Town was a two-story rock house completely furnished. Marion Nixon was the Chief Hostess for the San Antonio based eight hostesses, she also was in charge at the house. The household had no maid except for someone to do heavy cleaning. All hostess had their domestic assignment and a bulletin board in the kitchen kept tract of who was to do specific jobs.

Some had a roommate, Nellie Sauder and Marion shared a room. Each hostess was responsible for the room or sleeping porch she occupied. Downstairs chores were divided on a rotating schedule. Two hostesses kept the sun porch-library, two the living and two the dining room. Dinner was served each evening at 6:30 pm. Coffee was served without cream and meals planned for trim waistlines.

Special tasks were appointed. The collection for and the payment of the monthly rent; gas light and telephone bills; a "kitty" from which food was purchased. Time allowed for social time and sunbathing in the Texas sunshine. All eight came from other states but loved their San Antonio, Texas home.

Marion met her future husband, John Braubach, on a flight in 1946 while he was flying to Las Cruces, New Mexico to visit a war buddy. Marion today keeps in touch with her former roommates and friends for life from days flying for Continental as air hostesses and living at Girl's Town.

FLYING GETS IN THE BLOOD

American Airlines Continental Air Lines Chris Carleton Inboden 1943 - 1950s

"Oh, yes - Mother was right! It was her suggestion that I consider a career with the airlines. That was in 1943! Well, I considered and reconsidered, and finally joined American Airlines in New York that same year. What a great decision. Not only was there a wonderful training program, but the chance to know such super enthusiastic people. I was really proud to wear my American stewardess uniform and be a part of a great airline.

"Time raced by and so did I. For personal reasons, I found myself in Denver in 1947. A friend suggested that I check with Continental Air Lines regarding a position. Just entering their offices, I really felt a sense of family. I got the job as a flight hostess and a whole new way of life started for me. They felt me qualified to go on the line in a very short period of time because of my excellent training and experience with American Airlines. I loved my job, whether I was flying standby, on reserve, or flying almost every day while holding a line. I looked forward to going to work. I flew on DC-3 twenty-one passenger aircraft, Convairs, Viscounts and DC-6 aircraft.

"In 1950 I became Chief Hostess which was a 24 hour a day responsibility. It was an interesting experience watching those who "had it" make it, and those who fell by the wayside. Let's face it - times have changed, but what it takes to be a flight attendant hasn't.

"Fairy tales do happen. I met and married a wonderful, fun loving pilot who has since retired after flying thirty three years for Continental. We have one daughter - who, you guessed it, is also a licensed pilot...it just gets in the blood!"

Chris Carleton Inboden has kept her Continental friends. Golden Penguins, an association of former and current hostesses, was begun in Denver. Julie Borgman Looney was president and Chris became her vice president. Golden Penguins met socially and also raised money for community projects, McDonald House being one of their service endeavors. The group also met with the Denver Interline Association, a conglomerate of all airline flight attendant clubs, for one annual event. This group recently became Mile High Wings. Three airlines formed the chairmanship for 1993: Chris Inboden, Continental Airlines; Sally Olsen, United Airlines; and Cynthia Hastings, Eastern Airlines. Each year the three directors will change.

Chris is an example of the bonding of airline flight attendants past and present. The associations they form, not only enhance their social enjoyment with one another, but also provide community service in their various philanthropic endeavors.

Chris Carleton Inboden, Continental Airlines hostess in the 1950s. Chris joined the Continental hostess staff after flying as an American Airlines stewardess. She later became a Continental Chief Hostess.

PRIDE IN THE JOB SERVING COFFEE, TEA AND MILK

Continental Air Lines
Lee Butler Blanchard
1953 - 1954

Lee Butler Blanchard, Continental hostess, 1953.

"After my four weeks training at Denver's Stapleton airport in May 1953, I was off to fly in the skies for Continental airlines. I was now an air hostess, a job I dreamed about for glamour and excitement. While I was a student at the University of Missouri, I decided to make the job a reality for me.

"After graduation, I was sent to Tulsa, Oklahoma for temporary duty along with several other hostesses. We were so busy with long hours, but it was exciting! I served sandwiches, coffee, tea and milk, flying mostly on DC-3 charter flights, and I loved it!

"This experience followed with an assignment for reserve flights at El Paso, Texas. I didn't like reserve as I couldn't plan anything. Fortunately, schedules came two months later. I remember the pride we had in our job, our appearance and for our company. We worked long, hard, and horrible hours. All for $200 a month, but we didn't mind, we liked our job as air hostesses. We met so many interesting people on every flight. No drinks were served on the small planes, we were free to spend a lot of time visiting with out passengers.

"Our aircraft in El Paso were DC-3s, DC-4s, Convairs, DC-6s, but no jets. Travel time to Houston and to other cities varied, but most of our flights were three hours. On the DC-3s between El Paso and Denver we had many stops, it seemed every 30 minutes we landed somewhere. I really liked flying the DC-6s and the Convairs — I thought they had a lot more *class.*

"I met my husband while flying. He was a career military officer. I had to quit when we married, as that was the rule. I have continued to travel and now find it difficult to stay in Florida.

"I loved my job as a Continental hostess and I always spoke of it to anyone who would listen. I influenced my daughter, Barbara Blanchard, to become a flight attendant with Continental, she flies out of Dallas as her domicile and likes her job as much as I did."

A BRIEF HISTORY OF PAN AMERICAN AIRWAYS

Prior to 1928 travel to other countries from the United States was only available by ship. The general public did not travel, as it took too much time on a two-week vacation and was too costly for the average person.

Juan Trippe founded Pan American airlines October 28, 1927. He had purchased two Fokker F-7 tri-motored aircraft for his airline. The plane trip to Havana, Cuba from Key West, Florida took one hour and ten minutes and carried only mail. Pan American had only 24 employees at that time.

Three months later, the first passengers were carried on the Fokker for a fare of $50 one way. In 1929, Pan American added male stewards dressed in navy blue uniforms with brass buttons who served refreshments on board the flight to Havana. This was the beginning of Pan Am's inflight service.

In 1930 the name *Clipper* was given to Pan American's Sikorsky flying boat. Since then, all of the airlines' multi-engine aircraft were given the name Clipper.

By 1939, the Boeing B-34 *Clipper* had a dining room that seated fourteen passengers. Every over-seas passenger was assigned a berth. A private suite in the rear of the aircraft was called the *bridal suite*. The service on board the Clippers could be compared to any first class European hotel. Shoes were even shined overnight.

During the war years, 1942 through 1945, the Clippers were used to transport troops, but after the war the public wanted to take vacations in Europe, and Pan American's goal was to bring foreign travel within the reach of everyone.

In 1944, Pan Am hired the first seven stewardesses. They were trained for shorter flights out of Miami. The seven young women were given the same two-month intensive training as the stewards.

In 1946, the Douglas DC-4 transport replaced Pan American's slow flying boats. The DC-4 had proved itself in World War II. It was a fast and fuel-efficient aircraft which enabled the airline to lower its fares. In the same year, the Lockheed Constellations went into service for Pan American. These were the first pressurized aircraft, and they could fly high above turbulent weather.

In 1948, Pan Am celebrated its twentieth anniversary. It had started as an airline with two aircraft and 24 employees, with one route to Havana out of Key West. Twenty years later it employed 19,000 people. In two decades, Pan American had flown seven million passengers to 62 countries. Inflight service had been established with elegant service and comfort for passengers. The Stratocruiser was luxurious, with sleeping berths and a bar lounge.

Pan American took on a new name, Pan American World Airways. A new slogan was introduced, *The Most Experienced Airline*, a slogan that was never disputed.

In 1955, jet aircraft, which provided more economical air transportation, were introduced. Flying time was lessened by half, and now a traveler could go anywhere in the world in hours instead of days. Six-abreast seating and less elegant food service made economy fares available in the new quiet and smoother jet planes.

The Boeing 747 was introduced in 1966, and Pan Am's smaller jets were phased out. The big 747 was like a small cruise ship and passengers could walk around during a flight. First class passengers were served in an upstairs dining room with luxurious service.

The Lockheed L-1011 joined the Clipper fleet in 1980, and at the same time, Pan American merged with National Airlines. A coordinated merger of the two companies combined aircraft, facilities and personnel. Marketing was directed to use the Pan American image and to get flight attendants and crews in the same uniform as soon as possible. This merger has been called the *Pan-A-Marriage*. Everything was well planned and orderly. Pan American added quality people and a domestic route system and 45 years of National's rich history to make a combined heritage of nearly 100 years of aviation experience. Its' demise in 1991 is truly a *Lost Horizon* in flight, of a regal airline and its service to the world . . . *Pan American World Airways.*

A steward serving in the 14-passenger dining room of a Pan American B-314 Clipper, 1940. (Pan Am Photo)

Pan American's first flight stewardesses: Elsbeth Erhart, Lois Smith, Gloria Smith, Dorothy Mills, Doris Stimson, Lois Taylor and Dorothy Larsen.

THE FIRST SEVEN LUCKY STEWARDESSES

Pan American Airways 1944

Pursers were used on all Pan American flights until it was decided to try women on special flights. The requirements were stringent for the seven stewardesses that Pan Am would hire in 1944. Trim, attractive, a friendly smile and pleasing personality - these were just some of the prerequisites for the job as a Pan American stewardess. Much more than that, she must perform the duties of a combination purser and stewardess.

The Clipper, Pan Am's house magazine, described the new stewardess as follows:

She travels on a merchant seaman's passport because she flies for an international airline. She is responsible for the health and comfort of her passengers en route. She not only checks on passengers, but also continues to check vital papers from the port of departure to the port of entry. She supervises the loading of mail and cargo, and is familiar with domestic and customers regulations and international mail. She handles coded messages for reservations and takes care of all other documents and priority ratings. It is wartime, so she also checks papers vital to national security.

These are just some of the things that her gold Pan American wings stand for. She has earned them by completing rigorous courses and examinations. In fact, her course was identical to that of the stewards, including lifesaving and first aid. Says Joyce Swartz, who was purser on Pan American's Alaskan route, "The qualifications of landing this job were so stiff that no one in our original group is quite sure yet how she made it. Good health, brains, fluency in a foreign language, looks, charm, poise and character beyond reproach were only half of it. None of us felt we were so perfect that we had all these traits," she added.

The first seven to pass their pre-flight exams and earn their wings to fly on the Clippers were: Gloria Gene Smith, Detroit, Michigan; Doris Stimson, Chicago, Illinois; Lois Smith, Peoria, Illinois; Dorothy Elizabeth Mills, Stratsburg, New York; Elsbeth Erhart, Omaha, Nebraska; Dorothy Larsen, Atlanta, Georgia; and Lois Taylor, Lancaster, Pennsylvania.

Each stewardess was outfitted in a trim powder blue uniform with a collarless tailored jacket, a wide soft collared white blouse, a tailored A-line skirt with a kick pleat, brown shoes and a Robin Hood style hat with the

Pan American crest. She wore her gold wings proudly pinned over her left breast.

The first seven stewardesses were placed on the shorter routes out of Miami. They were so successful that Pan American gave the first class its stamp of approval and issued the go-ahead for recruitment for additional classes.

THAT PAN AMERICAN SOUTHERN CHARM

Madeline Cuniff 1945

Hospitality Pan American style included organizing parties and sporting events during layovers.

Hospitality Pan American style included organizing parties and sporting events during layovers. Prior to 1944, all of Pan Am's flight attendants were male couriers and pursers, but during World War II men were in short supply. Out of necessity, Pan American hired its first women flight attendants in 1944. Women flight attendants, called stewardesses on Pan Am, were limited to working flights other than those to Europe, because the airline deemed it unsafe for women to fly to Europe during the war.

Pan American stewardess Madeline Cuniff spraying aircraft before arrival in the US, 1945. (Pan Am Photo)

A lovely, soft-spoken lady from Alabama, Madeline Cuniff went north to New York in 1940 to visit her sister who worked for American Airlines. Soon Madeline was working for Pan American Airways in passenger service.

Madeline and her sister had grown up in the thirties when women in aviation were new and bold. They had both idolized Amelia Earhart and were great fans of air shows. The two had also observed the growth of women in the airline industry, starting with Ellen Church in 1930. In New York the sisters became licensed pilots, and Madeline flew for the Civil Aeronautics Patrol during the war years. When Pan American finally started hiring women, she jumped at the chance to become a stewardess in 1945.

"People were really afraid to fly, and I wanted to show them what it was all about," Madeline says. "My first flight was on a Boeing B-34 flying boat, New York to Bermuda. I felt very chic in my new blue uniform, but I didn't look chic for very long. I opened a chute to empty garbage in mid-flight and instead of going into the ocean, it backed up the chute and onto me.

"Our flights were long, and we were on duty up to eighteen hours at a stretch. The male pursers didn't like having women on board. They did half the work for twice our pay of $160 a month. Meal services were very elegant. We served meals on china which had to be washed. Much of the food was prepared in kitchens on board the Clipper. My two-month training program and Pan American's kitchen duty prepared me for many responsibilities.

"We had a special honeymoon suite on the flying boats, complete with bunks," Madeline recalls with a smile. "Newlyweds were given several bottles of champagne and left alone.

"Our crew duties were not over with the flight," she adds, "hostesses were responsible for entertaining passengers, sometimes for several days at a time on layovers. I've organized dances, bridge and golf tournaments, and you-name-it."

Madeline's southern hospitality, warmth and zeal for her work has made her many friends, among whom she numbers celebrities and royalty.

She continued with ground duty after turning in her wings. In 1980, Madeline celebrated forty years with Pan American World Airways. She continued to welcome passengers to the Clipper Club at John F. Kennedy International Airport until she retired in July 1984. Her enthusiasm and charm reflect her love of people. "I've had so many wonderful experiences. I treasure them, but I live for today," she says with that soft southern accent and charm.

United's World War II years and the 1940s

FIRST CLASS
United Air Lines
Catherine "Kay" Park Haney
1941 - 1942

Flying with celebrities on board is not an unusual experience for flight attendants. In the thirties and forties, before Air Force One, even the First Lady traveled on the commercial airlines.

Kay Park Haney, United Air Lines stewardess, 1942.

"My father was a pilot during World War I and his interest and love of flying rubbed off on me as a child. By the time I was twelve years old, I had determined that I was going to be a stewardess," pretty auburn-haired blue-eyed Kay Haney says. She was reflecting on her job as stewardess for United air Lines during 1941 and 1942, when she was based in her home town, Salt Lake City.

"Up until the time that I applied for training, nursing was a requirement. I applied for United's first class that accepted college girls.

"I cannot imagine another job as exciting, rewarding and fulfilling as being a stewardess. I liked the travel, meeting the passengers and working with the crews. I also enjoyed the high regard that was accorded stewardesses.

"We were taught that we should treat passengers as if they were guests. With only twenty-one passengers and long flights, we got to know each of them, so that we called them by name and developed a friendly rapport with them by the end of the flight. I am probably prejudiced, but I think the flying public in 1940 was nicer than many of the travelers of today. All of our passengers, too, were first class.

"Many of my passengers were military personnel that were either going to war or returning. I remember how proud I was to have known them for just a few brief hours. Among the non-military celebrity passengers I had on my flights were Bob Hope and Eleanor Roosevelt.

"On one flight I remember Mrs. Roosevelt typing her daily 'My Day' column for the newspapers. We were flying in violent weather, Denver to Salt Lake City. It was in fact so turbulent that we had to make an emergency landing in Rock Springs, Wyoming.

"Mrs. Roosevelt was a most gracious person. But with all due respect to her, one thing she wasn't, was petite. Many items were rationed during the war and required ration stamps to purchase. One of my passengers, after looking at Mrs. Roosevelt's feet, quietly asked me if she required two ration stamps to buy a pair of shoes big enough to fit her large feet.

"Although I didn't meet my husband on a flight, my experience in flying added to our common interests, since he was an Air Force pilot. My training and experience as a stewardess helped immeasurable in the transition to being an Air Force wife."

"Unless you were there at that time it would be difficult to understand the pride, the excitement, the reward and the satisfaction of being a stewardess on United air Lines in the 1940s."

Instructor Florence Pond demonstrates natural make-up for United Airlines stewardess trainees.

The United trainees have won their wings at stewardess school.

A TEST DID THE TRICK

United Air Lines
Libby Doyle Woodfill
1943 - 1947

Inflight careers take many forms. The following two stories are examples.

"I am a farm girl from middle Illinois — small town of Henry. After many years of living elsewhere, I now am back in the general area. Today we live along the beautiful Illinois River (when it isn't flooding) near Peoria — home of Caterpillar Tractor company. We purchased a home in Sun City, Tucson, Arizona this year for the purpose of wintering there and summering in Illinois.

Libby Doyle Woodfill, United Air Lines stewardess, 1943.

"I went to the University of Illinois, flunked Chemistry, so went with an airline career. My housemother at that time suggested that I apply for a stewardess position since the nurse requirement had been lifted because of World War II and they wanted girls with certain contact experience. I applied and couldn't pass the physical because of a low hemoglobin count. I went home, ate lots of red meat, including liver (which I hate). Again did not pass, but I convinced the Personnel Office that I had to have a job, so they made one for me in Accounting. Two of the men from Personnel heckled me for a month, *how's the hemoglobin kid today?* Next time I passed the physical. I'm not sure it was because I was tired of the heckling, or I really wanted to fly.

"There were eight in my class. We trained in the basement of the headquarters of United at Midway Airport in Chicago. I graduated and got my wings in August 1943. My stewardess roommate was Jean MacDonald Rowe. We also had two other roommates who worked in offices. This was a good idea, they always had the meals ready for us when we came home. When Jean and I were home, we did the cooking. I keep in touch with several of the ladies that flew at the same time that I did.

"We were domiciled in Chicago and I flew mostly

Climax of training course—final exams.

ALL OVER AMERICA—SMOKERS ARE CHANGING TO CHESTERFIELD
UNITED AIR LINES
"CHESTERFIELDS ARE PROVIDED EXCLUSIVELY on all United's Strato-cruiser flights to Honolulu. We have found our passengers prefer Chesterfields."*
VICE PRESIDENT, UNITED AIR LINES
DALE ROBERTSON
gets his Chesterfields from
Stewardess Audrey Jones
See him starring in
"LYDIA BAILEY"
A 20th Century-Fox Production
Color by Technicolor
CHESTERFIELD
Wherever you go-Sound Off
for MILDNESS_ plus
No Unpleasant After-taste*
*FROM THE REPORT OF A WELL-KNOWN RESEARCH ORGANIZATION
...AND ONLY CHESTERFIELD HAS IT!
1952
Chesterfield
CIGARETTES
LIGGETT & MYERS TOBACCO CO.
CHESTERFIELD
Try them Today!

out of Midway Airport to Denver and Cheyenne on DC-3s. I worked a Press flight when they dedicated the University of Illinois Airport. On my flights, most passengers were *Ferry Command* crew members flying on priority after delivering an aircraft to either coast. It was World War II and all passengers needed a priority for a seat. If there was an empty seat then we had other people as well.

"I had some notable personalities on my flights: Kay Francis, actress; Broderick Crawford, actor; and Dee Merrick. Ellen Church flew on one of my flights. She was a lovely lady.

"I flew for about two years, then trained stewardesses for about the same length of time. We had classes in a hangar at Midway Airport, then the Tucker Plant (automobile plant) in Chicago. Training was then moved to Cheyenne.

"I left the company to marry a United agent in 1947 and moved back to Chicago. One of the United Air Lines executives called to ask if I would like to work part time in reservations, on a temporary basis, we then moved to Denver. By that time my job was full time.

"While in Denver I set up the Stewardess Department for Challenger Airlines. I hired, trained and wrote the manual for them. They eventually became Frontier Airlines. I also taught at Denver University in their school of Aviation Stewardess Training course as an instructor.

"I joined Clipped Wings when the Denver Chapter was founded in 1947. Pat Jacobson was the founder, but I was their first elected President in 1953. However, Ginny Long Hitch finished the term as President, as we moved to New York. From there we moved with United to New Jersey and back to Denver. Altogether I worked 20 years at the different bases.

"I have been a member of the Denver, Chicago, and New Jersey Chapters of Clipped Wings and have been a MAL (Member At Large) since 1965. I still miss the monthly contact that you have in the chapters, but am fortunate to be able to go to Chicago and O'Hare chapters once in a while. I was National Treasurer in 1952, President for two terms 1953 - 1955.

"I presided at conventions in Denver and San Francisco. At the San Francisco convention they did a newsreel of the event. It appeared on Paths News in all the theaters throughout the country. The principals were Mr. Patterson, Ellen Church and a fleeting glance of yours truly. My movie debut and finale!!

"With working so much of my life it was difficult for me to do any volunteering, except with Clipped Wings. I am involved with the Handicapped Olympics and am also a *Pink Lady* with a local hospital in Peoria, Illinois. I find it very rewarding, and especially enjoy being with families who have patients in ICCU. They really enjoy having someone to listen to their problems.

"I have had so many wonderful things happen to me through United Clipped Wings that I surely will *die with my boots on* being loyal to them wherever I am, and wherever I go."

UNITED CLIPPED WINGS HISTORIAN

United Air Lines
Vicy Morris Young
1946-1949

Vicy Morris Young has been involved in aviation since her first introduction to flying as a United stewardess in 1946. She had good qualifications along with her dark beauty. She had been born in Tennessee, but spent her growing up years in Alabama. She attended the University of Alabama, but transferred to Northwestern University in Evanston, Illinois due to a double major in speech and journalism and they excelled in both. She graduated and then worked for a Junior college as a student, public relations assistant and assistant teacher all at the same time. She received an additional Associate degree for her two

Vicy Morris Young, United Air Lines stewardess, 1946.

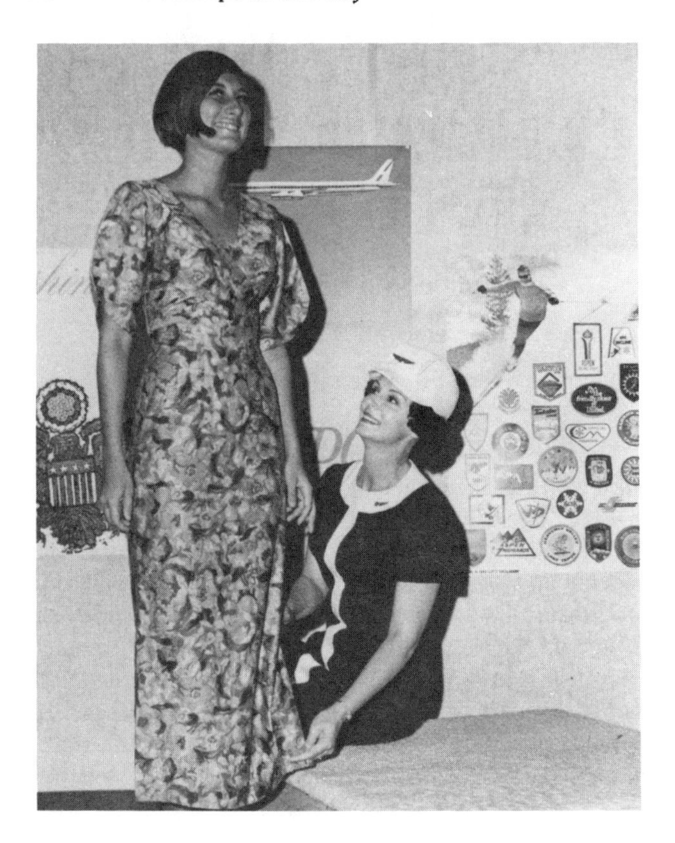

Vicy Morris Young, former United stewardess instructor and program director at an airline college.

years work.

Vicy joined the early Spring class for United stewardess training in 1946 and says, "Our classes were held in a hangar at Midway Airport in Chicago for six weeks. This facility had first been set up in 1938. We were bused daily from the South Shore Del Prado Hotel where 46 of us were housed. We all had round trip familiarization flights from Chicago to Cleveland before our graduation April 27, 1946. Then we all went to our respective domiciles on United's system. I enjoyed my job as a stewardess and while working met United Captain Bohzelsdorf. I had to resign when we married, as stewardesses had to be single at that time. We lived in Los Angeles and raised four sons. After my divorce I later married Dick Young, who was Director of Contract Services for United. I then became a ready reference for United airlines' historical items and United kept me well informed. I have assisted with over 27 Television, newspaper, magazine and book projects of major importance plus many minor ones. I have enjoyed it all.

"Most satisfying for me was seeing the changes in inflight to the present. I had a close relationship with Steve Stimpson, called 'the father of stewardess service,' as well as Ellen Church Marshall, the world's first stewardess who worked with Steve to hire and train the other seven Registered Nurses as stewardesses. They were known as the 'Original Eight.' None of them flew very long, several years at most. Margaret Arnatt is now the only one living today.

"I had met Ellen in some public relations affairs prior to the thirty-fifth anniversary of stewardess service in 1965. She had never married until age 60 when she married the widower of her best friend. This was just a year before a tragic fall from a horse. She died of head injuries.

"Since my husband flew out of Los Angeles, I became involved with the LA Chapter of United's Clipped Wings. I was active for 23 years and, while president of the chapter, we invited Steve Stimpson, who became the darling of the LA Chapter. He and his wife attended many meetings and social events. When he became ill and could no longer attend functions, Eva, his wife, was made an honorary member until her death. I always had a special relationship with Steve due to our sharing an interest in aviation history and United.

"I visited the United Training Center many times due to my involvement in college programs and teaching stewardess and airline training in Southern California. At one time there were 7 programs which lasted for about 12 years when there was a great need before the no marriage rule was dropped. These courses gave a sampling about airline careers. It was emphasized that this training would not prevent further training by the carrier who would employ them. I sat on boards that planned all of these programs, it was a great experience. At the same time I was National President for Clipped Wings. I left California when I remarried and went to Chicago. I still served for 2 years on Advisory committees for programs in Junior Colleges in California that the state was always ready to

The nursery liners for mothers and babies, a United promotion in the mid-1940s. (United Airlines Photo)

embrace new ideas.

"I feel like a pioneer, especially being lucky enough to have known Steve and Ellen as friends, as well as to have flown in the forties when airline service was building. We served such nice meal services. In 1936, Don Magarell was hired and brought United a Swiss Chef in the first airline flight kitchen to prepare meals and also special holiday meals with menus.

"Inflight service has come a long way since I was trained in Chicago. In 1947, the training school was moved to Cheyenne, Wyoming, where trainees lived in a dormitory sleeping room. A housemother provided a touch of home and monitored the 11 p.m. curfew. Buses transported trainees to a converted B-17 hanger. The five week course was intensive and mock-up Mainliner cabins provided on-hand training.

"In 1961 the Training Center was moved to Chicago near O'Hare airport in Elk Grove, Illinois. The new 8 story facility housed dormitory units, a cafeteria, beauty salons, classrooms and swimming pool. It is large enough to yearly train 2,000 trainees in inflight service and management. Men and women were now known as flight attendants. The last housemother was Ruth Ferber when the job was eliminated due to changing times. Classrooms are in constant use for training and seminar programs."

"With all the changes into the jet age, Vicy is still the keeper of the archives and historian for United's Inflight Service for Clipped Wings. Vicy has walked and talked this great legacy she shares with so many.

FIRST IN FIRST OUT
United Air Lines
Barbara Barton Frank
1946 1948

Tight turnabout schedules and rooming with friends are part of the life of a flight attendant. Sometimes dispatch calls at the most inconvenient time possible.

Bobbie Barton had just stepped from the shower when the telephone rang. It was Cheyenne's United dispatch saying she was first out for a trip to San Francisco, and she had one hour before the crew taxi would pick her up at the hotel.

"First out!" Bobbie Barton, United stewardess, exclaimed. "My clothes are all wet — my uniform blouse, my hose, and all of my lingerie — and my hair . . . It is freezing outside — I'll turn into an icicle!"

Dispatch firmly stated that her crew was the first to turn around after adequate rest. All of United's flights into Denver, Salt Lake, and Chicago had been diverted to Cheyenne, Wyoming, The winter of 1947 had brought a blizzard that dumped two feet of snow on Denver. The runways at Denver's Stapleton airport were buried in deep drifts and all transportation was immobilized as the city came to a complete standstill.

"This type of operation out of Cheyenne may last up to two weeks until Denver can dig itself out," the dispatch agent said. "We will see you in one hour, Miss Barton."

Bobbie was fortunate that she had naturally curly hair; a towel dry would be sufficient to make her presentable when the rest of the crew arrived at the hotel. Her wet clothes made Bobbie feel cold and uncomfortable as they hung limply from her tall frame. None of the other stewardesses could loan her anything to wear.

Bobbie later recalled this incident with good humor.

Barbara Barton, United Air Lines stewardess, 1946.

"This was more or less standard procedure in the winter, especially between Denver, Salt Lake City, and San Francisco and to the Northwest," Bobbie recalls. "Winter storms over the mountains were violent and Operations closed airports. We were fortunate in Cheyenne as we stewardesses had hotel rooms. Although the pilots and co-pilots always got a hotel or motel room, that wasn't always true for the stewardesses. When hotels and motels filled up due to mass cancellations en route, stewardesses stayed on board the aircraft with passengers. Sometimes a hot air blower was connected to the aircraft on the 21-passenger DC-3 and the 44-passenger DC-4."

"When all through flights were cancelled at Salt Lake City, blowers had to be rotated. Passengers kept their coats, hats, and gloves on, and we passed out blankets and pillows. We served hot bouillon, cocoa, tea, and coffee and kept a vigil all night while everyone slept. Everyone seemed to cope well with the circumstances. We tried to make the best of it and had a good time, but we got sleepy and tired. Our time on the ground was not considered flying time, that was only block to block. In other worlds, when the block was pulled and the wheels of the airplane started to roll."

Bobbie's attitude as a stewardess was service oriented. She had many an "Orchid Letter" from passengers forwarded to her and placed in her file. And it was no wonder: Bobbie's cool, dark beauty was punctuated with sky blue eyes and her sophisticated charm could placate any situation.

"I wanted to be a stewardess when I caught the 'bug' to fly in the fall of 1945, my senior year at UCLA. I applied to Western Air Lines and was turned down; I'm tall, I hope that was the reason. I applied to United Air Lines in Los Angeles and was told to reapply after I graduated from college, because being a college graduate was a prime prerequisite. When I received my degree in Psychology in June 1946, I applied again to United and was hired for the August six-week training class in Chicago."

THE HOUSE ON HIGH STREET

After receiving her United Wings, Bobbie was sent to Denver. "Six of us got together and rented a house on High Street," Bobbie said with a grin. "We each had a roommate: Irene Flynn was my roommate; Dove Call and Kay Kahley; Fay Steinsiefer and Virginia Riley.

"I had lived in Los Angeles and had never seen snow before," Bobbie said laughing. "Was everyone mad at me when early one November morning I woke everyone up to see the snow coming down -- I was fascinated!

"That house on High Street was something else. It was the meeting place and the talk of the whole neighborhood. Our neighbors saw us come and go at all hours of the day and night. They probably thought we were running a house of ill repute because we received several unexpected visits from the police. When we threw a party, all of the parking spaces within a block's radius were taken. The hi-fi got a little noisy, as did the crowd. Many a romance started at our house. Stewardesses brought their dates or came alone, as did the unmarried crew members and United station agents. Boy met girl, me included. I met Walter Frank, a United copilot. We were married in the fall of 1948.

"I kept flying after our marriage. That is, until the word got around, then I had to quit because of company policy. At that time a stewardess could not be married. But my United friends," Bobbie adds with a smile, "have always been a part of my life. Some of us who flew out of Denver meet every year. We call it our United Bash. We laugh a lot...we are the friends of the 'Friendly Skies.'"

FUN EXPERIENCES

United Air Lines
Fay Steinsiefer Barr
1946 - 1947

Inflight service cements special friendships in experiences shared.

Fay Steinsiefer was born in Oregon. After college she worked as a secretary for Standard Oil Company of California in 1946. "An article in the newspaper by United air Lines wanting to interview candidates for stewardesses prompted me to answer the ad. I loved travel and people and this sounded great to me," said Fay. "I interviewed, was accepted and graduated with wings August 1946 from a six week training at United's Headquarters' stewardess School in Chicago. As luck would have it five other girls I liked a lot were also going to be domiciled in Denver.

"The six of us decided to look for a place to live. We found a neat house with three bedrooms which was just what we needed and we each had a roommate. Mine was Gini Riley who ended up flying for United 43 years and Number 2 on United's seniority list of flight attendants when she retired in 1989. She has been my life long friend. Gini was based in LA and still lives there. We try to get together often. Bobbie Barton Frank lives in LA, Dove Call Kreger in Denver. Irene Flynn and Kay Kahley have both passed away. The four of us have reunions every other year and my friend Betty Bailey who lived in Denver and is now in Illinois, joined our gatherings in 1983.

"Our house on High Street was the party spot," Fay adds. "All the neighbors wondered just what was going on, because we were coming and going at all times of the day

Fay Steinsiefer Barr, United Air Lines stewardess (wearing the summer blue uniform) in the doorway of a DC-3, 1946.

and night and bringing part of our crew home for a cup of coffee, and parties, lots of parties. I spent time at Betty's home in Denver, too. We double-dated, played golf. I deadheaded on many of her flights.

"My four children have heard my fun stories," Fay related, "such as my first reserve flight to New York with one of my roommates. Dove and I went together on a DC-4. We were so excited we took our fur coats. We were like tourists in the big city. We were so excited!

"On my trip with crew members Spicklemier and Spitler, a passenger looked at our name plates and said, 'You all have sauerkraut hanging our of your ears.'

"I was sent on a plane deadheading only crew members to Omaha. Since there were only crew members on board, the pilots weren't too careful about taking off and descending rapidly. I had a cold and my ears plugged up. Upon arrival, I took a taxi to a doctor out in the country near the airport. He gave me a sedative to help. Help? I remember trying to keep awake on my flight out of Omaha.

"During layovers in Milwaukee, I'd go with the crew to visit the breweries. Being German, I like beer. They held open house at the breweries with refreshments and sometimes a band and dancing. What fun!

"On the 'Casey Special' out of Salt Lake City, Captain Casey always gave the stews a back rub.

"I had a great spirit of adventure," Fay says with enthusiasm. "I loved my job as a stewardess. Our trips out of Denver went to Chicago, Milwaukee, Cheyenne, Salt Lake, Spokane, and San Francisco. Sometimes on reserve we flew to New York. And there were charter flights. I liked where I flew and the travel, but most of all I liked the people on my flights. I only had a few celebrities like Xavier Cugat and his band. That was exciting."

During the fourteen months Fay was a stewardess, she met a young law student. In November 1947 she resigned her job to become Mrs. John Joseph Pickett. Three daughters were born before the marriage ended in divorce.

"I returned to my home state of Oregon with my girls. I was a legal secretary in Medford, Oregon when I met my second husband Jack Barr. We have a son in college. Life has been good to me," says Fay with a smile.

"My experiences flying are fun to remember. I tried to influence my three daughters to become stewardesses. My youngest, Leslie, took the cue and flew for Pan Am for over six years before the demise of Pan Am in 1991. She speaks both Spanish and Portuguese," Fay says proudly. "I traveled on many a pass on some of her flights.

"In August 1983 the four remaining High Street stews and Betty Bailey held a reunion at my home in Medford.

"For this United Bash Bobbie came from LA; Gini Riley was returning form a flight from Germany with a connection in Denver; Betts from Illinois; Dove lived in Denver - and all got on the same flight. Picture this, we are all 'sixty something.' I saw three wheel chairs being rolled out to meet their only flight to Eugene, Oregon. I got to thinking they might pull one on me to all meet me in wheel chairs! Ha! But no, they were for three real senior citizens because *we* are so young at heart! We laughed everyday, all day, and half of every night remembering the good times working for United. My husband Jack, said of our get together, that he'd never seen five women have such a good time.

Good fiends and good times are still cemented by the friendly skies of years gone by.

ROOKIE HAZING

United air Lines
Virginia Olstad White
1945 - 1949

Inflight service is hard work, but it's a lot of fun too. Crews have always enjoyed hazing new stewardesses.

Pretty blond Virginia Olstad was a senior at the University of South Dakota with graduation coming up in June 1945. She was known by her nickname, *Ginny*. In the early spring of 1945, she and her friend Dorothy Krell, also a senior, had heard about the job of being an airline stewardess, and decided to interview with United Air Lines in Chicago.

"The job of travel to new places sounded appealing to us," Ginny says. "In the interview we were told we were both too tall for their height requirements."

"Both Dorothy and I majored in Business and Merchandizing. After graduation in June 1945, we both were hired by Marshall Fields in Chicago in their Field Flyer Program in training to become buyers. I had worked there one year when I saw a United ad with new requirements of height for stewardesses. I applied, and

United stewardesses Ginny Olstad (left) and Ginny Hegge on the steps of a United DC-4, 1947. (United Air Lines Photo)

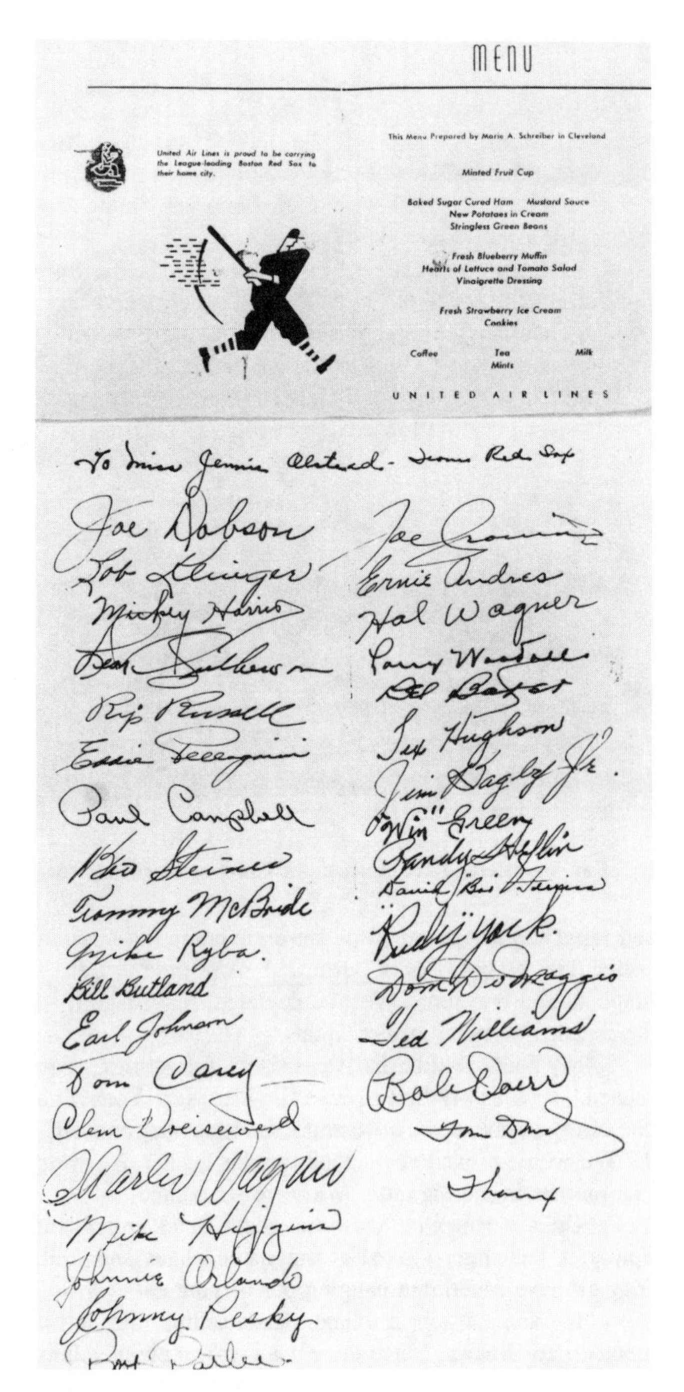

MENU

United Air Lines is proud to be carrying the League-leading Boston Red Sox to their home city.

This Menu Prepared by Marie A. Schreiber in Cleveland

Minted Fruit Cup

Baked Sugar Cured Ham   Mustard Sauce
New Potatoes in Cream
Stringless Green Beans

Fresh Blueberry Muffin
Hearts of Lettuce and Tomato Salad
Vinaigrette Dressing

Fresh Strawberry Ice Cream
Cookies

Coffee   Tea   Milk
Mints

UNITED AIR LINES

United stewardess Ginny Olstad had the Boston Red Sox on a charter flight in 1948. They signed the special menu for their flight.

since I'd had a good interview in early spring, except for my 5'6" height, they said I was accepted and would begin stewardess training the next week in Chicago. I was excited.

"After a training of six weeks I was based in Chicago. My first trip was on April 1, 1945 on a 21 passenger DC-3 to Milwaukee. Since it was April Fool's Day, I wondered what tricks my crew might play on a brand new stewardess, and so the story goes...

"Everything was going according to schedule and I seemed to be doing quite well in spite of my nervousness.

The interphone light went on, notifying me that the Captain wanted to talk to me. The crew wanted coffee.

"I filled two cups with coffee and approached the cockpit door. I put the tray on the floor while I opened the door with my "100" key - or so I thought. I pulled and pulled, but the door wouldn't budge. I knocked on the door and pulled again. I thought to myself, one of them must be holding the door so I can't get in, or they've locked it from the inside. I returned to the galley and called the cockpit.

"'You'll have to come back and get your own coffee if you want some.' It wasn't long before the co-pilot emerged from the cockpit. He helped himself to the coffee from the galley thermos and, took the two cups of brew with him. He hadn't said one word to me.

"In the crew car in Chicago, I asked if dispatch in Denver had told them that this was my first trip. I was surprised to learn that they hadn't known that it was.

"'I thought you held the door so I couldn't get in the cockpit! You must think I'm a bear, and I'm embarrassed, I apologize.

"The crew agreed with me that they had thought me a real grump. They told me the cockpit door must have been stuck when I tried to open it.

"On the return to Denver the following day, thunderstorms produced very turbulent air. One by one, all of my twenty-one passengers became airsick. I too, felt nauseated. The copilot came into the cabin and helped me take care of the passengers. I decided crews were pretty nice, and I would never in the future believe stories I had heard from my instructors."

Several months later Ginny was discussing her first flight with several other new stewardesses, and learned that she had been fortunate, as pilot's pranks on new stewardesses were a common occurrence. One stewardess related that on her first flight the crew had summoned her to the cockpit of the DC-3 shortly after takeoff to issue her special instructions on the operation of the toilet. The captain had pointed to a lever on the floor, "See this," he had said. "This is a wobble pump (which was used by pilots to put fuel into the engines), when a passenger uses the toilet, you must immediately come to the cockpit and pump three times to assure the toilet is flushed. Furthermore, before landing put the toilet lid down and the plug in the sink or you will have a terrible mess." The directions had been followed even though such an operation of toilet facilities had not been mentioned in stewardess training.

Another stewardess laughed as she added that it must have been the same wobble pump that her DC-3 crew had asked her to pump before landing on her first flight. They said it was to help secure the landing gear.

All heartily laughed as they agreed that fooling around and hazing of new stewardesses was fun for pilots and worth a good laugh by them.

Ginny continued about her experiences as a stewardess, "I transferred to Denver as my domicile early in 1947 and one of my roommates, Jo Leeper, never ironed anything! She encouraged me to save time and only iron the collar of my blouse, which I did. On my trip to Milwaukee weather was very hot and humid and I just *cooked*, I couldn't take off my jacket - and perspire I did in my *wrinkled* blouse! I never did that again.

"I was dating a salesman who traveled a lot. He said to meet him at the Denver Airport, if he was in town he'd meet me Saturday night at six o'clock. I took a cab to the airport on Saturday and I waited and waited for over an hour. A good looking tall United passenger agent, Lloyd White asked me if I'd been stood up. I told him, I guessed so. He asked if he could take me home -- this started a romance that has lasted a lifetime.

"I did return to Chicago and I flew the DC-6 to New York, Boston and Washington DC until October 8, 1949 when I became Mrs. Lloyd White. I thought being a stewardess was a great job, a fun job and all the time treating passengers like they were guest in your home."

REMEMBERING
United Air Lines
Helen Schmidt Carlson
1947 - 1951

Each day in inflight service brings a new flight, crew, passengers and a variety of experiences.

I WAS HOOKED!

"We had a very special treat at one of our Girl Scout meetings when I was growing up in a suburb of Chicago - a United Air Lines stewardess came to tell us about her job, a new career for women. It was in the 1930s and United was flying Ford TriMotors.

"I was in absolute awe - I had never seen anyone so glamorous! She wore a jaunty beret, oxford-like shoes, a tailored uniform and blouse with a mannish tie, and a big cape swirled from her shoulders. We all sat cross-legged on the floor in a semicircle around her as she perched on the corner of a desk, swinging her leg and smiling as she described what she did on her flights. I had never even been in an airplane, but I was hooked! From then on it was my dream to someday be a United stewardess.

"As soon as I turned 21, I applied to United and was hired. For four years I flew the friendly skies before I married a mining engineer, moved to a mining camp 10 miles round-the-mountain from Pioche, Nevada, and became the mother of four little boys. When my husband's

United Air Lines stewardess Helen Schmidt Carlson, 1947

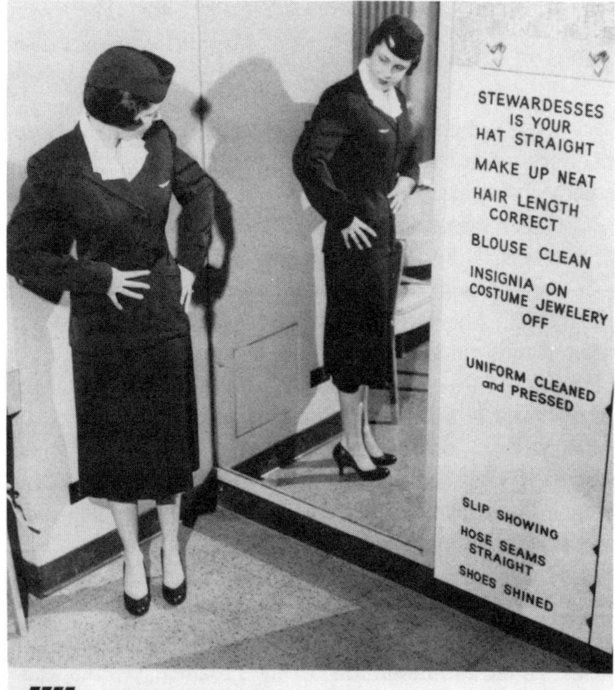

CHIC CHECK: This 1951 United Airlines stewardess had many pre-flight responsibilities, includin grooming check to guard against such fashion faux pas as crooked (stocking) seams, runaway sli and scuffed shoes. May 15, 1980 marks the 50th anniversary of United flight attendant service. (Ur Airlines photo)

work took us to Denver in 1962, I lost no time in joining Clipped Wings Association of Former Stewardesses.

"One of my first meetings was a spring luncheon and I was a stranger. Seated beside me was a very gracious lady, Agnes Hurt Bitterman. She asked me how I happened to become a stewardess, so I told her about that long-ago Girl Scout meeting. Aggie began to laugh, *I was that stewardess!* She was based in Chicago and, in addition to flying her schedule, United asked her to do public relations talking to small groups. Aggie and I became good friends and, not surprisingly, she always felt very motherly toward me.

"Helen was based in three domiciles in her four years with United: Salt Lake City, 1947-1949; Chicago, 1949-1950; and Seattle, 1950-1951. The following stories are some of her experiences as a United stewardess."

BUMPY AIR AND BURP CUPS

"Lack of oxygen was not the only problem on the unpressurized western flights caused by the topographic elevations. Our daytime flights during the summer were frequently brutal because of extremely rough air caused by the heat from the sun colliding with the reflected heat from the ground. We routinely flew at 12,000 to 13,000 feet. The pilots used oxygen and we occasionally used the pipe stem oxygen at our galley. The pilots did not have the luxury of climbing a couple thousand more feet to minimize the rough air - we just had to tough it out.

"The one-quart cardboard burp cups at each seat were no laughing matter, they were a necessity. On the DC-3's they were held by a clip underneath each seat. Once Floss Fotes reached down for a burp cup for a lady who felt ill, but Floss' timing was unfortunate. After washing her hair and her blouse in the tiny basin in the Blue Room (lavatory), Floss finished working the trip with her wet hair tied in a turban and wearing her winter coat. We quickly learned not to reach for a cup under the seat of a passenger who felt ill; it was much wiser to snatch one from under the seat of a passenger who still felt O.K.!"

MRS. COLE'S MISSING TEETH

"In 1947, passengers always wore their best clothes; the men always wore suits and the ladies wore hats, gloves and, if they had one, a mink coat. But air travel was no longer just for the wealthy and for business executives - it was becoming the preferred mode of travel for the middle class. Consequently, we had many first-riders who preferred to travel in mid-summer, and they always took daytime flights so they could see everything.

"One hot summer day, I was scheduled to take a DC-3 trip to Denver, leaving Salt Lake around noon. The incoming stewardess reported the air had been quite rough the last hour and several passengers had been airsick, especially Mrs. Cole, and elderly lady, a first-rider, flying from Portland, Oregon, to Denver to visit her son.

"A few minutes after take-off, Mrs. Cole rang the call button. When I got to her seat I noticed she was holding a new burp cup and was squirming about in her seat. 'I can't seem to find my lower denture, can you help me look for it?' I got down on my knees and checked under the seats and I shook the burp cup she was holding, but in my heart I knew her lower denture was no longer on board. I headed for the cockpit to ask the pilots to radio back to Salt Lake City for someone to check all the used burp cups to try to find the missing lower plate. I never did know what was done with the filled burp cups, but I visualized a warehouse full of them in Salt Lake City that blistering summer day!

"She was a very dear person and I truly wanted to help her, but the crew thought I was joking! By the time I convinced them it was true, the three of us were laughing hysterically at the incongruity of the situation. First the captain tried to radio Salt Lake City, but he again started laughing and had to break the transmission. The copilot tried, but his luck was no better, the captain tried again with the same result. By this time the ground radio operator became quite angry, thinking a bored crew was playing games with the radio. Finally, the copilot was able to maintain his composure enough to get the message through and to assure them it was no joke.

"On arrival in Denver, the passenger agent opened the cabin door and handed me a taped message from Salt Lake City stating the missing lower plate had been found and would be forwarded to Denver on the evening flight. Weak from her long ordeal, I helped Mrs. Cole down the few steps to where her son was waiting on the ramp. I got his name and address so United could deliver the lower denture to his home that evening, and I assured him his mother would feel O.K. once she had been on the ground for a while. I also suggested that on her return trip she might be more comfortable if she took an evening flight. Mrs. Cole patted my hand and thanked me for my many kindnesses, but she had decided to take the train back to Portland!

"I don't know how they learned of the story, but several days later, I saw a paragraph in a newspaper carrying a United Press dateline telling of the loss and retrieval of the denture."

EAST MEETS WEST and VISE VERSA

"In the olden days of the DC-3s, it was routine that after the passengers were loaded, the engines fired up, and everything set to go, we would wait at the gate until the passenger agent came running out with the latest weather report. He would open the cabin door waiting. We would then hustle up to the cockpit with the weather report as the plane left the blocks.

"It was also standard practice for the stewardess to collect their tickets from passengers after they had boarded and were seated.

"The pilots were several minutes late in boarding, so I had ample time to settle my passengers and collect tickets while preparing for a flight from Chicago to Omaha. When I took the weather report up front I stayed to chat a minute as we taxied. 'What are we going to do in Omaha this evening?' The captain replied, 'I don't know what you're going to do in Omaha, but we're going to play golf in Newark.' They were serious! I couldn't convince them we had a full load of people expecting to go to Des Moines and Omaha. How could I possibly explain to my passengers why we were flying over Lake Michigan on a west bound flight? I dashed back to the cabin for the manifest. 'Look, I wouldn't have all these tickets to Des Moines and Omaha if the passengers expected to go to Newark!' By this time we had taxied to the end of the runway with just one other United DC-3 ahead of us in line for take off.

"Suspicious at last that something might be amiss, the Captain called the tower. The tower held our flight as well as the DC-3 ahead of us while they checked into the matter. After a few minutes the engines were shut

United's uniforms on display. The models are members of the Denver Chapter of Clipped Wings. 1993 United captain (far left), retired captain Dale Cavanaugh (center) in his 1940s uniform. On his left is his wife Nan in her 1947 summer uniform. Helen Schmidt Carlson (far right) in her 1940s winter uniform.

down and a very embarrassed crew came bumping through the cabin carrying all their pilot paraphernalia - and their golf clubs.

"They deplaned through the cabin door, walked across to the DC-3 in take off position, threw their gear in through the cabin door, and hoisted themselves up into the cabin. Meanwhile, the other crew came over and crawled in through our cabin door. Yes, the crews were mixed up. The pilots got the FAA registration numbers of the planes for their respective flights from dispatch, and dispatch had inadvertently reversed them."

"ELKO, ELKO!"

"Shepherding is a very lonely job, and the many sheep rancher out west had trouble finding men who would spend months at a time in the wilderness alone with only their dogs and the sheep. In 1947 it was a common practice to offer a two year contracts to Basque shepherds from the Pyrenees Mountains in southern Europe. They were excellent shepherds who could tolerate the isolation. By the end of his con-tract, a Basque could save enough money to return home to his village and live like a king.

"After their arrival in the U.S., they would be boarded on a United DC-3 flight originating in Newark, New Jersey, which made *every single stop* on United's Mainline. It took more than 24 hours from Newark to Elko, Nevada, the Basque's destination. They spoke either French or Spanish, no English, so they had always been ordered, "DO NOT get off the plane for any reason, until you get to Elko!"

"One day I picked up my return flight from Denver to Salt Lake City, the DC-3 flight that had originated in Newark, and there were four Basque among the 21 passengers. When we landed in Cheyenne, Wyoming, I was advised that our equipment would be going into the DC-3 maintenance base (then located in Cheyenne) for a scheduled major overhaul. I told the passengers we would be transferring to another DC-3 parked on the tarmac which had just completed its overhaul. All the passengers deplaned - all but the four Basque shepherds.

"Using my best sign language, I indicated to them that this airplane was going no farther, but, pointing to the other plane on the tarmac, that plane was going to Elko. The Basques had been well coached - they refused to get off the plane until it reached Elko. I continued to try to convince them to transfer to the other DC-3, but they were adamant. Meanwhile, I could envision them staying with the plane for the next two weeks as it went through the maintenance base. Seated together, the four Basque passengers each sat with his arms folded across his chest, his head lowered, and his dark face glowering at me.

"We had reached an impasse when the cockpit door opened and Captain Warren Kimball stepped into the cabin. Seeing passengers still on board, he asked me why they had not deplaned. From their expressions, it was immediately obvious we had some kind of a major problem. I explained that the passengers did not speak English, and when they had boarded in Newark they and been ordered to *stay on the plane* until they got to Elko.

"The Basques apparently recognized that Captain Kimball was not only the man in charge, he was also the airplane driver. The captain pointed at each man individually, asking, *Elko?* and each man in his turn nodded vigorously, tenaciously declaring, *Elko!* Then, with a grand sweep of his arm, Captain Kimball marched off the plane shouting *Elko! Elko!* The Basque shepherds glanced quizzically at each other for a moment, then with a jubilant whoop, they leapt from their seats to charge after the captain, cheering and grinning!"

CELEBRITIES

"Most of our western states are sparsely settled with vast distance between towns, and the towns are small by East Coast standards. Before television, recreation was very limited in the rural west.

"It was a Sunday afternoon as my DC-3 trip landed in Rock Springs, Wyoming - the one trip each day to go into Rock Springs. As we pulled up to the gate I noted a throng of people crowded behind the chain-link fence.

"Something important must be happening to draw such a crowd — maybe they were boarding the Governor. When the passenger agents opened the cabin door I asked, 'Who's the celebrity today?' 'You are,' he answered.

'*I* am?' "Sure," he explained, 'in a town like Rock Springs there's nothing much to do on a Sunday afternoon so everyone drives out to the airport to watch the plane land and take off.' Before we left I stepped outside the cabin to wave and the crowd cheered!"

FLYING HIGH

"In 1948 the DC-6s were the only pressurized passenger planes flying; the unpressurized DC-3s and DC-4s were much more limited as to the altitudes they could fly. Although the union contract stipulated that a stewardess was not required to serve meals when flying at 10,000 feet or higher, passengers in the west would never have eaten if we had exercised the option. It is necessary to circle to 12,000 or 13,000 just to clear the Salt Lake Valley, and then there are mountain ranges to cross in all directions. Yes, it was very tiring but those of us based in the Rocky Mountain West had no choice if we wanted to be United stewardesses - besides we were young and strong.

"After flying out of Salt Lake City for two years, I transferred to Chicago where one of my first trips was a DC-3 trip to Newark. I was serving dinner as we flew over Ohio in a mild rainstorm when the crew called on the intercom. We were going to climb to 10,000 feet to get out of the rain. Puzzled by the message, I asked, "So?" An equally puzzled pilot responded, "We just thought you'd like to know." Used to routinely flying at 11,000 to

13,0000 feet minimum, I had forgotten that in the east they seldom flew above 7,000 or 8,000. When I went up front to have a cigarette, I thanked the crew for the message, explaining that I hadn't understood because I had just transferred in from Salt Lake. They found the situation very amusing, explaining that the girls who flew in the east would complain bitterly if they had to fly at 10,000 feet and would just sit and suck on an oxygen pipe!"

AN UNSCHEDULED LANDING

"On a non-stop flight from Denver to Chicago continuing on to New York, a distinguished older man boarded escorting a handsome younger woman, probably in her thirties, an acquaintance who just happened to be booked on the same flight. We served dinner out of Denver, but his friend said she was not hungry and didn't eat. We were cleaning up the buffet when he came back to talk to us.

"His companion was not feeling well. She had become unusually quiet in the terminal, and she admitted to him she didn't feel well enough to eat. Her condition had progressively grown much worse until she was unable to sit up in her seat because of the pain in her abdomen. It sounded like appendicitis to me, so I made her as comfortable as I could and notified the captain.

"We could make an unscheduled stop in Omaha, but the captain left the decision to the passenger. He knew such a decision was not to be made lightly, but he was very concerned about his friend who by now was extremely ill. Yes, we would stop in Omaha.

"The passenger wanted to talk to somebody, so standing at the buffet chain-smoking with sweat rolling down his face, he told us the real story. He had known the lady for several years and the two of them were headed east for a long weekend. Recently married, her new husband in Los Angeles thought she was merely going to Salt Lake City to spend a few days with a cousin. What was she going to tell her new husband? How could she explain being in the hospital in Omaha, Nebraska? He was concerned that this unexpected development might jeopardize her marriage.

"As we approached Omaha, I went through the cabin checking seatbelts and advising passengers of the unscheduled landing; we would be met by an ambulance and they would bring a stretcher on board to remove a very ill passenger please stay seated and we will leave immediately afterward for Chicago.

"Trying to make points for United, the Omaha passenger agents repeatedly assured the man that he need not discontinue his business trip; they would take excellent care of his friend and see to her every need. He firmly protested, 'No, I wouldn't consider it — a very dear old family friend — I would never forgive myself, I personally want to make sure she's all right.' So, carrying her elegant mink coat, he deplaned and rode off in the ambulance with her. Later I learned that she had, indeed, been operated on that night for a ruptured appendix. I've often wondered what the *very dear old family friend* told her new husband, and how he took the news."

GO WEST YOUNG MAN!

"Our DC-6 was taxiing for take-off from Chicago when a young passenger, a sailor, asked me if we expected an on-time arrival. His leave was almost up and he wouldn't get back to his ship in San Diego if the flight was late. Yes, we expected an on-time arrival. The problem was we weren't going to San Diego - we were going to New York!

"The captain radioed the tower, and the tower stopped the San Diego plane which was also taxiing for take-off. United sent out a vehicle with a hydraulic lift generally used to lift cargo into the plane. The frantic sailor deplaned through the forward cargo door just behind the cockpit onto the extended lift of the cargo carrier, which then ferried him across the field to the San Diego flight. I hope he got back to his ship in time!"

A SECOND CHRISTMAS GIFT
United Air Lines
Mollie Drown Dear
1952

"After one year of college at Iowa State College in Ames, I worked as a secretary and discovered I disliked this type of work. I was bored and knew I must find something far more interesting than typing letters. I applied with United, American and Northwest. My preference was United. Their interview was very understated and made me very comfortable. I cannot say the same for American, but perhaps it was the gentleman who interviewed me as he stated to me he preferred blonds! Northwest at that time hired only through airline schools which you had to pay yourself and there was no guarantee you would be hired. United had their own training school. American did also. I wanted to be a stewardess because of the travel, adventure and working with people.

Mollie Drown Dear, United Airlines stewardess, 1952.

"In 1952 we had to be between 21 and 28, also single. United made us feel we were very special and to be proud of ourselves, and that we had been picked from a large field of applicants. This has carried over to what I do with everything I attempt now. It gave me confidence to tackle many jobs later in life. Also, I love entertaining in my home, and have passed this on to our three sons.

"United gave the IQ test to me at their main travel center in Des Moines which was sent to Chicago to be evaluated. I was then sent a ticket to travel to Chicago for an interview. I was told the school had no openings at that time and I would be contacted. I was very disappointed, and thought they were not interested in me. Much to my delight the day after Christmas I received another ticket for another interview in Chicago. I was hired to attend school in Cheyenne the third week in February. I loved every minute at this wonderful school. My best friend at the training center has become my life long friend. She also introduced me to my husband Bill.

"The training was at United's training center for five and a half weeks. We were paid $1.00 per day, fitted for our uniforms and pictures were taken for hometown newspapers all in the first week. The course was very intent and thorough. We were in class by 8:00 am, a break for lunch and then on until 4:00 pm. We were to be in skirts or dresses, girdles, hose and heels, with makeup and to be on time. There were no excuses for missing class, late three times and you were on your way home.

"There were 21 in our class and we graduated March 31, 1952. My close friends Jackie Trolle Montero and Connie Hess DeJulian and I were the three who were lucky enough to bid for San Francisco domicile right out of school. We were immediately placed on reserve the first month. We did not question this as it was United's policy. We soon learned if we wished to shampoo our hair, wash our blouses, go on a date, to call dispatch first to see when we were scheduled for a trip. It did not bother me to be on reserve as it rolled around approximately every six months. As for bidding, the lower your seniority number affected the type of equipment you would work. I bid DC-3's for several months until I hurt my back. The company doctor said I could not fly this equipment any longer because of the heavy work it involved. This was a great disappointment to me because I loved this plane. Some of my fondest memories were on these trips. I then bid DC-4's, the coach trips of those days. I only flew DC-6's when on reserve, or if I was asked to trade a trip.

"The perk of the job for me was the fact *I was a stewardess*. There were not many in those days. We did receive passes for our parents and mine were able to leave the state of Iowa for the first time and came to California to visit me.

"Food service was all like first class of today (except for the DC-4 coach trips which only served coffee or tea). Everything was on fine china, linen and silverware. We took coats hung them in closets returning them to the passengers before landing along with gum and mints. We were to address each passenger by their name. We did not serve nor sell liquor.

"We had one carry on piece of luggage. Our weight could not exceed 120 pounds and were to be between 5'2" to 5'8". The reason for this was on the weight manifest of each flight the stewardesses were always listed as 125 pounds.

"I had the privilege of wearing the classic navy blue

Lilli Ann uniform. I wore this uniform which I can still get into, to the San Francisco airport when United celebrated 60 years of stewardess service. I was overwhelmed by the current flight attendants who just wanted to see and feel. One said '[look at you in your navy blue wool gaberdine with your sterling silver wings, and me in my polyester and plastic wings!' As you can tell, I loved being a 1950s stewardess."

1953
Now she's ready to serve you in the Mainliner Manner
This young lady is graduating from a girls' school you perhaps never heard of, yet it's one of the most exclusive in the nation. It's United Air Lines' Stewardess School, where only one out of 35 applicants qualifies to enter.
In money her tuition is low—in fact, zero. But it's extremely high in qualities that money can't buy—like good sense, good humor, fine character, a genuine liking for people, and an ability to serve them with tact and understanding.
So it's no wonder she's excited and proud as she steps up to receive her wings and diploma, with her classmates, her folks, and United Air Lines officials looking on!
As she joins us on the big United Air Lines team—clad for the first time in Mainliner blue—radiant in all her youthful enthusiasm—she's a living symbol of Service in the Mainliner® Manner. The right kind of people, trained in the right way, assure you of this fine and friendly service whenever—and wherever—you fly United Air Lines.
UNITED
AIR LINES
Serving you coast-to-coast, border-to-border and to Hawaii. For reservations to anywhere in the world call or write United or an authorized travel agent.

During the World War II years, American, like other airlines, dropped the requirement that a woman had to be a registered nurse in order to be a stewardess.

AMERICAN'S LADY IN RED

Lorraine Peterson 1941

For some of the veterans of inflight service, there has been a transition from a short term job to a lifetime career.

Lorraine Peterson began her career as a stewardess for American in 1941, and ended it as a flight attendant forty-three years later. Her first trip was a DC-3 flight from New York to Boston. Her last trip was in a Boeing 747 from Los Angeles to Honolulu.

Lorraine's flying career has taken her through four decades of change. What started as a job became a profession during the war years, when the nursing requirement was dropped. Later, anti-discrimination laws forced airlines to change rules which had previously required stewardesses to retire at age thirty-two. More and more men and minority group members started to enter the field, and "stewardess" was changed to "flight attendant" by the Civil Rights Act in 1964.

High spirited, red haired and freckled Lorraine used to bristle at some of the rigid airline rules, which included using only red lipstick. The weight restrictions were especially irritating. "At one time," she says candidly, "I was put on a liquid protein diet to reduce a few curves. I was put on suspension for being overweight and having a *corn fed* look."

American Airlines President and CEO, Robert Crandall, presenting American Airlines flight attendant, Lorraine Peterson, an award at her retirement. Lorraine is wearing the 1980s Hawaiian muumuu uniform. (American Airlines Photo)

Lorraine's flying experiences included an emergency landing in Colorado when two of the DC-7's engines failed to function. "The passengers panicked," she says. "I had to manhandle a few of them to save their lives." American presented her with their highest service award for her efforts in that incident. But for Lorraine it was all in the line of duty. She had flown military charters as a nurse during the Berlin airlift, and in Vietnam as well.

She was notorious for being a spunky redhead. She was known as the "red hot mama" and the "wild one" according to autographs from celebrities who had flown with her. "I treasure my autographs," says Lorraine, "and I keep them in a scrapbook with the rest of my stewardess memorabilia."

She wasn't forced to retire, as American has no mandatory retirement age. Instead, Lorraine chose to retire at age sixty-five. I was tired of pushing heavy carts," Lorraine confides. "Besides, flying is no longer the deluxe experience it used to be, and I miss the time I used to have to get to know my passengers."

Other American Airlines flight attendants arranged a party for Lorraine to show their appreciation for her efforts before her retirement. Lorraine was presented a distinguished service medal by the Federal Aviation Administration for her contribution to aviation. She will be represented in the Douglas aircraft Museum in Santa Monica and the Honolulu airport Museum in Hawaii. Lorraine certainly deserves the recognition. This vital woman is always ready to serve, even in retirement.

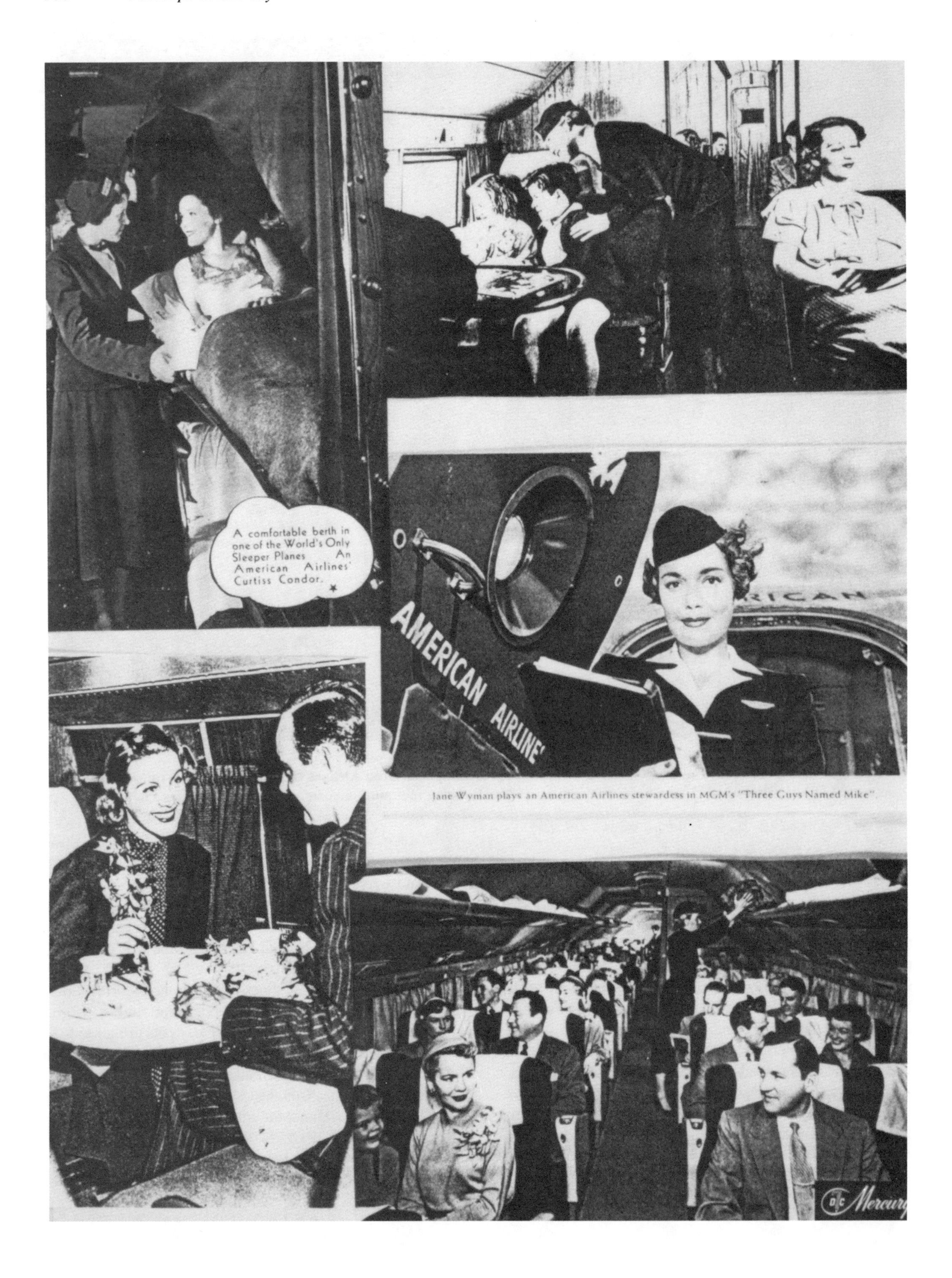

Jane Wyman plays an American Airlines stewardess in MGM's "Three Guys Named Mike".

American Airlines stewardess, Priscilla Engwall Seeds (second on left), shown with her crew in 1945. (American Airlines Photo)

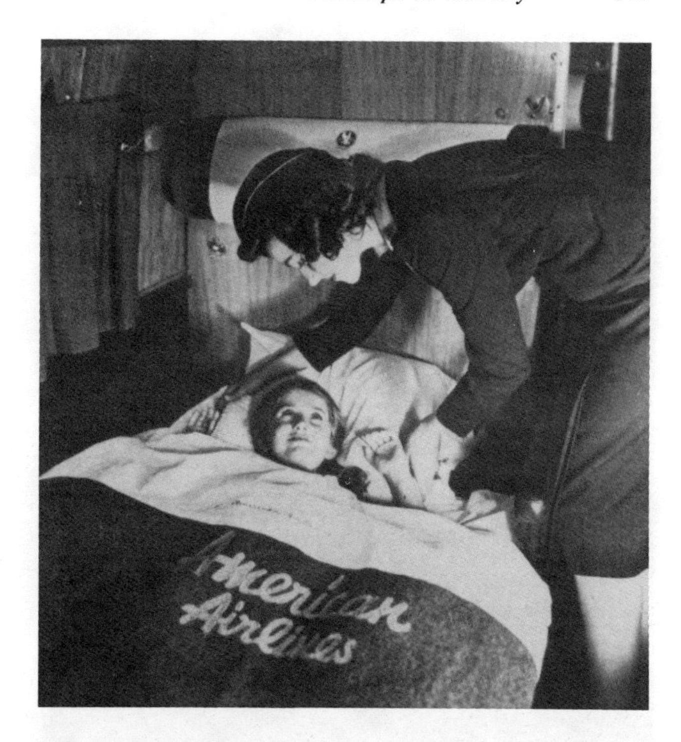

An American Airlines stewardess tucking in a passenger on a DST sleeper in 1942. (American Airlines Photo)

PRISCILLA HAD TO CHOOSE

American Airlines Priscilla Engwall Seeds 1945 - 1947

Marriage, or an advancement in management.

During the time she was a post-graduate student in nursing at the University of Illinois, Priscilla Engwall met a dental student, Bob Seeds. The romance was getting serious when Bob entered the Army in 1944. Priscilla had dreamed of being an airline stewardess, wanting the travel and the glamour the job afforded. She applied to American Airlines in Chicago and was accepted in 1945.

Training with American was at Great Neck, New York. The three week course included the types of aircraft, meteorology, scheduling, food service, safety, cabin service, first aid and grooming. Priscilla was first based in Tulsa. She flew on the 21-passenger DC-3's and worked American's first DC-4 flight in 1946.

In the meantime, her romance with Bob Seeds had continued through letters and planned meetings, as their separate schedules would permit.

In 1947, American asked Priscilla to accept the position of Chief stewardess at the New York base. At the same time, September 1947, her "standby suitor," Bob Seeds, was becoming very impatient. He felt he was on the back burner while the airline had first preference in Priscilla's interest and time. It was then he made his declaration. "It's American or me." Bob knew that stewardesses had to be single, so Priscilla ended two and a half years with American and became Mrs. Robert Seeds. She returned to nursing while her husband changed to a new career and entered law school.

Priscilla raised a family of four children and became a grandmother of nine. She was involved in the Moline community in which she was born and to which she returned to after her marriage. She kept her interest in the airline she loved through her involvement in the American Kiwi Association of Former Flight Attendants. She attended conventions and supported their work with mentally retarded children. Priscilla passed away in 1986.

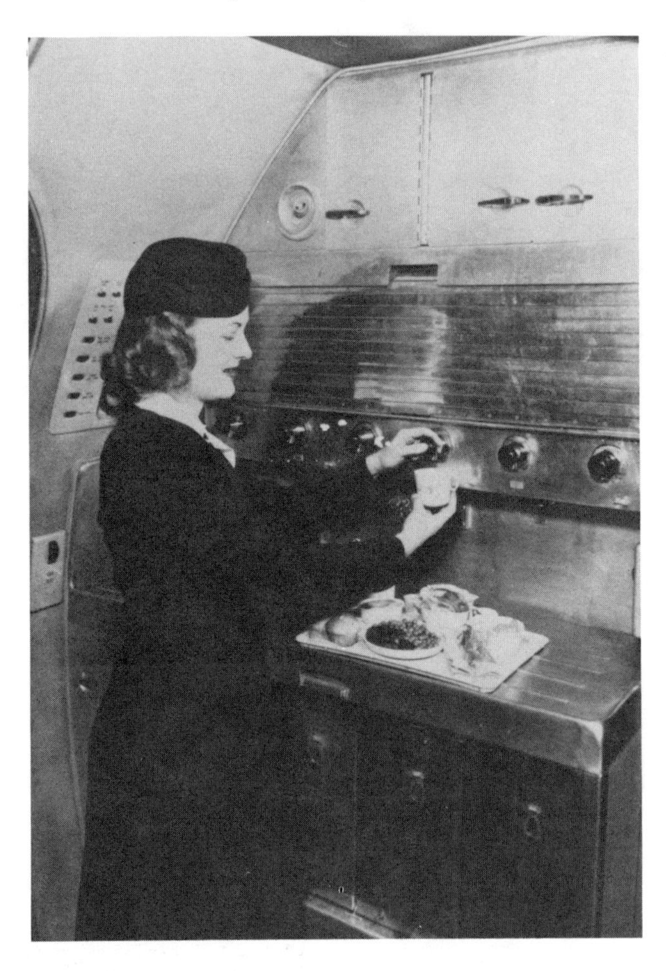

American Airlines stewardess in the galley preparing a meal tray, 1940. (American Airlines Photo)

1940s stewardess with a dinner tray. (American Airlines Photo)

HEY GIRLIE!!

American Airlines
Marilyn Clayton Harris
1953 - 1954

Marilyn Clayton was born in Mississippi which is evident by her soft southern drawl. She graduated college in 1953 with a degree in Education with a double major in English and History. Her goal was to teach either subject in a high school. A representative of American Airlines visited Blue Mountain College at the end of her senior year. Marilyn says about this development in her career plans:

"I talked with American's representative. I had never traveled and this appealed to me. I'd also never flown in an airplane. The interview went well. I found out I had been accepted and would be flown to Dallas for a physical. I accepted, but knew I'd have to diet for a goal of 124 pounds by the date of the physical. Dorm food wasn't exactly *Lean Cuisine*, so I ate oranges and carrots and also skipped many dinners. The physical went great.

Marilyn Clayton Harris, American Airlines stewardess, 1953.

American Airlines' largest class ever graduated: 128 stewardesses in July, 1953. (American Airlines Photo)

"I graduated from college and flew to Chicago for stewardess training in August 1953. There weren't enough airport faculty dorms, so some us were housed at the Shoreland Hotel. Our training was for six weeks and I enjoyed it a lot.

"The six of us got along really well, so we all decided to bid for Dallas as our home base. They were all from the East and they kidded me about my Southern accent.

"Rules were different. No married stewardesses, impeccable grooming, pressed uniform, short hair. Once I was written up for not wearing colored nail polish. Weight control was absolutely a must.

"Pay scale was low, there were no unions. It was all so wonderful and thrilling to me I guess I didn't mind. All the plus parts of the job — I got to travel to New York, San Francisco, Los Angeles and to *Mexico City*! I do remember that I tried to use my college Spanish with my Southern drawl and nobody knew a thing I said!

"I remember my indignation when a passenger addressed me as *Hey, Girlie!!* I replied, 'Are you addressing me, *sir*!'

"Our uniforms were navy for winter and tan for summer. We also wore high heels.

"The food was much better than now. We served filet mignon, swordfish steaks, etc. Now food tastes plastic unless you are in First Class.

"Being a stewardess was truly one of the high points of my life. I met my husband at an open house my roommates and I gave. He was stationed at Ardmore Air Force Base 100 miles from Dallas. We fell in love. We were married February 12, 1954. In those days your career ended when you married."

THE GREAT AMERICAN CHANGE

American Airlines Connie Chapman Harman 1963 - 1968

"I miss the interaction with people," said Connie Chapman Harman. Connie is a former stewardess, reflecting on her five years with American. "Flying was considered a job to do until you got married. Not that the job was easy to get, but it was considered a glamour job at that time..

"When I first started to fly, in 1963, stews couldn't be married, but this changed while I was with American. Attitudes changed along with marriage. Flight attendants seemed to settle down when they got married. They were more safety conscious and responsible. Husbands liked the good pay, too, and trips weren't missed unless you were really ill," said Connie.

Flight Attendant Connie Chapman Harman, 1963-1968.

Flight attendants started to stay longer. Connie flew with Lorraine "Pete" Peterson. "I flew with Lorraine in the sixties when she was in her forties and I was less than twenty-five years old. Passengers would come on board and make comments on her age.

"Pete had such a wonderful sense of humor and manner of interacting with people. She could handle any situation. Before the flight was over, those passengers who made remarks about her wished they could eat their worlds."

American presented stews with special gold wings at the end of five years of service. Connie was admiring her gold wings when she overheard her Captain say with some disdain that not all of the stews were golden wingers . . just old stewardesses.

"I was in my early twenties. I felt it unfair of that captain. I'm glad that now the traveling public as well as airline employees realize that older flight attendants add a sense of real charm to flying."

American realized how older flight attendants relate to any situation. Pete Peterson saved lives in a crash when she had to think for people and shove them to safety.

Connie had a close call on a Boeing 707 out of New York to Phoenix and Los Angeles. The aircraft was on descent into Phoenix when a private plane appeared out of nowhere. The pilot put the 707 into a sudden steep bank.

"The plane shook like a cocktail shaker," declared Connie. "So violent was the shuddering from the near stall, that the overhead compartments emptied, oxygen masks came down, and people lost false teeth and shoes. Everything was everywhere! From my jumpseat, I was trying to keep the exit clear by shoving things with my feet. I didn't have time to be scared until later," Connie added.

"The Captain averted a collision and we were okay. He continued the flight to Phoenix where the FAA agents came on board. We'd handled the situation by cleaning up the mess and returning personal effects. I used a megaphone to direct the return of items while another stewardess held up a purse, briefcase or shoe for identification. We served the meals we had on board, but they looked like hash. Nobody seemed to care. We served free drinks and champagne."

Connie had many experiences and several uniform changes in her five years with American. Overseas caps were part of the uniform in 1963. The American Beauty collection soon changed the look to mini-skirts with a choice of color, and washable uniform separates. "It was so great not to worry about dry cleaning one uniform and getting it back in time for a flight. With our bouffant hairdos, we had a mini-cap and then no cap at all."

Connie was trained on Convair 240s in Dallas. She also flew on DC-6, DC-7 and Boeing 707 aircraft. She had two domiciles during her five years, New York and Los Angeles.

"Time changes bothered us a lot, and we got jet lag," stated Connie. "Half the month we would fly to Hawaii and the other half of the month to London. Time never seemed to catch up, when you really felt 100 percent good. The airline realized this before too long and our schedules improved."

Connie has a friend who flies for American as a returning mother. At the time Connie flew in the sixties, stewardesses could be married, but could not have children and remain employed.

"Bonnie Pitt has returned in 1984 after eleven years, and has the same seniority as when she left, plus the eleven years. Her husband is a Captain and she has more seniority than he does. Stews had to take the airlines to court to win the right to work after becoming mothers."

Connie feels that the great camaraderie of airline employees is always there. When she moved to Brazil with her husband Dennis, not long after leaving American, there were some things we couldn't buy. Airline people going to Brazil would write and ask what we needed and bring it with them or send it with a friend.

"Working for an airline is very special. I'm an Air Force brat. My folks always said how great the *esprit de corps* was in the Air Force. I've known that too, it's the same with the airlines. Being an airline stewardess has made me appreciate people in all walks of life. Every day was a new experience and new challenge. I feel I appreciate everything more because I had that great job working with people. I call it the great American way of life!"

TWA's post war years was a time of growth, giving rise to an airline that flew many celebrities and became known as the "Glamour Airline."

A GLAMOROUS ERA AS AIR HOSTESS FOR TWA

Mildred Drews Gesell
1945 - 1948

"When airplane fever overcomes you, it's a love the rest of your life. My introduction to the airline industry came through working at the Lockheed air terminal in Burbank, California, in 1943. Our country was deeply entrenched in fighting World War II. The Burbank terminal, heavily camouflaged and difficult to recognize even on the ground, served the entire Los Angeles area and Lockheed aircraft Corporation. Commercial airlines, P-38's and bombers were constantly utilizing the airport. Blackouts were staged at night and aircraft flying over the area were spotted by searchlights to determine if they were "friendly." The commercial planes were DC-3's and looked quite intriguing to me from the ground. Watching them, the flying bug caught me.

TWA hostess, Mildred Drews Gesell, by a Constellation.

"In the fall of 1945 I applied for the air hostess position with Transcontinental & Western Airlines, Inc. Time lapsed with no word from TWA, so I returned to their office to apply for another position, maybe ticket counter. They then informed me a telegram advising me of a hostess interview had gone unanswered. Problem was I had not received it. The Personnel Manager then notified me of the next hiring for hostesses. Four hostess applicants were hired out of fifty prospects: a brunette, Joyce Clark; a blonde, Mary Woodward; a redhead, Shirley Bell; and myself, Mildred Drews, a light brunette. This day was the beginning of nine exciting years.

"Making the move from Los Angeles to Kansas City, TWA's home base, was by train. World War II ended in August, 1945, and this was October. We four were all eager to fly to Kansas City, but due to the postwar air traffic there wasn't space available. In fact we spent two nights and two days on what seemed to be a troop train filled with servicemen about to be released from the military and on their way home."

HOSTESS TRAINING

"Upon arrival at Kansas City we joined the rest of the hostess class, which totaled eighteen hired from all over the USA. We stayed at the residence of a Mrs. Carroll. Breakfast and dinner were served and we were instructed to give her our rationing books, stamps for sugar, meat, etc. Rationing did continue for a short time after the war.

"Five weeks of study were reduced to four weeks of hard work because hostesses were needed. We were issued student uniforms, a tailored dress, and required to buy our uniform shoes, navy blue calf with a heel not less than 2 inches or more than 2 ½ inches. Nylon hose were still a very difficult item to find on the market, due to the war. At one time TWA's commissary had hose available for hostess purchase.

"Every day seemed to offer an interesting experience as we learned aeronautical nomenclature and equipment, flight procedures, food service, safety and emergency procedures, station data and personnel regulations.

"Time and time again we were told to treat passengers like a guest in our home. Between boarding time and take-off a hostess would try to collect coats (tag them and hang them in coat rack in the rear of the plane), check overhead racks (good for hat only and small articles), check seat belts and offer mints, and most important begin the collections of tickets for the ticket manifest holder which also served as a seating chart. Passengers would check at the ticket counter and receive directions as to which plane to board, and the hostess would remove the portion of the flight being traveled. Ticket handling on the plane was very time consuming as it stimulated a lot of conversation about connections, etc. When air travel increased ticket handling was assigned the ticket counters, a salvation for us.

"TWA had been serving food on flights for many years and had become very efficient in this service. Thermos jugs were used for hot casseroles and tray size boxes were easy to assemble. A hot lunch or dinner consisted of soup, salad, hot entree, butter and roll, dessert, coffee or milk. Each tray was set up with a linen napkin, silverware, and paper doilies making an attractive presentation.

"A point to bring out here is that the silverware was neatly packaged in cellophane and ready for use. In 1945 it was a hostess duty to check out from the commissary a metal box filled with clean silverware prior to flight time. When the flight came in, the incoming hostess would help the outgoing hostess straighten the cabin and pass on any necessary information, then leave. The hostess leaving the plane would mistakenly take the clean silver at times. This could leave you at 10,000 feet washing silver and boiling it in the hot cup before a meal service, hoping nothing else would develop like turbulence, airsickness or too many questions to erode the time.

"When safety and emergency procedures were introduced to the class we listened closely. Of course the exits, fire extinguisher and first aid were thoroughly reviewed. The day Mr. Mutchler, Director of Passenger and Cargo Service, spoke to us of a TWA plane crash and how hostess Nellie Granger had crawled down a mountainside for help. He told us our chances of survival of a crash were good because of our location in the plane, and should this happen get to a telephone and call the nearest Station Manager. Needless to say there were eighteen future hostesses mulling this over in their minds and wondering who might face that problem!

"The class then experienced a personal appearance evaluation, proper use of cosmetics and hair styled short above the collar and given a permanent. The latter not too popular with some classmates. Beside being coached on good grooming we were reminded of the height and weight qualifications, which were as follows:

5′2″	100 to 107	5′5″	112 to 125
5′3″	107 to 115	5′6″	117 to 130
5′4″	112 to 120	5′7″	122 to 135

"If a hostess' weight would be below or above the standard weight requirement she could be taken off schedule until she was within the approved limits. If she would be off the payroll for this reason for 30 days or more in any four month period she would be subject to dismissal.

"While in class and the first three months of flight service I was paid $120 monthly. Expenses reimbursed when on layovers away from my domicile. After a few months of service the salary increased to $140 monthly.

"The hostess uniform was blue with the letters TWA cut out and trimmed with red on the upper right hand side of the jacket. It was a very unique look and the uniform was popular with everyone. We were told Mrs. Jack Frye, wife of the TWA president, and Oleg Cassini, the prestigious fashion designer, collaborated in designing this uniform.

"When placed on active duty we were required to purchase uniform accessories which totaled $26.90 with tax:

Winter hat	$4.75	2 Name Plates	$2.10
2 Blouse slips	$8.36	Blue Purse	$8.50
Baggage tag	$1.05		

Mildred Drews Gesell on a TWA tug for a publicity shot by a DC-3, 1940s. (TWA Photo)

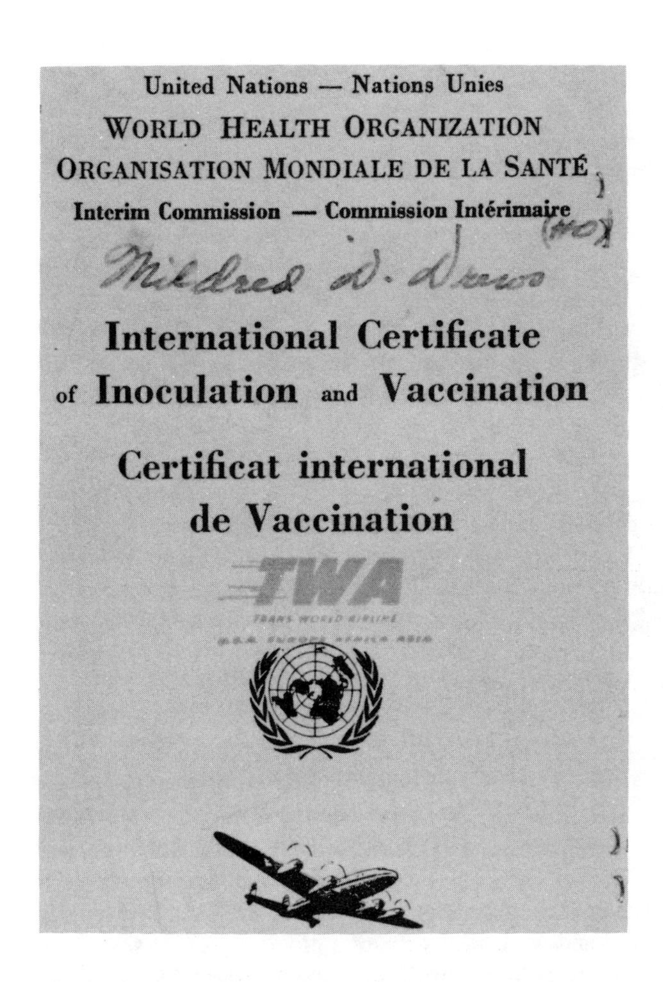
United Nations — Nations Unies
WORLD HEALTH ORGANIZATION
ORGANISATION MONDIALE DE LA SANTÉ
Interim Commission — Commission Intérimaire

International Certificate
of Inoculation and Vaccination

Certificat international
de Vaccination

TWA

TWA international hostess certificate of vaccination.

"Also, we were required to purchase the first winter uniform (winter suit and topcoat) totaling $100.25 through a salary deduction plan of $5 a pay day. Summer uniforms were loaned by the company, and after a couple years seniority all uniforms were issued on loan."

OUR WINGS AND ON THE LINE

"The day finally arrived when we received our Wings. We were also given our first flight assignments, nerves surfaced. New hostesses were usually assigned the Kansas City to Albuquerque run, a night flight. That was my good fortune. Served a snack service and stops scheduled for Topeka, Wichita and Amarillo on a DC-3. All went well. The return trip was partial daytime with a dinner service which was more of a test. I gained some self confidence and knew I liked this job.

"In 1945 there were three major airlines flying coast to coast: United Airlines - northern route; TWA - central section of the country; American Airlines - the southern part. The main airlines operating north and south were Colonial Airlines, Eastern Air Lines, Pennsylvania Central Airlines, Northeast Airlines, Western Airlines, Continental Airlines, Braniff Airways and Delta Air Lines.

"Equipment in 1945 was primarily DC-3s and a few airlines had some four-engine equipment. TWA had four Boeing Stratoliners which was a four-engine aircraft a comfortable roomy cabin, 38 passenger capacity, pressurized and crew of five (2 hostesses). This was a very safe plane, the public paid an extra fee for this flight.

"Speaking of the Boeing Stratoliner, I'm reminded of a problem that arose more than once on the same plane. The hydraulics that controlled lowering the gear and locking in place was malfunctioning and we were over New York City. The Captain coached my partner and me, we in turn informed the passengers that the Flight Engineer would take up the floor of the cabin (a section of the aisle) and crawl into the baggage area where he could crank down the gear manually. He did so, the wheels locked in place and the passengers just leaned over their seats and watched. No problem. Everyone took it in stride.

"My first couple years of flying were spent on DC-3s. Air travel was beginning to appeal to all travelers, however there were few women and children in 1945 and early 1946 as passengers. Also there were many first time riders during this period. We were traveling in a plane with an altitude possibility of 12,000 - 13,000 feet and no pressurization. Flying in the western regions of the U.S. turbulence often times prevailed, or perhaps a thunderstorm over the plains. It wasn't unusual to have half the passengers airsick. Then to add to that leg of the flight, I had a meal service, not too welcomed by some.

"Airsickness was always a concern and the company continually sought a good remedy. One hostess meeting we were introduced to a new air sick remedy which had been tested and seemed to be a huge success. I then had a passenger who boarded in Albuquerque and informed him of the flight plan. He knew we would encounter turbulence and cautioned me he would be sick, always, always became sick. He had gone so far as to tie paper grocery bags around his waste and under his suit because someone said that would help, but to no avail. I told him about the new remedy we now carried, he was glad to take it. This was bumpy a ride and he didn't become ill. Then to my surprise the company removed the remedy because of being ineffective!

"Having flown to Albuquerque for a couple of months my roommates and I could hardly contain ourselves before we would fly to New York and other cities east of Kansas City. It was December 20, 1945 when I left on that first trip east to New York City. The Christmas season was upon us and the cities reflected it with beautiful lights and decorations. During the layover the crew and I went to Radio City Music Hall and saw the fabulous Christmas show featuring the Rockettes, also took in Rockefeller Center's huge beautifully lit Christmas tree. On the return trip to Kansas City a winter storm was moving into the Midwest. There was no instrument landing system (ILS) in 1945 and pilots relied on radio beams and visibility. Upon arrival in Chicago discovered Kansas City airport was closed because of weather. We stayed in Chicago and the next day Scheduling sent us east to Pittsburgh. After rest,

FINAL

DAILY NEWS

NEW YORK'S PICTURE NEWSPAPER

QUEENS BROOKLYN LONG ISLAND

New York, Wednesday, February 6, 1946

2 Cents

(NEWS foto by Edsar)

Paris-Bound. Crowds attend ceremonies at LaGuardia Field as commercial air service between New York and Paris is resumed. The Star of Paris, 3,00 -mile-per-hour TWA Constellation transport, is ready for takeoff with record load of 36 passengers and eight crew members. Ship got into the air at 2:21 P. M. yesterday on scheduled 17-hour flight.

went west again and Kansas City was closed. My crew and I flew every day for ten days back and forth between the east coast and Midwest, celebrated Christmas in Pittsburgh and finally on December 30 arrived back in Kansas City. What a help the ILS has been to the airline industry of today!!!"

JANUARY 1946 - NEW YORK, HERE WE COME!

"After proving ourselves as air hostesses and qualified for a transfer, four of us decided to move to New York. My friends making this move were Joyce Clark, Mary Woodward, Guyla Thomas and myself, Millie Drews. First step: found an apartment on Long Island and proceeded to get acquainted with the big city of New York. After each trip we gave a full accounting at the apartment, it was a great time. One night a plane had struck the Empire State Building in downtown Manhattan per the evening news on the radio (no TV then), and three of us were very anxious because the fourth roommate was due to come in that evening. As it was, she was not involved in the crash but we always harbored the possibility it could happen.

"The two-engine DC-3 had been proven to be a safe plane in many ways, one being it could maintain altitude if one engine malfunctioned and had to be feathered (turned off). My three roommates had all experienced this and I secretly hoped I would also. Well the day came when we were to land at Pittsburgh on a very windy day and we had a full load of 21 passengers. That airport was located on a mountain (Pennsylvania Mountain) top and there was a small building serving as a makeshift terminal. Captain Hal Blackburn, an experienced pilot who had been with TWA since its earliest beginnings and had also served in the military during the war, handled the plane with special skill and we landed without a problem. There were some passengers who vowed they would never fly again, and how could I stand my job!!!!

"Engine problems on propeller-driven airplanes could easily be detected in flight by the pitch of the engines. As we worked the flights our "antennas" were up at all times. On a DC-3 we also had a visible way of detecting a potential engine problem during a flight. A small trickle of oil would start creeping down the cowling covering the engine and could readily be seen from a cabin window. I would report it to the Captain, who in turn asked the First Officer to please check. The trickle would increase and the First Officer would report it. Chances were before the trip was over that engine had to be feathered.

"Equipment used for overseas travel was the Constellation, a sleek and distinctive plane with its shark-like fuselage and unique triple-finned tail assembly. Some particulars:

International 749A - Constellation

38 passengers -	Ambassador Flights (berths): 2 pursers, 1 hostess
49 passengers -	First Class: roomy seating, pressurized cabin
9 Crew members -	Captain, Relief Pilot, First Officer, Navigator, 2 Flight Engineers, Radio Officer, purser, hostess

"In February, 1946 TWA inaugurated regular service to Paris and the International Division was established. Airline personnel, including my roommates and I, and the general public made up a good crowd at LaGuardia Field for a big send-off. At that time seniority or a foreign language were not required to bid the International Division. This gave us food for thought and a wonderful opportunity to see Europe.

"Summer in New York was very pleasant. It was then I was assigned my first charter trip, the Washington Senators Baseball Team. We flew the Boeing Stratoliner from the Midwest to New York and they were scheduled to play the Yankees. I was given a couple tickets to the game so Guyla and I went to our first major league baseball game, and, at the famous Yankee stadium!!!

"In the fall of 1946 the four of us decided to transfer. Mary stayed in New York and bid International, Guyla and Joyce moved back to Kansas City, and I chose to live in Los Angeles."

AUGUST 1946 - A TRANSFER TO LOS ANGELES

"Being back in Los Angeles was a treat after having lived there in the early 1940s. The airport for commercial use had been relocated from Burbank to Inglewood. The first flights I bid were DC-3s to Albuquerque, New Mexico. The scenery was most interesting for we flew over the Continental Divide, Grand Canyon and Hoover Dam, the Painted Desert and the vast desert and mountainous areas of the Southwest. These flights would stop in Phoenix, a small city then, and on to Albuquerque. From the Los Angeles domicile we could be assigned the daily round trip flight to San Francisco. The Golden Gate Bridge would peak through the morning fog rolling into the Bay and often we would have to circle until that fog moved out. Beautiful sight.

"Eventually I bid Constellation flights to Kansas City or Chicago as the layover points. The Constellation was one beautiful airplane and a joy to work, and work we did! Two hostesses shared this work.

"First class flights would have 57 passengers and daytime flights a full meal service. We still gave special care, picked up and tagged coats, took them to the coat closet in the rear of the plane. Seemed as though we walked constantly. The galley was located forward of the passengers. The trays were full size and delivered one at a time. This meant walking down the aisle 114 times by the time they were all collected again. Flight time to Chicago, approximately 6 hours 45 minutes non-stop from Los Angeles. This would be a routine trip.

"Not every trip proved to be routine, and the exceptions are never forgotten. There was the child who was choking on a mint given out prior to landing. I took the child from the mother during the landing as the mother was panicking, the passengers supported me in the aisle and I held the child in a position which forced the mint out of her throat. There was the man who boarded, threw a pistol on the seat and casually said he was with the FBI. I passed the word along to the Captain pronto and he did some checking through the control tower before takeoff. Another time a passenger had a seizure and the Captain started to descend for an emergency landing at Las Vegas for medical reasons. The passenger was revived before having to land and we continued on to San Francisco. Once an elderly man in the men's lounge put a match to a paper towel and let it float to the floor. I saw it on the floor for there was a little space between the drape covering the doorway and the floor. I extinguished the fire and asked him what he was doing. He replied he didn't know what to do with the towel. Then there was the incident when an elderly

UNITED STATES - FRANCE
INAUGURAL SCHEDULE

EASTBOUND—Read Down | WESTBOUND—Read Up

FLIGHT 900 Thurs. Only			FLIGHT 954 Tues. Only			INTERNATIONAL SCHEDULES Effective Feb. 5, 1946 U. S.-PARIS					FLIGHT 955 Wed. Only			FLIGHT 901 Fri. Only		
LT		GT	LT		GT		City	Airport	Deviation from EST		LT		GT	LT		GT
......		......	•11:50	Tues.	1650	Lv	Washington, D. C.	National Airport	0	Ar	5:10	Thurs.	2210	......	......	......
......		......	1:00		1800	Ar	New York, N. Y.			Lv	3:50	Thurs.	2050	......		......
2:00	Thurs.	1900	•2:00p	Tues.	1900	Lv	New York, N. Y.	LaGuardia Field	0	Ar	3:05		2005	7:25	Sat.	0025
3:25		2025	......		......	Ar	Boston, Mass.			Lv	......		......	•5:50	Sat.	2250
•4:25	Thurs.	2125	......		......	Lv	Boston, Mass.	Bedford Airport	0	Ar	......		......	5:05		2205
10:05		0205	7:35		2335	Ar	Gander Field, Newfoundland			Lv	•10:20	Thurs.	1420	•12:20	Sat.	1620
•11:35	Thurs.	0335	•9:05	Tues.	0105	Lv	Gander Field, Newfoundland		1 hr. later	Ar	9:20		1320	11:20		1520
2:00		1300	9:25		0825	Ar	Limerick, Ireland	Shannon Airport		Lv	•4:15	Thurs.	0315	•4:50	Sat.	0350
•3:00	Fri.	1400	•10:25	Wed.	0925	Lv	Limerick, Ireland	Shannon Airport	6 hrs. later	Ar	2:45		0145	3:20		0220
6:00	Fri.	1700	1:00	Wed.	1200	Ar	Paris, France	Orly Field	6 hrs. later	Lv	12:00	Wed.	2300	12:00	Fri.	2300

ORLY FIELD

Paris

From far-away places across the world — from New York, Detroit, and Chicago, from Rome, Cairo, and Bombay — TWA's swift, frequent flights meet at Orly Field, airport of Paris.

TRANS WORLD AIRLINES

Mildred Drews Gesell (left) on a TWA float in New York City.

passenger was boarded by a family member. After takeoff it became apparent the passenger was mentally confused, as she was trying to open the door and kept declaring no one cared. The plane was pressurized so no door could be opened, but caring for her six hours was a challenge.

"In November of 1948 an "Air Transportation Day" was held at the Los Angeles airport. Planes were on display and TWA was proud to show the Constellation. I was on hand with other crew members, and a record showed 7,000 people had filed through the plane."

GLAMOUR

"Celebrities were always interesting to have on board, and we would strive to maintain their privacy. Cary Grant boarded a night flight. Tony Martin and Cyd Charise were returning to Los Angeles from their honeymoon. Jimmy Stewart traveled to Chicago and when dawn broke the Captain invited him to the cockpit to enjoy the beautiful scene. Linda Darnell was a very pleasant lady. Robert Young and his wife were a joy to have aboard. Margaret Whiting hummed a few tunes in the back of the plane one night. Tony Curtis was traveling on the east coast. Peter Lawford, also a memorable passenger. One of my favorites was James Melton, a famous operatic passenger. Mr. Melton traveled on several of my flights. Also a frequent traveler and usually going to St. Louis was Stan Musal, Stan the Man as they say in the baseball world. Stan Kenton, talented big band director, boarded in Pittsburgh and slept. Eddie Rickenbacker, then President of Eastern Air Lines and also well known war hero.

"Los Angeles as a domicile placed us in the heart of the movie industry. There was a charter flight our crew boarded in Kansas City for Los Angeles with the cast of the Greatest Show on Earth, a movie which had been filmed in Florida. Cecil B. DeMille, one of the most talented movie directors in Hollywood, was a pleasure to have as a passenger.

"The Los Angeles Dons, a professional football team, had many charter trips to the Midwest, and to which my flying partner and I were assigned. Food service was a big item on the sports charters.

"Howard Hughes was the major stockholder of TWA during my employment. We were thankful he loved the airline, the Constellation and carried such an interest. Mr. Hughes had the reputation of being a recluse, in fact two TWA Presidents never met him. There was this story floating about of how he went to a hotel and had a problem with a hotel employee. He bought the hotel and fired the employee. Somehow this story always had our attention on the line.

"One day the Schedule Clerk phoned to tell me to stand by for a special assignment and I would be notified of details within the next twenty-four hours. On *hold* in the apartment, I slept and ate and ate and waited. When I finally phoned the Schedule Clerk and asked how this flight plan was progressing and what exactly it was, he replied, 'Well, they're taking some seats out of the Connie and putting in a double bed.' This got my attention and asked for the full story. 'Well, it's Howard Hughes and he wants to fly William Randolph Hearst, Sr. to the state of Washington. Hearst has a heart condition and they don't know if the doctor will let him travel by air.' I waited and waited for the final word, a little apprehensive because that hotel story was caught in my mind. After a thirty-six hour hold the flight was canceled, the doctor said no flying for Mr. Hearst. I was a mite bit sorry for it could have been an interesting trip.

"Howard Hughes depended a great deal on Noah Dietrich, his right-hand man so to speak. One evening my flight was ready to depart and the cabin door had been closed. Suddenly the Passenger Agent opened it again and asked if I would announce a seat was needed and would anyone consider taking a later flight. After a couple such announcements and a minor ground delay, a serviceman volunteered to change flights. The man who needed the seat was Noah Dietrich on a mission for Howard Hughes.

"Whenever an airliner crashes, airline people are most interested in the who and why. On October 24, 1947 I was preparing to leave Kansas City when the story broke, a United Air Line DC-6 crash on the rim of Bryce Canyon in southern Utah. A friend of mine was a stewardess on United. It broke my heart to find out Helen Morrissey was on the flight and there were no survivors, 52 killed. A few days later her friends told me something unusual, almost as if Helen had had a premonition. A note was found in her knitting bag giving instructions in case of a crash."

TWA purser George Denny receives the transit pouch with documents for an international flight. It is the last item on board and the first off at the destination and no flight can leave without it. (TWA Photo)

1948 - A TRANSFER

"For some reason I felt a yen to live in the Midwest again, so transferred from Los Angeles to Kansas City in December, 1948. During the next couple of years I worked on DC-4's (60 passengers), Martin 202 (36 passengers), and the Constellation (57 passengers). I bid the Constellation flights and had great flying partners. There was Joyce Clark, my friend since the day we were hired in LA, who left the hostess job when she married. Pat Longacre and I were a team for a long time and solved many a problem together. For instance, there was a dinner service scheduled out of New York. Commissary was loading the plane when suddenly there was a cloudburst. When setting up trays we found lettuce floating in rain water in all 52 trays, that part of the meal was ruined, not to mention doilies and napkins. Thank goodness the entree was protected. Not a good experience."

APRIL 1951

"I accepted a promotion to Hostess Flight Instructor in 1951. In this supervisory position I was required to check hostesses on the ground and also in flight which meant a lot of travel coast to coast. It was an interesting job and led me to some very good friends who were also Flight Instructors: Ruth Daugherty, Ivanelle Garthwaite, Marge Mossman, Harriet Barnes and Ruth Brockman, who at one time had also been a flying partner. Jeanette Phillips and Margie Jones were special friends who worked in management. The special person in charge of us all was Mrs. Miriam Filkins who we felt was a great supervisor.

"During this year of Flight Instructor assignments I instructed a hostess class. It was most rewarding to have a student earn her wings and become a success."

FEBRUARY 1952 - INTERNATIONAL

"The time seemed right to request transfer to the International Division, it was approved and I packed my bags again for New York. Attended a school where I became well indoctrinated with overseas flight procedures, such as food and liquor service (liquor served on International only), money exchanges, customs and their forms, emergency and survival training, and schedules. As part of the survival training we went out to a Coast Guard Station Rockaway, NY, and took part in a ditching drill. This meant inflating life rafts (carried on planes), board the raft, send flares, dye in the water as a marker, sending signals with a mirror, operate the emergency radio and steps to survive at sea. Knowledge we all hoped would never be put to use but felt well prepared before that first flight to Europe. Expenses during a layover were nominal for we had a crew bus which transported us to and from the airport, we signed the register at the hotel and our uniforms accounted for the fact we were TWA employees, and the dining room accepted our signature as payment of the meal - the essential layover expenses were billed to TWA. Actually, my first trip to Europe cost me 10¢ and that was a phone call in New York prior to departure.

"International flights from New York had layovers in the gateway cities to Europe: Frankfurt, Paris and Lisbon, with stops for fuel at Gander, Newfoundland; Shannon Airport, Limerick, Ireland; London; or much further south, the Azores Islands en route to Lisbon.

"My first trip to Europe was to Paris on February 21, 1952 - New York, Shannon to Paris. There were only twelve passengers so it was a very easy trip from my standpoint. International travel was still in its infant stage and also the winter season had some effect, thus light loads in February. The travel to Europe increased in the spring and every flight was filled to capacity the rest of the year for this was the Holy Year for the Catholic Church and there was an unending pilgrimage from the United States to Rome. This was the period of time when the travel agents were accompanying tourists and tour groups were becoming established.

"The layover in Paris was exciting and the fear of struggling with a foreign language vanished as many French people spoke some English. The crews stayed at Hotel Windsor, the Celtic or Hotel Reynolds and the prices (in 1952) were near 2000 francs for a single room, or $6 a night. The hotels were close to *Les Champs-Elysees*, proclaimed as the gayest and most famous avenue in Paris and perhaps the world. It was a delight to go shopping on the Champs for perfume, leather gloves, visit dress shops. The restaurants were another grand experience, or one of the innumerable sidewalk cafes. On those first trips to Paris I managed to visit the Arc de Triomphe, towering Eiffel Tower, and toured the Louvre which houses original works of art such as the Last Supper and the Mona Lisa.

"On our long international flights we were allowed three hours rest with *bunk time*. The bunks in the Constellation were next to the cockpit. The Captain at the beginning of the flight would schedule all nine crew members three at a time to rest. We all hoped that our "bunk time" would come later in the flight after working and being on our feet for a long time.

"Crossing the Atlantic Ocean afforded little scenery, water and more water. After eight or more hours in flight, Ireland looked like an oasis with its green countryside. Truly the Emerald Isle!! Recalling one crossing, a boarding passenger asked me if we ever saw any ocean liners, to which I replied *no*. Famous last words! That very trip, and the one and only time out of one hundred and eight crossings I made, we flew over the Queen Mary. It was exciting and she looked beautiful. The Captain had everyone's attention when he announced we were circling over the famous liner and that our Radio Operator was in touch with their's.

"Flights to Frankfurt, Germany took over thirteen hours flying time from New York. The crew stayed in a village outside of Frankfurt called Bad Homburg and at the Ritters Park Hotel. This was a fine hotel with a gracious and attentive staff. It was but a short drive to Frankfurt where the crews would go shopping or sightseeing. Scars of World War II were everywhere for Frankfurt had suffered from heavy bombing. There were blocks of rubble and shops established in buildings that were partially bombed. All this even seven years after the war was over.

TWA purser fills out 38 types of required forms for an international flight. Local customs, immigration and health forms are required at every foreign airport. A round trip to Paris requires 500-600 forms. The passenger manual serves as a guide. (TWA Photo)

"On one return trip from Frankfurt we received instructions to ferry (travel without passengers) the plane to Munich, Germany and, as a charter flight pick up Jewish immigrants coming to the United States. The day before our departure for Munich the Russians had forced a U.S. Air Force reconnaissance plane down in Russia. The Cold War was on at this time. Our flight to Munich took us down the same corridor and near the Russian border. All crew members kept a watchful eye as we ferried to Munich. The crew went into the terminal while the plane was being serviced. I was shocked at the obvious suppression the people had experienced for their faces and attire showed it. Upon entering this huge building I noticed the starkness. The people were quiet and seemed dejected. Somehow I felt strange in my blue uniform, nylon hose and high heels.

"There were times when after our legal rest we would be required to deadhead (travel as a passenger) to another city beyond the gateway cities. In one instance I deadheaded to Geneva, Switzerland to work a flight back to the USA. A very memorable such assignment was from Lisbon, Portugal to Rome, Italy with a lengthy layover in Rome. The tour guides were a salvation for I saw the Coliseum, the Forum, Michelangelo's statue of Moses and many other interesting historical sights."

TWA pursers George Denny (left) and Ernest Belshaw making up a berth on the Paris Sky Chief, 1949. (TWA Photo)

EMERGENCIES

"Night flights could seem long for everyone is sleeping and lights are dimmed. We were westbound and over the Atlantic Ocean, cabin pressurized and it was a smooth flight. As I made a cabin check halfway up the cabin I heard a hissing sound, even above the noise of those propeller driven engines. After identifying the source, the hissing was from a seal on the window, I checked all the seat belts of the passengers in that area to be sure they were fastened and then told the Captain of the problem. The Flight Engineer confirmed we had a leaking window so the remainder of the flight to Gander was flown at a lower altitude to eliminate depressurization and the possible loss of a window. There was a mechanical delay at Gander to repair the window.

"By 1953 we had some International flights that left from Detroit, and such was my assignment. After takeoff the purser and I were working in the galley. We had been gaining altitude over Detroit when suddenly number three engine, which was located just outside the galley, went out of control, a runaway prop. This same incident had happened on an Eastern Air Lines plane some months before and the propeller had come off the engine and cut

Millie Drews Gesell, a former TWA hostess, worked at the Quad City Air Show aboard a restored Constellation in 1993. The aircraft was restored by the *Save The Connie* Project and flies to many airshows in the US.

through the fuselage killing a stewardess. We left the galley in a rush, made emergency landing preparations. The plane carried enough gas to take us to our destination so it had to be "dumped" for a safe landing. The gas was released through a fuel valve in the wing tips and in the meantime the cockpit crew was struggling to feather the engine. They finally succeeded and we all breathed a big sigh of relief.

"There was a lighter side of hostess work. Laurence Olivier and a very attractive companion boarded in Paris. This was the Ambassador flight, which was deluxe in every way including berths for sleeping accommodations. There were two pursers and a hostess on this plane. The pursers had made up the berths and passengers were retiring. Mr. Olivier was in the top berth and his friend in the bottom one. As I came down the aisle, I noticed he had a watch in his hand which was thrust through the berth's curtains trying to pass it on to the hand below. They were a foot apart. Well, to the rescue. I planned to help with the transfer and as I took the watch from his hand he gave my hand a BIG squeeze thinking he had made contact with his companion. I didn't say a word but thought of the line which was noted on the bottom each of page in the hostess Manual: *Nothing in this manual replaces the exercise of good judgment on the firing line.* I often wondered if they ever discussed the *squeeze*.

"Customs inspectors were thorough as we entered any country. The most thorough however was when we arrived in New York and the *black gang*, as the crew called them, met our plane. There were eight Customs men dressed in black coverall type suits who inspected the plane even as the last crew member was deplaning. They took everything out of the galley, covers off the seats, check light fixtures and every crack and corner for anything possibly being smuggled into the country. This type of search was done infrequently and one wonders what prompted their search."

APRIL 1953

"After having had a good sampling of flying to Europe, I transferred back to the Midwest and Kansas City. It was good being back on Domestic and also seeing my friends again. Settled into an apartment with Guyla Thomas, an ex-hostess, and flew to either coast on the Constellation. One day Ruth Daugherty-Bush introduced me to a handsome fellow named John 'Al' Gesell, who at one time had worked for TWA (1941-1948). We became engaged that fall and planned a spring wedding."

ROMANCE

"There is romance on the airlines and this is my story with some suspense added. Al had given me a beautiful engagement ring and we were busy making plans for the wedding. He took me to the Kansas City airport for the 11 p.m. flight to San Francisco and bid me adieu. Ruth Brockman had been my flying partner for some time and I was glad she was with me that night. We were on the Constellation, took off and just as we started to gain altitude over downtown Kansas City number three engine broke out in a big blaze. Two first-time air travelers were in the forward seats, thanks to my suggestion when they boarded, and had a real good view of the fire. Ruth and I prepared for an emergency landing: moved able bodied men by the exits, coached the passengers, and kept hoping that fire would be out. The plane turned for an approach to land and the fire truck had lined up with the runway. Miraculously the engine fire was extinguished, another good job by the cockpit crew. The passengers and crew waited for a change in equipment so Ruth and I went to the coffee shop to steady our nerves. There was my future husband, calm and collected reading a newspaper and eating apple pie. He looked up rather surprised and said, 'What are you doing here?' From that day forth he watched the plane until it was out of sight.

"On October 16, 1953 Flo Windsor and I were assigned a very special charter trip, the press flight which accompanied President Eisenhower's plane, the Columbine, to Salina, Kansas. The President went to Abilene to dedicate the Eisenhower Memorial Foundation Museum and visit the house where he lived as a youth. The Columbine was the President's private plane, also a Constellation, and flown by Colonel Draper. While the President's party and the press were in Abilene the Colonel invited our crew to tour the Columbine. Very interesting seeing the flying office of our President. On the return trip to Kansas City our plane landed before the Columbine as the Secret Service and press corps were to be on hand as the President deplaned. Flo and I were surprised when the press took some pictures of us with President Eisenhower. This was a most thrilling experience."

TWA Stratoliner Luxury

APRIL 1954

"On April 15, 1954 I resigned from the hostess position to marry. The rule read *when you marry you can no longer work as an air hostess.* As I reflected upon the past nine years I realized I had traveled approximately three million air miles with people from all over the USA and the world. There were many kind, interesting and thoughtful passengers who had shared their sorrows and joys, business knowledge, family matters, personal life or had given advice. I had accumulated nearly 10,000 hours flight time and had worked with the most capable and dedicated flight crews. Trans World Airlines had been a great company to work for and every department was comprised of congenial and qualified personnel. From that day in April, 1954 I have been in awe of the mushrooming growth of the commercial airline industry. The 1945 - 1954 period seems like but a seedling to the present jet-age operation. So now, when I see a jet winging its way across the sky I still look up and am intrigued."

Millie, as she is called, has two children: a son, Drew, and a daughter, Nina. She also has three grandchildren. Millie and husband Al are active in the "Save a Connie" restoration and donate time at air shows to show it to aviation enthusiasts. TWA also has a museum at Kansas City to preserve its proud history.

FLYING HIGH

TWA

Joyce Richardson Austin

1952

TWA was the glamour airline. With a president like Howard Hughes and so many celebrities traveling on TWA, how could it miss?

"'You're not twenty-one years old, you're not five feet two, and you can't weigh 100 pounds!' the TWA supervisor snapped. The words of supervisor Ellen Johnston came as a shock. She took one look at me and almost shattered my hopes before I even sat down for the interview," said Joyce Richardson Austin.

"My best friend had finally convinced me that being a 'stew' was a great job and that I should apply to TWA. Their headquarters were in our hometown of Kansas City. I followed up on her suggestion, and after a somewhat hectic interview, I got the job in March of 1952. My friend promptly quit and got married."

It took some doing to get a job with any airline in the fifties, just as it does today. The requirements were strict, all applicants had to be single and had to pass intelligence and personality tests. If an applicant passed the test and met all the requirements, she could expect to earn $165 a month as a hostess for TWA.

Joyce was trained at the Kansas City Municipal airport in the "Little Red School House" - the fire department. The regular six-week course was condensed into four weeks, as twelve trainees were needed on the line as soon as possible.

Joyce received her wings and was domiciled in Detroit. She worked on DC-3's which cruised at 180 mph and carried twenty-one passengers, and on the DC-4 "Delta Connection" routes between Cincinnati and Detroit. She flew on Martin aircraft 202As and 404s as well. When the 300 mph Constellations started operating out of Los Angeles, Joyce transferred there.

Out of LA Joyce worked on the first "Champagne Flights," non-stops to Chicago Midway airport. Walter Winchell, the famous and controversial news commentator, was on one of her first Champagne Flights at the request of Howard Hughes, TWA's president and owner.

"We left Los Angeles at nine pm and arrived the following morning at six am in Chicago. Our layover was 36 hours before returning to LA on a daytime flight. I got five days off on my return to my domicile. That was really living," said Joyce as she remembered the good times.

"We had Walter Winchell on many charter flights out of Los Angeles," she recalls. "We would be waiting on a 'Connie' in the hangar. The crew would fly Mr. Winchell, along with a dozen hamburgers, to his home in Philadelphia. Howard Hughes insisted Winchell loved them, but he never would eat them," Joyce smiled. "We didn't let them go to waste though. the crew ate them."

Once Joyce flew a charter trip from LA to Tampa for the premier of the movie "Underwater" at Silver Springs. "Howard Hughes had Jane Mansfield doing public relations for the movie in a skimpy red bikini. The crew thought that was fantastic," she said with a laugh.

"You could see the movie in the lake in an underwater theater, or at the movie house. Guess where I

Joyce Richardson Austin (left) as a hostess for TWA, 1952.

saw it?...In the water."

Joyce was based in Los Angeles for three years before deciding to transfer to Kansas City. It was not long before she was asked to become a Hostess Supervisor.

As a supervisor, she was responsible for fifty hostesses in and out of uniform, an she worked the flights supervising new girls.

"Uniforms at that time were light blue with the red TWA cutout on the left breast. Under it we wore a navy blouse-slip. we were living dangerously and could be fired if we took the jacket off while on duty," Joyce said. "During the fifties rules were strict. Our hair had to be above the collar line and its natural color. Lipstick and nail polish had to be true red. We had to wear navy high heeled pumps. A girdle was a must, and girdle checks were made on a regular basis. Sometimes unofficial girdle checks were made by playful crews! Jewelry was limited to a tailored watch and one ring. Above all, no smoking was allowed in public while in uniform."

"I liked my job as a supervisor, but much preferred to fly the line. The VIP charter flights were really fun...that was a very special time with TWA. We really were known as the glamour airline, because so many celebrities flew TWA. It was a time of really flying high."

Joyce remained a supervisor for four years until she met and married Fred Austin, a TWA executive. Today, Joyce and Fred live in Los Angeles, and are the parents of three grown sons.

Fred is a Vice President and manages the U.S. operations of Short Brothers Aircraft, Ltd., of Belfast, Ireland. "We travel extensively, and I still spend a great deal of time living our of a suitcase," Joyce added, "Travel gets in the blood and becomes a way of life."

The lounge in the Constellation, 1945. (TWA Photo)

TWA IN HER HEART

Jerrlea Costello Currigan 1963 - 1966

TWA became an ongoing part of her life.

"I think my interest in flying and the idea of pursuing an airline career came in high school after attending a career day program at which a Braniff hostess was a guest speaker. After high school I attended Wichita State University; joined Delta Delta Sorority; and graduated with a B.A. in Education. During that time three of my sorority sisters quit school to fly for TWA.

"January of my Senior year I decided to interview with TWA and felt if I didn't make it I would know before they held the teaching interviews.

"I found out the days and times for the interviews and drove from Wichita to the airport in downtown Kansas City. I remember walking in and seeing all the other girls with the same dream of becoming a hostess. After I gave the receptionist my name, the first thing I was handed to sign was a form stating that I would retire at the age of 35. I thought this was strange since I hadn't even had an interview, but maybe it was a good sign. I had my three interviews that day. My first letter from TWA arrived January 29, 1963 saying that my application for the position of hostess had been approved. Final approval would be subject to the satisfactory completion of my routine employment processing, which would include a physical. A definite class date would be assigned to me later.

Jerrlea Costello Currigan, TWA hostess, 1963.

"My class date was set up for May but I informed them that I would be graduating in June and asked for reassignment. I reported for class the week following graduation. The training classes lived at the Casa Loma Hotel on the Country Club Plaza and we took the city bus downtown each day for training. Our accommodations consisted of a one bedroom apartment with three twin beds and a bed that pulled down out of the wall in the living room. It was so hot and humid in Kansas City that summer and we had a window air conditioner that didn't work, so many an evening we had to wet down towels and lay them across our bodies so we could cool off enough to sleep. We did our own grocery shopping and cooking. We also had a curfew that stated we had to be in the hotel by 7:30 pm and in our rooms by 10:00 pm.

"The training lasted five weeks. The first week everyone was marched down to Harzfeld's (a department store with a beauty shop) to have our hair cut and a perm. Everyone got a perm even if you had naturally curly hair and your hair could not extend below your collar. Persian melon was the popular lipstick and nail color at that time and of course we all had to wear girdles. Only one ring and a watch were allowed with the uniform.

"Domicile assignments were assigned according to the openings and TWA had bases in Boston, New York, Newark, Chicago, Kansas City, San Francisco and Los Angeles. Each student had three choices and then according to birth date the oldest got first choice and on down the line.

"At the time I was flying, TWA was flying the Constellations 749 and 10496, Boeing models 707, 131, and 331, Convair-880, B-727, and DC-9.

"The four of us that were assigned to Kansas City found a new completely furnished apartment just a couple of miles from the airport. Everything from furniture, TV, dishes, pots and pans, and linens were furnished for $62.50 each. We also had a doorman.

The first month was reserve and on the Connie. I would fly the milk run which was a four day trip with 11 stops a day and the layover would be just eight hours. From block in to block out and then hit all the same cities the next day.

"The 50s and 60s were the glamorous years to fly. I remember thinking that my $350 a month was as much as a legal secretary made at that time and I only worked 15 days a month. I loved the travel and made some lifelong friends. At that time there were only females on domestic and we always shared a layover room and flew with the same crew all month.

"By the time I got married the rules had changed so I could fly until I started my family. My years as a hostess were some of the best years of my life and I wanted to keep in touch with TWA and my friends. I joined Clipped Wings and held chapter offices before serving as international Vice President and President for the past eight years. I have also worked for TWA in a consultant capacity since 1986. At the present time I am working for the TWA Hotel Administration Department doing the field work for the crew accommodations. I also substitute teach at the state school and help my husband who is a manufacturers representative for a ladies apparel line."

DELTA'S MOTHER MARY

Delta Air Lines
Mary Ruth Rouse
1950

Delta's Training Director for Stewardesses and Flight Attendants, Mary Ruth Rouse, 1986. (Delta Air Lines Photo)

If the business of flight attendants is to take care of their passengers, who takes care of the flight attendants?

Her door has always been open. Delta Air Lines' Chief Training Instructor, Mary Ruth Rouse was thought of as a mother confessor for her trainees. She encouraged them to come to her and discuss any problems they might have. Her advice was gentle and encouraging, and she listened. Mary had an innate warmth and compassion for people. This was reflected in the affectionate nickname, *Mother Mary*, given to her by Delta's stewardesses and flight attendants, who have shown their loving respect for her over the years.

Mary joined Delta in 1950. She was chosen to become Chief stewardess Instructor by Delta's training department in 1963.

In this position, Mary's rules for beauty went further than skin deep. She felt that there weren't any shortcuts or special tricks for real beauty and said, "You can learn how to coif your most becoming hairdo and apply the most appropriate makeup and wear the most flattering clothes style. All these finishing touches are wasted unless the real you is a beautiful person."

Mary adds, "The girl who passes the rigorous acceptance standards to become a flight attendant has the potential to be beautiful in her own right. That is what we have always concentrated on in Delta's training department...the potential for beauty in all of us."

Mary stressed that attitude is important. The way a person feels about himself shows in everything he says and does, the way a person stands tall, walks and talks creates poise and charm. Self assurance is reflected by good health and vitality and by a person's approach to life.

"Good grooming reflects the way you feel about yourself, and how your want the world to perceive you. Being well informed is also important for an alert mind. A healthy outlook consists of keeping problems in their proper perspective. Being positive helps. The happiest people I have met have this approach to life."

The responsibilities of a flight attendant are great. Passengers comfort and safety are in their hands. "Under conditions of extraordinary stress, a person's emotional and physical condition could mean the difference between life and death for passengers, fellow crew members and oneself."

Mary's philosophy of life applied to both men and women. Each person has the potential to be a beautiful inner person according to his or her own attitude. Mary summed it up, "It's what you do with what you have that counts."

Mary Ruth Rouse represented the dedicated, friendly professionals in whom Delta has taken much pride over the years. Being called *Mother Mary* reflected her own inner self, her giving way, and of her own principles of life.

The lounge in a Delta DC-6.

CONTINENTAL'S "SAIGON TONI"

Continental Airlines
Toni Carpenter
1966 - 1983

MAC (Military Air Command) flights are a common occurrence during wartime for commercial airlines to contract airlift of troops...

"I came from an aviation family; my great aunt was one of the original Powder Puff Derby entrants, and my father was with one of the small airlines that merged into American Airlines. My mother once said that she supposed it was inevitable that I would end up connected with aviation somehow, considering the number of people in my family with pilot's licenses. I think I decided this at the tender age of eight, when I was flying from Chicago to New York. The stewardess put her hat on my head, and sent me around with the gum to the businessmen on the flight! If there had been a way for a woman to get her commercial ticket (license) at the right time in history, I'm sure I would be flying up front. As this wasn't to be, I ended up with a private license plus a lot of years flying in the back of the plane.

"I moved to California when I left college, and my first job was as a bookkeeper for a restaurant near a number of airline offices. The local managers of some of the airlines encouraged me to apply as a stewardess, and I finally succumbed. The first airline I visited hired me on that day, and I was to begin hostess training with Continental in January. They offered me a place in the class already in session, but I opted to wait until after the holidays. Had I known then about the importance of seniority, I would have jumped at the chance to graduate earlier.

"There were about 35 trainees in my class. I remember reading an article in the *Reader's Digest* at about that time which stated that there were about 700 applicants for every position, and that the average *life* of a hostess, or stewardess was one year, ten months and twelve days. When I was first hired, we were required to resign if we married, or reached the advanced age of 32.

"Everyone at Continental was very friendly to me but it was a two-edged sword. Continental was a southwestern based airline, and because my father was then station manager for American Airlines in El Paso, many of the executives from Robert Six on down soon learned that I was Ross Carpenter's youngest daughter. I had deliberately avoided applying to American. None of my fellow trainees wanted to sit with me in the company cafeteria, because Mr. Six or one of the many vice presidents would sit down to chat.

"We had about four weeks of accelerated training with classroom studies for six to eight hours a day. We did a lot of our practical training at night, while the aircraft were in the hangar for service. We even flew to Denver one night to check out on the DC-9, which was not flying into Los Angeles. The training department used a *mock-up* of a cabin interior to assist in teaching serving techniques. We also had a number of drills in emergency evacuation, first aid, fire control and every conceivable thing the training department could imagine. I agreed to think it over. The trainees also got lectures in diet and weight control - and we got weighed every week - plus we got extensive beauty makeovers. I was the first hostess ever hired by Continental whose blonde hair came out of a bottle at the time she was hired. I was counseled seriously about the importance of maintaining my hair coloring to their strict standards. Our hair could not touch our collar. We had our make up checked and we all had eyebrows drawn on to our faces. The training department encouraged us to wear a particular brand of makeup which came in a tube like tooth paste. It was applied by slapping it into the skin. I believe this makeup is on the market still, although no flight attendant I know still wears it. Privately we referred to it as Crisco, and it did resemble that product, although tinted.

"I believe the first black hostess Continental had was in our class. This was long before the days of male hosts. I entered training on 1/14/66, and graduated 2/12/66. Because of my modeling experience and my teaching degree, the training department wanted me to fly for six months, and then become a supervisor or go directly into training.

"While on duty, we were required to wear a girdle, carry extra nylons (pre-panty hose!) and carry an extra pair of white gloves. We also had to wear our hats at all times when not actually on the aircraft. Our total appearance was observed at all times by our supervisors. Any hostess who did not meet standards could be sent home without pay. Weight infractions were monitored strictly as well. On the first flight or every month we were weighed in uniform. Any hostess over her maximum was put on weight check. She was weighed weekly, and had to lose two pounds a week. If she failed to do so, she could be suspended without pay until the weight was lost. Three weight checks in six months could lead to termination. We were on probation for six months. We had at least one check ride during that time by our supervisor, and we had lots of checks before and after flights to make sure we had those hose, our manuals, and those clean white gloves!

"Before my probation was completed, I had decided that I did not want to become either a trainer or a supervisor; as a matter of fact, as soon as my probation was up, I became a union activist. But I also started flying our military contract flights to Southeast Asia - MATS (Military Air Transport Service), later changed to MAC (Military Air Command). I felt as though I had come home. I had the longest assignment to MAC of any Continental flight attendant. Continuous service from June, 1966 to the last Continental MAC flight into Travis air Force Base in March, 1973.

Toni Carpenter, Continental Airlines hostess, wearing the designer-look uniform, 1966.

"I flew in and out of Hawaii, Alaska, the Philippines, Wake Island, Guam, Thailand, Japan, Okinawa, and of course Vietnam. We carried troops, USO shows, civilian government employees, and military families. We flew long range Boeing 707's, with only one class of service. 165 seats in three and three configuration. Some of the flights were 12 hours long. Believe me, we made our own inflight entertainment: we used to put on talent shows, play charades, hold various contests and generally clown around with the troops that were so afraid to be going off to war, but too proud to show it. Many of these young boys were just that — young boys — and they welcomed the chance to let off some steam, no matter how silly the situation.

"Over the years, I carried several of the soldiers three or even four times. I had in excess of 250 landings in the war zone. I have been sung to and shot at, spent time holding the hand of a young man with a *Dear John* letter, and traded quips with Bob Hope in Cam Rahn Bay. I sat in a bunker in Danang while it was being shelled and visited the control towers in Saigon, my picture was on the front page of the *Stars and Stripes* wearing a side arm (pistol), while the troops were boarding. The gun was specially provided for the occasion by a colonel with an eye for the news - and the ladies. There are still pilots with Continental who call me Saigon Toni, which dates back to that newspaper photo.

"I was mascot for a Marine F-4 squadron, an honorary GIB (Guy in Back) for an Air Force Squadron, mascot for a Recon Battalion, and also for an Army LRRP (Long Range Recon Patrol) team. I received a letter of commendation from the United States Marine Corps for my efforts which they believed saved the life of one young Marine who experienced an allergic reaction to some medication while on board my flight from Honolulu to Okinawa. I have received uniform fatigues with my name on them from both Army and Marine groups. They both fit perfectly I guess the guys had plenty of time to take visual measurements during those long flights. I corresponded with many of the men from my flights, old and young. I was even mentioned in the will of one Sergeant Major who didn't return from his last tour of duty.

"People asked me why I stayed out in the Pacific so long. I always said that it was important for me as an American to make sure that the last flight over or the first flight back was as good as I knew how to make it. Some of the most heart wrenching, yet rewarding experiences came with the hostess' own cooperative effort. We didn't have much in the way of amenities to offer the passengers, but I believe we made up for it in good humor and sincere effort.

"For a long time, each flight that left the USA would save the unopened cartons of fresh milk and pack it in dry ice. This precious commodity was handed over from crew to crew until the flight arrived in Vietnam, or at Clark Air Force Base in the Philippines. There was a big burn center and orthopedic unit at the base hospital. We used to take this fresh *state side* milk up to the wounded soldiers who were patients there. I also used to spend some time in the MARS stations in Clark and in Okinawa. I could practice my radio techniques and bring a surprise to some G.I. in the jungle at the same time. Instead of hearing the same radio report coming in at the same time by some man, the G.I. got to *talk* to an American girl. I also did my stint at the jungle survival school for aviators in Clark Air Force Base as well. It was all probably very illegal, but the man in charge of the school for two years was an old friend from high school, who figured that the military pilots would rather look at me than at the Sergeant. I lectured on various kinds of poisonous snakes they could encounter if shot down, plus some of the booby traps to watch out for. There was a lot of very top secret material which I did not get to hear about. We were in Clark during the POW release, and we even managed to get into the hospital to visit some of these real American heroes. One of the hostesses even later married one of the POWs she met that day at Clark.

"After Continental stopped flying the MAC flights, I transferred to our overseas operations in the South Pacific. I flew to Guam, Fiji, Samoa, New Zealand and Australia. During the last months of my flying career I flew to South America.

"Throughout this whole time, I had some time off flight status to negotiate some labor contracts for the Continental flight attendants as well as for some other airlines. At Continental, we negotiated the very first maternity leave in the industry. I was also chairperson of the flight attendant Systems Board of Adjustment (grievances) and put on arbitration cases for the Continental flight attendants and other union groups. I was also chairperson of the flight attendant's first ever retirement board, and had fiduciary responsibility over the funds in the retirement plan.

"After the retirement of Bob Six, deregulation and labor disputes, it seemed to me that the heart had gone out of the airline, at least for me. And with the 1983 strike, I retired early. One event for which I am remembered most frequently, and my only real *claim to fame* came about after I had left the airline. I was approached to work with the screenwriters for the movie *Wall Street.* The writers wanted some help from an airline union person who had the kind of experiences I had. I helped them with dialogue to make the movie believable, when the Michael Douglas character met with the heads of the pilot, mechanics and flight attendant unions. The writers needed to know what kinds of questions would be asked by the union heads, and what kind of promises would have to be made to the unions in order for these people to support a takeover of the airline. Because of the help I gave them, the screenwriters named the character who was the head of the flight attendant union, Toni Carpenter. that is as close as I have ever gotten to fame and fortune, but I would not trade my 17 years with the airline for anything. The experiences, the memories and the friends that came from that time of my life give me a different kind of riches.

"I still travel a great deal of the time, and still to Asia. As the overseas director of a wholesale courier company, I lived in Hong Kong for almost three years; now I make eight or nine trips overseas each year. Nowadays, I am sitting in the seat, not serving coffee with a smile."

Northwest Airlines Stratocruisers — Finest ... Fastest

Lower Deck Club Lounge *Northwest Airlines Stratocruiser*

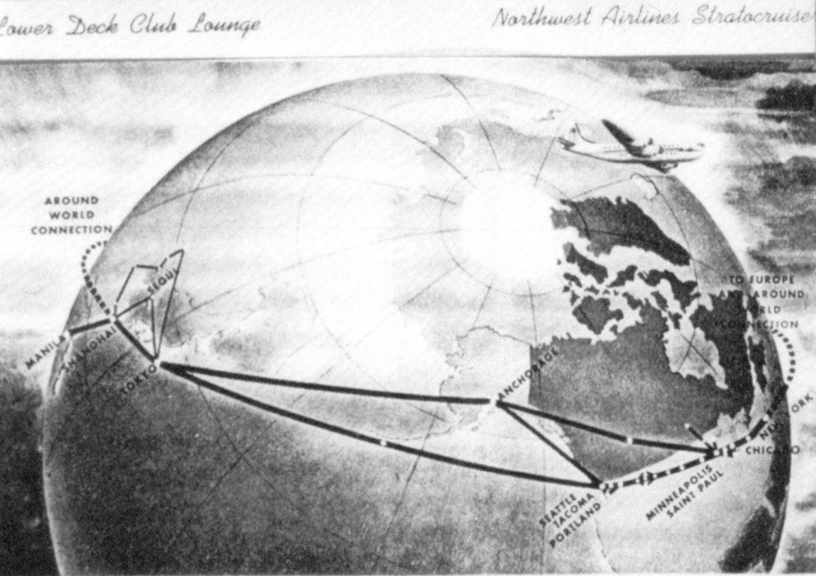

AIRLINE UNIFORMS THROUGH THE DECADES

BEAUTIES FROM 53 AIRLINES THAT TOUCH DOWN IN THE U.S.

The symmetrical symposium of international beauty gathered belo
would have been ungatherable a generation ago. These girls repre
sent 53 of the some 60 airlines now serving the U.S. Of the girls, 2
work for foreign airlines, the rest for U.S. carriers. Although the

NOREEN SMYTH
Trans Canada

EILEEN DAY
BOAC

MARTY KLINGENSMITH
Lake Central

CELIA FALCON
Trans Caribbean

PAULA STRIBLING
Southern

DIANA BULLOC
Central

RITA MUELLER
Lufthansa

BILLIE BOYD
Continental

CORRINE FINK
Allegheny

COLETTE DURANTHON
Air France

HELEN JONES
Pan American World

JOAN ROBER
Frontier

TILLY KOSTERMANS
KLM

MICHELINE RIKIR
Sabena

RITA HERZOG
Swissair

VIOLETTE KRAUSS
Alitalia

FANNY DAVILLA
Lav

MARY LOU ROGNAS
Capital

ROSA GARC
Guest Aerovias M

JANICE UNDERWOOD
American

ANGELA McCARTHY
Irish Airlines

MARY MIDDLETON
Eagle Airways

LOIS MURRAY
Northeast

BETTY YUHAS
TWA

YOKO MAYUZUMI
Japan Air Lines

GERI WIERS
Northwest

are alike in their youthful vitality. they come from such dissimilar places as Tokyo. Tacoma and Tel Aviv. wear everything from parkas to shorts and. among them. speak at least 16 languages.

Like the Americans. the foreign girls are mostly in their 20s and are cast in the same slim. trim mold. They earn less than Americans. fly more widely and stay on the job longer before they marry. The girls below and their airlines are identified at bottom with the top row of names matching the top row of girls and so on down.

EN LYDIA RODRIGUEZ Caribair — HELEN BAILEY Bonanza — ERNA HJALTALIN Icelandic — WENDY PILBEAM Varig — HELEN BEARD Ozark — ANNE HULSEY Eastern

ITTA LINDMAN SAS — EYBE BROCKDORFF Avianca — JOANNE McGANDY North Central — JOAN McCLURE National — JUANITA MUSTY Western — SHARON JENKINS West Coast — JANA HART Pacific Northern

EDES JIMENEZ Iberia — ILA HAREL El Al Israel — MARY LYNN Flying Tiger — MARGARET COHAN Qantas — ELISA VILLARREAL Aeronaves de Mexico — HELEN WITTWER Mohawk — SYLVIA TORRES Cubana

MOORE lta — SALLY JO LEE Alaska Airlines — KATHRYN PEDERSEN Wien Alaska — MARGE ESTES Northern Consolidated — ANNETTE MOORE Braniff — RUBY McGEE Trans Texas — NANCY BOESEKE United

May 15, 1930, the "Original Eight" modeled their dark green double-breasted suits with matching capes and hats. *Upper left:* Ellen Church, *upper right:* Alva Johnson, *front, left to right:* Margaret Arnatt, Inez Keller, Cornelia Peterson, Harriet Fry and Ellis Crawford. Margaret Arnatt survives today. (United Airlines Photo)

1930 Classic beginnnings. The first uniform for the "Original Eight" was designed by Steve Stimpson and Ellen Church in dark green wool. Long flowing capes were lined in gray. The hat was designed like a shower cap — in the style of the day.

BOEING AIR TRANSPORT

May 15, 1930

Left to right: Myrtle Fredrickson (1936), Mildred Roper (1939), Marie Hess (1933).

UNITED AIR LINES

(photos: United Airlines)

Summer uniform, 1939.

Winter uniform, 1940s.

Stewardess Doris Eng Brennan with her crew, 1940s.

UNITED AIRLINES

Steve Stimpson with stewardesses in 1959. The uniform on the right was designed by Raymond Loewy in a pink-beige color. The hat was a sugar scoop design. The uniform was worn from December 1959 through April 1963 with varying styles of jackets, with our without a collar, and various versions of pleats for the skirts.

Left to right: **stewardess wearing the 1930 uniform; Steve Stimpson, the father of stewardess service; stewardess wearing the 1959-1963 uniform.**

Brightly colored A-line double-knit dresses with matching Kepi-style hats were designed by Jean Louis in 1968.

1970. Hawaiian print muumuu and jacket uniforms were worn on United's flights to Hawaii.

1970-1972. United flight attendants wore the long skirt in the B-747 upper deck. Men wore matching jackets. Street length uniforms were worn in the main cabin.

1980s

UNITED AIRLINES

In 1980, United's flight attendants numbered 8,700. The jet aircraft flew 550 miles per hour and carried up to 374 passengers. Half of the flight attendants were married; one in five had children; Thirteen percent were men; Seventeen percent were minorities. The average seniority was eight and a half years. The average salary was $1,700 for seventy-five hours of flying time.

United's 1986 uniform was dark navy worn with burgundy accessories — a well-tailored look carried over to the 1990s.

United's Cipped Wings 1940 fashion show was held in Chicago to raise money for St. Luke's Hospital. Gail Allemana and Howard Stiles pose in children's sized crew uniforms beside a United float. Gail and Howard are the children of United captains.

AMERICAN AIRLINES

(American Airlines Photos)

American Airways, 1933.

1934

1936

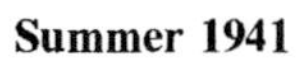

Summer 1941

1943

Summer 1952

AMERICAN AIRLINES

Summer 1959

Summer 1960

1964

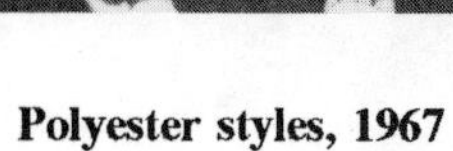

Polyester styles, 1967

American Beauty Collection, 1969

Americana Collection featuring red, white and blue plaid and Daniel Boone-style cap, 1969

AMERICAN AIRLINES

Field Flower Collection, 1971

1980

1983

AMERICAN AIRLINES

American Airlines' Uniforms 1985-1990s: variation scarves, ties, sweaters and dress styles for women.

Hawaiian muumuu and shirt jacket in red, white and blue.

DELTA AIR LINES

(Delta Air Lines' Photos)

1940-1942

1958

1969

1979

1980s

First uniform, December 25, 1941

CONTINENTAL AIR LINES

Summer 1942: navy skirt with white jacket. Summer 1943 had a navy jacket.

Brown winter 1943-1944

Light gray summer 1944

Dress-type summer 1945

The Golden Penguins model uniforms form 1950-1990 at continental's 50th anniversary of hostess service. Mildred "Tommie" Heck Carlisle models the Hawaiian muumuu. She was in Continental's first class of hostesses, 1941.

Photos by Peggy Mass

Pink hostess uniform of 1960: white stockings, pearls and pink beret cap

Designer uniform of 1970 featured pearls and red beret cap.

1990s classic dark navy with various options.

TWA's first hostesses wore wool serge uniforms, 1935.

TWA

1944 — the famous TWA *cut-out* uniform

TWA winter uniform, 1950

Summer uniform, 1968

TWA hostesses in 1971 uniforms

TWA

Late 1950s: the first jet class for the B-707

Summer uniform, 1966

English barmaid

Roman togas

In 1968, TWA used paper uniforms on transcontinental flights to advertise their flights to Europe and the cuisine of each country served. One size fit all.

French cocktail dress

New York lounge pajamas and French cocktail dress

TWA's classic dark uniform of the 1980s and 1990s. Pictured here is hostess Annie Gilmore Schmitt.

The 1958 classic uniform featured a matching hat.

NORTHWEST

Classic uniforms of the 1990s feature maroon on the women's lapels and white round-neck blouses.

EASTERN AIR TRANSPORT

Eastern Air Transport's Chief Hostess, Mrs. Anne Porter Cullum photographing four hostesses.

EASTERN AIR TRANSPORT 1931

Hostess Miss West with refreshment hamper before a flight on a Curtiss Condor.

National Uniform 1940-1942

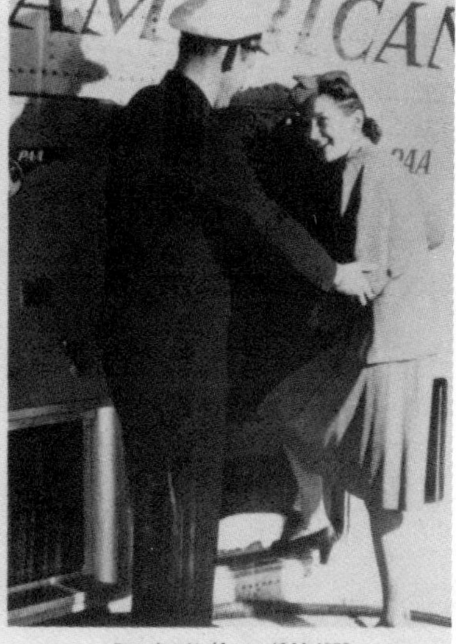

Pan Am Uniform 1944-1952

NATIONAL

AND

PAN AMERICAN

(Pan Am Photos)

National Uniform 1951-1962

Pan Am Uniform 1952-1959

Pan Am Uniform 1959-1965

Pan Am Uniform 1969-1971

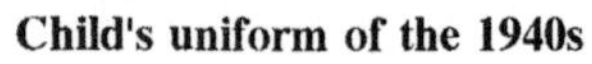

Child's uniform of the 1940s

Pan Am uniforms of the 1980s

Braniff Airlines' hostess Jeanne Braniff Terrill.

BRANIFF AIRLINES

and

NORTHEAST AIRLINES

FRONTIER AIRLINES

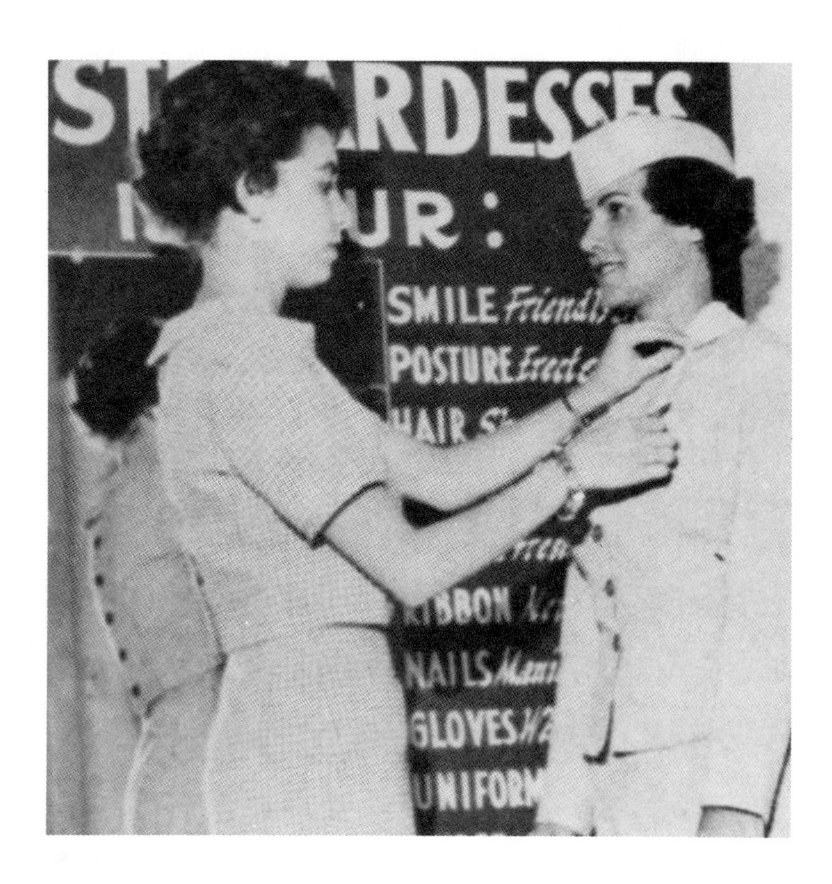

Selections of the stewardess uniform for Frontier's hot pants of 1967.

Colorado-based Frontier Airlines' stewardesses with actor Jimmy Stewart.

ALOHA AIRLINES

Begun in the 1940s, Aloha Airlines is now a flourishing commuter between the islands. The first flight attendants played the ukelele.

LOST HORIZONS

Mergers

1961 Capital Airlines - United Airlines
1966 Ozark Air Lines - Trans World Airways

Bankruptcies

1991 Eastern Airlines
1991 Pan American World Airways

Fly UNITED
Capital Airlines
PENNSYLVANIA
PCA
CENTRAL
CAPITAL AIRLINES Gives You a Bird's-Eye View of Everything Along the Way
Capital Airlines
Capital
AIRLINES
"KNOWN FOR YEARS AS PCA . . . ONE OF AMERICA'S PIONEER AIRLINES"
The Nation's Capital City Is an Inspiring Sight from the Air by Day or by Night
Capital Airlines
Capital
AIRLINES

Capital
AIRLINES
AMERICA'S LARGEST JET-POWERED FLEET
APRIL 26, 1959
A MILLION JET-POWERED MILES
WITHOUT SPILLING A DROP
Capital Airlines' Jo Humbert—first hostess to welcome the jet age. Jo has been pampering passengers aboard the vibration-free Viscounts for a million jet-powered miles.

Capital Hostess Jo Humbert was the first air hostess to fly a million jet miles in the Vickers Viscount. The *Capital Timetable* and various magazines and newspapers featured her photo in 1959.

PENNSYLVANIA

CENTRAL'S CLONES

Betty Turner Hines
1943

There were other stewardesses in the 1940s who, like Eastern Air Transport's Trudy Von Hoven Pracny, found themselves hired before they knew it.

During World War II, in the spring of 1943, a young, attractive widow was at the Washington, DC airport on her way to her parent's home in Massachusetts. Betty Turner Hines had been working in Washington when she learned that her husband, an Army Air Force pilot, had been killed in action in Europe. She needed a change and decided to quit her job as a secretary and go home for awhile and get her life together.

As Betty waited for her flight, a ticket agent for Pennsylvania Central Airlines struck up a conversation with her. He told her that Pennsylvania Central needed stewardesses and knew that one of the women scheduled to start training the next day had been hurt in an automobile accident and had dropped out of the class. He suggested that Betty find out if she could get the job. He knew the company hired widows, and she was young and attractive. He told Betty that the travel and the change would be good for her.

Betty decided that she would give it a try. A job as a stewardess might be the change she needed, after all. She caught a cab across the field to the hangar where Penn Central's offices were housed. The ticket agent had called ahead to inform Personnel that he was sending over an applicant for the stewardess position.

Betty couldn't believe that all this was happening to her. In just an hour's time she found herself hired and scheduled to start training the following day. She called her parents to say she wouldn't be coming home after all, she'd just gotten a new job.

"We learned all about the DC-3, the routes, interline service ticketing, service aloft, and emergency procedures," says Betty, recalling her six-week training session in Arlington, Virginia. "On the last day, just before we received our wings, we were sent to Elizabeth Arden's studio in the city to do our makeup and hair. It turned out to be an all-day affair. We all had our hair cut and permed, and then had our own personal makeup applied by a professional makeup artist. When we got back from our all-day beauty overhaul, we all burst into tears. We couldn't believe our eyes: we all looked alike - we were clones of each other!

"I was based in Detroit after I finished my training. I flew between Detroit, Cleveland, and Washington, DC. We didn't stay at a hotel on layovers in Washington; the crews bunked at the airport in separate rooms for pilots and stews and we all slept on cots. It wasn't very glamorous.

"I was airsick a lot. I resigned after having a scare in an electrical storm, after nearly a year of flying. Being a stewardess was a nice interlude for me, because it helped me get my mind off myself and my problems by serving other people," Betty says reflectively. "I'm glad I got the job. My daughter Frances was a flight attendant with Eastern."

In 1948, Pennsylvania Central became Capital Airlines and grew into the fifth largest carrier. But in 1961, financial troubles forced Capital to merge with United Airlines. Fortunately, United hired all of Capital's employees, preserving the welfare of the 7,600 people who would have otherwise lost their jobs.

Pennsylvania Central air hostesses, 1942: Betty Turner Hines is sixth from left.

THE UNEXPECTED PICNIC
Pennsylvania Central Capital Airlines Florence Wiese Espy 1946 - 1947

Being a flight attendant, Murphy's Law applies, the unexpected happens and they cope with the situation.

Florence Wiese worked in a bank while attending the University of Wisconsin. After finishing two years of college she heard about airlines wanting college girls for their stewardesses. She thought this sounded new and exciting and applied to Pennsylvania Central Airlines.

Her training was six weeks at Washington National Airport in Washington DC. Her first domicile was Milwaukee and later Pittsburgh. Her first flight from Milwaukee was to Washington DC in a 21 passenger DC-3, she relates the experience:

"My first flight was memorable. In those days the Hostess, as we were called, was responsible for bringing the silverware on board. I was so excited about my first flight that I walked out of operations and left the silverware behind.

"Wouldn't you know, we were serving steak that day. I explained my plight to my 19 passengers. One man suggested steak sandwiches and plastic spoons for the rest of the meal. (We always had plastic spoons in our supplies for coffee.) The passengers didn't leave one scrap of food and they all laughed and referred to it as a picnic! Needless to say, I never forgot the silverware again!

"We were paid a monthly salary. I flew over a hundred hours many months and loved it. We had more time to talk to individual passengers, pass out flight logs, and help calm fears for first riders. It was glamorous to arrive at airports and to have crowds waiting at the gates just to see the planes take off and land.

"It was a new and exciting occupation and almost glamorous except for the burp cups. Many of the same businessmen traveled the routes weekly. We called passengers by their name. The atmosphere was friendly and a wonderful job I'll always remember."

Capital Airline hostess Florence Weise Espy, 1946.

WHAT'S A GIRL TO DO?
Capital Airlines Eleanor "Ellie" Keller-Werner Sherwood 1949 - 1958

Safety came first - this flight attendant had to take out of the ordinary action...but it worked!

Ellie Sherwood received her BS degree from Northern Michigan University. At 43 years, after her children were all in school, she returned to finish her college education and received a MA from Michigan State University as a Mental Therapist. She tells her story of being employed by the airlines between 1949 and 1958...

"I started hanging around airports when I was fifteen. I learned there were different kinds of airplanes, but also that there were lucky ladies that worked on airplanes while they were airborne.

"I was offered a job at an airport in Rochester, New York. When my employer couldn't pay me, he would ask one of the flight instructors to take me up for an hour and give a me flight lesson. Since I didn't know the difference between a magneto and a spark plug, I had difficulty learning aerodynamics. (At the present time I was a student pilot and I was learning to fly in a Tomahawk Piper Cub.)

"I wasn't all that interested with those first lessons, as I wanted to fly, but I wanted to be one of those ladies in the attractive uniforms helping all those passengers. So I enrolled in a school in Kansas City that trained for the airlines. I had a futile trip to Los Angeles, where no airline would hire me because I was too young. I then returned to Kansas City and was hired by Continental as a counter Ticket Agent. Because I couldn't load baggage, I was sent

Eleanor Keller-Werner Sherwood, Capital Airlines hostess, 1949.

to their new Houston base. While I worked there as a Ticket Agent I met many celebrities including the New York Giants, and movie stars. Jack Benny was signing his autograph on a personal check and I alarmingly told him not to do that as anyone could cash it! He laughed, he'd signed it *George Burns*. I worked for Continental until 1954 and then transferred to Capital Airlines. I'd often traveled on passes on Capital to my home town of Rochester. They hired me first as a Reservations Agent and then as a Hostess. I finally was one of those ladies working on the airplanes! I signed a contract that when I married I would have to resign flying as a Hostess.

"My first trip was on a DC-3 on a route that had thirteen stops. Most flights on this route were eighteen minutes to forty minutes from city to city. At one point I had to ask the agent when he opened the door, 'what city is this?' This was a morning flight and I was supposed to serve breakfast complete with scrambled eggs. I could not find the silverware! (This was before plastic.) I held off serving the meal and when we finally landed at Rochester (my old stomping grounds), I asked one of my former co-workers where the silverware was kept. It was under the last seat where I would never have thought to look. Well, the folks working on the ground crews had a nice, unsolicited breakfast -- as that was our last stop.

"Another incident, I was frightened in extremely turbulent weather flying in a DC-4. I had three very young boys between the ages of three, five and seven traveling by themselves. They had been seated together. I made sure their seat belts were fastened and showed them the burp bags and kept an eye on them. We suddenly had a fire in a propeller. The boys were so frightened, three passengers volunteered to each have a boy sit by them. I was impressed by their thoughtfulness.

"Another flight I was flying on a Viscount which was a jet propelled airplane and very quiet. Anything that was said in the rear of the cabin could be heard by most of the passengers. We were arriving late at New York's LaGuardia Airport, when a man decided he would be first off the plane. He stood by the exit door in the rear of the cabin near the galley and hostess jump seats. I had already made our landing announcement and checked seat belts. I asked the man to be seated as it was FAA rules everyone was to be seated with their seat belts fastened. The man was very angry and stood his ground by the exit door and refused to move! I told him I'd have to *cool him off*. I filled up the coffee server with water and told him I'd pour it over him if he did not return to his seat immediately. Well, after a *long* pause, he went to his seat and *all* the passengers clapped! I felt sorry I'd done this nasty deed, but what does a five foot two inch, ninety-eight pound girl do? So — that's what I did!

"I was living and based in New Orleans when I met and married the only Yankee in the crowd. I resigned when I married. My husband was based in Biloxi, Mississippi with the Air Force. Upon his discharge we moved to his home in Detroit, Michigan. We are the parents of three children.

"I enjoyed my job as a Capital Hostess and I always felt sorry for those girls that had to work day to day in an office."

CUPID TOOK ME OUT OF THE GOLDEN SKIES

Capital Airlines
June Porter Rittenhouse
1953

June Porter became a Capital hostess in 1953. This is her story:

June Porter Rittenhouse, Capital Airlines hostess, 1953.

"There's always a story behind the job with the airlines, isn't there? Well, mine began the summer after graduation from the University of Kansas. Regrettable, I became engaged to a young man eight days before he left for Korea and the summer before my junior year in college. What was supposed to be six months in the fighting in Korea and then six months back stateside, turned into twenty-four months in Korea and Japan - right through my junior and senior years. When I should have been having the social time of life, I was sitting home on weekends in the sorority house wearing a diamond ring. I know I was unprepared for the engagement, but when I realized what a mistake it was, I just could not write the *Dear John* letter to a boy fighting a war in Korea. And when he got home, all we had were two years worth of love letters written overseas. It was then I felt I *had* to get out of that small Kansas town in which everybody kept asking me, 'How is David Dean? And when are you two getting married?' One dear lady told me, 'When you get married, you're married a long, long time.' She was warning me against what she perceived was an early marriage, and at twenty-one, I thought I was so grown up!

"I had a B.S. degree in Education; but the idea of going out to teach physical education in western Kansas at a beginning teacher's salary in 1953 did not overwhelm me. I began looking into the *excitement and glamour* of hostessing on trains or planes, even though I had never been up in an airplane in my life! Weren't we adventuresome? And, being out in the middle of Kansas at the time, I didn't know the airlines had their own schools. I gave the ring back, applied to McConnell Airline School in Minneapolis, Minnesota, and escaped the Kansas wedding. My parents were relieved.

"While in airline school, my first flight was from Minneapolis to Rochester, Minnesota, to see my family who were there with my very ill brother at the Mayo Clinic. I remember being quite disappointed because I thought there would be this *rush* feeling of exhilaration upon lift-off. I found it was like taking off in a bus.

"At that time, smaller airlines came to Downs in New York and McConnell in Minneapolis to interview and recruit stewardesses. Capital wanted Helen and me, so we had a wonderful trip out to Washington DC. We had a ship change at the Cleveland Airport which, at that time, didn't announce flights in their little restaurant. Well, we didn't know that nor see the sign, so of course, we missed our flight. *How to make an impression on your airline job interview* . . . had to await the next Capital coming through to DC. Helen had checked her things, complete with long designer umbrella, into one of those small half-lockers. When the flight was called, she couldn't get that darned umbrella out of the locker, and I thought we were going to miss the last flight! I never really trusted that airline after that - because they hired us anyway!

"Following graduation and my trip back to Kansas to get my things to move to DC, I still took the time to stop at the United Offices in Chicago for an interview. They offered me a job and I could have gone to the January class in Cheyenne; but this was August, and I had the job with Capital to begin right away! Funny, due to that merger in 1961, I would end up in United's Clipped Wings which has become such a big part of my life. I don't regret going with Capital. Looking back, had I waited to join United in January, I would never have met Ritt in DC. Fate preceded Cupid that day and I've never regretted it.

"I had a ball with Capital, I loved every minute of our DC-3s, DC-4s and *Connies* (Constellations). I was truly *walking on air*. I lived in Alexandria, Virginia, in a basement apartment complete with wood burning fireplace, no real kitchen, and a shower curtain in the furnace room around the toilet. We called it *Hernando's Hideaway*. My roommate was Helen Fassett. Later we moved to a bigger apartment when her sister joined us to work in reservations. We still only had one bedroom with a doubled and a hide-a-bed in the living room. It didn't matter as the three of us never were home to sleep on the same schedule.

"I remember Helen telling me that on one of her flights, a lady rang for her and when Helen arrived to inquire of her need, the lady said, 'Put out your hand.' When Helen did, the woman spit out her gum in her outstretched hand. Of course that was not as bad as the time during turbulence and storage of many used burp cups, a woman asked me to go back and search through the vomit for her partial plate!

"On the Capital Connies, we had parakeets in cages up in the *Cloud Club*. We had to remove them when an outbreak of Parrot Fever hit the states.

"Guys used to like to think it was their uniform that captured the girl's heart. In our case, it was as much my uniform as his.

"Early in Jack's and my dating, I traded another Hostess to get his flight home on leave to Milwaukee for Christmas. I let him take me out to a farewell dinner, but then showed up on his plane for the flight. Surprise! When we landed in Milwaukee, I had a ship change on to Minneapolis as we only kept two attendants on board to serve dinner out of Chicago. He deplaned and walked over to his waiting family, then came back to get me for

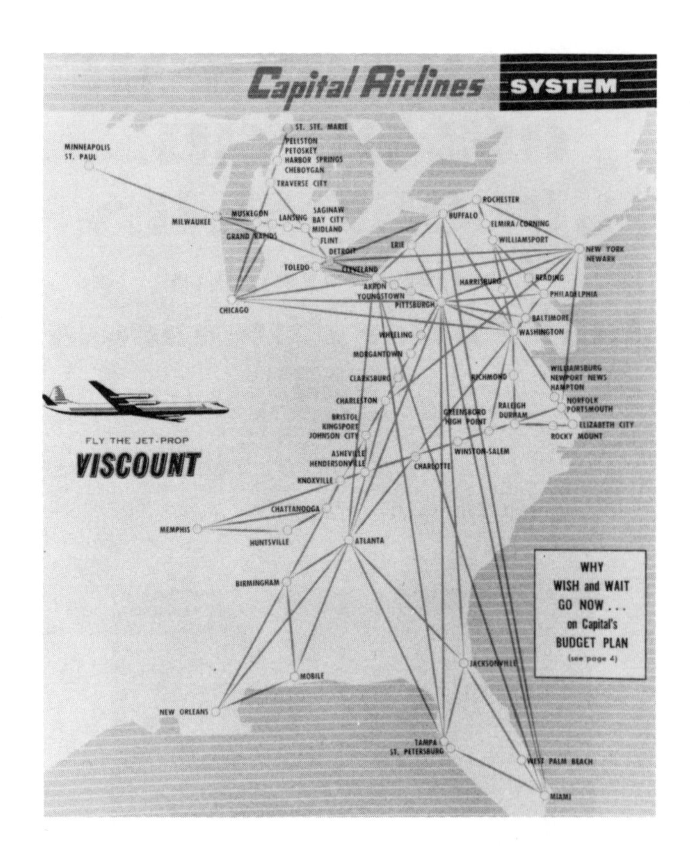

introductions before escorting me to my second plane. He kissed me at the bottom of the Connie's stairs. Then, he had to walk back to his open-jawed family — especially the high-school-age sister who was absolutely taken with my job.

"I, on the other hand, had to climb those steps to the stares of the enplaning stewardess and two passengers in the doorway. They wanted to know if I knew that soldier. 'No, I told them, but that's part of our good Capital service to the fighting men.'

"I dated Jack Rittenhouse in DC. After flying a year's stint with Capital when I began to feel it was more important to land on schedule to see Jack than it was to get overtime pay flying. I knew Dan Cupid's arrow had stung me to take me out of the golden skies. I married Jack and have a dividend of four children.

"While my flying days were short, my membership with United Clipped Wings spans the last twenty years. Capital merged with United in 1961. I was elected their National President in 1982. I enjoy being an active member today. Clipped Wings affords me a golden circle of friends.

"I've gotten more mileage out of my year of being a stewardess than my 38 year marriage, 32 years of motherhood and 15 years of career combined. You were a *stewardess*? Talk about walking on air, it's like I walked on water! My stock just about rises 100%! This nation is still enamored by the perceived glamour of the airline flight attendant from whatever era. We are right up there with the cowboys and the astronauts. And its still so much fun receiving that acknowledgement."

Capital Airline hostesses with President Marcos. Left: June Porter Rittenhouse.

THE TICKET
Capital Airlines
1959 - 1961
Northwest Airlines
Carol Cleary Kubiak
1990s

Flying is a way of life. Carol has flown for two airlines and as a hostess for a Corporation's private executive jet.

Carol Cleary Kubiak tells her story with wings for two airlines and as a hostess for a private jet for General Motors Air Transport:

"I was born in Union Beach, New Jersey and when my twin brother Hank and I were orphaned at the age of sixteen we went to live with an Episcopal minister and his wife in Keyport, New Jersey. After High School in the late 1950s there did not seem to be much opportunity for a girl to travel and see the world. I thought about the airlines and this seemed to be the *ticket* to travel and see that world. I worked three jobs in 1958 to pay for the Grace Downs School in New York City. It trained for prospective stewardesses. Since I was not yet 20 years old, I lived in the village in a girls dormitory until I was called by Capital Airlines for an interview by Joy Geddes, the Chief Hostess. I was hired and trained for five weeks in Washington, DC.

"I was then domiciled for domestic flights in Detroit, Michigan. Think how it was to be 20 years old, on one of your first trips standing at the top of the stairs - and with a gasp I saw both Chubby Checkers and Paul Anka coming to board *my flight*! Most of my other trips have been with the general public, not celebrities, but that trip set the tone for me. I knew then that I had picked the right career.

Carol Cleary Kubiak, Capital Airlines hostess, 1959.

I planned on transferring bases every six months, but I met the man that I married 14 months later. Detroit had been my last choice for a domicile, but its a hard city to leave and I'm still here!

At a clam bake in Portland, Maine in May, 1993, United's Mainliner Club's convention honored United's number one flight attendant, Jo Humbert. Back row: host and manager of United's Portland station, James McLendon. Left to right: Carol Cleary Kubiak, Arlene Kauffman Laurie, United Clipped Wings President and Jo Humbert. All were former Capital hostesses before the merger. Author, Helen McLaughlin, far right.

"I was next employed in Detroit by GMAT (General Motors Air Transport) to be a hostess on their Convair. It was my job to make GM officials and engineers feel comfortable and safe, and in return they made me feel I was an important member of the General Motor's team. On GMATs I finally saw the world, from Norway to Australia and parts in between. It was the best of jobs.

"I am flying again for an airline, Northwest, also out of Detroit as my base. I retrained for six weeks in Minneapolis. I fly on DC-9s to B-747s aircraft. Having flown from the late 1950s to the 1990s I have seen so many changes in the airplanes, the flying public and the equipment! But I must say that becoming a stewardess (which is how I always think of myself - not flight attendant) was the turning point in my life.

"The friends, the situations and people all over the world have made me appreciate my family, my friends and my country much more. That could have only come from doing something you love."

Carol is one of many former Capital hostesses that have joined United Clipped Wings Association. Capital merged with United in 1961 and United invited Capital hostesses to join. She joined in 1966 and became an active member. She has attended all the Conventions since 1970 and the most recent one in 1992.

She has been involved with their philanthropic project, the Special Olympics. She worked in Minneapolis in 1991 at the first International Special Olympics and in Salzburg, Austria in March 1993. She says of this opportunity, "it is involvement with an organization who gives help to others that helps me enjoy life more abundantly."

TWA - OZARK MERGER
October 26, 1986

Ozark began their operation in 1950 with a flight from St. Louis to Chicago. Each of four DC-3s was painted a different color so that the public would know they operated with more than one aircraft.

The proud airline had 36 years of service before the merger with TWA on October 26, 1986. Ozark's employees brought many attributes to TWA and was one of the smoothest mergers in the industry. Professional flight attendants from Ozark and TWA blended into a team to serve TWA's customers.

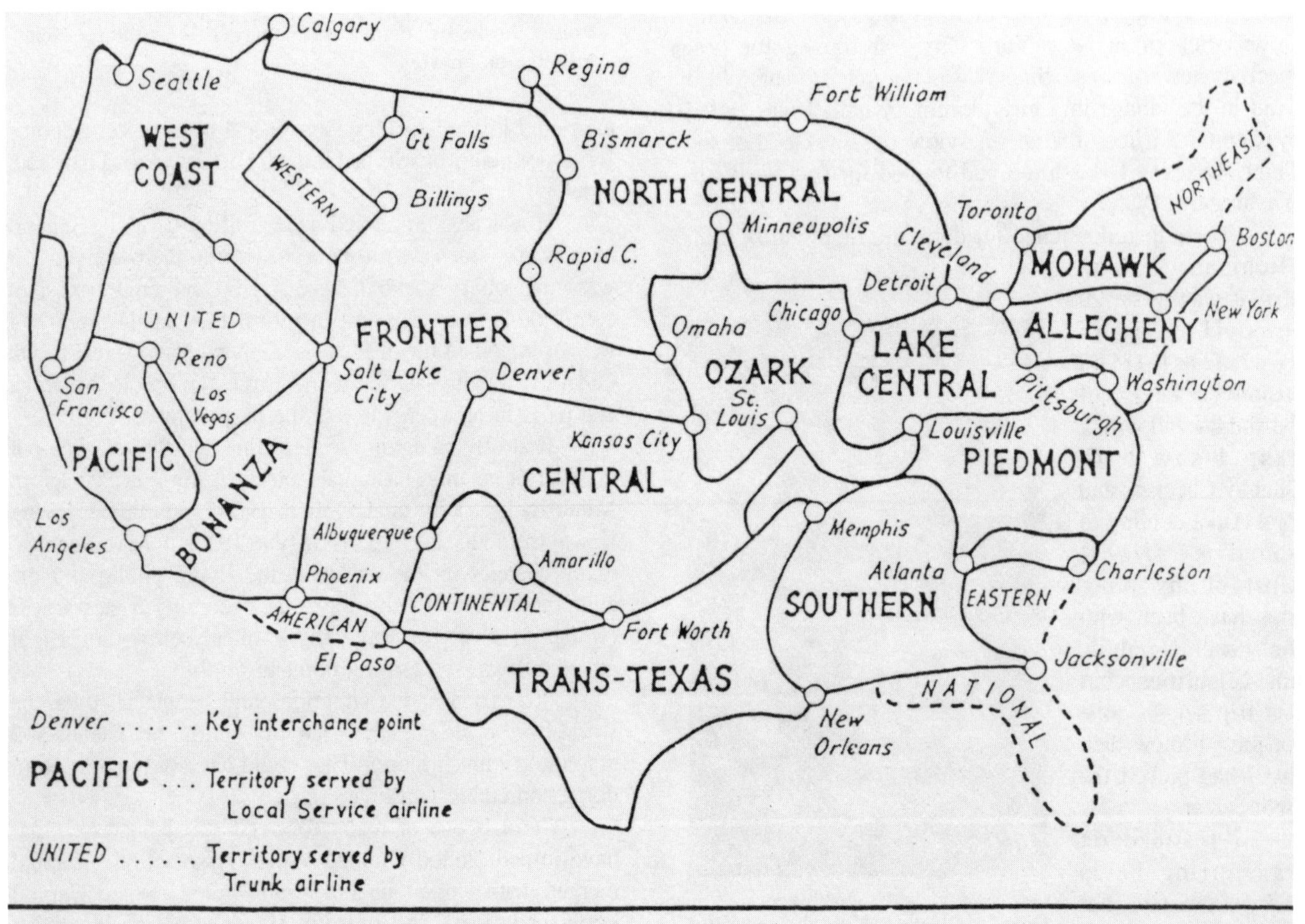

Local Service Airlines—Territories Served during the Early 1960s.

Eastern Airlines faced bankruptcy and lost on January 18, 1991. A 60 year old airline left the sky. But people make an airline. The following stories reveal Eastern's great legacy beginning with Trudy Von Hoven Pracny, one of Eastern Air Transport's first seven hostesses, and continuing through the 1990s. Eastern Silverliners International, an organization of flight attendants, has information concerning its activities. Their address is in the Appendix. Trudy's story is in The Early Era.

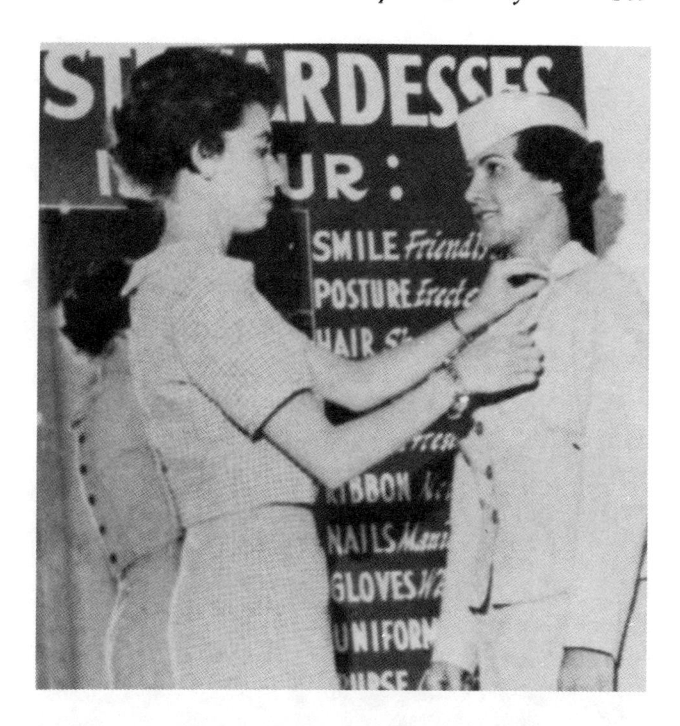

Frontier Airlines' uniform rules, 1962.

EASTERN'S PRIDE FOR FORTY-THREE YEARS

Margie Boyle 1944

*This Eastern vignette features a lady who was with the company forty-three years and who has transported at least one **very** strange passenger.*

For Eastern Air Lines, the abbreviation "EAL" represented the qualities "energetic, attractive and lovable" that described flight attendant Margie Boyle. Margie was number one on Eastern's seniority list, a petite, dark-haired Irish colleen with green eyes and a smile that melted every heart.

On February 15, 1944, Margie joined Eastern just six days after she graduated from the University of Illinois with top honors and a BA in Journalism. She was tiny, measuring 34-23-34 and weighed about 105 pounds.

She kept her 1944 measurements by her favorite hobby, walking. On April 28, 1984 she walked fifteen miles for the March of Dimes. On the job over the past four decades, Margie has probably "walked halfway to the moon."

How could an airline have been so fortunate to have someone with so much charm and personality representing their service for forty-three years? Especially someone with her TLC and compassion for the people she served? Turn that around, and Margie felt that Eastern provided the setting for a career to serve people. People made life interesting for Margie.

"I learned something from everyone I met. I liked travel and when I told a passenger goodbye I felt like they

Margie Boyle, Eastern veteran of 43 years, in her 1944 uniform.

Captain Eddie Rickenbacker, President of Eastern, presenting and award to "Little Bit" Margie Boyle.

had momentarily been a friend and I was losing them as they deplaned."

Margie first won recognition in a contest writing about "My Job and Why I Like It." This achievement revved her interest in winning Eastern's "Happy Holiday" sales contest in 1952. She won a trip to Mexico City. In 1953 she won again and was presented a trip to Buenos Aires by President Eddie Rickenbacker. Margie had caught his eye. This was the second time she had won Eastern's system-wide contest. She was a tiny dynamo of energy and personality. He said to her, "You're not very big 'Little Bit,' but you surely have what it takes to make things happen. I'm proud of you, and Eastern is proud of you."

Eastern's Bev Griffith, the manager of Eastern's public relations in New York, noticed Margie, too. From that time on, Margie was asked to carry out public relations assignments for cities all over Eastern's route system. In uniform, she represented Eastern at travel shows, career days, sales blitzes, airport dedications, conventions and presidential charter flights. She has given travel tips on clothing, cosmetics and baby's needs to calm the fears of women flying. As a free lance writer, Margie presented the women's point of view in many U.S. newspapers.

Seniority afforded her additional opportunities. She was selected as personal stewardess for the Dwight Eisenhowers before the purchase of the "Columbia." She was also stewardess for campaign trips in 1959 for Nelson Rockefeller and for many charter flights for celebrities.

On February 16, 1984, Eastern honored their number one flight attendant with a special celebration at her Atlanta base. Eastern's Vice President of Inflight Service "Winnie" Gilbert presented Margie a plaque to commemorate Eastern's appreciation of her forty years of dedicated service. In Margie's own words, the ceremony was "fantabulous." Saint Valentine's day 1985 marked her 41st anniversary and 21 million miles in the air as an Eastern flight attendant.

She complimented her flight attendant experiences by traveling to every country she wanted to see. Her favorite place to visit is Ireland, the Emerald Isle. Margie feels she has roots there, as she is Irish. She spent vacation time in 1983 at a temporary residence in a purportedly haunted castle. Since her retirement from Eastern she still likes to go home to the quiet, tiny, rural town of Fairmont, Illinois as she did when she had a busy schedule flying for Eastern.

REMEMBERING AND THE WINDOW SEAT REQUEST

"That's a record, not only for Eastern Airlines, but for every company in the world. I couldn't believe it when they told me Margie Boyle had never been late, never taken sick leave and never missed a flight," said Jack Bell, who was Eastern's manager of military operations.

In 1967, when Eastern signed a Military Airlift Command contract, Margie bid the MAC schedule. She flew on Eastern Airlines first DC-8 flights, including fourteen trips to Vietnam during the conflict there. She also flew on MAC flights to Germany, Libya, Japan, Greece, England, Italy, Hawaii, Korea, Iceland and Scotland.

Eastern flight attendant Margie Boyle in her 1980 uniform.

In 1984 Margie bid the MAC flight to Guantanamo Bay, Cuba. Every week she commuted from her home base in Atlanta to Norfolk, Virginia on Monday, to go to work on Tuesday. She said of this arrangement, "This was far more beneficial exercise that the rich and lazy get from the Main Chance or the Golden Door."

On one trip, Margie came very close to not taking her scheduled flight. It happened on an L-1011 MAC flight to Panama. Eastern was scheduled to pick up marines who had been on a survival training mission in the jungle. Margie had been up front in first class. The Marines had boarded in battle fatigues with all their gear: guns, helmets, knives and a huge sack that several of the men helped to load. They were joking about *Willie*, a first rider whom they thought should have a window seat. Margie agreed: a first rider should have a window seat.

"I'd like to meet Willie," Margie said. "I'd like to welcome him aboard and show him around our L-1011."

The Marines pointed to the big sack lying on the floor.

"Is he dead?" she exclaimed. "You have to be kidding!"

One of the Marines grinned and said, "No, ma'am, he ain't dead, that's for sure!" The big sack seemed to slump and momentarily had looked like it moved.

Margie's eyes opened wide. "What, for heaven's sake, is in there? It moved, I saw it!" she cried.

"Now don't get excited, Miss. Willie is our boa constrictor. I froze him so I could take him home. I think he may be thawing, but he's bagged so he can't get out," the Marine said, trying to reassure the distraught Margie.

She hated snakes. Even garter snakes frightened her.

"No way!" she said, trying to maintain her composure. "No way is that snake staying on this plane." She turned on her heel and marched off the aircraft.

"That Willie is off the flight or I refuse to go!" Margie told the Colonel in charge. The man had no idea what she was talking about and said, "I can't quite place Willie, Miss, but I'll be glad to sit by him myself if he's offensive."

"Your bet he's offensive," Margie had retorted. "Willie's a boa constrictor!"

The Colonel then made arrangements to have Willie spend his first flight on Eastern Airlines in the cargo bin. sorry to say, he didn't get the window seat.

Margie moved from number one female flight attendant to number one of *all* Eastern's 6,500 flight attendants on August 1, 1984, when Eugene Wallace retired. At the time of Wallace's retirement, eight other senior flight attendants retired with a total of 317 years of Eastern Airlines service. Margie was asked to speak at a special ceremony to honor the "Magnificent Nine," on October 25, 1984. She had previous plans and had to decline, but she wrote a speech to be read that was a parody of their duties: "How lucky they are to never again have to eat standing up, or to awake in the middle of the night wondering if the bids were due at 8 am that day, to never have to struggle with the "Frequent Flyers" garment bags heavy enough to weigh down a full-grown rhinoceros, and carry-on baggage of an assortment tied with breaking string, and no place to stow it."

Every day continued to be an adventure for Margie Boyle. She's still called "Little Bit," the nickname given her by Eddie Rickenbacker. Everyone who knew her agrees it was more than a little bit of luck the day she joined Eastern. The pilots thought so too. She was asked to join the Retired Eastern Pilot's Association, and in July, 1985, Margie was the first woman flight attendant ever to be given this honor. Margie retired before the 60 year old airline left the skies on January 18, 1991. Eastern is still sadly missed but has left a great legacy in U.S. aviation as has Margie Boyle in the hearts of many.

BAPTISM BY FIRE

Eastern Airlines
Jack Nee
1946 - 1984

Flight attendants who stayed with Eastern since the forties witnessed the airline's growth and transition from propeller craft to the jet age of commercial air travel.

"My baptism by fire into airline management happened suddenly in 1957. I came from a pie in the sky job as a steward for Eastern," says Jack Nee, looking back on his 38 years with Eastern Airlines.

"I started flying as a purser in November of 1946 after spending some time in the service. I wanted to do something different, something unconventional. Eastern was offering employment at that time, and I jumped at the opportunity to travel. I was born in New England, and I'd really only seen the Northeast coast. My training as a cabin attendant took place in an old theater building in Queens, New York. After that, I was domiciled at Eastern's Miami base. I wanted to partake of Miami's glamour." Jack's stay in Miami was a short four months. Eastern opened a new crew base in Boston in 1947. Miami, however, remained his favorite route. "I then transferred to Boston. It was small and only had 25 crews. I was glad to be a New Englander again. Miami was all right for overnight stays, but I didn't like living there. I missed the charm of New England, and my roots were

Jack Nee, Boston inflight supervisor until his retirement in 1984. He was an Eastern steward in 1946.

there.

"Our route structure out of Boston was skimpy, but we covered fourteen stops on our round-trips to Miami with stopovers in Atlanta and St. Louis. I soon realized what it meant to 'earn my wings every day,'" Jack says, recalling many long hard days of work. "Time flies when you fly, and eleven years as a flight purser went by quickly for me."

In 1957, I was appointed the first Inflight Supervisor of Inflight Service. Prior to this time we had been supervised by a manager called a Senior Flight Attendant," he remembered. "Nobody seemed to know just what a supervisor was supposed to do, so I had to 'wing it.' This was to be my baptism by fire," says Jack with a grin.

"My responsibilities were varied. I made crew assignments and when a crew member failed to show up for a flight, I covered it. I was responsible for scheduling vacations and sick leaves, bid sheet flying schedules, and training and retraining crews on new aircraft. I also doubled as a father confessor. I was always learning."

With the sixties came the jet age. Eastern introduced the DC-8 and the B-727 jet aircraft.

"I was fortunate to get in on the ground floor," says Jack. "I was assigned to the Douglas DC-8 assembly plant in California. After training there, I instructed cabin attendants in the required FAA ground school course. I traveled to all of Eastern's crew bases to introduce the new jet equipment."

The Boston base grew from 25 crews in 1947 to a complement of about 175 active crews. The supervisory staff grew to five. Out of Eastern's 6,500 flight attendants, 3,500 were male. When Eastern ceased operations, bases included Boston, New York (Kennedy and Newark), Miami, Chicago, Washington, Atlanta and San Juan, Puerto Rico.

"I've flown in everything from DC-3s to L-1011s," Jack says. "When I was first employed, Captain Eddie

Eastern pursers in the 1950s.

Rickenbacker was Eastern's president. His most quoted words were, 'It warms the cockles of my heart.' Thinking about my experiences, I would agree. It warms the cockles of my heart."

Jack's most amusing incident was connected with his 30th anniversary with Eastern. Washington base sent him a congratulatory letter which read:

November 16, 1976

Dear Jack,

On your 30th Anniversary with EAL, we would like to ask you a personal question: Was it hard serving meals in the open cockpits?

Seriously — our heartiest congratulations on such an important mile-stone!

The very best!

Sincerely,
Inflight Services
Washington

Jack replied:

November 19, 1976

Dear Washington Staff,

Your congratulations certainly "warmed the cockles of my heart."

I agree with you, during the past thirty years many things have changed. We used to have a President who enjoyed floating around the Pacific Ocean in a rubber raft, eating sea gulls; and now we have one who walks on the moon, playing with rocks.

The answer to your question is "Yes:" it was difficult serving meals in open cockpits. The major problem seemed to be keeping the napkins on the trays.

Thank you for your note.

Jack Nee

Jack's recollections span the history of inflight service. He says in reflection of his 38 years in aviation, "One could never have imagined that what the Wright brothers began as an experiment would develop into the giant of an industry it is today." Growing with it has been very gratifying. Jack Nee retired in February, 1984. He was one of the many in Eastern's rich history whose training and expertise helped flight attendants attain professional status.

A FLIGHT STEWARDESS'S WINGS OF PRIDE

Eastern Air Lines
Elinor Smith Lykins
1946 - 1947

A nurse with a love affair with travel and service.

"My love affair with flying began on a sunny afternoon in Stanley, Wisconsin, my birthplace, when I was seven years old. My mother took me to a neighboring farmer's field where an old biplane was giving rides to those brave enough to put on the helmet and goggles, get strapped in the open cockpit and thunder across the open field. I was overcome and begged, pleaded and cried for a ride, to no avail. She said it was far too dangerous for anyone to attempt. I was crushed and right then decided that someday that thrill would come my way.

"I graduated from the eighth grade in a one room country school, then went on to high school in a small town. I attended college for a year and then St. Luke's Hospital School of Nursing in Chicago for three years. When I graduated as a registered professional nurse, my life was ready to really "take off."

"After a year and a half as an operating room scrub nurse, I decided it was time to go flying. I had interviews by Eastern Air Lines in Chicago in late 1945 and was thrilled beyond words to be accepted for training as a flight stewardess as we were called. In February of 1946 I had my first plane ride. At the time I lived in Boston, so I flew on Eastern to Newark Airport to begin my wonderful adventure. We were housed at the forest Hills Inn on Long Island. I went to flight school five days a week for one month and graduated on March 15, 1946. Our diploma was signed by Captain Eddie Rickenbacker and to this day I proudly display it in my home. There were 25 women and nine men in the class at that time, and our picture was taken standing by a DC-3.

"I was one of five women sent to the Newark, New Jersey, base where we rented an apartment, sharing expenses and commuting to the airport by a city bus, sometimes getting up at 4:30 a.m. to be ready for an early morning flight. My first flight was trip 81 to St. Louis, Missouri, and return on trip 80. Names were included on the manifest of passengers. We always addressed them personally as we served them. We enjoyed a warm and interesting relationship with our passengers because we only had 21 seats. We could give more freely of ourselves and our services which would include a well-balanced meal served from our small galley at the left rear of the plane. Cold food was cold and hot food was hot. Meals were served on a nice tray after placing a pillow in the passenger's lap to give support. Rough weather was quite common, and liquids at times flew around along with the food. Air sickness was quite prevalent, and burp cups were used on a regular basis. We sometimes had a real *clean up* in very rough weather, but it was all part of the work we did.

"In 1946 Eastern flew what was called the 'merry-go-round.' We left Newark early in the morning, flew to Boston where we had a several hour layover and back to

Elinor Smith Lykins, as an Eastern stewardess. (Eastern Photo)

Eastern stewardesses and pursers, 1946. Elinor Smith Lykins is on the right in the first row by the pursers. (Eastern Photo)

New York, then on to Philadelphia, Baltimore, Washington and Richmond, Virginia. Our shortest meal service of the day was accomplished in 20 minutes between Washington and Richmond. It was very hurried, but a good full meal. We then left for the last leg of the trip leaving Richmond and arriving in Newark around 10 p.m. On night flights we served lovely trays of assorted sandwiches and a choice of hot coffee, tea, bouillon or hot chocolate, before making all passengers comfortable and secure for their trip. We conversed with those aboard and made many friends along the way, as we had time with 21 people to give personal and caring service.

THE UNIFORM CODE

"Our uniform code was very strict, and we all took great pride in looking the part of an Eastern stewardess. We wore beautifully tailored gabardine navy skirts and off-white jackets with red stripes on the sleeves with *Eastern Air Lines* in red on the left sleeve. *Flight Stewardess* was embroidered on the left upper arm of the jacket and our blouse was white. The uniform hat was worn forward at an angle over the right eyebrow and had our Eastern insignia the *Duck-Hawk* in red and blue on the left side of the hat. It was distinctive and very immaculate look and we were not permitted to ever look anything but our best. In the summer, rules stated that in the cabin we could take our jacket off, but at all other times we were in complete uniform. I must say, our topcoat was so handsome. It was a lovely royal blue gabardine with a red satin lining and we felt so special. We wore white gloves, and the only jewelry we were allowed to wear consisted of one small ring, an ID bracelet and a wrist watch. Glasses were not permitted, and perfume was not allowed. We always had to keep in mind that when in uniform we were to stay in complete uniform except in the hot summer when, as I stated previously, we could take our jacket off in the cabin while serving passengers.

"One of my favorite flights was to St. Louis. We stopped on Washington, Louisville, Evansville and went on to St. Louis, which took a total of five hours. We always had a good layover, and the city was full of interest. On one flight, as we were fairly close to St. Louis, the plane encountered extremely severe turbulence. I had all the passengers strapped in, but was talking with a passenger, who had an immediate need. Suddenly, I was thrown from the top of the plane to the floor and from side to side - flying around as if in space! A passenger grasped hold of me and held me until we passed through the turbulence. I was bleeding from my nose and had severe contusions on both knees. The captain came back as soon as he was able and saw one sorry looking stewardess! Ha! I was most disheveled and in complete disarray. And just like any woman, my greatest worry was my hose, the precious silk stockings of the day. They were all runs and completely unusable. As we all know, this item was so hard to obtain in 1946 and we always gave them extra care.

"After the captain surveyed the situation and found that all passengers were just fine, he proceeded back to the cockpit for the landing. I chose not to see a physician and spent my layover in bed in the hotel room. I had very stiff knees and a cracked nose, but bought new hose and had my uniform cleaned, and worked the trip back to Newark. I can never forget the concern and caring of Captain Piollet, a most kindly gentleman, but then Eastern Air Lines was known for their exemplary employees.

"Some of my modern day flight attendant friends have asked, 'Whatever in the world could you have served for a meal on a little DC-3?' My instant reply was, 'We served the most delicious food in a most orderly and efficient manner, pleasing our passengers with still another outstanding service Eastern provided in 1946.' At the time we did not serve alcoholic beverages aboard, but we did serve lovely food.

"When we started serving a meal, we took our napkin tray covers and soiled linen bag out of the buffet. We started our service from the rear forward, asking groups of six passengers at a time if they would care to have dinner. We placed a pillow on their laps, spread tray covers over them and inquired if the passengers would care for juice or soup, serving only one beverage at a time. If soup or juice was not desired, we asked the passengers if they would care for coffee or milk. If we had a limited amount of time between stations, we paged our passengers for the next station and served them first. They then had a maximum amount of time to eat. We picked up the trays as soon as possible after the passengers had finished eating, repacked casseroles in the jugs, put the soiled linen in the bag, and stored it in the buffet pit.

"Captain Eddie Rickenbacker flew with us on different occasions, boarding the plane as any other passenger taking a seat, and sitting quietly. He always wore his hat sitting squarely on his head and gave you a nice smile and thank you as he deplaned.

"I loved flying for Eastern, but was not using my nursing skills much. After giving much thought as to what to do, I resigned and interviewed for a position as a courier Nurse with the Santa Fe Railroad with headquarters in Chicago, Illinois. We were required to be experienced nurses as there were many needs aboard the trains. My runs were form Chicago to Los Angeles aboard the El Capitan, one of the finest coach trains of its day. With 396 passengers we carried two nurses to serve. We had a well equipped bedroom built in the Club Car as it was always in the center of the train. I served the Santa Fe Railroad from 1948-1951.

"I married Robert Lykins on September 16, 1951 in Chicago and started a new life at age 31. We have lived in Nashville, Tennessee since 1952 and I am now considered a Southerner. We have one son John, and two grandsons who live in Kansas. We travel there as often as we can for visits.

"In 1980 I asked an Eastern flight attendant aboard an Eastern plane if they had an organization of retired and current flight attendants. She told me about the Silverliners and I decided that I would get involved.

"I was able to organize and establish a chapter of Nashville Silverliners. It was so wonderful to again become a part of Eastern Airlines. We were able to work for them doing public relations, giving community service in their name. We called on accounts as a courtesy and gave wonderful functions for terminally ill children, disadvantaged youth, and children with a variety of illnesses. We had a yearly fund raising event to make money for projects in our area. I was privileged to go to the annual convention at Washington, DC in May 1980, as president of the Nashville Chapter. I saw first hand former and current flight attendants who had so much to offer to so many.

"From 1980 to 1991, I was most active in the organization and made many wonderful friends along the way. As I was then retired my time was given to Eastern and it became a way of life for me. I am so very proud to have served this wonderful airline and a sadness remains as I think of our loss, with its demise in January 1991. My memories will always give me great joy and a feeling of knowing I have been a part of an outstanding, unique and a totally *people* committed airline, our Eastern Airlines. Thanks for the memories!"

SNAP DECISION

Eastern Airlines
Edwina "Winnie" Gilbert

Vice President of Inflight Service

1956 - 1991

More and more, today's flight attendants are able to move into management and to enjoy successful careers in other areas. The following stories illustrate this

The airlines' first woman Vice President worked up to an executive office from being a flight attendant. "In

Vice President of Inflight Service presenting an award to flight attendant Margie Boyle, 1984.

1956, I made a snap decision," Edwina "Winnie" Gilbert declared with a snap of her fingers. "I was tired of working a nine to five job as a bank teller and also being a full time student at the University of Miami. I was driving down N.W. 36th Street in Miami when I noticed an Eastern Air Line stewardess crossing the street. It flashed through my mind that being a stewardess would get me out of my rut and it would be a refreshing change of pace from the hectic life I'd been leading, trying to juggle my job and school."

Winnie parked her car near Eastern's headquarters and walked into the Personnel Department. Several hours later, she walked out as Eastern Airlines' newest stewardess trainee.

At a very young age she had a natural spontaneity about life. She was born in White Plains, New York. Her parents moved often and she had to constantly adjust to new places and people.

She was in eight schools in one year when she was a small child. Her family moved to Miami and Winnie later graduated from Miami Edison High School. She majored in science at the University of Miami, because she wanted to excel and be like Madam Curie. However, this didn't work out for Winnie, so she joined a management-trainee program for the First National Bank. At the same time, she continued to take classes at the university.

Winnie's working career changed a great deal when she joined Eastern. She was correct in assuming that the job would be an interesting way to travel and to learn about the world and aviation.

She loved her job, but she also wanted to get married. In the sixties, Eastern's stewardesses were not permitted to be married and she quietly rebelled along with other stews. On the sly, she married Frank Gilbert and kept her job. She kept quiet about the marriage.

Her husband never answered the telephone, in case it was Eastern's scheduling department. But it wasn't long before the constant traveling and trying to keep her marital status a secret made her life very difficult. She typed a letter of resignation but before she could turn it in, Eastern offered her a promotion to instructor of stewardesses at Miami. She accepted, and three years later became the manager of the school.

Winnie handled the management of the training school with ease. Her position as Manager of the flight attendants involved her with upper management. Even though she didn't have the college degree it required, she knew she could handle more responsibility. In 1977, she was called into a company meeting, and she thought she might be offered the directorship of flight training. Instead, she was promoted over the current director to Vice President of Flight Training.

She was overwhelmed and realized it was a tremendous obligation. Winnie talked it over with husband Frank. The job paid $75,000 a year and she would be the first woman vice president at Eastern, in fact the first woman vice president of any airline. She accepted.

In her own way, Winnie was very much in favor of the women's movement and she had fought against male prejudice on the corporate level. As a top executive, she made quick, spontaneous decisions, directing over 6,000 flight attendants. She managed a $295 million dollar yearly budget to maintain Eastern's quality of inflight service. She saw to it that passengers got safe, friendly and courteous service.

Winnie tried her best to keep her employees happy. In fact, she tried a new concept to keep from furloughing and laying off flight attendants. Her program enabled senior flight attendants to take an unpaid leave of absence, and let Eastern cut costs by keeping its junior flight attendants.

A flight attendant was allowed up to one and a half years of maternity leave, using their sick leave and then six months with no pay. An additional six months after the baby's birth was allowed, if she elected to nurse her baby. In this way, the flight attendants retained their jobs until they returned to active status as a line flight attendant. In addition, Eastern had an employee profit-sharing plan and an employee purchase plan.

She kept abreast of the problems of labor management and was there at the last in the plea to save that fateful day toward Eastern's demise.

A CAREER
Eastern Airlines
Brazellia Wilson Baker
1970 - 1991

This flight attendant was selected for her poise, charm and expertise for management.

More and more, today's flight attendants are able to move into management and to enjoy successful careers in other areas. Bebe Baker was no exception: a young woman who had beauty, tact and personality, and a good business sense. Eastern Airlines spotted these qualities in Brazellia "Bebe" Wilson Baker while Bebe was a student at Spelman College in Atlanta in the late sixties. Eastern Airlines career representative, Ginny Henry, was at the Spelman campus recruiting flight attendants, and Bebe was an energetic volunteer helping with the program on weekends.

Bebe graduated in the spring of 1970, as an honor student with a major in piano and a minor in secondary education. Her plans were to teach, but volunteering for Eastern piqued her interest in becoming a flight attendant. After graduation, the airline hired Bebe as a part-time agent in air freight until a flight attendant class started in September 1970.

The six-week course involved eight hours of ground school and safety training in each type of aircraft, service procedures and food service in all aircraft, first aid, personal appearance and grooming.

Bebe's first assignment took her to Atlanta where she worked twenty days on duty and eleven days off each month. She was assigned to DC-9, DC-8 and Boeing 727 aircraft.

"We flew many charter flights for the Houston Oiler football team," says Bebe. "My first celebrity was really special. Flip Wilson was on a flight in first class, and since my maiden name was Wilson too, my crew insisted I work in first class. I enjoyed that so much, I gave him my Eastern wings. That caused a stir when I put in a request for another pair, which I had to pay for, but it was worth it. Flip gave me a big kiss and an autographed photo of himself as *Geraldine* that I really cherish."

In August 1972 Bebe was promoted to management as a personal appearance supervisor in Atlanta. She was responsible for regular personal appearance evaluations for over 200 flight attendants. Her job responsibilities involved overseeing around-the-clock checks on uniforms and grooming, as well as weight control.

"My office was across the hall from crew check-in," said Bebe. "Every flight attendant was weighed before his or her flight. If a flight attendant was one half pound or more overweight, one week was given for weight loss before that person was removed from the payroll until the weight was lost."

Bebe remembers one humorous incident. "I was weighing a senior male flight attendant, John George, who was one half pound overweight. As I looked away to record his weight he exclaimed, 'Don't put down that weight, Bebe, it's gone!' I couldn't believe my eyes. He'd dropped his pants to get rid of the extra half pound!"

Eastern Airlines flight attendant class of 1970 in mini-skirt uniforms. Bebe Wilson Baker is second from the left in the first row.

In May of 1975, a class action suit was brought against Eastern on weight control. The lawsuit claimed it was an unlawful practice. flight attendants thereafter were weighed semi-annually. At the same time, the words "steward" and "stewardess" were dropped and the nonsexist term "flight attendant" was adopted by the profession.

A class action suit on maternity was also brought against Eastern, who routinely took pregnant flight attendants off the payroll. The airline lost the case and adopted a new policy. Maternity was now considered an illness, and from the 28th week of pregnancy on, a flight attendant could take sick leave. Insurance covered the employee for hospitalization and physician's care. a new maternity uniform was added to the uniform selection.

Meanwhile, Bebe's career was still going up and up.

Eastern Airlines classic uniform, March 1980-1989.

In February of 1981, she was named Manager of Planning and Administration at the Boston base. She took on the responsibility of Manager of Administrative Staff members and coordinator of six supervisors. The duties included overseeing worker's compensation, maternity leave, audits for both liquor and shuttle flight monies, uniforms, a profit plan budget and monthly updates. Discipline problems were also under her supervision, and Bebe also acted as base manager in the manager's absence.

Base Manager Joe Callena nominated Bebe for the Black Achievers Award for the Greater Boston YMCA. Bebe won hands down for her work with the inner-city youth in seminar career planning, showing them how to interview for jobs.

"It gave me a sense of personal award in working with the children and giving to them and to the community. I was a role model and it was an honor to be nominated by Eastern."

Bebe was chosen by public relations as one of the Eastern flight attendants to appear in the movie "The House on Skull Mountain." Each flight attendant used in the movie was paid $213 and had the opportunity to enjoy a unique experience.

"Because of my work as a personal appearance supervisor I also judged a Miss Bermuda beauty contest and was given an all-expense-paid trip to Bermuda," said Bebe. "I enjoyed doing these things in public relations representing Eastern."

Bebe requested relocation from Boston to Atlanta in May 1981, in a decision to establish permanent residency and to marry Rodney C. Baker. She took a short-lived downgrade to supervisor. Bebe's career took off in a big way when she was chosen Manager of Supervision of Inflight Service in March 1984. One thousand flight attendants were domiciled at Atlanta, Eastern's largest base. Bebe had the responsibility of directing the activities of these flight attendants through ten supervisors who reported directly to her.

She represented Eastern in a positive way wherever she was and says of her career, "I've never stayed in a job long enough to get stagnant or bored."

Bebe had the quality of making any job look easy, she did it so well. People who need and like people have careers that take off like Bebe Baker's.

HER GRIT PREVAILED

Eastern Airlines
Joanne Fletcher
1965 - 1991

It's not always easy to pursue an inflight career. In the thirties the flying nursemaids were resented by the pilots. In the forties, UAL's Stewardess Union rejected Hawaiian native girls. In the sixties the United States was struggling with civil rights issues, and this story demonstrates the triumph of determination over racial bias.

"My story is of grit, and of determination to be all that I can be regardless of being black." says Joanne "Joni" Fletcher, who flew with Eastern for over seventeen years. "I had to learn the hard way that my very black skin did make a difference, even after the Civil Rights Act of 1964 became a law that prohibited job discrimination on the basis of race, sex or marital status."

Joni graduated from Roosevelt High School in Washington, DC in 1964. During her teens, the civil rights issue had erupted in violent confrontations in the U.S. In 1965, Joni was the first black woman hired by the Department of Agriculture Credit Union in Washington, DC. While working as a teller at the credit union, Joni became friends with Karen Collins, a white teller. Karen had interviewed with Eastern Airlines and was turned down for a flight attendant position because of a physical condition. Karen's interview sparked Joni's interest, and she asked Karen to outline the qualifications for the job. Joni was not a college graduate, but she had experience working with the public, she liked people and she wanted to travel. She knew this was a difficult job to get, but she was determined to do it. For the next eight months she made applications to most of the major U.S. airlines.

Joni's applications were mostly well received. In personal interviews, however, she was turned down. Undaunted, she applied again. As the months went by, she was repeatedly rejected in interviews, the inference being that she was too dark in color and that lighter skin tones were preferred.

"I got the idea that I was too noticeably black, and that my personality and other qualifications didn't count, and this hurt. I couldn't accept that skin color made that much difference, and I was more determined than ever to get a job as flight attendant. It was my third interview with Eastern Airlines at their headquarters in Miami, that Lorraine Roxie admired my persistence and my qualifications, and hired me for the July 1967 class.

"Our training began immediately. The night before we were to receive our wings, the entire class went to a Miami night club to celebrate. There were two blacks in the class, myself and Myra Tillson. Myra had light brown skin and mine was *black* black," declared Joni, with eyes flashing, remembering the incident. "The manager came over to our table to inform just me that I could order food and drink, but that I was not to dance with any whites. I was crushed by his remarks and began to cry. Suddenly I realized that even though my classmates had accepted me and I had earned my wings, I was going to have a difficult time being accepted by society."

Joni was placed on reserve status at her domicile and hometown in Washington, DC and soon thereafter was called for a flight.

"I went happily for my first flight in my new uniform and my snow white gloves that contrasted with my dark skin. On boarding the aircraft as a reserve flight attendant, I soon realized that the entire crew was unprepared for me. I received stony stares; not a single crew member introduced himself. The senior flight attendant crisply assigned my cabin station and then left me alone to my own resources. No one talked to me or even knew my name. I felt so alone among all those people on that airplane. I did my job, but at the end of the flight the tears came. When I returned to my domicile, it was only with the encouragement of my supervisor and my friends and family that I returned to the job that I'd worked so hard to get."

It wasn't long before a passenger made a scene that proved a turning point for Joni. She was serving dinner trays in her cabin zone when a woman passenger shrieked at her and pushed away the tray Joni offered.

"No, I will not take food from those colored hands!"

Joni returned to the buffet, put down the tray of food and approached the woman a second time. She placed her hands in front of the woman palms down and said, "No ma'am, I won't serve you from these colored hands, but I can serve you from these hands." Joni turned the pink palms of her hands up for the woman to see.

"She still refused to let me serve her, and later refused to let me hand her her coat with my colored hands. Other passengers, however, had observed my humor in handling the situation. Through the years I've used my sense of humor in difficult moments; it helps the hurt and eases the tension and makes everyone feel better," said Joni with a smile.

"My friend, Joseph Griffen, also black, is a former Air Force Major, now with the Federal Aviation Administration in Washington, DC. He has also helped me a great deal. He gave me some words of wisdom:

Joni, you represent black women wherever you are. Always be a lady, neat and clean and never wear a wrinkled uniform. Don't ever have a run in your stockings, or chipped nail polish or messy hair. You be yourself. You like people and it shows in your manner, your beautiful smile and in your voice. Be the very best you can be and life will be good to you.

She put her pain in the past and she wore her Eastern Wings with pride. She proved that being black and the hurts she encountered gave her a better perspective on life. Her personable warmth and genuine regard for people was evident to all those who worked with her and to all the Eastern passengers she served so well.

THE REPLY, "EASTERN!"

Willie Podesta Young 1957 - 1964

People working together as a team - an esprit de corps that lives on.

Willie Podesta Young was a professional model 1954-1957 while attending St. Louis University as the House Model for Bridal Originals and Sylvia Ann Formals. She had attended the Patricia Steven's Modeling School in 1954 and St. Louis University until 1957. She later in 1979 received a BA degree from Stevens College majoring in Business Administration with a minor in English and Political Science. Through the years she has continued part-time modeling. Her story as an Eastern stewardess follows...

"In the fall of 1957, I did not return to college because, foolishly so, I did not feel the need of continuing my education. At that time BLAW KNOX, a Pittsburgh Company, built a plant in my home town, Mattoon, IL. It was not unusual for our family to entertain many of the new arrivals and the BLAW KNOX people were no exception. I soon became friends with Captain Paul Duke (BLAW KNOX' pilot) and his wife Delores and reveled in the stories Paul told of the airlines. IN the fall of 1957, at the invitation of the Dukes, and permission of the President of BLAW KNOX, I flew to Pittsburgh to *fill and empty seat.* During that week a seat was available and I accompanied the plane to New York. While the BLAW KNOX people conducted business, Captain Duke took me on a tour of Newark.

"Being from a small town in the middle west this was truly the *big times* and I wanted to become a part of this exciting industry. It was a that time I told Captain Duke that I wanted to be a stewardess. When he asked, *Which airline?* I looked up, saw a sign that read: *FLY EASTERN AIR LINES* and without hesitation said *Eastern!*

"We inquired at the counter about an application and, after checking to see if there were any *cornstalks* caught between my toes, the agent suggested we go to 10 Rockefeller Center where interviews were being conducted. With three hours remaining before a scheduled return flight to Pittsburgh, we boarded the subway and my *life with Eastern* was about to begin. After filling out my application I was asked to wait and take a written test. Captain Duke explained why this was not possible (we were scheduled to return to Pittsburgh in an hour) and it was back on the subway to Newark. Because I could not take the test I never dreamed that I would hear from Eastern.

"Within a week a letter, hotel voucher and ticket authorization arrived for an interview in Miami! I remember walking into the conference room thanking the interviewer, Lew DeVane, for the ticket and the opportunity to be interviewed. He looked at me and said, 'congratulations and welcome to Eastern Airlines!' Excited? You bet! I became a part of the December 1957 class. Later I read the book *From The Captain To The Colonel* and found it interesting that Lew was known for hiring girls with hips! I trained at Eastern's Miami Springs Villa for five weeks after graduating I was given a ten day leave because I was not yet 21!

"My first trip was on a 60 passenger Connie with the final destination Montreal. The weather in Canada on January 21, 1958, was marginal shall we say. Several delays and six stops later, we canceled in New York. To say I was exhausted and ready for bed is a gross understatement. Even the fact that the room was really

Eastern Airline stewardess Willie Podesta Young in 1957.

small (we used to say *the rooms at the Paramount were so small that you slept with your head in the closet and your feet in the bathroom*) did not keep me from sleeping the entire layover.

"During the Golden Years it was not unusual to be able to hold a bid after a few months. On graduation day, I had the dubious distinction of being last on the seniority list; two months later I held a bid.

"During the early days, I flew many Chicago and St. Louis trips and had a tendency to fly the same trip for many months. When Minneapolis became a destination, it became a favorite layover city. Those were also the days that crews stayed together and not only did we work well together, we developed lasting friendships.

"Occasionally, I was asked to fly publicity trips for Eastern, a particular favorite was an open house at Wright Paterson Air Force Base. Captain Dick Merrill headed that crew. His stories were always wonderful and I feel privileged to have flown with this aviation legend.

"For two years I was privileged to fly with the Dodgers, when their players returned to Los Angeles after spring training. On our return trip to Vero Beach we stopped in various cities to pick up the minor league players.

"I always enjoyed flying the Super G-Constellation. This was a friendly plane, and being left handed, I truly like the galley. During my career it was not unusual to see many of the same passengers. We pulled our own tickets which gave us the opportunity, if interested, to learn passenger names. Many times people would gather in different areas of the plane, either to talk or play bridge. Those were also the days when front end crews were allowed to spend time in the cabin, meeting and greeting our passengers; it was also an era when children experienced the thrill of sitting in the Captain's seat.

"People made the flights memorable and in those days, time was available to sit and converse with them. On the Washington-New York Shuttle I met many very interesting people, not just from government, but form all walks of life. It was wonderful having Congressman William Springer from my home district in Illinois board and call me by name and telling his companion: "I crowned Willie when she was Centennial Queen."

"How can I ever forget November 22, 1963. My bid took me from Miami to Philadelphia with stops in Dallas and Miami. The B-727 was now part of the Eastern fleet. This trip had a two hour Dallas layover giving us time to go into the Love Field terminal for ice cream. On this day several men were around our airplane *doing things*. I asked the gentleman who seemed to be in charge, 'what's going on?' It so happened, he was the Director of Advance Communication for the White House and Air Force One. President Kennedy was arriving at that gate the following day; their job was to see that 18 phone lines were ready, so that they could be connected to Air Force One upon arrival. What transpired the following day stunned the nation. Our crew heard the news in Philadelphia that President Kennedy had been shot and killed.

"There are many things that come to mind when I look back on my days with Eastern Airlines. Most of all, I remember people working together to make our airline America's favorite way to fly. We were professional and considered it an honor and privilege to be a part of Captain Eddie's Airline. After all these years, I still retain friendships from my flying days.

"Many of us were extremely fortunate that Eastern allowed us to continue our association after our flying days ended. Like many other airlines, we have an alumnae association; ours is called Silverliners International. Fortunately, Eastern saw the value of using people in our organization to promote the airline. I am one of 12 women who are particularly fortunate, we were President of this International organization while Eastern was still part of the airline industry. My Eastern years were and continue to be a most important part of my adult life."

At the present time Willie is active in Eastern's Silverliners and attends conventions. She also manages Buck Grove Indian Trails, a public golf course in Mattoon, Illinois which is owned by her parents.

HAPPY BIRTHDAY TO THE USA!

Eastern Airlines
Jean Seluta-Brown
1964 - 1989

For a very special Bicentennial birthday party, Pan Am saluted America with a special flight to London. flight attendants were selected from 18 other airlines to represent America - Jean Seluta-Brown represented Eastern Air Lines.

Jean Seluta-Brown was born and educated in the Boston area. She worked in Personnel for a bank after graduation and then as a receptionist for Eastern Airlines. She then decided to apply for a position as a flight attendant as she wanted to experience the adventure and travel and she liked people. She says of her time flying:

"I was on reserve in Boston after six weeks of training in Miami Springs. Eastern was expanding very rapidly in 1964 and I lucked out only staying on reserve one month. I flew on all of Eastern's aircraft, but my two favorites were the A-300 and the B-757. Both were a pleasure for both the passenger and they were designed to make service easy for a flight attendant."

Jean's attitude of trying to make Eastern proud that they hired her paid off when she was chosen out of all Eastern's flight attendants to represent Eastern in 1976 for a very special flight.

PAN AM SALUTES AMERICA WHILE SOARING FROM A SIX AND ONE-HALF MILE HEIGHT

America's Bicentennial celebration soared to new heights on July 4, 1976 when Pan American World Airways threw a 200 birthday party at 35,000 feet aboard it's 747-SP Clipper Mayflower.

Flight 1776 carried 180 passengers and crew members which included a special compliment of 18 cabin attendants from U.S. domestic airlines. The participating airlines were:

For Pan American's salute to America's Bicentennial, 18 U.S. airlines were represented on flight 1976 to London. The flight attendants became celebrities in their colorful uniforms. Jean Seluta-Brown represented Eastern Airlines, sixth from right. (Pan Am Photo)

Air California
Air New England
Aloha
American Airlines
Continental Airlines
Delta Air Lines
Eastern Airlines
Frontier Airlines
Hawaiian Air
Airwest
National Airlines
North Central
Ozark Airlines
Piedmont
Southern Airlines
Texas International
United Airlines
Western Airlines
Pan American World Airways
Hughes Airways

During the six hour flight, each guest Hostess handed out a variety of mementos such as playing cards, inflight magazines, key chains, match books and route maps. The inflight menu featured typical American fare. The special printed menu was of special interest to passengers, many of whom had their copies autographed by the entire Pan Am and guest crew. Passengers were entertained by a selection of three feature films.

Arrival in London was heralded by a welcoming party at the Skyline Hotel. During the three day visit, the cabin attendants were hosted to a tour of London's famous landmarks, including: Buckingham Palace; Piccadilly Circus; Fleet Street; and the Tower of London. They were accompanied by members of Pan Am's London flight service base who acted as guides for their visiting colleagues from across the sea. The distinctively attired group became a tourist attraction in their own right as they paraded from site to site in uniform.

During their sightseeing tour stops were made at two of London's largest travel agencies, Thomas Cook and American Express. At each location the ladies dropped by to invite Briton's to visit the USA and to distribute promotional material about their airlines and travel in the United States.

Later that night the group was honored at a banquet dinner at the Mayflower Hotel prior to attending a musical review called *What's A Nice Country Like Us Doing In A State Like This* (a satirical look at America on the occasion of its 200 birthday) in which Tommy Tune was one of the stars.

This great salute to America was the idea of Mr. Neil Reyer, Pan Am's Director of Catering Services Planning who worked with Jeff Kriendlen, Director of Public

Relations. Not only did it promote Pan Am, but also promoted domestic carriers in the U.S. with the professional flight attendants chosen to represent each airline.[2]

OUT OF THE ASHES INTO THE FIRE

The impact of deregulation has affected every major airline in the United States. Some have had to reorganize and some have been bought out by other companies and some have lost the battle to survive.

The trauma experienced by Eastern Airlines in 1983 was nearly disastrous for the airline. The financial loss of the company amounted to $183.7 million.

President Frank Borman, in a letter to all company employees, said, "Part of the reason for the loss is that we spent most of the year fighting one another rather than the competition. If the year 1983 had any redeeming qualities at all, it was that out of the trauma emerged a clear commitment of *all* employee groups to do whatever is required to succeed. The Phoenix that arises out of the ashes is a promise for the future."[3]

The airline industry changed dramatically following deregulation in 1978. New low-cost airlines entered the free market. As a result of this competitive impact, many companies failed during the transition from a regulated to a deregulated industry.

Flight attendants were a vital work force involved in the Eastern trauma. Eastern was unique in its employee involvement and ownership. The flight attendants, along with other employees of Eastern Airlines, by forgoing wage increases and other benefits, had been given the opportunity to share in whatever profits the airline might generate. They had all become part-owners of the company through an employee stock ownership plan. This had a dramatic impact within the company through greatly improved morale of the employees and greater productivity.

The employees of Eastern took the ball in their own court. More productive personnel contracts with flight and ground crews improved communications with all personnel by establishing clear-cut objectives. Productivity goals were established, as well as service quality standards and a spirit of working together as a company.

At the same time, innovative marketing moves were made. A new Eastern hub at Kansas City was established. Another money maker for Eastern Airlines proved to be the "Midnight Specials," special flights with low fares, where freight contracts paid for the cost of flying the trip. This operation was the 'brain child' of Russell Ray, Jr., Senior Vice President of Marketing.[4]

Eastern was awarded a new international route from its Miami hub to London, with service inaugurated on July 15, 1985. Since Miami was a major hub, this new service gave London passengers access to most U.S. markets and connections on Eastern to the Caribbean islands, as well as to Central and South America.[5]

First class passengers to London were introduced to "Golden Wings" service, a seven-course dinner consisting of caviar and lobster served with champagne, a Caesar

In 1990 Eastern changed uniforms to a dark navy to represent THE NEW EASTERN shortly before its demise on January 18, 1991.

[2]Excerpts from *Pan American Passenger and Inflight Services,* September/October 1976, pp 16-17.

[3]Letter from President Frank Borman to Eastern Airlines employees, 29 February 1984.

[4]1991 interview with Major General (retired) B.W. McLaughlin, former Eastern Airlines Vice President of Marketing and Sales, New York Region.

[5]Ibid.

salad and standing rib roast with vegetables. A fruit and cheese course was served, followed by a dessert of Sacher torte or English trifle and international coffees. Excellence in dining was keynoted in all cabins. Executive service offered dinner and breakfast served on china and with linen. Economy class passengers received hot towels and a choice of dinner entrees, as well as a Continental breakfast.

For a while Eastern rose out of the ashes of near disaster to spread its wings. Profitability, however, was short-lived because of a highly competitive operating environment and the continuing high cost of Eastern's labor force. Wage concessions gained from employees were only temporary. With no long term wage concessions from employees, the airline found that in February 1986 it was unable to meet and service its debt and remain a viable company. The management and the board of directors were forced to sell the company to Texas Air. The rest is history — a sixty year old airline ceased to exist with the demise of Eastern Airlines January 18, 1991. The *Wings of Man* still exist in its many former employees' hearts.[6]

YOU GOTTA BELIEVE
Lynne Grubb, RN
Eastern Airlines
1991

A tribute to an airline whose spirit lives after its aircraft and crews have left the skies.

"In 1989, my common sense told me that I'd better take a computer course in order to gain a skill. My twenty year career with Eastern Airlines looked like it would be coming to an end. I ventured to Miami-Dade Community College to sign up for a class.

"At age 40 I began my education 22 years after I graduated from high school. May 1993 I graduated from the Medical Campus, with Phi Theta Kappa honors and I earned an Associate degree in nursing. I passed the Board Exams and I am currently working as a Registered Nurse at Camillus Health Concern, a health facility for the homeless.

[6]1991 interview with Major General (retired) B.W. McLaughlin, former Eastern Airlines Vice President of Marketing and Sales, New York Region.

Lynne Grubb, flight attendant for Eastern Airlines, 1990.

"Years ago Eastern had a slogan, *You gotta believe*. These are great words to live by. You have to believe in yourself. Because people believed in me. I believe in myself. If you become overwhelmed and discouraged, think - "if they can do it, I can do it."

"When I wrote the *Miami Herald* with the demise of Eastern in December 1991 to express my feelings, the *Miami Herald* chose the slogan, *Thanks for the Memories* for the title. The Eastern Silverliners decided this would also be appropriate to put on our shirt and other items."

THANKS FOR THE MEMORIES[7]

To The Editor:

As any flight-crew member can tell you, flying for a living is not a job, it's a way of life. And oh, what a life! My 22 years at Eastern Airlines were filled with memories that I will always treasure.

Dancing in Dallas with Bob Hope, being snowed in in Syracuse, holding the hand of a POW returning from Vietnam, driving a courageous old woman with concentration-camp numbers tattooed on her inner arm to South Beach because she was afraid of getting lost, sharing a child's joy of his first flight, listening to an articulate Muhammad Ali personally acknowledge his fellow passengers on the shuttle, getting Whitey Ford's and Hank

[7]Lynne S. Grubb, *Miami Herald,* 1991.

Aaron's autographs, calming the fears of nervous flyers, sunsets in Los Angeles, sunrises in Puerto Rico, being a fairy godmother to some very special passengers on Flight 5 to the North Pole . . . and of course, Eastern's most valuable asset, my fellow employees, who are now my extended family.

No, flying was not just a job, any more than Eastern was just another airline. Eastern Airlines may now be put to rest alongside Captain Eddie Rickenbacker — but Eastern's spirit will live on in its people.

Lynne S. Grubb
Miami

Pan American World Airways folded it's wings in 1991. The entire world felt this loss . . . the airline that contributed so much to commercial aviation and its golden wings of excellence.

AN ERA GONE BY

Prestigious Pan Am's Training

Pan American employed interesting people. Some had law degrees, some had teaching degrees, and some were nurses. One flight attendant based in San Francisco was a part-time dentist between flights. And some flight attendants were just out of high school.

Pan Am's most famous of flying boats, *Atlantic Clipper*, the B-314, as shown, lifts away for a transatlantic flight to Europe, 1939. (Pan Am Photo)

Being a flight attendant for Pan Am sure beat a nine-to-five job. The pay was good and the benefits were excellent, if you liked variety and could pass the many steps in the hiring process.

Variety it was: in the schedule, the hours, the people and the international routes. The average age of flight attendants was thirty-four. No one was quitting, and the average flying career lasted between ten and fifteen years. Pan American had not hired any flight attendants since 1980.

Since Pan Am's merger with National Airlines, some basic requirements changed most notably the second language requirement. Not many of National's flight attendants could meet this requirement but the person with a second language was given hiring preference.

Earning the coveted Gold Wings was a long and arduous process. The first step was an application which identified the general basic requirements. The minimum age was eighteen, and one must be a high school graduate to qualify. Most of Pan American's flight attendants, however, had several years of college to their credit. Weight requirements were in proportion to height, and the minimum height five feet, three inches, in order to be able to reach the overhead bins.

The next step involved a series of interviews. The first: A group interview and if it was satisfactory, a letter was sent to the applicant arranging a second interview conducted by two interviewers. This second session lasted between one and two hours. If the applicant passed, a third interview was arranged within two weeks. The third meeting was approximately thirty minutes long and was conducted by a supervisor. If the applicant successfully passed this final interview, a company-paid physical examination was arranged by the airline.

On arrival at the Pan American flight attendant Training Center in Hawaii, a home study course of at least thirty-five units was assigned each trainee. The course was to be completed by the perspective flight attendant at his or her own pace. Written examinations and performance tests were given in mock-up situations. The entire self-study course had to be completed by the end of the fourth week.

The training was rigorous. Trainees were taught grooming, the use of makeup and uniform fitting as part of the four week course. Other study units included: a week of emergency procedures on all types of aircraft; nutrition and all types of food and bar service for first class I and II and economy class; the operation of galley and cabin equipment for all types of aircraft; intercultural communication; airport codes; documentation; special passenger handling; flight procedures; Pan American people; travel benefits; bidlines; deadheading; conduct guidelines; coping with stress; and how to project the correct image of a flight attendant.

Trainees who successfully completed all of the training and performance tests were awarded silver wings and were sent to one of the following domicile bases: London, New York, Miami, Houston, Los Angeles, San

Francisco, or Honolulu. At the end of a six-week probation period, the flight attendant received the coveted Gold Wings of Pan American World Airways.

The era of Pan American World Airlines will always remain a highlight in world aviation history. Its' proud history lives in the hearts of many who were chosen to wear the Gold Wings that exemplified its service.

AN ANGEL WITH WINGS

Pan American Airways

Elaine Zwiener Lee

1946

Pan Am's international routes in World War II post war days took crew members away from their home base many days at a time.

She had a goal: to work herself around the world. Born in New Richland, Minnesota, Elaine Zwiener had a natural gift for languages, and on graduation from high school she received an American Legion scholarship to the college of her choice. She majored in political science and completed four years of study in three years by attending summer school. She continued her studies at the University of Mexico, where she learned a great deal about the Spanish culture. On her return to Minnesota Elaine took a foreign service examination and enrolled in a course in Japanese given by the Army.

"I knew it would be a long time before I heard results from the State Department," she recalled. "On an impulse I took off for Miami to apply for a position as stewardess in Pan Am's Latin American Division. The man in my life, Herb Lee, needed time to start his radio station WKTY in Wisconsin, and I wanted to fly and see the world. I was born with a wanderlust and I decided I would work my way around the world." Elaine joined Pan American in 1946; her salary was $350 a month. Uniform cost was paid by the company and a *per diem* allowance paid for layovers overseas, including a tipping allowance. For eighteen months she flew DC-3s and DC-4s from Miami to Argentina, Columbia, Brazil, Venezuela, the Canal Zone,

Elaine Zweiner Lee, purser for Pan American Airways, 1950.

Elaine Zwiener Lee, Pan American stewardess. (Pan Am Photo)

Pan American purser, Elaine Zweiner Lee (first row, far right), shown with her Pan American Clipper crew, 1950. (Pan Am Photo)

Guatemala, Mexico, and the islands of the Caribbean. In October 1947, she worked on Pan American's 20th Anniversary Flight from Key West to Havana.

Her next assignment, 1948, was with the Pacific-Alaska Division based in San Francisco, where she was promoted to purser. This position made her responsible for official documents on all her flights, and she ordered all food served aloft. Elaine's flights took her to Honolulu, Wake Island, Guam, Tokyo, Shanghai, Manila, Bangkok, Calcutta, New Caledonia, Australia, and New Zealand.

The course in Japanese gave her real satisfaction, for the phrases she had learned to speak were understood in Tokyo. In her spare time she studied French, wanting to become more fluent in that language. In San Francisco Elaine leased a ranch house with five other stewardesses. It had a tennis court and pool.

"It was the gathering place for all our friends," she related. "I liked San Francisco a lot, but I still had Europe and Africa to see. I was already planning ahead for my next transfer to Pan American's Atlantic Division."

She was assigned to New York in 1949 and finally got to use the French she had been practicing. Out of New York, she flew to London and Paris on the Constellations and Clippers.

"I also studied Portuguese so I could get along nicely in that language. I flew to Calcutta and completed my last link around the world," she said beaming. "It took me three years and 600,000 miles of flying. It was slow, but I think I made a record, the slowest global circumnavigation in the history of air travel. It gave me a thrill to have reached my goal."

Many of Pan Am's trips were twenty to thirty days in duration. Layovers were two to three days at each point. It took twelve to fourteen hours to fly from San Francisco to Honolulu and another twelve hours to Wake Island, with an additional ten hours to Tokyo and six and a half hours form Tokyo to Shanghai. Flights from Shanghai to Calcutta took fifteen and a half hours flying time. From New York, with a refueling stop at Newfoundland, the flight to Shannon, Ireland was fifteen to sixteen hours. The trip continued to London, Brussels, Rome, Istanbul, Damascus, Iraq, New Delhi and Calcutta.

A thirty-day South Africa round trip went from New York to the Azores, Lisbon, Dakar, Leopoldville and Johannesburg. Each flight leg had stopovers. Trips were assigned by the flight scheduling department at each division, as trips were not bid at that time.

Elaine was chosen by Pan American to participate in their 20th Anniversary flight in 1947. The ceremonies were held at Meacham Field, the site of the original takeoff. A similar ceremony was conducted in Spanish in Havana.

Elaine appeared on the *Ed Sullivan Show* for being chosen to participate in Pan American's 20th Anniversary Flight. She was also honored on his show for being the first purser to complete a circuit of the globe and for speaking six languages.

Elaine was also on the press plane that flew President Harry Truman to Guam to fire General MacArthur. She was on flights returning Japanese War Criminals to Tokyo. All her flying encompassed 15 times around the globe.

In 1951, Elaine's thoughts turned toward the man at WKTY in LaCrosse, Wisconsin. Herb Lee's radio station had been a great success, and Elaine and Herb were married on April 21, 1951.

The years never changed Elaine's enthusiasm for people and travel. Life was good to this beautiful lady. She became the mother of eight children. Her family and grand children were a great joy to her. She had a real zest for life, and was active in her community and church, and an avid skier as well. Every chance, Elaine and Herb had to dance they cut a mean rug while everyone stopped to watch.

When she had been asked to sum up her experience as a flight attendant Elaine said, "Pan American presented me the greatest opportunity to use my college skills. The job offered travel, the use of foreign languages, service to others and leadership opportunities. I had a strong dedication to a great company. My years with Pan Am laid the groundwork for a rich and full life."

Elaine died in 1991 after a long illness.

PAN AMERICAN AIRWAYS

I met a lovely lady, Mrs. Paul C Keenan, who flew for Pan Am between 1953 and 1954. She wanted me to write about her roommate who was also a Pan Am stewardess. A story of care and love to give away to make Christmas special when she couldn't go home to loved ones. I have been given permission by both the author Marion F. Leach and the story she tells about Diane's roommate Lynn Peterson Schriver:

The December Without A Christmas Day

by Marion F. Leach

"The holidays were coming but it surely did not feel like it! For a young lady out of northern Illinois the balmy weather of Honolulu was not the least bit conducive to creating the Christmas spirit. Too warm, too green, too sunny, too flowery! All wonderful for sure but not for Christmas, thought she. It all made for a bit of longing for home. But that was not to be this December of 1952. Young Lynn Peterson was out on her own, a University of Illinois graduate earlier that year and just three months on the job as a stewardess for Pan American Airlines. It would be her first holiday time away from her family and just thinking about the warmth and love she'd be missing was depressing to say the least. She liked her job; youthful energy kept her tireless; natural friendliness made meeting new people easy and intellectual curiosity found satisfaction in the strange new places her flights took her. Nevertheless, as Christmas approached she felt a sense of longing of the old familiar holidays she'd known. She thought of her wonderful Swedish mother whom she would miss and something this perceptive lady taught her surfaced in her mind — *when you have a problem or get to feeling low, find someone for whom you can do something nice.* A sort of golden rule piece of advice and what a handy time to have it come to mind! Her flight layover in Hawaii at Christmas wouldn't be so bad if she could do something special for someone.

"That opportunity arose on Christmas Eve. Her stewardess roommate became ill and Lynn took her flight — Honolulu to Wake Island — an eleven and a quarter hour trip. Why not? If she couldn't be at home she might as well have Christmas in the air. Now, the flight was really a special airline airlift; Pan Am aircraft, American Airline pilots and forty-four men of various ranks headed for the Korean War and one stewardess, Miss Peterson! Christmas was so important to her that among her last minute preparations was a dash to find treats to have on board for her passengers. She got a comb for each man and wrapped cookies and candies, all good stocking stuffers, and secreted them on the plane. They were flying west and Lynn knew that meant they would cross the International Date Line and lose a day - Christmas Day! Perhaps all those men on board knew this too and missed their families at this season just as much as Lynn and that explained the gloom which invaded the cabin. But Miss Peterson didn't really intend to miss Christmas Day - she would celebrate as they flew across that date line. A word to the captain assured her she'd be informed as they approached the invisible divider.

"Just before they got there, she aroused her resting passengers with a cheery greeting — 'Close all the blinds, please, Christmas is coming!' Then she startled them by

Pan Am placed an order for 25 747s in April 1970. The aircraft made international travel safer. The navigation is the same system that guided the Apollo space flights. The upper deck first class lounge can convert into a dining room. (Pan American Photo)

requesting that each man take off a sock and find a place to hang it! Laughter filled the plane! 'Why?' they yelled. Lynn replied, 'Santa Claus is coming!' Off came the socks, down went the lights and as Lynn traversed the aisles stuffing all those warm socks with a comb, cookies and candy, she led them in Silent Night. They sang every verse of every Christmas carol they knew and music was never sweeter. Her little galley was lit by the only candle on board but it provided just the right atmosphere for the coffee and tea she served with the sweets. They had no Christmas Day but they did have Christmas! It was warm and wonderful and surely unforgettable. When they landed a few hours later on Wake Island, it was December 26th.

"Some of the men on board wrote to Pan Am and commended Miss Peterson on her originality, care and concern for her passengers and her love of Christmas. Her scrapbook carries the official letter of commendation Pan Am sent her.

"That was not the end of this December without a Christmas Day. After her layover on Wake, Lynn flew on to Tokyo and as luck would have it, on her return flight going east, she gained a day. Two New Year's Eves, one on Wake and the other in Honolulu. Dear roommate was still ill and had one more request for Lynn — replace her at a party. Again, why not, it might be fun! It turned out to be much more than fun — a true serendipity of enormous importance for there she met the handsome Marine flyer who would one day be her Mr. Wonderful!

"Jake and Lynn Peterson Schriver became our friends in Carlisle, Pennsylvania at the Army War College and today we are neighbors here in South Carolina's Low-country. When the holidays arrive we four will raise a cup of cheer to the December that had no Christmas Day but surely had the true spirit of the season," said the former roommate, Diane Keenan.

The Pan American upper deck first class lounge and dining room on a 747 in 1980.

THE GLAMOROUS JOB

Pan American Airways Stephanie Kimmel Knapp 1971 - 1977

Her friend had the glamorous job. She worked to fly to far away places . . .

Stephanie Kimmel Knapp, Pan American purser in the cockpit of a Pan Am Clipper.

Stephanie Kimmel graduated from Iowa State University in 1971 and landed a good job with Quakers Oats Company in Chicago. She shared an apartment with three other girls, and attended graduate school at night. Her social life came to a standstill as she burned the midnight oil studying for classes.

In comparison, one of her roommates, Marilyn, was living the glamorous life of a Pan Am purser. Marilyn had never learned to read the newly computerized bidlines, and was always on a reserve schedule. The Chicago lines at the time were the "double crossings:" Chicago - London - Detroit - London - Chicago, and rarely would any purser call in sick for fear of losing too much flying time. Marilyn called into flight scheduling from places like Bonwits and Bergdorfs. She wore fur coats, had attractive friends and took her parents on exotic vacations.

Stephanie looked at her own situation of all work and no play and decided that Marilyn's job was what she wanted. She had been an excellent student, she was attractive and she spoke French. After several interviews, Pan Am hired her as a purser.

Unlike the carefree Marilyn, however, Stephanie was assigned the New York Region and flew the European and African routes. She was always on an airplane flying somewhere, and logged between 85 and 100 hours of flying time each month. She did continue to see a young Naval aviator, Ken Knapp, when her busy schedule permitted.

Pan American pursers Stephanie Kimmel Knapp (right) and Lisandre Rockerback hamming it up in a 747 engine nacelle, 1970s.

She had met Ken when she lived in Chicago. The two were both native Iowans with similar backgrounds and much in common. Their romance flourished, with Stephanie commuting between New York and Ken's duty station near Virginia Beach, Virginia, and eventually they married.

Stephanie was very junior in seniority at the time of her wedding, and she was only given a few days off for the occasion. It was February and cold. After four days off she reported back to work in New York with a bag full of winter clothes, only to be assigned a fourteen day trip to Africa. She later confessed that Africa became one of her favorite destinations, but not when she was newly married and carrying a suitcase of woolen clothing.

On Stephanie's return to Virginia Beach, where the newlyweds were making their home, she found a note from her husband saying that he had been unexpectedly called for a shakedown cruise on an aircraft carrier, destination unknown. Within a month, Ken's ship was in Vietnam. Fortunately, Stephanie's position with Pan Am enabled her to meet him in Manila and other ports throughout the final years of the war.

But things were tough for her at home when she was between flights. During one month in Virginia Beach she attended four memorial services for members of Ken's squadron who had been killed in combat. She flew Monday through Thursday, New York - Frankfurt - Munich and return to New York. At home she attended memorial services and saw the American flag presented to little children. And then she was assigned a flight from New York to Lisbon and Barcelona. The following anecdote is in her own words:

"I worked a flight to Lisbon and Barcelona right after attending my fourth memorial service for friends of my husband. They were all in the same squadron stationed on an aircraft carrier off the coast of Vietnam. While in Barcelona I developed insomnia and, in retrospect, nearly suffered an emotional breakdown. I exploded in hives, and the Pan Am doctor in Spain said that I should deadhead to New York as a passenger.

"In Lisbon we stopped to pick up a full load of passengers. I learned later that they included a scientist who was developing a cure for poisonous scorpion bites. He had with him a case of three of the most deadly kind of scorpions. Somehow the case with its contents had escaped the skymarshals and the high security. They had eluded Lisbon's metal detectors for obvious reasons. As the flight progressed the scientist obliged travel-weary passengers by displaying his cargo to those passing by on their way to the aft lavatory.

"About three and a half hours from New York, the scientist noticed that there were only two scorpions for display. He informed the flight service crew of the dilemma and all the flight attendants sought my counsel with respect to whether or not the passengers should be informed. I found this request for my opinion flattering but hilarious, since I was the person being sent home with mental exhaustion. We all concurred that although panic was a possible consequence, the passengers should have the option to keep their feet off the floor and their children in their seats.

"The announcement was greeted with complete calm, and the passengers were absolutely nonchalant about the scorpion on the loose. Barefoot children continued to walk down the aisle as they had before and adults seemed altogether unconcerned. Even more amazingly, the purser placed the remaining scorpions in the COCKPIT for safekeeping! At this point I was certain that the entire world had gone mad, or that I was further over the edge than even the doctor in Barcelona had diagnosed. If anyone on board was going to be stung, I certainly didn't want it to be one of the flight deck personnel!

"After all the passengers, including the scientist with his last two scorpions, had disembarked in New York, I too left the aircraft. Then I remembered my uniform hat was still in the overhead rack and I returned to retrieve it. I was stopped by armed guards and asked whether I was the representative for the "Society." (Apparently, the S.P.C.A. had been summoned to meet the flight and direct the search for the errant scorpion.) I told them no, that I was a crew member. Our unpaying passenger was never recovered, the aircraft was fumigated, and we all lived to tell about it."

After a good rest Stephanie returned to flight duty and flew for a total of six years. When Ken returned from Vietnam the two had several extended honeymoons to Nepal, Iran, Africa, and the Orient, flying around the world. Stephanie's years as a Pan Am purser were enjoyed at the time and savored today, with memories of wonderful people and places.

Stephanie says, "I think the most important ingredients for being a successful flight attendant are a sense of humor and a strong sense of self-worth." She feels that a sense of humor is necessary to deal with the long hours and the improbable situations a flight attendant encounters. A sense of self-worth is necessary because the traveling public as a whole often undervalues the contributions of the individual flight attendants. She feels that many times their courage is tested, as in the case of Uli Derickson's extraordinary stamina and confidence during the long hijacking siege of TWA's flight 847 in the summer of 1985 and the crew in the Sioux City crash in 1989 of United's flight 232 where fast action of flight attendants saved lives."

Stephanie resigned her position with Pan Am in 1977 to attend graduate school at Columbia University. She earned her M.B.A. in 1979, and then worked for the Prudential Insurance Company. Ken resigned his Naval commission and is now an executive for an American commercial bank in London, where Ken and Stephanie and their three children live today.

The interior of a Pan American Lockheed L-1011-500, in the first class cabin, 1983.

THE NINETY-YARD DASHES

Pan American World Airways

Leslie Pickett Butner

1980s

Interviewing for a special job calls for poise and confidence. It helps to be ready and on time, too.

Chairman Seawell presents Pan American wings to National Airlines flight attendant Linda Miller and National Airlines Captain Don Lovern on January 7, 1980, the day of the National/Pan Am merger.

"Looking back it's a miracle that I ever got hired," says Pan Am flight attendant Leslie Pickett Butner. "During my last term at the University of Oregon, I began inquiring about the airlines. Pan American was interested, but their training class started a month before I was to graduate from college, and decided it wasn't worth it to quit school so close to graduation. Pan Am agreed, and said they'd interview me again in the fall." After graduation, Leslie moved to Portland. She decided to get some kind of job to support herself until she could reapply to Pan American.

"I worked three separate jobs, two of which were part-time, to get by," Leslie recalls. "I worked weekends at a boutique and weekdays at the Nike warehouse. I also tutored in Spanish. One of my students was a rich girl who was learning Spanish so that she could interview with Pan Am for flight attendant. She was very pretty, and I think she was putting all her stock in her looks, because she never studied her lessons and consequently never learned any Spanish. I was lucky if she ever showed up for her tutoring sessions."

Leslie Picket Butner, Pan American flight attendant shown in 1984. She speaks fluent Spanish and Portuguese.

Leslie's fall interview with Pan American was scheduled for the same day as that of her lackadaisical student. "Her interview was just before mine," Leslie says with a laugh. "When she came out of the office, I asked her how she did, and she said it seemed to go okay, adding, 'They asked me if I could speak Spanish and gave me a sheet to translate. I couldn't read it, but I did manage to pick out a few words I recognized.' Then she looked directly at me and said, 'I know you'll do just fine with the Spanish. I told them you were my teacher.'

"Who needs enemies when you've got friends like that? I wanted to curl up and die. Fortunately, I speak Spanish fluently, so that wasn't a problem. But with a student like that, they probably thought I was an awful teacher."

Leslie was notified of a second interview a few days later. She had to make up an excuse to get off work, so she told her manager at Nike that she had a doctor's appointment that afternoon and would have to leave early.

"My boss forgot all about it and took me out of town to a distant warehouse that was seldom used. It was so dusty that when we finished our business there I was a dusty mess from head to toe. I knew that I would have to wash my hair and change my clothes, but time was getting short, so I reminded my boss of the doctor's appointment. We rushed back to the main warehouse in town, and from there I immediately rushed home.

"When I got to my apartment, I found myself locked out and remembered that I'd left my jacket at the warehouse, and my keys were in its pocket. I panicked because I knew there was not time to go back to the warehouse and still get to my interview on time and looking halfway decent. I rushed to the manager's apartment and borrowed a key.

"Of course, this had to be the day I chose to use a new hair conditioner. My hair was a greasy mess and it took thirty minutes to get it right. What a day! But the funny thing was that I didn't have time to think about the interview itself. I got there just in time with no time to spare to be nervous. I flopped myself in front of the two interviewers and then I started to laugh. I ended up telling them the whole story. We all laughed about it. As it turned out, I guess they figured that if I could make all those ninety-yard dashes from one place to another and still get to the interview on time, they wouldn't have to worry about me being punctual.

"I was asked back for a final interview and finally got the job. I loved my job with Pan Am. It also afforded me the opportunity to give passes to my mother. She was even a passenger on some of my flights.

National Airlines merged with Pan American on January 7, 1980. The first National crew is shown with National's founder, G.T. Baker, standing in the center.

NewsWing

EASTERN AIR TRANSPORT INC.

REG. U.S. PAT. OFF.

A Division of North American Aviation, Inc.

Vol. 5 — Brooklyn, N. Y., March, 1932 — No. 7

THESE VIEWS SHOW SOME OF THE OUTSTANDING FEATURES OF EASTERN AIR TRANSPORT'S PASSENGER FLEET OF 18-PASSENGER CURTISS CONDORS

When Flying With Eastern Air Transport

WHAT SAFEGUARDS PROTECT THE PASSENGERS?

You have a right to know. Turn to Page 2 and read the article, "Air Service For the Passenger Provided by Eastern Air Transport." You will find these eight pertinent questions answered:

1. Why Only Multi-Motored Airliners for Passengers?
2. Why Two Pilots on All Planes of Over Six Passenger Capacity?
3. Why Two-Way Radiophones on All Passenger Planes?
4. Why 1,093 Miles of Leased-Wire Communications?
5. Why the Most Expensive Flying Instruments Provided by Any Transport Company in the World?
6. Why Is Costly High-Test Aviation Gasoline Used Exclusively?
7. Why Extreme Conservatism As To Suitable Flying Weather?
8. Why No "High-Speed" Planes For Passenger Service?

REFLECTIONS

Yesterday *and* Today

Old Logo
Eastern Air Transport

New Eastern Logo
We Have to Earn
Our Wings Every Day

1930s Curtiss Condor

1980 L-1011 A/C

Old Interior
1931 A/C

New Interior
1981 L-1011

EARLY DAYS

Marion Cook

The 1930's style of flying

Marion Cook Glynn of Meadville, Pennsylvania, first took to the skies in an 18 passenger Curtiss Condor. She was the first lady hired out of a group of seven young women who began flying for Eastern Air Transport, predecessor of Eastern Airlines, in 1931.

Early Qualifications — 1931
Age: under 28
Ht.: max. 5'4"
Education: college graduates or registered nurses
Wt.: maximum 125 lbs.
Flying time - 40 hours a week: $125.00 a month

Flight Attendant Duties *(as indicated in the first Flight Attendant Service Manual)*

- Offer newspapers, gum, cotton for the ears, and ammonia capsules for the passengers.
- Serve coffee from thermos bottles
  Offer bags of donuts
- Adjust the altimeter at each stop to confirm the altitude on the ground, and make certain the air speed indicators in the cockpit function.
- Assist station hands in a bucket brigade to fuel the airplane.
- Before each flight, clean the cabin, sweep the floor, dust off the seats, window sills, etc.
- Make sure that all seats are securely fastened to the floor.
- Warn passengers against throwing cigars and cigarettes out the windows.
- Carry a railroad timetable in case the plane is grounded.
- Keep an eye on the passengers when they go to the lavatory to be sure they don't mistakenly go out the emergency exit.

Eastern's 50th anniversary of inflight service, 1981.

Pan American's Sikorsky S-40 flying boat, *American Clipper*, the world's first commercial four-engine aircraft. All four-engine Pan American aircraft were called *Clippers*.

NEW HORIZONS

1970s - 1980s - 1990s

Deregulation in 1978 brought about the growth of commuter airlines.

In 1986, USAir is a result of both mergers and deregulation

"Pan American's Bicentennial Birthday Party Salute to America" was a special flight to London on July 4, 1976. Flight attendants were selected from 18 U.S. airlines to represent America on flight 1976, on a Clipper Mayflower, a 747-SP aircraft. (Pan Am Photo)

Lacy Woodcock, Jr., Piedmont - USAir flight attendant from August 16, 1960 to April 11, 1992. Lacy is shown in the engine nacelle of a B-767. He was in Piedmont's first class of pursers trained for international flights, May 1987.

USAIR HISTORY

A Product of Mergers and Deregulation

The predecessors of USAir are many. It was first formed in 1937 under the name of All-American Aviation. The airline had quick pick-up service of air mail to isolated communities that did not have airport facilities. By 1949 airports had been built on their route system and passenger service was begun on their DC-3 aircraft.[1]

Passengers were first flown from Pittsburgh to Washington, D.C. and routes expanded to New York, Buffalo and Cincinnati. The name was changed to All-American Airways with the introduction of passenger service.[2]

The name changed to Allegheny Airlines in 1953 when the operation included Boston and Cleveland in the eastern states and Detroit in the west. Other aircraft slowly replaced the DC-3, and operations and maintenance were moved to Pittsburgh from Washington, D.C. Allegheny merged with Lake Central Airlines in 1968. By 1972 a merger with Mohawk Airlines followed. As other routes were added to Arizona, Florida, Louisiana, North Carolina and Alabama, a new name emerged for the merger conglomerate in 1979 — USAir.[3]

Piedmont airlines merged with USAir in 1986. Piedmont's route from Charlotte to London further expanded USAir's system. In 1988 Pacific Southwest Airlines was also merged to develop a route system with USAir Express connecting 270 cities across the U.S., Canada, Bermuda, the Bahamas, Puerto Rico, London, Frankfurt and Paris. The USAir Shuttle operates from the former Trump Shuttle and Eastern Airline routing, flight crews and aircraft.[4]

In 1992 British Airways added Capital and ownership of 25% to boost USAir's cash flow. The London route structure is managed by British Airways, which is the airline trend for global airlines.

TREASURES OF 30 YEARS

Piedmont Airlines
USAir
Patsy Benton
1963 - Present

For flight attendants, flying is a way of life . . . some fly for decades. The next two brief vignettes of flight attendants give special quotes.

Patsy Benton started flying for Piedmont after a short stint working in a credit office. She had two years college prior to her first job. Flying as a flight attendant appealed to her. "I thought it would be fun," says Patsy. I've worked both domestic and international flights since the

[1] *An Illustrated Guide To The World's Airlines*, William Greer & Gordon Swansborogh, pp 276-277.

[2] Ibid.

[3] Ibid.

[4] Information provided by flight officer David Hobart, USAir Shuttle.

USAir merger, but I prefer domestic flights.

"I first checked out on the DC-3 so I've seen a variety of aircraft. My favorite today is the B-737-300. I have enjoyed it all. The last thirty years have been everything to me! The people I've met, the places I've been and the friends I've made are treasures that I'll never forget. I cannot imagine my life without being a flight attendant!"

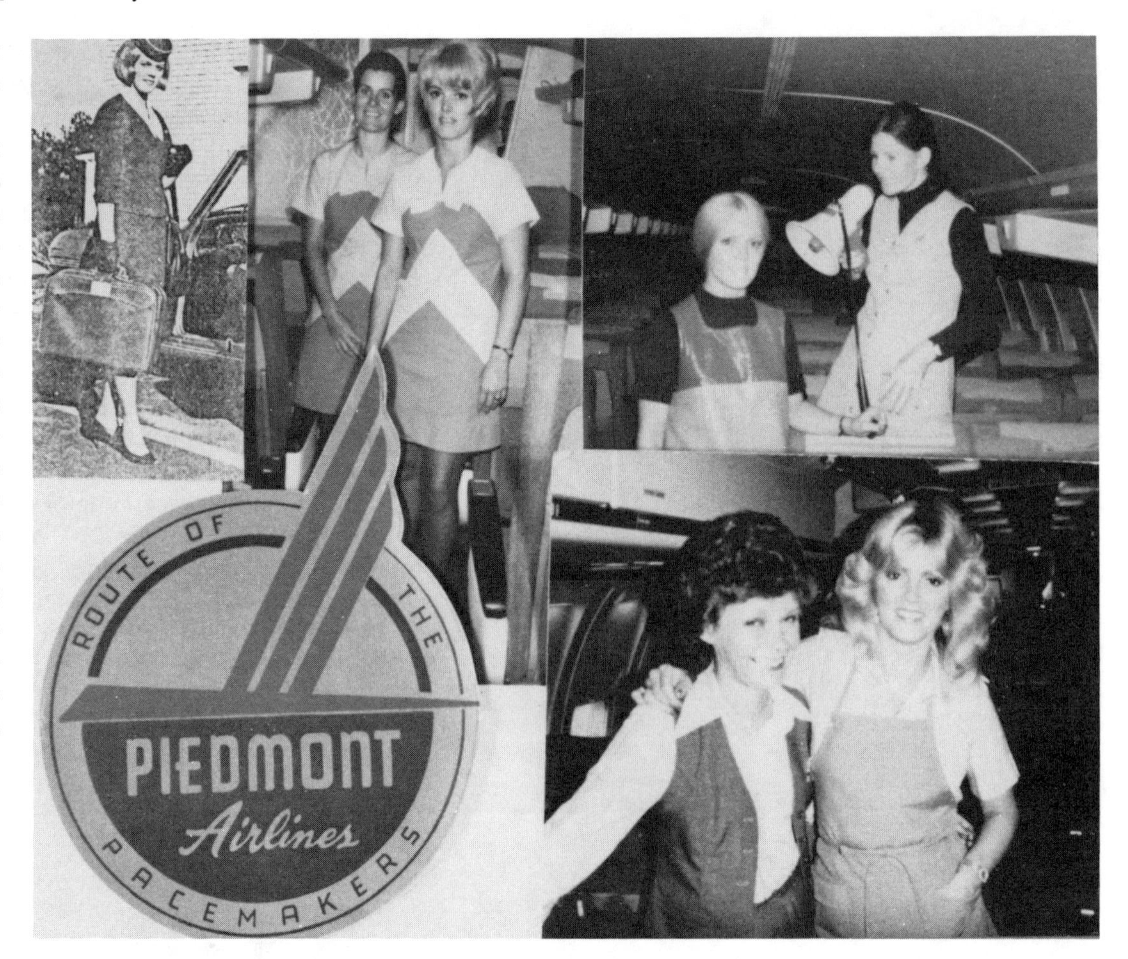

USAir flight attendant Patsy Benton was a flight attendant for Piedmont before the merger.

A SELECT SORORITY

USAir / Piedmont Airlines
Carol Fair
1963 - Present

Carol Fair needed a job to support herself. She was first employed as a flight attendant for Piedmont Airlines in 1963 and then for USAir after the merger.

Her flights are mostly international. To quote Carol, "I just love it all! I have flown on a variety of aircraft: The DC-3, Martin 404s, Fairchild 727, Boeing 737, the YS-11. My favorites are the oldest and the newest, the DC-3 and the Boeing 767. I spent 25 years

Left to right: President of Piedmont Airlines, Tom Davis; Linda Roberts; Aloma Gudger; *Carol Fair*; Carol Hewett and Amelia Moss, April 3, 1963.

with Piedmont Airlines, an airline gone with the wind, but, like Margaret Mitchell's novel, never forgotten.

"I've been based in the South, including Roanoke, Virginia; Knox-ville, Tennessee; Atlanta, Georgia and my present base of Charlotte, North Carolina. It has all been so interesting as well as the places I fly to.

"My whole world is a very select sorority and the flight attendants are my sisters. I really can't remember doing anything else but this wonderful job."

AROUND THE WORLD IN A LOCKHEED L-1011

Pacific Southwest, USAir
Sherry Hendry
1969 - Present

Sherry Hendry loved people and wanted to travel. After receiving a Bachelor's degree in Business Administration, she joined Pacific Southwest Airlines in 1986. With the USAir merger she became a flight attendant for them in 1988 to the present time.

With her business degree, management positions became natural to Sherry. Pacific Southwest Airlines chose her as Supervisor of Inflight Service first in San Francisco and later as a check flight attendant in Los Angeles. In the 1988 merger, USAir realized her talents and made her the Regional Director of Inflight. With downsizing and streamlining in 1990, the position was eliminated. Sherry was then made the Base Manager for Charlotte's Inflight Service, a position she currently holds. She relates:

"My most interesting experience was my opportunity to participate in an Around the World Tour in a Lockheed L-1011. We logged 46,000 air miles, and went to 24 cities and 21 nations. We were the flight crew responsible for all of these countries' dignitaries to see the L-1011.

"We took the heads of state and dignitaries on half hour flights whereby they could experience the wonderful L-1011 inflight. As a result many companies purchased this aircraft and the L-1011 is still operating today.

"I was again selected in 1975 to tour South America: Peru, Chile, Argentina, Brazil, Ecuador, Jamaica, Panama and Mexico in the Lockheed L-1011. All of this provided me with travel to see the world and enhanced my career opportunities. It has also allowed me to share my wonderful experiences with family and friends and give them exposure of my travels around the world!"

Pacific Southwest flight attendant, Sherry Hendry, with Kuwait customers on the "L-1011 Around the World Tour" in 1974. This tour was to acquaint countries with the L-1011 aircraft. Sherry is now an inflight manager with USAir.

Far right: Sherry Hendry, USAir Base Manager for Charlotte, NC, giving out awards to flight attendants, 1992. Debra K. Wolfington, Charlotte Supervisor (on left), is holding an award.

MONKEY BUSINESS
Piedmont Airlines
USAir
Lynda "Scotty" Lennon
1970 - Present

These weren't hijackers — but they terrorized the passengers. . . .

Lynda Lennon, known as Scotty, was born in the U.K. and left to come to the United States at age 19. Her family stayed in Scotland. She completed four years of Business College and worked first for a large lumber company and then for a chain of beauty salons. She then joined Piedmont as a flight attendant in 1970.

"The job appealed to me," says Lynda, "I wanted the interaction with people, the opportunity to upgrade my salary and become well traveled. Also I thoroughly wanted the 'freebies' to get to the old country to visit my family."

With the USAir merger, the opportunity to fly international flights to Europe as a flight attendant became a reality. She occasionally picks up an international flight for shopping or a family wedding, but prefers domestic flights and prefers the B-737-400, as Scotty says, "with a great workable galley, but an aircraft small enough for total people involvement and communication." Scotty tells this story.

"Another glorious sunrise - the airport quiet and deserted. The first flight crew arrives with double Java juice in hand to cross the tarmac to the airplane. It is sitting dark and ghostly against the horizon. Six stops ahead and more and more seats occupied as the morning wears on.

"After the third stop, take off into the puffy whiteness above us, just about to climb into 11,000 feet when all of a sudden, blood curdling screams! I was up front and turned around to see 40 monkeys leaping through the cabin screeching, defecating all over everything and everyone, pulling people's hair, grabbing food from their trays and causing havoc! Everyone was terrified!

"We apparently had crates of monkeys going to the Cincinnati Zoo and they had managed to gnaw through the containers when the tranquilizers wore off. They escaped from the rear baggage compartment into the passenger cabin to terrorize. All ended when we landed. Thank goodness for terra firma that day! The job of corralling them was left to somebody else!

"The airline is a magnificent opportunity to help one become totally independent, broaden horizons, be all things to all people. Also, to offer these great opportunities to your children who also become more self assured due to travel. This educational experience has given me a completely wonderful life.

USAir flight attendant Lynda "Scotty" Lennon, shown as a flight attendant for Piedmont Airlines before the merger with USAir.

I WANTED TO SEE THE WORLD

Piedmont Airlines
USAir
Debra K. Wolfington
1976 - Present

"I joined the airlines as a flight attendant to see the world - at least outside of North Carolina! I am a single, professional with a black chow named Boo Boo and a cat named Jake.

"My first regular route with Piedmont without being on call for reserve was on a B-737 for a one day turn out and back leaving at 6:20 p.m. and returning at 11:45 p.m. for 26 days a month! Things did get better.

"The merger with USAir in 1986 provided a good schedule. My favorite aircraft is the B-767 and to me a flight attendant's dream. It is comfortable for passengers as well as flight attendants.

"I feel the personal growth and life experience I have achieved with this career have been immeasurable. No other work could have been as well suited to my potential and allowed me to enjoy my life as much."

USAir flight attendant Supervisor Brenda Long (left) and Sherry Hendry (far right), Base Manager of Inflight Service for Charlotte, NC at an awards ceremony in 1992.

THE HIJACKER

Piedmont Airlines
USAir
Brenda Long
1976 - Present

Hijacking has become a threat to the airlines - a form of terror for crew members and passengers. The flight attendant has to deal with the situation.

Brenda Long's home was Charlotte, North Carolina. She graduated from the University of North Carolina at Chapel Hill in 1975. She worked as a Dental Hygienist after graduation until she decided the "Glamour" of being a flight attendant was the job she wanted. She was hired by Piedmont in the early fall of 1986 and trained at Winston Salem for three weeks. She later was in the merger with USAir in 1986 to the present time.

A serious and yet somewhat humorous experience stands out in Brenda's mind while she was a flight attendant for Piedmont. She relates:

"I was non-reving on a flight on a smaller turbo-prop YS-11 aircraft which boarded passengers at New Bern, North Carolina. I was a newly hired employee at this time. An elderly gentleman informed the flight attendants he had a gun and to take him to the cockpit. The captain called me on the P.A. system to come up front to the cockpit. The captain then asked me to bring a scotch and water to the elderly man who appeared intoxicated. I brought the drink back to the man. The captain proceeded to inform the passengers over the P.A. system that we were being hijacked to Cuba!

"En route the male flight attendant who was in the cockpit grabbed the scotch and water from the hijacker and threw what was left in his face and then pushed him out of the cockpit into the cabin and yelled, *Grab him!!* at which time all 17 Marines on the flight jumped on him! I actually had his leg at one point. They tied his hands with a necktie and the man passed out!

"We then had to administer oxygen to the hijacker. We were over Myrtle Beach by this time, The captain turned the aircraft and landed at Wilmington, North Carolina. It turned out the man did not really have a gun; he had been drinking heavily and thought it would be *fun* to hijack a plane. He hadn't realized how serious was his intent!

"In 1976 Piedmont did not have any training program procedures to follow on hijacking. Since this calamity of events Piedmont and now USAir implemented a thorough training session on hijacking.

"Since that time I've flown domestic flights on a variety of aircraft. I have been a supervisor for flight attendants in Miami and presently at our Charlotte base for USAir."

A CHRISTMAS GIFT
USAir
Sandra Travis
1989 - Present

Flight attendants get homesick too, especially when they're scheduled to fly on holidays.

Sandra Travis says, "I left home very young, at age 16. I returned at age 21 years to attend college for two years. I have always worked in restaurants as a waitress and in management. I wanted to become 'a waitress in the sky' for money, benefits, a stable future, respect and experience of travel. I am a safety professional, however I serve more cokes than I save lives. Also, I add, *THANK GOD!*

"My most memorable experience was from a man who took the time to write a letter over the holiday season (Christmas and New Years). He thanked us for working so he could be with his family, knowing that we would not be with ours (for days). I was so very homesick, and this gift of a passenger's time meant a lot!"

THE CONTEST FOR SEAT 19D!
Piedmont / USAir
Sandy Mixon
1984 - Present

Passengers can get "territorial" for that assigned seat. Flight attendants have to direct and appease individuals or groups in all situations.

Sandy Mixon sought a position as a flight attendant with Piedmont Airlines in 1984 after teaching early childhood education for 10 years. She says, "I wanted to expand myself and life experiences. I wanted to be able to travel and broaden my knowledge of other areas of our country and of other countries and their cultures." She relates a humorous experience:

"In the first months of my career as a flight attendant we had experienced a weather delay. In reboarding the flight we had gone to 'open seating' due to double seat assignments and concern for as timely a departure as possible. One male passenger was last to board, almost missing the flight. He had been absent from the boarding area during reboarding and was unaware of the 'open seating' arrangement. His original seat assignment was 19D. He rushed to the aft portion of the aircraft to take his seat, which was at this point already taken. Only 19E was available. He threw his bags on the floor and refused to take any other seat but 19D. Due to FAA safety regulations regarding passengers being seated during taxi, we had to inform the captain to stop the push-back until this passenger could be accommodated.

"The Captain, frustrated with the weather delay, deplaning, reboarding, and now possible delay in take off, came out of the cockpit, hands-on-hips, staring down the aircraft aisle asking, 'who's delaying this flight?' The passenger was standing in the aft galley doorway, hands-on-hips, staring down the aisle toward the front of the plane. At the same time, I asked the passenger seated in 19D to please move to 19E so this man could be seated and the aircraft could begin taxi and take off. I apologized for the inconvenience as I knew we had told passengers they could take any available seat.

" The scene was so comical, even though it was serious. These two grown men were standing at opposite ends of the aircraft aisle, hands-on-hips, faces set in growling stares as if ready to reenact a shoot-out from the Old West. I thought what a parallel to my former first - third grade students, attitude wise. I had to giggle to myself as I thought of relaying this account to them on my next visit. This traveling passenger was only a larger version of my former students. 'He's in my seat, get him out of my seat, *I want my seat*!' Yes, adults were as territorial over their assigned seats as students were in the classroom. I guess we *did* learn it all in kindergarten!

"I flew domestic routes and I liked the long layovers in cities on our route system as I had never experienced areas much beyond the southeastern states until my association with the airlines. My first trip to Denver, to the Colorado mountains and skiing was wonderful. As a former school teacher I have always wanted to soak in the history and culture of each area. The Continental Divide and Great Rocky Mountains were magnificent. New York with all its hub-bub of activity: the plays, the museums, the ethnic food - all were invigorating. San Francisco's fog and rocky coastlines were so different from our flat East Coast beaches. The Peabody Hotel, Rum Boogie Cafe and Graceland in Memphis were now real places I had experienced and could share with students I used to teach.

So many images now were authentic to me, not just things or places I had read about in a book. Hawaii, Germany, Paris, Amsterdam, Venice - the list goes on and keeps growing.

"The airlines has opened up all these experiences for me. It has given me the opportunity to meet the most ordinary and most famous of people. I have been able to spend a small amount of time with each of them adding smiles to their day (I hope) while trying to deliver quality personal service during their travels."

Training classes for USAir. ***Upper left*****: fun in make-up class;** ***upper right*****: CPR training;** ***middle left*****: Sandy Mixon and another USAir flight attendant;** ***middle right*****: operation of the oxygen mask;** ***lower left*****: Sandy Mixon, 1994;** ***lower right*****: evacuation slide.**

NORTHWEST AIRLINES
Some People Just Know How To Fly.℠

Northwest Airline flight attendants ready for a flight, 1994.

Northwest culture training for international route system.

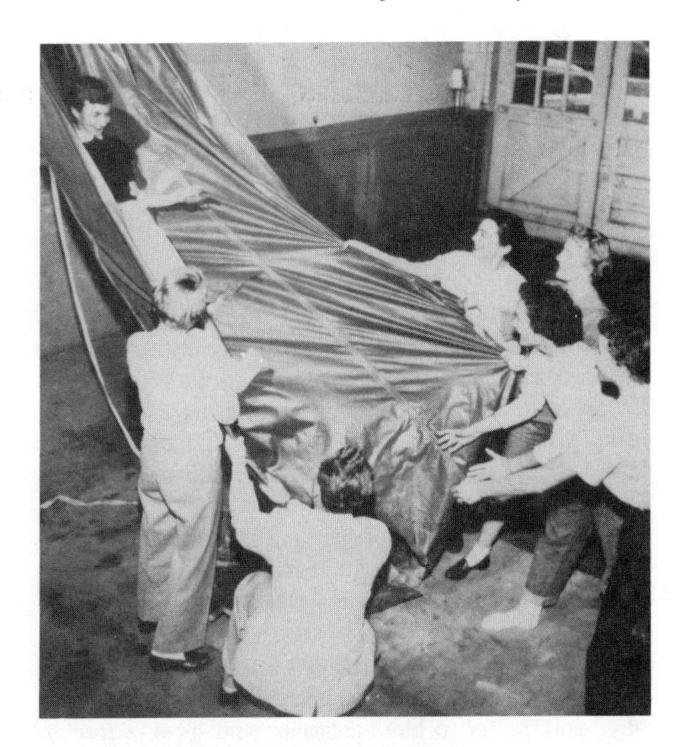

Safety training in action.

Northwest Airline flight attendant safety training.

TWIN CITIES REGIONAL AIRLINE[5]

Mesaba

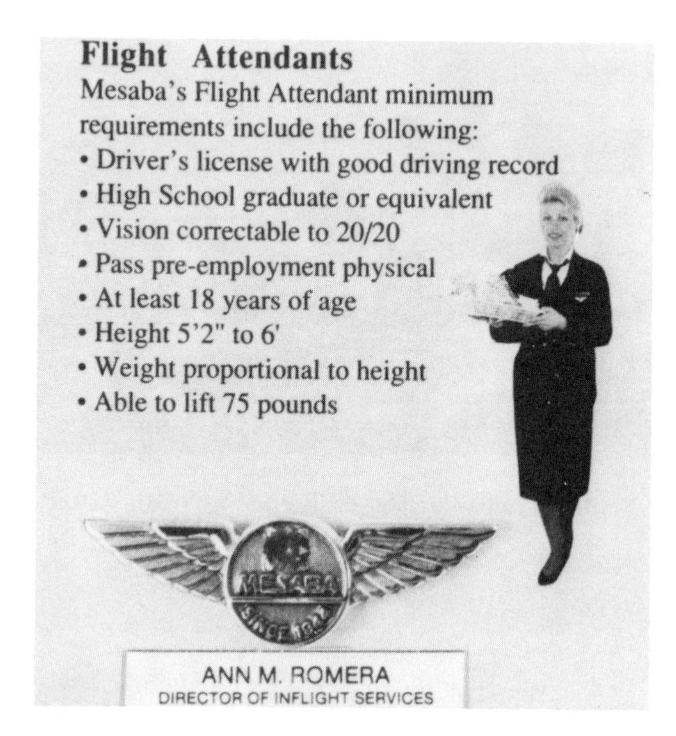

Flight Attendants
Mesaba's Flight Attendant minimum requirements include the following:
• Driver's license with good driving record
• High School graduate or equivalent
• Vision correctable to 20/20
• Pass pre-employment physical
• At least 18 years of age
• Height 5'2" to 6'
• Weight proportional to height
• Able to lift 75 pounds
MESABA
SINCE 1944
ANN M. ROMERA
DIRECTOR OF INFLIGHT SERVICES

Mesaba is a regional airline headquartered in Minneapolis/St. Paul. Through a marketing agreement, they operate as one of Northwest's "airlinks." Another airlink with a hub in the Twin Cities is Express I. Other carriers based in the Twin Cities are Northwest and Sun Country.

Northwest is one of the "major" airlines - as are American, Delta and United, to name a few. They operate a variety of jet aircraft, some of which can seat up to 400 passengers. Northwest employs about 10,000 flight attendants. Many of the "major" carriers not only have domestic routes, but also have international routes. That is why many prefer to hire applicants who speak a foreign language. Starting salaries range from $1050 to $1337 a month.

Sun Country is a charter airline. Sometimes charter carriers furlough flight attendants during the slow vacation travel season. Salary - $1200 per month for 75 hours.

Mesaba is one of 29 regional airlines. They serve a certain region of the country, and often feed passengers into a major airline hub from smaller cities. Turbo-prop aircraft are operated, some holding only 15 passengers without a flight attendant, and some holding 60 passengers with two flight attendants. Mesaba's F-27s and DHC-8s require only one flight attendant. Starting salaries for regional carriers range from $807 to $1013 per month.

Mesaba Aviation was founded in 1944 in Grand Rapids, Minnesota as a fixed base operation. The company specialized in flight lessons, charter flights, aircraft maintenance and fuel sales. The company continued to grow throughout the mid-century until it began scheduled service in 1973 between the Twin Cities and Grand Rapids, Minnesota.

When airline deregulation occurred in 1978, Mesaba began to expand its route system even more into cities abandoned by major carriers. Throughout the early 1980s the regional airline expanded into the states surrounding Minnesota.

In 1984, Mesaba signed a marketing agreement with Northwest Airlines under which the airline operates as Northwest Airlink and feeds regional traffic to three of Northwest's domestic hubs. Originally, Mesaba served only the Twin Cities hub as Northwest Airlink, however in 1988, Mesaba expanded its services to Detroit.

Today Mesaba has a base in Minneapolis/St. Paul and in Detroit. The airline currently operates a fleet of seventeen 19-passenger Metro-III aircraft and fifteen 44-passenger Fokker F-27 aircraft and seventeen 37 seat De Havilland DHC-8 aircraft.

Approximately 350 pilots and 90 flight attendants are currently employed. Mesaba Airlines provides air service to 45 cities in 15 states and Canada.

[5]Information provided by the Manager of Inflight Service, Mesaba Northwest Airlink

ANOTHER GIRL FROM CRESCO

Mississippi Valley Airlines
Air Wisconsin
United Express
United Airlines
Margy Montague

From a handful of carriers in the thirties, the airlines industry has grown to cover all parts of the U.S. An enormous network of airlines of all sizes now serves small towns as well as major cities. Experience on a smaller airline sometimes leads to bigger things.

Margy Montague is shown with her crew after the 1985 MVA merger with Air Wisconsin. Margy later became a United Airlines flight attendant.

From a handful of carriers in the thirties, the airline industry has grown to cover all parts of the U.S. An enormous network of airlines of all sizes now serves small towns as well as major cities. Experience on a smaller airline sometimes leads to bigger things. Major airlines use them to feed their route systems today and are called Express, Connection, etc.

A teenage girl took notice of her hometown's pride in Ellen Church's accomplishments. Margy Montague's family are neighbors and friends of the Church family in Cresco. Margy knew that Ellen Church had pioneered stewardess service for the airlines, in fact for the entire world. She was especially interested in the celebration of United Airlines' 50th Anniversary which honored Ellen and brought fame to Cresco. This event sparked an interest in aviation for Margy, and she was determined to become a flight attendant.

She attended college for two years before making an application to Mississippi Valley Airlines. She had found that information on the airlines varied. There were commuter, regional, national and major airlines throughout the United States. Each airline had its own route system, types of aircraft, and requirements and training time for flight attendants. Margy applied to Mississippi Valley Airlines because it was a large regional airline with its headquarters in Moline, Illinois, and it flew into Cedar Rapids. That would make it easy to get home to Cresco, when time allowed.

Margy completed three weeks of training in Moline to earn her wings. Her enthusiasm and pride were not diminished by joining a smaller airline, as she knew Mississippi Valley Airlines was the seventh largest among the regional carriers at that time, and was sought after by other regional airlines to train their inflight staff. During her training she learned that Mississippi Valley Airlines was one of many small airlines that had grown out of the 1978 Airline Deregulation Act, which had eliminated monopoly routes. The new regional airlines are similar to the feeder airlines that flew passengers to smaller towns on "milk runs" in the forties.

Regional airlines often work in a team effort with major airlines. Mississippi Valley developed a working relationship with United at O'Hare in Chicago, and was connected to United's Apollo automated reservations system. Mississippi Valley Airlines was also a feeder for TWA at their gateway city, the "St. Louis Connection."

Margy had been trained for three types of aircraft, and for the special features of each in passenger safety and service. Mississippi Valley Airlines had a fleet of wide-bodied Short SD-330s that carried thirty passengers, the Short SD-360s that could seat 36, and the larger pressurized Fokker F-27 that could carry 48 passengers. One flight attendant could work the aircraft inflight service, as FAA regulations require one flight attendant for less than fifty passengers. Mississippi Valley Airlines' well-trained flight attendants were polished, service oriented, public relations agents for their airline.

In July 1985, Mississippi Valley Airlines merged with another, larger regional, Air Wisconsin, headquartered in Appleton, Wisconsin. The Moline base was added to its other bases at Fort Wayne, Indiana and Richmond, Virginia. Air Wisconsin, like Mississippi Valley, had an agreement to feed United's Chicago O'Hare hub. With the merger, Air Wisconsin was catapulted into the status of a national airline, due to the growth in size and its gross annual revenue. All flight crews and flight attendants were meshed into one seniority list. Margy's domicile remained at Moline. She was still under the supervision of Judy Barack, former Director of Inflight Service for Mississippi Valley Airlines, in the same position for Air Wisconsin's Moline base.

Jet aircraft were now a part of Air Wisconsin's fleet of aircraft: 100-passenger BAE-146 jets complimented 48-passenger Fokker F-27s and the Short 36 passenger turbo-props. All crews were constantly scheduled for recurrent training to meet the FAA's safety regulations.

Margy made application to United and was accepted by United to train at their flight school. Her experience with both a regional and a national airline made the transition to a major airline easy. Margy's charm, friendliness and professionalism will enhance the friendly skies of United.

And so the girl from Cresco, Iowa follows in the footsteps of the other girl from Cresco, Ellen Church. Margy has more than met her dream.

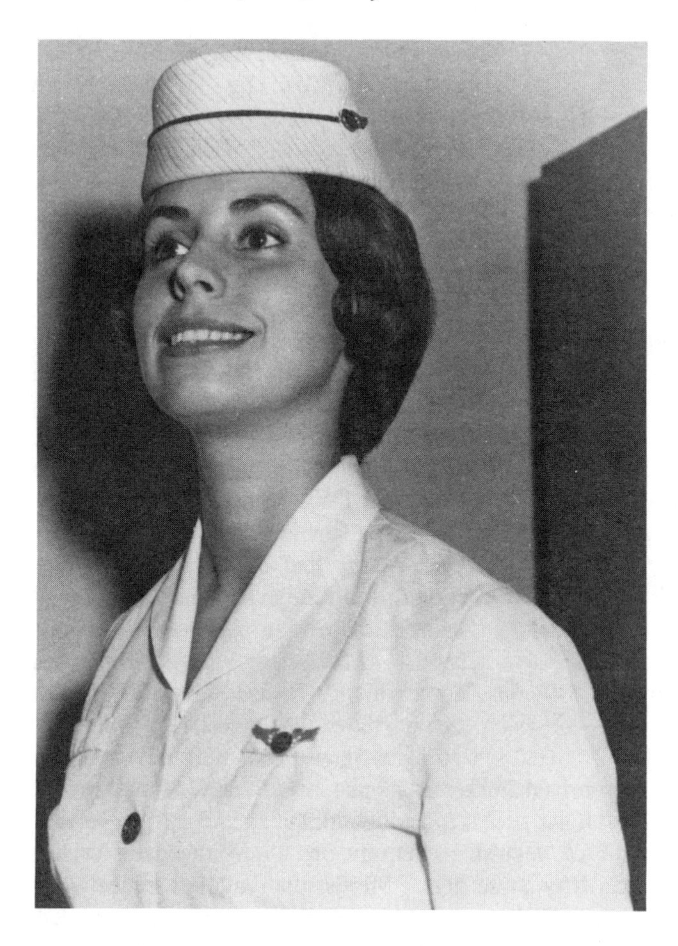

Stewardess Stephanie Knowles, Central Airlines, 1962.

Stewardess Stephanie Knowles (center) in a Frontier Airlines uniform in 1967. Central merged with Frontier.

MANY WINGS IN FLIGHT

Central Airlines People's Express Frontier, United Stephanie Knowles 1962 - Present

With mergers and bankruptcies, many in inflight have flown for more than one airline.

Stephanie Knowles, a United Airline flight attendant, can look back at many changes as well as mergers and all wrapped up in a statement of her 31 years with wings winging through the sky with Central Airlines, People's Express, Frontier Airlines and United. She says, "I've had an interesting life and difficult as it was to go through airline mergers it was also a lot of fun and I've met a lot of terrific people." Here is her story. . . .

"I was born in Breslau, Germany in 1942. After World War II, Breslau was called Wroclaw, East Germany.

"After the upheaval of the war we lived in a refugee camp in Bavaria in West Germany between 1945 and 1951. My father made application to come to the United States under the refugee quota. We were lucky and we landed in New York harbor on Labor Day, 1951. We were very disappointed to learn Americans don't work on Labor Day and we had to spend an extra night on the ship before we could be processed.

"My family ended up settling in Warren, Pennsylvania. I started off in first grade again as I knew no English. I graduated from high school in 1961. Before graduation a representative from various colleges, trade schools and from various professions came to speak to us. This is when I learned about being a stewardess. I met a representative from Humboldt Institute that did airline and secretarial training.

"At that time I had never flown, nor did I know that airlines do their own training. The Humboldt representative made it sound so easy, that if I took the course I'd get placed in a stewardess job.

"In February of 1962 a representative from Central Airlines came to the school to interview for stewardess positions. Almost every girl in the school had an interview. I was the first. At the end of the day two were selected and I was one of those. I was so excited! The training class for Central was to begin May 1, 1962. I did finish my course at Humboldt and graduated early in April.

I went home for two weeks to pack and get ready for a new experience.

"Thirteen girls from many states checked in at the Western Hills Inn in Ealers, Texas. A van picked us up each day to take us to a hanger where our classroom was. Our training was for 2 weeks and our instructors were the Chief Stewardess and her assistant. Our training included: the operation of a flight, safety/evacuation, makeup and hair styling.

"When I started to fly, no food was served, only beverages. We had a *stew kit* that we picked up at the hangar before each flight. It was an inexpensive brief case that contained instant coffee, tea, lemonade mix in summer and hot chocolate mix in winter months. We also received 2 water jugs, one hot and one cold. This was our service. We were also encouraged to talk to our passengers, but to avoid controversial subjects of religion and politics.

"We also had freshly laundered linen headrests, pillow cases and magazines for each flight. We had to put the clean linens on the head rests and pillows at the beginning of a flight and strip them at the end of a flight and leave them in the rear seat.

"We flew on DC-3s seating 24 passengers. One trip to Denver in a DC-3 had 14 stops. From Fort Worth we made many stops through Oklahoma and Kansas with a shuttle back and forth from Liberal, Kansas to Guyman, Oklahoma. The Captain called ahead for a pick-up of hamburgers for the crew and for any passengers that wanted to participate. Sometimes I would take a sandwich on my trips. From Guyman we'd fly into Colorado with stops at Lamar, Pueblo, Colorado Springs and finally Denver. A full day's work!

United Airlines flight attendant Stephanie Knowles, 1994.

"Since there was only one stewardess, we got our own room except in larger cities layovers like Little Rock, Kansas City or Denver. We would share a room with another stewardess and never know who our roommate would be.

"An amusing incident happened at Stapleton Airport in Denver. We were just about ready to board passengers when a gust of wind blew off my wig! I had no idea where it landed. I got a scarf out of my suitcase and tied it around my head and cheerfully boarded passengers. A Braniff Agent drove up to the DC-3 door and handed me my wig before we took off. He had seen the whole episode and retrieved my wig from the roof of one of the lower buildings where the aircraft was parked. I went in the *blue room*, put on the wig and proceeded as normal. None of my passengers said a word about it and I laughed to myself!

"Before 1967 and prior to the Civil Right Act we were not allowed to be married. On a flight I was supposed to take, a reserve stewardess was called to take my place as I had the flu. On a layover at Kansas City she was taken to the hospital. They refused to give the captain any information on her. This particular captain was very protective. As it turned out this stewardess had been secretly married and some of us knew it. She gave birth that night. After that happened everyone, including me, remembered that this stewardess had worn her rain coat all the time and would go straight to bed on layovers always claiming she was not feeling well. We never saw her again.

"In 1967 a Braniff hostess won a court case that marriage was permitted. All airlines did not immediately follow, but this change in marriage rules made the job a career.

"Another time prior to 1967 when the FAA regulations were not as strict as they are now, or else Central didn't stress things very much, an incident happened. I was sitting on the jump seat in the back of the Convair-240 right next to the *blue room* as we landed and was appalled at what happened. An old gentleman came out of the *blue room* and went toward his seat. He was not too steady on his feet. I immediately rushed to help him to his seat. I asked him why he stayed in the lavatory for landing and he said, 'A sign came on *return to seat*, so I sat back on the toilet!' I explained what the sign meant and I thanked God it had been a smooth landing!

"I married a Delta pilot in 1967 (which ended in divorce). At the same time Frontier took over Central, Frontier put *Miss* on all our wings. It didn't take long however, for many stewardesses to *come out of the closet* with a husband.

"On Frontier we flew 727 jets with a very small galley. To learn the *Frontier way* we worked with another stewardess. We had a lot of food and beverage service with no carts. We literally ran ourselves ragged.

"We wore the 'unfashionable hot pants' at this time and many of us wore wigs. I liked wigs because I hated to sleep with rollers in my hair.

"Our base at Dallas was kept open. All the Central people stayed there. Frontier's supervisor noticed I had my ears pierced and I got in trouble as this was a *no-no*. Not long after, we were to be fitted for new uniforms and I really was in trouble.

"I have a good small body achieved through exercise and running. After panty hose became popular and no more girdle checks, I stopped wearing underclothing altogether. Not to be sexy, just to be comfortable. Our blouses were double paneled and we wore a jumper. I was in the office of the secretary who handled the new uniforms. I tried on the uniform and I wasn't wearing a bra, etc. I *did* have on panty hose. I went directly to the airplane to take my trip. My supervisor called me at the gate to tell me I had to put on a bra or I couldn't work the trip. I didn't have one with me and they couldn't find anyone to work the trip without a delay so there I went! The supervisor never followed through with bra checks for me, so I went back to my old ways.

"With the unions and as men became stewards, we became flight attendants and we were treated like grownups and things changed for the better.

"Frontier grew larger after deregulation. We flew east to Toledo and to Atlanta and Orlando. We had full flights and I thought we were doing alright. Suddenly People's Express Airlines bought Frontier. We kept the Frontier name, but their management. All the food service disappeared and we had to sell a prepackaged snack box for $3.50 if the passenger wanted to eat. We sold coffee, tea and soft drinks for 50¢ each, coffee refills were free. We had to keep track of all inventory. Flight attendants got a percentage of the sales at the end of a flight.

"At the beginning inventory we got so many sleeves of cups, soft drinks and snack boxes and at the end of a flight everything had to balance. It made a lot of paperwork. We had to work more days to get our 85 hours of flying. It was almost a relief when Frontier went out of business in 1986. Frontier merged with Continental Airlines. I went to a United interview and hoped I'd be selected. I was and I enjoy working for them. I had 6 weeks of training and was sent to Newark, New Jersey. My seniority in the class was decided on the last four numbers of my Social Security. What a let down! Here I was 45 years old and the oldest one in training.

"I rented a room in a house in Cranford, New Jersey and commuted to Denver where I had a house. It was hard at best, as the first year we did not get passes. We were allowed to use the jump seat.

"A transfer to Denver came through for me on October 1, 1992. A happy day for me! Those first six years with United were hard commuting but I work for a wonderful airline and I married again in September 1993. Imagine, getting in a car and driving to the Denver airport to take my trips! It is wonderful!"

A LIFETIME CAREER
United Air Lines
Betty Lowry
1941 - 1978

A lifetime career in inflight service and another with United at the time of her retirement.

Betty Lowry, a pretty dark haired nurse had just graduated from nursing school at West Suburban Hospital in Oak Park, Illinois. United Air Lines was hiring nurses, a prerequisite requirement for their stewardesses. In 1941 Betty was hired and took her stewardess training in a room above the boiler room at Chicago's Midway Airport. She became one of the 150 stewardesses employed by United.[6]

Betty Lowry was first a United stewardess in 1941. Management jobs followed. After retirement, she became president of United's Silver Wings Plus Program, 1978. (United Airlines Photo)

[6]*Betty Lowry - Biography*, United Airlines Silver Wings Plus Travel Club, March 1986, pp 1-3.

Her first flight as a stewardess was on a 21-passenger DC-3. At first planes were unpressurized and planes flew low. Five percent of all passengers were airsick because of the turbulence. The flight between Denver and Chicago took seven hours and required a 45 minute refueling stop in Omaha. Betty Lowry saw many changes in the airline industry after this first flight. Her career in aviation lasted 37 years.[7]

She became an Assistant Chief Hostess and later a Chief Hostess for United Air Lines. During this time she participated in exchange programs for flight attendants of several overseas airlines. She made many friends and traveled to visit friends from Swissair.

She also has had many celebrities on her flights including Eleanor Roosevelt, wife of the President, and General Douglas MacArthur. When a young Frank Sinatra was on her flight she told him, "You don't have to sing for your supper." She was the First stewardess ("A" stewardess) for United's charter flights during Dwight D. Eisenhower's campaign for the Presidency in 1951. The same crew flew on all these campaign flights.[8]

As coordinator of appearance and uniforms she saw a wide variety of changes, from wool to polyester, mini skirts, pants for women and stocking seams to panty hose. The fabric trend returned to wool. She worked with many well known designers. Among her favorites was Jean Louis.[9]

For her last several months before retirement in 1978 Betty chose to return to flying on the line as United's *number one* flight attendant. She bid Chicago to the West Coast flights on 250-passenger DC-10s. A contrast over her first flights on a 21-passenger DC-3, the DC-10 was pressurized and had a movie screen and earphones.[10]

She says of her career as a United stewardess/flight attendant and in inflight service management, "People are the most enriching part of the travel experience -- whether you travel for pleasure or as part of your profession. The biggest change in the present and 1941 is passenger composition. For the 1940s, most passengers were businessmen and servicemen during World War II years. Now they are businessmen and women, families and from all walks of life. Flying has become more affordable for everyone."[11]

Following her retirement in 1978 Betty was asked to return to United for a special assignment for the Silver Wings Plus program as Club President. She agreed as she was over 65 years of age, loved travel and wanted to help provide information on travel opportunities for people in a very special time in their lives. This group for 60 years of age or over, people with flexible schedules wishing to participate in leisure travel opportunities with savings.[12]

Betty Lowry's career spanned over four decades of inflight service as a dedicated employee for United. The original silver wings she wore are on exhibit at the Smithsonian National Air and Space Museum in Washington, DC. A tribute to an aviation enthusiast.[13]

FORTY-THREE YEARS IN THE SKY

United Airlines
Virginia Riley
1946 - 1989

Her career with United bridged many changes in four decades and included management.

There are flight attendants who have been flying for forty years. It takes a lot of caring, and a wonderful sense of humor to serve the public for so long. Virginia Riley retired as number two on United's flight attendant seniority list in 1989. "Other flight attendants laughed when I told them about the things we used to do," United Airlines former flight attendant, Virginia Riley says with a chuckle. "Gini," as her friends call her, is best known for her sense of humor which permeates everything she says and does.

She met more people in a week as a flight attendant than a person one hundred years ago probably met in a lifetime. She regularly flew on 376-passenger Boeing 747 aircraft. Gini loved the variety of people who boarded her flights from Los Angeles to Honolulu. "I saw a cross-section of our country," she says. "My job allowed me to learn about their thoughts, habits, and ways of life."

Gini first thought about becoming a stewardess when, in 1946, she noticed a United Air Lines advertisement for stewardesses in the newspaper. At the time, she had just graduated from the University of Arizona with a degree in sociology and was working for the State Welfare Board and the American Red Cross in Phoenix, assisting returning servicemen and their families. Gini applied for the job and

[7] *Betty Lowry - Biography*, United Airlines Silver Wings Plus Travel Club, Betty Lowry, March 1986, pp 1-3.

[8] Ibid.

[9] Ibid.

[10] Ibid.

[11] Ibid.

[12] Ibid.

[13] Ibid.

United Flight Attendant Virginia Riley in an engine nacelle of a B-747 shortly before her retirement as #2 in inflight seniority in 1989.

was hired shortly thereafter, in August 1946.

After completing six weeks of training in her hometown of Chicago, Gini was domiciled in Denver, where she remained for the next four years. After 1950 she was domiciled at a number of bases, including Washington, D.C., Salt Lake City, San Francisco and Miami. In 1963, Gini was based in Los Angeles where she has spent most of her time.

From 1956 to 1966, Gini acted as supervisor under the Chief Stewardess, giving check rides out of Los Angeles. From 1961 to 1963 she was sent to Miami as an assistant to the Chief Stewardess to set up a new base there. In 1967 she returned to flying the line at her own request, as she missed the variety of flights and meeting people.

Red roses were presented to veteran flight attendant Gini Riley on May 19, 1973. She wore dark glasses to hide her tears. The occasion was the last scheduled Military Airlift Command (MAC) flight, number 282, that United would fly from Yakota Air Force Base in Japan to Travis Air Force Base in Sacramento, California.

MAC flights between Sacramento and Yakota had originated in July 1971. Crew members on that first flight included flight attendant Gini Riley and Captain John Grosso. Each was presented with a plaque commemorating the event. In addition, Captain Grosso received a letter of commendation from Colonel Douglas L. Campbell, Commander of Yakota Air Force Base. The letter read:

> May 25, 1973
> United Airlines, Inc.
>
> I would like to express my sincere appreciation for the fine service provided by United Airlines. I speak not only for myself, but for all MAC passengers, in saying, "Thanks for an exceptional flight."
>
> The competence and professionalism shown on every mission has earned United an outstanding reputation which is justly deserved. The extra care and personal attention furnished by United has produced a "First Class" atmosphere, a pleasurable trip, and a satisfied customer. For this I offer my personal thanks for a job well done.
>
> On behalf of the MAC family I now say "Sayonara" with the hope that someday United may once again fly the friendly skies of MAC.
>
> Douglas L. Campbell
> Colonel, USAF, Commander

Flight attendant Timmy Pang has welcomed passengers to his native Hawaii for over 40 years. Pang was one of United's first cabin stewards on island flights. He says, "there is no job on the ground that can duplicate it." (United Airlines Photo)

United stewardess in 1948 (right) with the new pet carrier cage. She's wearing the summer uniform.

At least a part of Colonel Campbell's wish has come true for United, for the airline is now flying regular routes in the Orient. United's excellence won the airline the approval of the Civil Aeronautics Board to inaugurate Royal Pacific Service to Tokyo in 1983. Service to Hong Kong followed and other cities in the Orient have since started service.

Gini continued to bid a schedule of flying United's MATS flights to Germany and Japan. She recalls a funny experience on one flight.

"The senior flight attendant is responsible for reporting an exact head count to the military representative before departure. On one particular flight from Germany, shortly before takeoff, the captain called me to the cockpit to say that he had received a radio message indicating that my count did not agree with the military manifest. He asked me to count my passengers again. I might add that the captain was a gruff, no-nonsense person.

"I made another tally and reported back to him. Somehow I had one less person than the original count I had given. The captain demanded to know how I could have made such an error. I had to tell him that I had accidentally counted a teddy bear as a person. The captain was not amused. 'It seems, sir,' I said, 'that someone brought a life-size teddy bear on board and put it in a seat. I was counting empty seats and I didn't notice that the occupant of that particular seat wasn't human.' In spite of himself, the captain started to laugh.

"My ex-roommate had a funny thing happen on a DC-6. A feisty elderly woman who obviously didn't hear too well stopped her and requested that she open a window because the cabin was too warm. The stewardess explained that this was impossible because they were flying at a high altitude and it was necessary to pressurize the cabin. 'Aw, go press your own eyes,' was the irritated old lady's retort.

"I could go on and on about fun things that have happened during the last thirty-nine years," Gini says with a chuckle. "My job has always been interesting and it's people who make it that way." Indeed, Gini's file is full of "orchid letters" from passengers who raved about her personal touch and superior service.

It isn't only the passengers who found Gini exceptional. Her fellow flight attendants honored her on her 35th anniversary in 1981 with carnation leis and a cake on board a flight form Los Angeles to Honolulu. Passengers took part in the celebration and enjoyed the special recognition of Gini's achievement.

Other fun events took place on the ground. In November of 1982, a group of Los Angeles based flight attendants marched in the zany Dor Dak Parade, a takeoff on the Rose Parade, in Pasadena, California.

"All of us were over thirty-five years old," Gini says with a giggle, "so our banner read *Old Birds Flock Together*. We older flight attendants poked fun at our age. After all, we don't fit the public image of flight attendants. We formed a suitcase drill team and dragged our flight bags behind us as we marched along. We weren't allowed to use any United identification in the nonsense parade, so we stripped our old uniforms of all insignia. We wore masks, silly helmets or paper sacks over our heads, and we all wore large foil wings. I pushed another flight attendant in a wheelchair just for fun. As we marched along we were pelted with marshmallows by our cheering section."

United Airlines flight attendant Virginia Riley (on a B-747 to Hawaii) wearing the muumuu uniform and a lei and holding a cake to celebrate her 35 years with United, August 1981. The muumuu uniform was discontinued by 1990.

United flight attendants are involved wherever they live. The Los Angeles based flight attendants first organized their annual Christmas party for orphans in 1981 under the direction of Denice Snavely. Individual flight attendants baked cookies, provided gifts, and volunteered to help with the party. United's Captain Bill Tishler and Captain Murph Rasenstein volunteered as clowns and Captain Murph Rasenstein volunteered as Santa each year. At the 1982 Christmas party, members of the Los Angeles Dodgers gave baseballs and helmets to each orphan. Activities such as these continue to give United Airlines its name: "The friendly skies airline."

In over four decades as a flight attendant with United, Gini saw the airline industry undergo many changes. "My salary was $155 a month in 1946," Gini remembers, "and that has changed. I made an excellent salary. But I did earn what I got with a lot of hard work for 43 years of service to United. The safety procedures training has also changed a great deal since I was first trained. Back then we learned from lectures and the stewardess manual. Now flight attendants receive real life situation training using all the modern equipment, and each flight attendant is retrained periodically.

"But the biggest change has taken place in the equipment itself," and she adds, "in 1946, one stewardess flew on the 21- passenger DC-3, and the 44-passenger DC-4 flew with two stewardesses, and we became fairly well acquainted with a passenger by the end of the flight. Nowadays, the aircraft that carry two or three hundred passengers or more, like the B-747s and the B-767s, fly with eight or more flight attendants on duty. Flying has became another form of mass transportation with a lot of paper work. We never used to serve liquor on flights; you can see how much that has changed over the years!"

Gini's uniqueness lies in her sense of humor and her enduring warmth and friendliness. These are qualities United Airlines has always sought in its sky girls. For Gini, her love of people has remained steadfast through her long career of dedicated service. She could even make an "old bear" of a captain laugh about a teddy bear on board.

"Being a flight attendant has been an interesting career for me, but I never dreamed I would fly for forty-three years," says Gini reflectively. "Being a flight attendant is not just a job, it's a profession. I was away from my domicile for days at a time, but it's a way of life, and I made a lifetime of friends." Those who worked with her found Virginia Riley's keen sense of humor and her enthusiasm catching. She's the "friendly" in the friendly skies airline. They honored her with a party for her retirement, she will always remember.

Gini meets with former Denver United friends for their yearly bash, friendship cemented by the High Street House roommates plus the lucky ones getting to join in the fun! That includes me (the author), Nan Bowman Cavanagh and Ginny Olstad White.

United's O'Hare-based international flight attendant, James Pettus says about more international markets, "United's global expansion has enabled me and thousands of other employees to expand our careers. I've been trained about different cultures and customers so that, as a world-wide carrier, United can deliver world-class service to all of its customers." James is a 1994 United flight attendant. (photo and caption permission of public relations, United Times, 1992)

HE BROKE THE MOLD

United Airlines
H.C. Brantley

A planeload of disgruntled passengers is no laughing matter, but flight attendants know how to turn a bad situation into an enjoyable one.

On a February day in 1984, clouds hung over the Eugene, Oregon airport and a steady rain was falling. United's flight 756 out of San Francisco with service to Denver was over an hour late for its regular noon departure. The luncheon hour had passed and the expectant passengers were hungry. Some were edgy about making their connecting flights at Denver.

The United agent announced the arrival of flight 756 as the sleek Boeing 727 broke out of the clouds and thundered down the runway. The agent announced the expected departure time to the waiting passengers who would be boarding as soon as the Eugene passengers deplaned.

A friendly crew greeted the boarding passengers and quickly seated everyone. The aircraft was nearly full.

Among the flight crew was one particular flight attendant who caught the attention of the passengers, a good-looking man of medium height. His good humor was immediately apparent as he joked with passengers, revealing a broad smile under a neatly groomed mustache.

"H.C. Brantley at your service, folks," he said with a twinkle in his eyes. "We know you're hungry and unhappy that we're late, but we'll get this show on the road. So buckle up and here we go."

The aircraft started to taxi as the senior flight attendant greeted the passengers, introducing herself and her crew with an apology for being late, and asking the passengers to give their attention to the safety instructions.

Brantley knew safety instructions were routine and boring to many. In fact, some frequent travelers had heard them so many times that they now completely ignored the instructions, even though aircraft types have different cabin configurations and safety features. But H.C. had his own way of getting people's attention.

When the Senior asked the passengers to look at their safety cards, H.C., stationed in the forward section of the coach cabin, suddenly yawned with gusto and, with a bored expression, flapped the safety instruction card over his head upside down. He yawned again and turned the card right side up, cupping his left ear with his hand in an exaggerated effort to hear the Senior's instructions.

"Place the oxygen mask over your face first, then your child's," the instructions continued. H.C. started to hyperventilate and took the oxygen mask, putting it on as a party hat, and then fumbling to put it on correctly. He cradled an imaginary baby in his left arm and rocked it to and fro. Then he took off his mask and with great effort put it on the imaginary infant as he beamed and nodded his head.

"The seat cushion can be used as a flotation device—" H.C. grabbed a seat cushion, put his arms through the straps and flailed them wildly in mock swimming strokes. The passengers watched, dumbfounded, and looked to the Senior for signs of disapproval.

H.C. cast a ho-hum look at the Senior and yawned as she spoke endearingly of the inflight magazine.

"It's really okay," H.C. whispered, "but I prefer *Playboy* myself."

At the conclusion of his lighthearted performance, he bowed from the waist and with his lips silently formed the words "thank you," and then hurried to his jumpseat for takeoff. They had paid strict attention to H.C.'s rendition of safety instructions.

H.C. kept the passengers laughing all the way to Denver. After takeoff, the Senior designated *no smoking* sections of the aircraft.

"This is the stewardess with the mustache speaking," H.C. added when the Senior was finished. "Remember now, no smoking in the lavatory. That's a definite no-no, and if you get caught, remember: we'll have to put you off the plane."

The Rocky Mountains were in full view as the Boeing 727 broke out of the clouds on its final approach into Denver's Stapleton Airport.

"The stewardess with the mustache speaking," H.C. said as they headed down into Denver. "On your right is good old Pike's Peak. I heard tell it got its name from the famous explorer Captain Zebulon Pike, who set out for the Rockies in 1806, following the Arkansas River across the Great Plains. He was known for getting his bearings mixed up. One day in November, there was a peak protruding out of the clouds and, by its size, he thought it was close by. Well, he kind of underestimated how close it was and days later he was still wandering around in the snow. Then one of his scouts said, 'There, Captain Pike, is that mountain you've been looking for. Better take a peak.' And that, ladies and gentlemen, is how Pike's Peak got its name."

And that's how a young flight attendant named H.C. Brantley turned a delayed flight with nervous and unhappy passengers into a pleasant and relaxing trip.

H.C. Brantley is really *the star of the show* in his own right. Fellow flight attendants at his Denver base were happy when United Inflight Service selected H.C. as 1984s flight attendant of the Year for Denver. They feel that H.C. has broken the mold, adding personality and humor with just the right touch. H.C. watches for white-knuckled passengers and puts them at ease, and he salves tempers with good humor.

H.C. joined United in December 1972. In 1974 he became a Supervisor of flight attendants in Los Angeles and in 1976 he became an Instructor of Flight Training. Beside his career as a flight attendant, H.C. and his wife, who is also a United flight attendant, are trying to get a computer software business off the ground. Before joining United, H.C. spent two years in the army and studied at California State University for two years.

"It's a great job with travel and people . . . I like the people."

H.C.'s fellow flight attendants are glad he broke the mold and added his special personal touch to his job.

Vickie Cole Wolfe, flight attendant for United Airlines, 1994.

RETURN TO THE SKIES

United Airlines
Vickie Cole Wolfe
1961 - 1966
1983 - 1990s

The flip side of humor is tragedy. Although air crashes are rare, any flight attendant who has survived a crash never forgets it. It is often a flight attendant's swift action and concern for the passengers that saves lives.

Vickie Cole Wolfe was born in Washington state and attended Colorado Women's College in Denver for two years before becoming a United stewardess in 1961. She loved her job and interacted with people saving lives in a crash at Salt Lake City in November 1965. By April of 1966 she was in love with William Wolfe and left United to marry. The couple made their home in Denver and became the parents of a daughter and a son. Vickie says of her job as a stewardess:

"People are wonderful and my job as a stewardess was very fulfilling. I enjoyed the passengers and I liked the people I worked with on United. I missed flying even though I was a wife and mother.

"In 1983, new work laws made returning mothers acceptable as flight attendants through class action suits brought against the airlines. Each flight attendant was given a hearing and rulings were made on an individual basis. I was notified on July 2, 1983 that I had won my hearing in the McDonald class action lawsuit and could start training on July 12. I had a choice of Denver or Chicago as my home base. I naturally chose Denver, my home. I was on the line by August 20, my family are 100% supportive of me. I fly with 1977 bidding seniority and my original 1961 seniority for pay, passes and vacation bidding.

"There have been a lot of changes in the job, both positive and negative. The job itself, I feel is exactly what it used to be, *pleasing* the passengers from point A to point B. But now there is twice the paper and computer work to go along with it.

"The passengers have changed the most. No more classy white gloves, hats, etc. It is now Levis and shorts most of the time.

"I bid and work *first flight attendant* or *first class aisle* most of the time and enjoy that very much. Most of my flying partners have about eight years seniority and that is great. They are usually younger but that keeps me on my toes."

THE CRASH

"With no warning, it happened. It was November 11, 1965, about 6 pm, a cold day but good weather. A United B-727 was en route from Denver to LA with a stop at Salt Lake. After a sharp descent, the B-727 hit the runway in Salt Lake with such force that the main landing gear strut

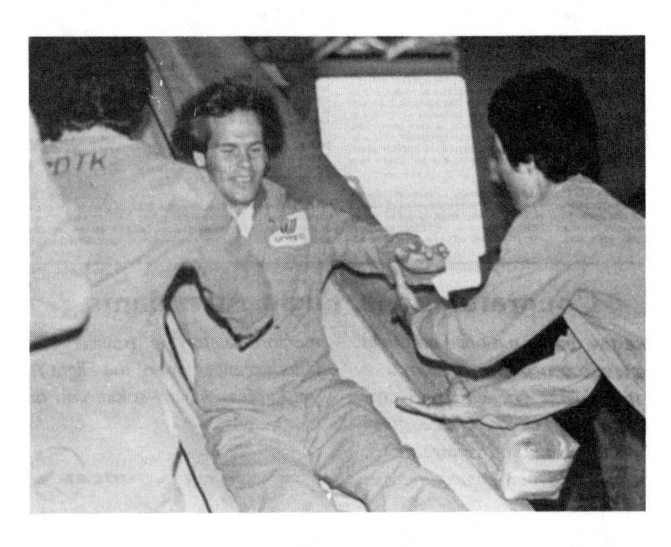

The slide evacuation training. Flight attendants receive *realistic* training. Procedures are reproduced with smoke and sounds of a crash. Recurrent training is mandatory in all aircraft configurations.

United's Janice West says she has today's safety professionals to rely on in emergencies. "Self-confidence and trust in every flight attendant crew member - because we've all had the same training." (United Airlines Photo)

drove through the wings.

"A ball of flame rolled down the aisle and the plane swerved back and forth on the runway. The B stewardess was on the jumpseat next to me by the cockpit door and she tried to jump up, she was so frightened. I pulled her back into her seat with such force that I broke several of her ribs. We were always taught to stay in our jump seats with the seat belts buckled during landing.

"The C stewardess was in the aft jumpseat by the stairwell. Smoke was so thick and black you couldn't see your hand in front of your face, even though the emergency lights were on. It seemed to take forever for the plane to finally come to a stop on the runway. People were immediately crushing at the entrance door where they had boarded the flight. I couldn't get the plug-type door open because it had to come into the plane a little before it opened. Passengers were pushing at my back and smashing me against the door.

"Somehow the flight engineer got out of the cockpit and squeezed by my side. Together with all the force we could muster, we got the door open! People poured out like a flood, flailing in all directions down the slide, which had automatically opened. The next thing I knew I was on the ground at the bottom of the slide.

"The C stewardess was trapped in the aft stairs with two passengers. She found a crack to push her hand through and moved it back and forth. Luckily, a fireman saw it. Rescuers had to cut a hole in the side of the aircraft to get her and the two male passengers out. One of the men died the following day. Out of 86 passengers, 43 were saved, as well as our crew of six.

"I wasn't seriously hurt in the ordeal. I was hospitalized three days for treatment of smoke inhalation, a deep scratch on my arm and badly bruised back muscles. But when I returned to my Denver base I developed pneumonia. I had bid a December schedule, but didn't fly again until mid-January, when the hearings on the crash were starting in Salt Lake. I was subpoenaed to almost all of the hearings, since I was the A stewardess on the flight.

"The crash was so horrible, and the hearings were almost as bad. They dragged on and on for nearly two years. I can bear to think about it now. United was so wonderful to us. They offered us all a trip to anywhere in the world. I had taken my vacation only the month before the accident and had gone on an extended trip around the world. I was in love and really didn't want to be away anymore. In April 1966, I became Mrs. William Wolfe and United paid for our honeymoon to Bermuda.

"I had to attend those hearings until 1968, until United said I didn't have to go anymore. I was then six months pregnant with our daughter.

"Getting back on the line has made me feel ten years younger and totally agrees with me. I have done some special assignment work for the Denver Inflight Office and I've enjoyed that also.

"After the wonderful honor of System-Wide flight attendant of the year in 1989, I was asked to represent United Airlines in London at the International flight attendant of the year convention. My husband and I spent four wonderful days there and I was named Runner-up in

Over-wing evacuation training is for all types of aircraft configurations.

the event. Wonderful honor!

"In May of 1991, I was requested to go to United's Chicago Inflight Center and become an instructor for our new-hire program. I did and enjoyed it very much. It was very rewarding for me and allowed me to have some favorable input into the training program. During the nine months I taught, I hopefully had a positive influence on those 200 trainees now flying the line.

"In December of 1991, I was then asked to take the position of Implementation Coordinator for the domestic Service Quality project that was to be presented to some 15,000 domestic flight attendants.

"I remained in Chicago, commuting on weekends to Denver until December of 1992 completing the implementation aspects of the conferences. Start dates of November and December were set for Chicago and San Francisco and a January start was set for Washington, D.C.. I returned to schedule flying January of 1993 in Denver and am delighted to be back "on the line" as that is my first love in this career. It's hard to believe that I've been back as a McDonald for ten years now. I plan to work until retirement.

"My commitment to this job and United Airline customers is to provide the service and attitude they expect and appreciate. Our business customers need a different type of response to their needs compared to the vacationing families who have perhaps saved for sometime to enjoy the benefits of air travel. I feel it's my responsibility to initiate the *do unto others* attitude."

ROMANCE TOOK FLIGHT

United Airlines

John T. Corpening

Inflight Training Instructor
and Author of *First Steps*

1984 - Present

John T. Corpening, United flight attendant and Inflight Trainer at United's Headquarters in Chicago, 1994.

"My love affair with flying began as a young boy when I visited my Grandfather's farm whose farmhouse just happened to sit in a deep *holler* at the very end of the runway of the Bennedum Airport in Clarksburg, West Virginia. From my vantage point on the second floor sleeping porch I eagerly awaited the takeoff of the red and white Capital Airlines' DC-3s. Barely airborne with it's gear still down, the passengers were clearly visible in the ship's windows.

"The romance continued after my family moved to Phoenix. I literally *hung out* at the old Sky Harbor Airport, knowing by heart the schedule of when the American DC-6s and TWA Constellations would roar in over the desert for landing. Before long the early jets arrived, but I departed for college and an eventual 20 year career in nursing and health care education. My heart however still longed for the skies.

"The romance took flight in 1984 when I was most fortunate to be accepted for training as a United Airlines' flight attendant. I have been able to combine my teaching experience with flying by serving in the capacity of Inflight Training Instructor since 1989. Introducing flight attendant Trainees to their new career has been a pure joy. Their enthusiasm and excitement is nothing short of remarkable. Graduation morning is a particularly special time when the pride on their faces is almost tangible. Pinning on their wings and sending them into the skies to embark on what I consider to be the world's best career is a special moment indeed.

"The *kids* as I call them will only know jet flying with it's pressurized cabins, above the weather altitude, flush toilets, on board entertainment, seat-back telephones, engineered galleys, and jetways. I suppose that most of us mourn what has passed, but if you don't know what was, then you can't dream about working just one trip in a DC-4 as I do!

"The flight attendant legacy is a proud, wonderfully colorful, and at times, a heroic one. I am trying to preserve this legacy of what has passed forever with a collection of inflight service memorabilia that includes wings, uniforms, photographs, and other artifacts that chronicles our proud past. When my collection finally resides in a museum, it will be my way of honoring those who walked the first footsteps in the sky as well as those who will walk after me."

FOOD SERVICE THE UNITED WAY

In the last sixty years, the airlines have grown and developed in many ways. Not the least of these is the kind of meals served in flight.

The thirties was the era of chicken. Chicken was served either from a thermos or cold. On the 12-passenger Boeing 80-As the Original Eight stewardesses served food cold. The menu included fried chicken, rolls, fruit cocktail, fruit and cake. Hot coffee and bouillon were served from thermos bottles. At that time, the food service was prepared by Palmer House in Chicago and carried on board

DC-4 food service: 2 stewardesses, 44 passengers, Henry Dreyfus serving tray, 1940s.

by the stewardesses.

In 1936, United opened its own flight kitchens. Henry Dreyfus designed a combination lunch box and serving tray that was first used on the 21-passenger DC-3 and later on the 44-passenger DC-4 aircraft. The tray was constructed of papier-mâché and plastic. Before serving, a stewardess turned the cover of the lunch box upside down and placed the tray on top. During food service, she would place pillows on the passengers' laps to support their food trays.[14]

Food was kept hot in individual casseroles wrapped in heavy paper for insulation. The individual casseroles were packed in boxes that were then sealed and placed in the galley of the DC-3. In 1946, the DC-4's galley had equipment for warming food. During this period of airline history, all service was one class and no liquor was ever served on board. United had a variety of meals which included a Continental breakfast, a complete breakfast, lunch, a midday snack, dinner, a special dinner with a menu for holidays, and a late evening snack (after 8 pm).

In 1947, United added eight DC-6s to their fleet for their Hawaiian service. The combination tray was no longer used because each seat now had its own individual tray for food service.[15]

The Boeing Stratocruiser was added to the Mainliner fleet in 1949 for service from the West Coast to Hawaii. This was the first United plane to have a passenger lounge, where drinks were served. The airplane had a stateroom in the rear with seats that made into beds at night. It was frequently reserved by honeymooning couples.[16]

In 1956, United retired the last of its 21-passenger DC-3s after twenty years of service. The DC-7 followed with non-stop transcontinental Red Carpet service. Liquor was now served to passengers, and stewardesses were sometimes referred to as "flying barmaids" instead of "nursemaids" like the Original Eight.[17]

In 1936 United was the first to have its own kitchen to supply passenger meals. The kitchen is in Oakland, California. (United Airlines Photo)

The retirement of the DC-3s proved to be temporary. In 1961 after the United merger with Capital Airlines, the DC-3 was again put into use on routes between Washington, Harrisburg, Elmira and Binghamton. The DC-3 was later replaced by Vickers Viscounts.

In 1969, food service changed drastically with the

[14]Frank J. Taylor, *High Horizons*, McGraw Hill, Inc., New York, 1964, p. 268.

[15]Ibid.

[16]Ibid.

[17]Ibid.

Stratocruiser to Hawaii with a lounge, honeymoon suite and elegant food service.

introduction of the Boeing-747 jumbo jet. These two-level 350-passenger aircraft are used for United's Royal Hawaiian service, and transcontinental Ocean to Ocean service. The food is prepared by the galley staff in the belly of the aircraft. Partially prepared and frozen meals are set up, cooked and arranged on food service carts, which are then taken by elevator to the passenger serving level.

United more recently started its international service to Tokyo with the Boeing-747 and to Hong Kong with the DC-10. An elegant food service with Oriental as well as Western meals, is served aloft. Other routes have been added in Asia as well as South America and Australia with international food service.

United was the last of the major carriers to drop one-class service, and the last to serve liquor aloft, to show movies on long flights, and to provide VIP lounge clubs known as the Red Carpet lounge. However, United was first in its food service, having its own flight kitchens and chefs. This is largely attributed to President W.A. Patterson's hiring of Don Magarrell in the 1930s. Magarrell pioneered the creation of a variety of inflight meals that could be served from a small galley space. These meals had an appetizing appeal for passengers, were served on special size china, and were a vast improvement over the standard cold fried chicken.[18] Don Magarrell's expertise, United's flight attendants, quality service have helped make United the global airline it is today.

Today flight attendants are multi-talented. A flight attendant in one month may fly on six different aircraft types with numerous configurations and galleys[19] New emphasis is being placed on special meal choices. Today United offers a wide variety of meal choices and they are appetizing as well as responsive to dietary and religious dictates. The customer will not be faced with a compromise in appearance or taste.

UNITED'S SPECIAL MEAL CHOICES

Asiatic / Indian
Baby
Bland
Diabetic
Friendly Skies
Gluten-free
High-fiber
Hindu
Kosher
Lacto-vegetarian
Light Choice
Low-calorie
Low-cholesterol
Low-protein
Low-purine
Low-sodium
Moslem
Non-lactose
Special meal
Vegetarian (pure)

Children's meals feature McDonald's popular foods for breakfast, lunch and dinner plus activities and a toy. These are available on more than 80% of United's meal flights across the U.S. United gets requests for McDonald's Friendly Sky Meals from people traveling on both domestic and international flights.[20]

On many international flights United offers regional specialties. For example: on a flight from Glasgow, Scotland to Washington, DC's Dulles Airport, first class customers can choose an appetizer of Loch Fyne Salmon, an entree of medallions of venison and Scottish scones for tea. The menu choice was created through the United

[18]Frank J. Taylor, *High Horizons*, McGraw Hill, Inc., New York, 1964, p. 268.

[19]*United Times, Corporate Communications*, August 1993, vol. 6, no. 7, p. 4.

[20]"Making Meals Special," *United Times, Corporate Communications*, vol. 6, no. 6, July 1993.

Kingdom's Hotel of the Year, One Devonshire Gardens of Glasgow. The tea service was designed with the help of the Gidleigh Park Hotel in Devon, England.[21]

Employees in United's Catering Division today are creating meals with varied and innovative choices.[22] Meal service has come a long way from the chicken of the 1930s and United is continuing to cater to the culinary requests of its customers.

First class international passengers fill out a card at the beginning of their flight, indicating when they would like to eat and sleep, and whether they prefer a leisurely "early seating" meal served in courses or a briefer meal presentation.[23]

The premium food service includes pre-departure beverage service, premium food and liquors including beluga caviar and Godiva chocolates. United feels investment in first class international service anticipates passengers needs and provides them with the personalized service they pay for.[24]

FULL CIRCLE TO AMERICAN

Mohawk, Eastern, Presidential, Qantas, and American Airlines

Kathy Gifford

Agent - Stewardess - Flight Attendant

1960s - 1990s

"When I was twenty, I wanted to be a *stewardess* because it was an honorable and respected profession that allowed me to grow and expand. When I was forty, I wanted to be a *flight attendant.* After working on the ground for a while, I discovered I missed the clouds, the people, and the constant challenge and changing circumstances.

"I was a *stewardess* in the 1960s and a *flight attendant* in the 1990s. I have had the pleasure and pain of seeing changes of standards lowered. Some airlines accept applicants who are eighteen years old with little or no work experience and fail to really realize what we are and why we are there and undo the image that we as professionals have worked hard to create.

"I stand by my statement of years ago when mothers would ask if I would recommend this profession for their daughter. You bet! It is the greatest hands on, in depth, heart wrenching, gratifying education you could ever ask to receive. You see it all! At age 46 years just when I feel I have seen and heard it all, I find out I'm just a babe in the wood with a lot to learn.

"I graduated from high school in 1964. I graduated from college in 1983 when my youngest child was age four. My airline experiences have been: A Reservations Agent for Mohawk Airlines which is no longer in business.

Kathy Gifford, Eastern stewardess of the 1960s.

I was a stewardess in the 1960s for Eastern. I trained six weeks in Miami, Florida and flew both domestic and international trips because I was dual trained. I left Eastern in 1968 to marry and raise a family. While a stay-at-home mom I was involved in volunteer community service and politics. I organized political campaigns and functions and helped communities become more educated in government.

"I returned to the airline industry in 1987. I became

[21]"Making Meals Special," *United Times, Corporate Communications,* Vol. 6, No. 6, July 1993.

[22]Ibid

[23]*United Times, Corporate Communications,* August 1993, vol. 6, no. 7, p 7.

[24]Ibid.

a flight attendant for Presidential Airlines after three weeks training in Washington, DC which was a domestic airline. It is no longer in business. I worked in a supervisory position for Qantas, for emergency preparedness recurrent flight attendant training (EPT) that flight attendants are required to do once a year.

"As a flight attendant for American Airlines, I fly domestic only because of the no smoking on flights. I trained five weeks in Dallas/Ft. Worth, Texas and was first based in Washington, DC and currently in Dallas. My favorite aircraft are the 767 and 757s for performance, safety and reliability.

"Those of us that work in the clouds see the experiences, the tragedies and joys of life every day. It is an education in life. Institutional study, as valuable as it is, can not substitute for the reality of life as it happens. The ability to be a dedicated, professional flight attendant is a gift.

"As I am a single parent I have had some worrisome times. My youngest daughter, who is seventeen, has had some serious health problems and has been hospitalized 19 times in the past five years. My job has helped, as when I go to work I see people with handicapped and terminally ill children and I think how lucky I am, as Lauren is fixable and is getting better. When I see someone who is ill and will not get better I have an attitude adjustment and I become better for it."

Kathy Gifford, American Airlines flight attendant, 1994.

Golden Graduation

I love flyin' far and wide to see the land I love,
Climb to find the blue horizon, the sun and the sky above.
It's my flight and I know it's right, and I just smile inside.
From the sunrise in the east to the sunset in the west,
We're AMERICAN AIRLINES, Doin' What We Do Best.

Forty-eight young voices sang those words May 2, sang them in harmony and with conviction. It was a special moment for those women and men of AA flight attendant class 83-2, as well it should be.

But the gathering and the singing was special for the spectators, too, for a little bit of history was being played out that day at the Learning Center.

Class 83-2 was symbolic because its members graduated 50 years after the first four stewardesses for American Airways accepted their wings and began flying between Chicago and New York — the very next day.

The Golden Anniversary was marked by an array of special guests, topped by a keynote speech by a man who knows quality when he sees it, Stanley Marcus, chairman emeritus of Neiman-Marcus. In his talk (see text below), he praised AA's flight attendant corps, saying its members have always been a standard of quality for the airline industry.

Also on hand with greetings were President Robert L. Crandall, Thomas G. Plaskett, senior vice president-marketing; Patsy Underwood, senior director of flight services and training, plus the smiling graduates' families and friends.

With wings freshly pinned, red roses in lapels — and in most cases — moistness in their eyes, the Golden Anniversary class accepted the good wishes of every person watching.

And the next day, just as their predecessors did a half-century ago, many of these flight attendants were off flying their trips, Doin' What They Do Best.

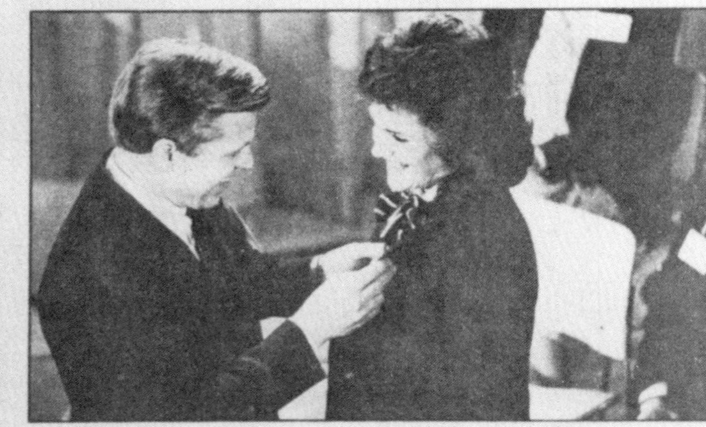

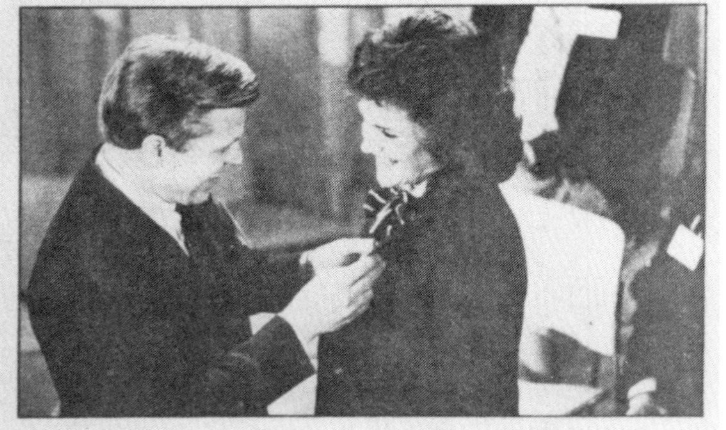

Class of 83-2 (photo left) sings AA theme song at graduation. (Photo above) Two future flyers on hand for their mother's graduation were 3-year-old twins Dana (in foreground) and Kathy Reed. Mom is DFW-based Paula Reed. President Robert L. Crandall pinned wings on 48 proud graduates (upper right). This one is Melissa Stockton, who will be based at Chicago. After the new flight attendants received their wings, Stanley Marcus presented each graduate with a copy of his book *Quest for the Best*. Shown with their copies are (lower right, from left) F/As Paul Duchesne, Trish Kennedy, and Laurel Debeaudry.

AMERICAN PREMIUM SERVICE

People's Express Continental, American Todd Matthew Powell 1980s - Present

Flight attendants sometimes change airlines and domiciles too. Todd is an example of this and today is a Premium language speaker with American.

A personable young man impressed me with the ease and gracious manner in which he conducted the service and cabin crew responsibilities as the premium flight attendant. His announcements in Spanish following the English version were spoken like it was his native tongue. It was obvious that he liked his job.

I had the good fortune to fly in American's first class flight on a 757 aircraft to Costa Rica with Todd, and asked him for information for a book on professional flight attendants I was researching. This is his story. . . .

"My full name is Todd Matthew Powell and I am from Peoria, Illinois. I graduated from Quincy University in Quincy, Illinois, with a B.S. in International Business. I had known for sometime that I wanted to be a flight attendant, but I thought it best to get a college degree first.

"After graduation from college, I was hired by the upstart discount airline, People's Express, as a flight attendant and was based in Newark, New Jersey. The airline was not much on service, but offered low fares. In addition to serving food and beverages, we had to collect tickets and forms of payment. You can imagine the chaos on the Newark to Boston flights with 150 passengers and thirty minutes flying time.

"Eventually, People's Express was bought out by Continental Airlines, and I had the opportunity to become a flight attendant for Continental for two years. I flew mostly the route Newark to London on the Boeing 747-200 aircraft. It is a beautiful, spacious aircraft to work on. It is my most favorite of all.

"It was an unstable time for Continental and they were in Chapter 11 Bankruptcy. I applied to American Airlines, as I wanted better stability. I was hired by American in 1988. During my training in Dallas at American's Learning Center, I qualified as a Spanish speaker.

"Our training at the Learning Center lasted five weeks. It was a very comprehensive course in aircraft specifics for safety and service, food service, and grooming We were closely monitored each week for our weight.

"On graduation, I was sent to New York. My pay was $800 a month. I remained in New York two and half years flying to Europe and the Caribbean routes. At the end of two and a half years I was also able to qualify as a Portuguese speaker and fly trips to Rio de Janeiro and Sao Paulo, Brazil. I find these trips interesting and it is much cheaper to live in Florida than in New York as my base.

"I have been a premium flight attendant for nearly a year. In May 1993 I had a refresher training in Dallas on procedures and policies of American, as well as the responsibilities of a first flight attendant in charge of the cabin crew. I enjoy my position as a premium. I have control of what is going on and I also prefer to work in the first class cabin - American's service is premium quality."

Todd Powell, American Airlines Premium International flight attendant, 1994. Todd speaks fluent Spanish and Portuguese and flies South American routes.

FROM MUSKEGON TO MUNICH

American Airlines
Terrance G. Koegler
Flight Service Manager
1985 - Present

Flight attendants can use their flying experience to go into management positions in inflight service.

Terry Koegler is an American Airline Flight Service Manager at Chicago's International Airport. He supervises 170 domestic and international flight attendants at American's busy hub. He is one of many managers in a demanding job in inflight supervision. Terry tells his story, that began as a young boy.

"I became an aviation buff at age nine when I had my first flight aboard Eastern Airlines in 1972. I knew I wanted to target a career in aviation in later years. I took flying lessons at Waukegan airport near my home at age sixteen. However due to uncontrollable weather conditions I did not receive my private pilot's license until my first year at Embry-Riddle Aeronautical University in 1981.

"I majored in Aeronautical Science (flying). It was a difficult time for airlines and many pilots were being furloughed. I discussed the situation with my parents and it made sense to change my major to Aviation Administration. For a job, I could then apply in many areas. I graduated with a degree in 1985 and faced reality - the job market.

Terry Koegler (center) and other American Airlines flight attendants having fun before boarding passengers, 1994.

Terry Koegler, American Airlines flight attendant (center) and an O'Hare inflight supervisor, 1994.

"To my disappointment, I was told all major airlines *do not hire* into entry level management. They explained that I should get *my foot in the door*, and then move up. I was now regretting my decision to deny my F-15 pilot slot in the Air Force ROTC in school. A ten year commitment had been frightening at the time to a 19 year old.

"Since I had to get 'my foot in the door,' I decided to target a specific job. I didn't want to work in reservations or on the ramp. It was between ticket agent or flight attendant. I decided flying would be a great experience. There was one major problem. There is a specific look for an airline crew member. I was nearly six feet tall and 220 pounds. Airlines would not look at anyone over 180 pounds with my height. So stress . . . I learned to say *no* to french fires and *yes* to jogging!

"I interviewed with American, Eastern, and Continental to no avail! I interviewed with United and all went well until I went to the medical department. Two weeks later I received a letter of rejection. Luckily, a neighbor knew a Vice President at United that found out I'd been three pounds overweight. They really do stick to the weight requirement.

"Another applicant was a flight attendant supervisor with Simmons (American Eagle) in Chicago. Her name was Elise. She talked me into interviewing with them. I did and I was hired!

"Two weeks later I was training in Marquette, Michigan. I had two and a half weeks in the classroom and one week working with another crew member. I was qualified on Short's 360s and the YS-11. At Eagle we flew four to twelve legs in a day with eight hour layovers making $12,000 a year — *Pure Glamour!*

"I decided to hit the major airline circuit one more time. I lined up two interviews in 1986. One with American, and the other with Northwest.

"At American I had a very structured interview which was successful — the magic was the scale?!?!? I was measured at five feet eleven inches and my weight could *not* exceed 160 pounds. I weighed in at 161 pounds! The interviewer allowed me a second interview and let the medical department take my official weight. Two nurses said 161 pounds and a little old nurse told me to hold my head straight — I was a little taller, so I was OK! They would let me know . . . .

"My Northwest interview was a group interview. This was successful. In two weeks I was set up for a second interview. In the meantime American called to confirm that I was accepted in the class of '86-4. I gladly resigned American Eagle to pursue my future with a major airline.

"At American's Learning Center my five and a half week training was both enjoyable and stressful. Every Monday was dreaded — you guessed it — weigh-ins! I managed to *survive* them.

"The last week of training before graduation the instructor entered the classroom with a bowl of apples, one and a half weeks later we were in *The Big Apple*, New York City! I flew two trips New York to Los Angeles and loved it. The following week I was back at the Learning Center (alias *Charm Farm*) in Dallas to be trained for over water, international flights. JFK needed flight attendants to fly the Caribbean.

"There were five of us in a one bedroom apartment in Manhattan — two men and three women. We flew San Juan turn around only so we were *all* home at night — talk about stress!

"After eight months of probation, I was fortunate to get a lateral transfer with a 23 year flight attendant at Chicago International. International bases are allowed to swap with each other.

"My first four months at Chicago International, December 1986 to March 1987, I flew only Honolulu because I wasn't trained for Europe. The following fall, I decided to teach Recurrent Ditching Training for International flight attendants for two years.

"Because of a wonderful Base Manager at Chicago International, I decided to interview for an International Service Manager and put my education to use. I started managing 40 international flight attendants and now have 170 domestic and international flight attendants under my supervision. They are a great group who want an approachable supervisor and one that its supportive. I try to be both.

"My most memorable and rewarding experience in years of management has been in flying the troops home from Operation Desert Storm. What a thrill to fly into the desert to bring those men and women home to safety. Flying them into the desert had been very humbling. All they had were their back packs, and gas masks and guns. Needless to say, the plane home was very somber.

"My job gives me the opportunity to be involved in aviation working with people, helping people and being productive as part of a team for American."

TRAINING AND WORKING LIFE, AMERICAN STYLE

Continental Airlines
American Airlines
Sherrill Dickey
1984 - 1993

"I'm a firm believer that deregulation caused a number of the problems the airline industry is facing today, particularly the demise of so many carriers. Each surviving airline has responded differently to the glut of experienced flight attendants in the job market, but none better than that inevitable trend setter, American Airlines.

"When Continental Airlines filed for its second bankruptcy in 1990, I had already served four of the six years that marked my tenure as a flight attendant there. I decided at the second bankruptcy filing that I was not prepared to deal with the personal stress and the career stagnation associated with working for a company in bankruptcy.

"Before I quit Continental, I began interviewing with other major carriers. I'd heard all the stories that 'this or that airline' wouldn't even talk to you if you'd worked for another carrier, and especially if you'd worked for Continental. This could not have been more false at American Airlines. In my group interview, my mentioning I was currently employed as a flight attendant drew a warm and understanding smile from my recruiter. In my one-on-one interview. I was encouraged to tell about my company volunteer work as a Continental Airlines flight attendant, to talk about my good letters, and to remember the wonderful memories I'd had as I'd come to love being a flight attendant.

"Not once during five and a half weeks of training at American Airlines was I made to feel as if my previous flight attendant experience was not acknowledged and

appreciated. In fact, one of our instructors faced the class on the first day and said, *for many of you who have flown before, we are not here to show you what American Airlines expects of you in our uniform.* The instructors showed genuine compassion in recognizing those who had flown for airlines now out of business (Eastern, Midway, Pan Am). Some of these men and women had invested 25 years of their lives at another airline only to be starting over at the bottom of American Airlines' Seniority list. To them, the instructors said, *We want you to know we are happy to benefit from your experience. We're sorry you lost your airline.* I've noticed that American doesn't over-use the word *family* in the media, and they didn't over-use it in training. The compassion and the love are just there. You could see it in their faces. And the pride in their company says it all in one word, American.

"With respect to training content, I was overwhelmed by the high technology laser disc computer equipment American Airlines provided us with in presenting our course materials. The laser disc actually turns a computer screen into a TV set but is different from watching a video in that you can *interact* with the course material by touching the screen. The student can start and stop, or repeat, any portion of the lecture at any time by a mere touch of his or her fingertip to the screen. One can answer computer-generated review questions by touching the screen as well.

"For example, First Aid was my greatest fear, always has been. I'd had no exposure to the world of medicine and my family is remarkably healthy, so a mental picture of a broken arm or seizure or even an asthma attack was next to impossible for me to muster. American Airlines' training modules in these areas are incredible. Each individual student can work at his or her own pace and view actual flight attendants on actual airplanes dealing with actors trained to simulate these medical conditions. What a higher degree of confidence I felt after seeing *actual* medical emergencies instead of studying anatomical drawings or talking hypothetically.

"The laser disc equipment also enabled us to see, at our own pace, actual aircraft interiors with respect to door operation and location of emergency equipment. For first time flight attendants, this was very valuable. And for those of us who had flown for other carriers, it helped reinforce American's way in our mind with constant visual representation."

DOUBLE DUTY
Continental and American

Sherri, as she is called, celebrated her one year anniversary party as an American flight attendant May 13, 1993, in Dallas. It was on a special flight in the refurbished Continental DC-3 she had worked on at airshows and special flights in a 1950 hostess uniform - besides her regular schedule when a flight attendant for Continental. Husband James Minor, Continental pilot arranged the party. Invitations were sent to her Dallas classmates living in the Dallas area for an early evening flight over Dallas. Champagne and dinner was served by Sherri at an executive airport. The refurbished DC-3 had originally been American Airlines Flagship, *Big Spring*. The aircraft did double duty for Continental and American for a flight attendant who had a very unusual celebration.

Sherrill Dickey, American Airlines flight attendant (left), in the cockpit after a flight, 1994.

This is not an unusual occurrence today as many flight attendants have worked for more than one airline...the blending of the great service that the airlines in America provide the traveling public.

I was asked to attend this flight over Dallas . . . alas, I had another commitment! It would have been particularly meaningful to me, as I had been a Continental hostess during World War II (1943-1945) working in Lockheed Lodestars. I later became a United Air Lines stewardess and I loved the DC-3 aircraft and preferred to be scheduled for its flights.

AMERICAN'S C.R. SMITH MUSEUM 1993

American Airlines celebrated its sixtieth anniversary of inflight service in 1993 with the opening of the C.R. Smith Museum at Dallas/Ft. Worth International Airport. The museum is situated adjacent to the airport and honors its former founder and President of American Airlines. Smith began a long career in aviation in 1927. He was first named President of American in 1934 and continued until he was appointed the U.S. Secretary of Commerce under Lyndon B. Johnson.[25]

C.R. Smith first developed the DC-2 and DC-3 in cooperation with the Douglas Aircraft company's engineers. This airliner became the most famous in aviation history and was known as the workhorse of the airlines in the 1940s. The aircraft is still in use today by some smaller commuter airlines.[26]

Nearly 10,000 items have been donated to the C.R. Smith museum. Volunteers collected and sorted the many artifacts. Betty Overstreet, John Milandra, Bob Swartz, and Doug Bauder all volunteered their time the past two years. They tagged and entered items from the 1920s to the present in a database. The museum's director, Greg Kennedy said that the museum became a reality because of their volunteer efforts.[27]

The museum is unique in its presentation of American Airlines' history. Museum visitors can use video/computer work stations to get data on each era since the 1920s.

The museum features a mock-up of an airline counter where visitors receive boarding passes and enter a theater through a simulated jet bridge. There, everyone is seated in First Class airline seats for take off on flight 1364 to Boston's Logan International Airport. All are briefed on safety features and a 15 minute, 70mm film is presented on a large screen.[28]

Visitors to the museum may also sit in a mock-up of a cockpit and experience the thrill of piloting a jet using flight simulators. Tools, materials and training for aircraft maintenance are explained by videos. The museum visitors are given a full scope of the airline's operations by items on display that include American's SABRE access terminals, as well as baggage sorting scanners, routing and scheduling. There is a computer model of an airport's operations. Children can see the science of flight using wind tunnels in a flight lab which teaches the principles of aerodynamics in a fun way.[29]

The C.R. Smith Museum is not only a tribute to American Airlines' excellence and to their founder...it also gives the museum visitor a visual and hands-on experience in U.S. airline history.

The C.R. Smith American Airlines Museum in Dallas, Texas opened its doors in 1993. The museum honors its first president and his great legacy of the airline he helped build. American celebrated 60 years of inflight service in 1993. (Learning Center and C.R. Smith Museum, American Photos)

[25]Jack Knight, *Air Log and AFA News*, Lindberg Notes, April-June 1993.

[26]Ibid.

[27]Ibid.

[28]Ibid.

[29]Ibid.

UP, UP AND AWAY
TWA

Air mail service started for Western Air Express in April 1926 between Salt Lake City and Los Angeles. A month later on May 23, the small airline carried its first two passengers. In the next three years, routes grew to include Denver, San Francisco and Kansas City. In the same time period, the Pennsylvania and Santa Fe Railroads founded TAT (Transcontinental Air Transport) to combine air and rail transportation. The new airline was known as the Lindbergh Line, named after Charles Lindbergh, the organizer of the operations.

A ten-seat Ford Trimotor called the "Tin Goose" operated three-stop service during the daytime between Los Angeles and Clovis, New Mexico. The Santa Fe train then carried the passengers from Clovis at night to the four stops between Waynoka, Oklahoma and Columbus, Ohio where the Pennsylvania Railroad began. This combined journey took forty-eight hours, which saved three days of travel on the rails alone.

A TWA hostess in the rear galley of a stratocruiser (a converted C-54) used after WWII.

Hostess for Transcontinental and Western Airline, Inc., Miss Lines of the first class (1935) is shown in her uniform of gray flannel complemented with overseas style cap and red silk blouse, gray oxford shoes and a black leather bag. She is ready to board a DC-3.

COURIERS

The first flight attendants were known as couriers. They were the sons of the men who financed TAT, and they took over the inflight duties of the co-pilot. They added a touch of class, wearing the white jacket of the steamship steward. They worked closely with the airport passenger agents. An "aero trailer" car was used to transport the passengers from the city to the airport. The courier picked up the food for the flight en route, weighed and tagged the luggage and checked the passengers' tickets.

Another responsibility of the courier was to load all mail and freight. On board, he explained safety belts and the aircraft's heating and ventilation system. En route he had to be alert for airsickness and dispense "burp bags" and he gave the passengers chewing gum to alleviate ear discomfort during ascent and descent.

Food was elegantly served. For breakfast, hot bullion was served with bread and butter sandwiches. Luncheon was served hot. Precooked boiled chicken was kept hot in Thermos containers. The chicken was served with salad, fruit, coffee and milk. In the afternoon, tea was served with cold sliced meats and fancy sandwiches. The passengers were served on a table and since galley space was limited, the meal was served in courses.

Newsreels and cartoons were first shown en route on October 9, 1929 in the new eighteen-passenger Curtiss Condors which nearly doubled the passenger load of the Ford Trimotors.

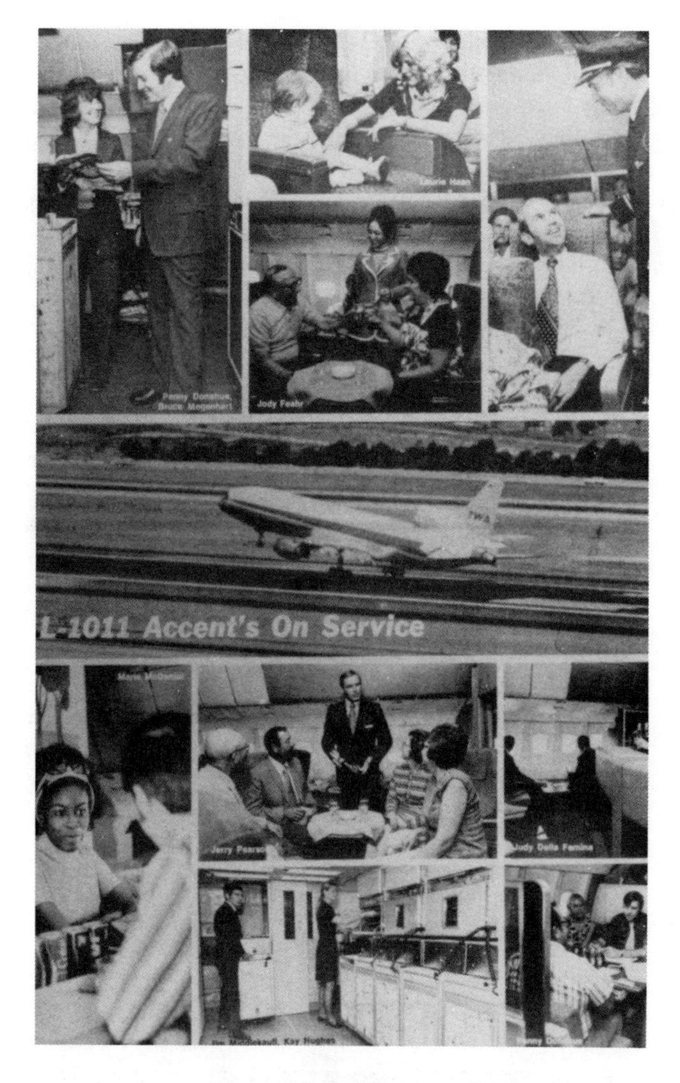

A merger with Maddux added San Francisco and San Diego routes on July 15, 1930. TAT and Western Air Express became Transcontinental and Western Air Lines and TWA was born.

HOSTESSES TWA STYLE

When TWA's directors decided to inaugurate hostess service, they imposed the nursing requirement because they felt that nurses were disciplined individuals. Some 1600 women applied in 1935 for the first hostess class. Only 30 were selected and graduated on December 6, 1935.

The first uniform was of gray wool serge, and was worn year around. A hostess was required to wear a jacket regardless of the weather, when passengers were boarding or deplaning.

The word "hostess" was preferred over "stewardess", as TWA's ladies of the sky were trained to greet passengers and function as a representative of the airline. Her duties were to arrive fifteen minutes prior to boarding time to check that the passenger count and the meal count were in accord. Passengers' names from her manifest were used in rendering all services. Newspapers, magazines, cards and checker games were dispensed after the aircraft was in flight.

Hot meals were boarded in Thermos containers in winter and cold box lunches were served in the summer months. Tea and coffee, kept hot in Thermos bottles, were available on all flights.

The Douglas Sleeper Transport (DST) was added to TWA's service in 1937. The hostess determined the berth assignments by the passengers' sleeping habits, sex and destination. Before each refueling stop en route, all passengers were awakened to relieve ear pressure. The hostess cleaned the lavatories during the night and served breakfast before landing.

By October, 1937, TWA had 69 hostesses based in Kansas City, Newark, Chicago, Los Angeles, San Francisco and Pittsburgh.

The Boeing Stratoliner was the first four-engine, pressurized aircraft used by TWA in 1940. It had the capacity to carry thirty-three passengers. For night operation, nine passengers had lounge chairs and sixteen had sleeper berths. Two hostesses were assigned to work the flight. The senior hostess set up trays in the galley and the junior hostess served the passengers.

TWA's first-class service on an L-1011, 1984. The serving smock is used to complement the dark uniforms with classic style - other airlines followed suit into the 1990s.

By 1946, TWA was awarded an international route to Europe. *The Star of Paris* was the first Constellation, and inaugurated TWA's service to France. The nursing requirement had been dropped and the hostess ranks had grown to number 350.

The first class of twenty-two pursers and twenty-six hostesses trained for international flights was graduated November 11, 1945. In 1946, a new uniform of blue wool with a TWA *cutout* was worn with navy blue accessories. This uniform was to become an all-time favorite.

The purser on international flights was male. He was trained to be a *maître d'* and exemplified TWA's quality service with his special flair. His duties were to coordinate the hostess responsibilities, handle all liquor and food provisions, all TWA and government forms and do all the heavy lifting. With the addition of the Paris route, Transcontinental and Western Air, Inc. became known as Trans World Air Lines. By 1950, TWA had inaugurated short haul, fast service via the Martin forty-passenger aircraft. One hostess served all forty passengers single-handedly. Oleg Cassini designed a new winter and summer uniform for hostesses in 1955 to give the look of the fifties and TWA started serving liquor on all its domestic routes in 1957.

The jet age was ushered in by the Boeing 707. TWA's coast to coast service began March 20, 1959. A new drop-type tray replaced the bayonet service table and provided faster food service. By 1960, *Flair in the Air*, a new jet age look in hostess uniforms was designed by Don Loper. A winged hat symbolized worldwide service with a TWA emblem surrounded by interlocking hemispheres. Along with the jet aircraft, Royal Ambassador service was introduced with new china, crystal, flatware and linen for first class passengers. The first hostess serving smock was designed by Pierre Balmain in 1966.

In the sixties, TWA's fleet had expanded to include the Convair 880, the Boeing 727 and the Douglas DC-9. Hostesses were given a *speed pac*, a prepacked liquor cart top. This was covered by canvas with a plastic window to take inventory and was secured to the liquor cart before take-off. The *speed pac* enabled the hostess to give quicker personalized beverage service.

In 1968, the *Up, Up and Away* advertising campaign promoted TWA's international service. Paper uniforms were designed by Eliza Daggs. They were throw-aways which could be altered to fit by scissors and were intended to match the cuisine of the city served by a particular flight: Rome, Paris, New York or London. The paper uniforms proved to be of short duration. They tore easily and were considered a fire hazard. They were discarded (literally) in favor of gold, poppy, orange and green plaid coordinated ensembles for summer. By 1969, an international base at Los Angeles was opened for Pacific Royal Ambassador Service with china table service designed especially for use on the Boeing 707s.[30]

[30]Excerpts from the TWA 1926-1984 Dee Meyer slide show script

The introduction of the 747 aircraft in 1970 again brought changes in hostess service. Now they had spacious galleys equipped with ovens to help in serving 342 passengers. The job of Flight Service Manager was created to coordinate the large cabin crew.

In 1968, the hat was no longer included in the hostess uniform. Slacks were introduced as part of the uniform, as were hot pants (short shorts). This radically new uniform was designed by Valentino of Rome.

By 1972, the name *hostess* was changed to *cabin attendant* to include both men and women. The term *flight attendant* was adopted to include pursers, flight service managers and cabin attendants. Male cabin attendants wore a gold half-stripe on their jacket sleeves to distinguish them from the higher-ranking pursers.

By 1975, TWA had suspended Pacific service with a swap with Pan American for new routes in Europe. By 1978, flight attendants were wearing the new "professional look" uniforms in navy wool created by Ralph Lauren. This distinctive look was emulated by other airlines and is still evident today.

TWA has always been considered America's glamour airline. It was first in many inflight services and excellence remains the company's goal. TWA's motto is *Being the best isn't everything, it's the only thing.*

TWA's hostesses into the 1980s

THE GOOD LIFE
TWA
Anna Gilmore Schmitt
1948-1983

With over three and half decades with TWA, a flight attendant became a role model by her example of teamwork and her love of people.

After nearly four decades of service as a flight attendant for TWA, Annie Schmitt flew her last trip on December 1, 1983. Her husband Joe, close relatives, friends and Chicago-based TWA managers were at the gate to greet Annie's flight 516, which marked the completion of thirty-six years with TWA. As she stepped off the plane, she was presented with red roses and a kiss from her husband.

During the ensuing festivities, Captain Don Carr and Annie's inflight supervisors reflected on her attributes as a role model for future flight attendants: her serene blonde beauty comparable to that of Grace Kelly, her poise, her charm, her teamwork, her warm smile, and her genuine love of people. As one co-worker commented, "Annie remains in the hearts of all of us who worked with her as a role model for the future."

Annie had always been fascinated with airplanes and aviation. After high school she worked for United Airlines at their general offices not far from her home in Chicago. She decided she needed more education, so after a year she quit United to attend Woodrow Wilson Junior College for a couple of years. "In one of my classes I became acquainted with a girl who wanted to be a stewardess," Annie recalls. "We decided to apply to United after we finished school. United wasn't hiring at the time, so we applied to TWA. I got the job but my friend was turned down because of poor eyesight.

TWA flight attendant Annie Gilmore Scmitt in the cockpit after a flight, 1983. The same dark, classic uniform is worn in the 1990s.

"McConnell Schools was training for TWA in Kansas City. The tuition was $325 for an eight-week course. The flight to Kansas City was my first ride in an airplane and I loved it! The training program included daily exercise classes, grooming, and practicing walking up and down stairs in high heels. Classes covered meals, meteorology, first aid, and airline familiarization, including drawing on a map all the routes of all the airlines. Twelve of us graduated and two of us flew for thirty-six years," says Annie, beaming.

Her first flight as a hostess was on a 21-passenger DC-3 from Chicago to Washington, DC, with eight stops. During her first few months with TWA, Annie flew from Chicago to Philadelphia. Since then her flights have taken her to nearly all the cities on TWA's domestic system and international routes.

TWA hostess on a DC-3, Annie Gilmore Scmitt, welcomes a pistol-packing passenger in 1948.

She remained based in Chicago except for one year (1968) when she flew TWA's international flights out of New York. Those flights included the grueling *double crossing* which involved six days on duty: New York to London, London to Chicago, Chicago to London, and London to New York. The polar flight, New York to London, London to Los Angeles (over the North Pole), Los Angeles to London, London to Paris, and Paris to New York also involved six days of flying.

"I didn't fly to all of the cities on TWA's overseas routes," says Annie, "but I have visited them on vacations."

The variety of aircraft on which she has flown since 1945 has required periodic upgrading of training in inflight service and safety for each. They include: the Douglas DC-3 and DC-4; the Martin-404; the Boeing-707; the Convair-800; the Boeing-727, 727-Stretch, and the Boeing Stratocruiser; the Constellation 049, 749, 1049, 1049G; and the Lockheed L-1011.

"The greatest changes have been in the meal service," says Annie, reflecting on all the changes she's seen during her years in the airline industry. "Meal service changed with the introduction of each type of aircraft. On the DC-3s I served on cardboard trays with inserts for the entree, salad, and dessert. The entrees were heated and put in thermos containers. I served a lot of cheese sandwiches for lunch. One captain I frequently flew with hated cheese and he'd throw the sandwiches out the cockpit window during the flight. I could imagine that the route from Chicago to New York was strewn with cheese sandwiches!" she laughed. "Meal service now is very sophisticated with flight galleys on the L-1011 and serving carts.

"The other big changes since the forties were safety, security and what the passengers are allowed to bring aboard the aircraft. She remembers one incident in 1948 when a passenger was going as a delegate to the Republican Convention in Philadelphia, toting a gun in a holster. As Annie says, "You wouldn't see anyone on board an airplane today with a gun."

As for humor, Annie recalls a 727 flight on which she was working first class. Amy Vanderbilt and her husband were on board. Annie was responsible for collecting garbage from the galley in large brown plastic bags. On her way to the lavatory to stow them for landing, she slipped and dumped the garbage all over the Vanderbilts. "They laughed," says Annie, "but all good etiquette went out the window."

And there are flights she remembers with fondness. "My favorites were the Chicago-Las Vegas turnarounds in the L-1011," Annie says with a sigh of nostalgia. It was on one of these flights that Annie met her future husband, Joe Schmitt. Joe was a widower from Dubuque, Iowa, and president of A.Y.U. McDonald Plumbing, Heating and Air Conditioning Company. He had been impressed with the beautiful and serene Annie Gilmore, who was hostess on his flight from Las Vegas.

As Annie recalls, "It was June, 1976. I had twenty passengers in my zone who had yet to decide what they wanted from the menu before takeoff. It was always a big hassle to get passengers to make up their minds. I was immediately impressed with Joe because he knew what he wanted and made up his mind very quickly. Apparently, sometime during the flight Joe asked my supervisor about me and discovered where I was domiciled and that I was single. When we landed in Chicago, he was the last to leave the aircraft and asked me for my phone number. The rest is history."

Annie became Mrs. Joe Schmitt. She continued to fly for TWA seven years until December 1983, when she ended a career that had started as a job in 1945.

"Now Joe and I still fly when we travel, I just won't be wearing wings anymore," Annie says. "Now that Joe has retired and we moved to Missouri, I am enjoying participating in TWA's Clipped Wings International Association of former hostesses."

PERSONALITY WITH A PLUS!

TWA

Marion Korenchan Wozniak

1954 - 1985

Weight checks have always been around for flight attendants. Marion was no exception.

TWA was fortunate to have Marion Korenchan as an Air hostess for 31 1/2 years. Her warm personality, good humor and love of people reflected in her service to TWA. Marion says, "I started on the Martin 404 and then flew on every piece of equipment TWA had. Each aircraft had something nice and different to like. I flew to every city on the Domestic system and I was also on many international routes.

"We trained four weeks in Kansas City and yearly for one day emergency reviews. I was first domiciled in Kansas City for two years. I had a great variety after that:

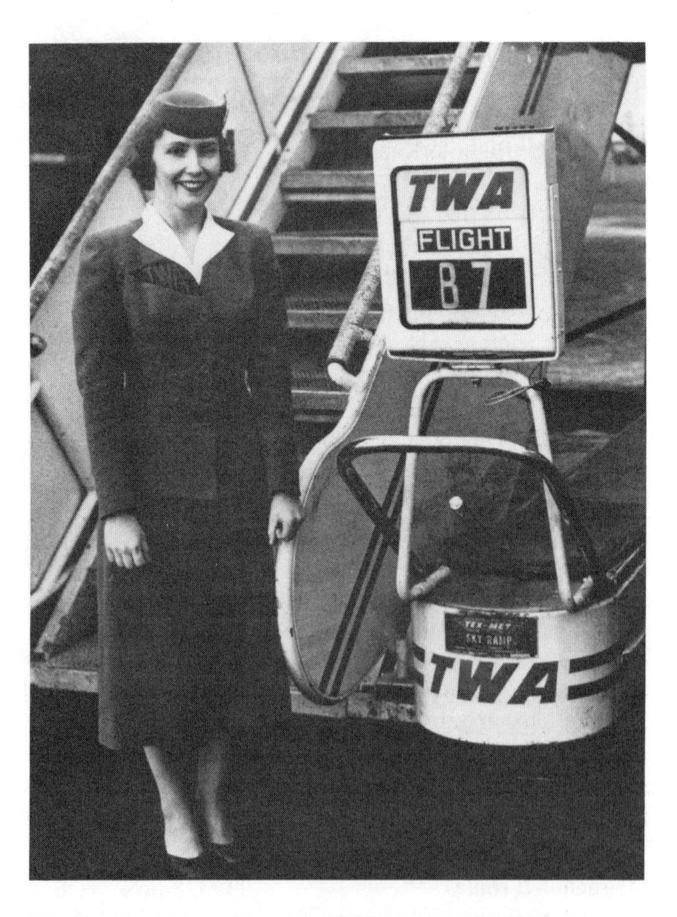

Marion Korenchan Wozniak, TWA hostess in 1953.

two years in San Francisco; two years in New York for international flights to Europe; six more years in San Francisco; four years in Chicago; two and a half years in Los Angeles to fly international routes in the Pacific; twelve and a half years in Chicago, and again one and a half years in New York flying international to both Europe and the Middle East. I loved the people and the travel."

Some of Marion's experiences show her personality with a plus. She has remained good friends through the years with flying partners and in particular with Ruth Ensley McFarland.

FRIENDS FOR LIFE
(How I Met Ruth Ensley McFarland)

"We were both based in Kansas City, but did not fly together until almost two years after I started with the company. Ruth started before me, my on line date was March 27, 1954. We were working a flight that made several stops, the last one being from Chicago to Kansas City. This piece of equipment, the 049, had the galley located up front, separated from the cockpit only by the eight seat lounge. There was a large step-down from the main cabin to this galley.

"We had a load of 87 people, which, to my recollection, was almost full, and we served a hot lunch. The flying time was usually a long hour. Knowing we were being checked, Ruth asked me if I could set up the trays or work the aisle faster. I replied I wasn't sure, so she volunteered to work the aisle. (Bear in mind that this included going up and down the step from the galley with full trays in her hands.) We completed the meal service, including all trays and loose cups picked up. Ruth looked at her watch and complimented me on a speedy job just two minutes longer than her best record! A flight report on our check ride showed that we did this *graciously and with enthusiasm*. Ruth and I have been friends ever since!

THE ZIPPER EMERGENCY

"Around Fall, 1956, on a Martin 404, going from Santa Fe, New Mexico to Albuquerque, the flying time was a short hour, and I had a snack to serve to a full load of 40 passengers. The Martin 404 was a one hostess airplane, with the galley up front right in back of the cockpit, and the lavatories in the rear, just before the aft stairwell.

"In Santa Fe a small boy about five years old was boarded by his Grandmother, who told me he was being met by his mother in Albuquerque, and please take good care of him.

"About midway through my snack service, this little voice coming from this sweet face sticking out from the lav door said, 'Marion, my zipper is stuck, can you help me?' I dropped what I was doing immediately, as I was rather embarrassed and I went to the back of the plane. I pushed the small boy back into the lav, and proceeded to fix his little zipper. I washed my hands, and proceeded to finish my service amidst comments like *would you help me with my zipper?* from teasing men. It was all good clean humor, and I actually enjoyed the attention.

"Upon arrival in Albuquerque, the little boy's Mother did meet him, and was told the zipper story by one of the other passengers. She proceeded to thank me very much. Down under, it was always comforting to be able to help someone.

THE MANHATTAN REQUEST!

"Picture this: a full coach cabin on a Boeing-707 going from San Francisco to Washington, DC, flight time about four and a half hours, give or take a few minutes. Our service was cocktails and lunch, plus anything else requested during that time. Three of us worked the coach cabin, which held around 125 passengers. Cocktails were free, with a two-drink limit per passenger.

"The majority of passengers were business men, either just starting or just ending their trip, and ready to relax. My flying partner and I had worked many flights together under these same circumstances, so not too much phased us in the line of requests, remarks, etc. We had just completed giving cocktails to the last five or six rows, and were in the process of pushing the liquor cart to the next position to take care of another group of rows, when a gentleman sitting in the middle of three seats yelled out that he just spilled his two Manhattans on his pant leg, and could he have *two more*! We both politely explained that we couldn't give him two more until we had finished the service, as our supply was very limited. We also felt it only fair that those who hadn't been served yet be given a choice as long as our supply remained. He wanted to know how he was going to enjoy his Manhattans before lunch if

he had to wait so long! I smiled and replied, 'perhaps you could suck your pant leg for awhile'. His traveling buddies broke into hysterics, and commented 'You'll never try that one again to get another drink!'"

WEIGHT CHECK!!

"And flight personnel think they have it hard today!! Bear in mind I started in 1954 at age 26 1/2 years old and I was hired at 128 pounds. Thirteen years later I was threatened with removal from the payroll if I did not lose the 5 1/2 pounds that I had gained when I was then pushing 40 years of age!!

"On a check on my appearance on July 19, 1967, I weighed 133 1/2 pounds. The following day I received a registered letter from the hostess Supervisor's Office that read as follows:

> Dear Miss Korenchan:
>
> This is to confirm our conversation of July 19, 1967, regarding your uniform appearance. As we discussed that when you were hired in 1934, you weighed 128 pounds, and now you weigh 133 1/2 pounds. Based on your height of 5'5", the maximum weight allowed in your case is 128 pounds.
>
> While weight is a serious problem in your case, mere weight loss is not the only answer as weight distribution plays an important role in your uniform appearance. You are 5 1/2 pounds overweight and are expected to lose those 5 1/2 pounds at the rate of 2 pounds per week. In order that this weight reduction may progress in an orderly manner, you are expected to report to this office once each seven days and have your weight recorded. On August 9, 1967, which is three weeks from our conversation, you will be expected to report to this office and your weight must be no more than 128 pounds at that time. If you have not reached this weight, you will be removed from the payroll and will not be permitted to return to the payroll until such time as you meet the prescribed weight and appearance requirements.
>
> Yours Very Truly,
> Trans World Airlines, Inc.
> Patricia Batzi
> Transportation Supervisor/Hostess

"I did lose the 5 1/2 pounds, but I had to report every 30 days for the next three months, just to be sure I maintained my 128 pounds. And, I did!!

"Several times thereafter I was on weight check for a few pounds, but as difficult as it was to maintain the weight, I am eternally grateful that they watched it for me. I always did have a fairly nice figure in my 31 1/2 years of flying. I retired eight years ago, and I have gained some 30 pounds at the ripe old age of 66 now that I don't have anyone holding a scale over my head!"

To sum up Marion's career she says, "The day TWA hired me to be a flight attendant was the answer to my prayers. It opened up a whole new world to me and it enabled me to see many places in the world. The *on line* education was better than any school could have offered me. To this day I continue to thank the good Lord!!"

THE REHEARSAL THAT PAID OFF

TWA

Ona Gieschen
1946 - 1988

At one time height requirements were for shorter flight attendants, This TWA hostess had an idea that worked for her.

Ona Gieschen, TWA hostess, 1946.

The Great World Air Cruise from New York, February 15, 1970. Ona Gieschen is 5th from the top with the crew on the steps.

"As a kid on the farm, any time that we heard an airplane go over, we would run outside to watch it. Then we would speculate whether it was an army plane or one of those big airliners that carried passengers. You could spend quite a while wondering where it came from and where it was going, who might be sitting up there right now looking down at you.

"Later, near the end of WW II, I worked for a while as a foreman clerk at Pratt Whitney, where they tested aircraft engines. My boss was an old time barn stormer. He could tell the most wonderful stories. Anyway the war ended and I started working in the credit office of Peck's department store. *Boring!!!!!!* One day I just took myself off schedule, walked across the street to TWA's employment office and said that I wanted to be a hostess. Miss Johnson sort of looked me over and said, 'Fine, why don't you sit there and take the typing test.' A typing test to be a hostess? There was more to this job than I realized. Anyway, after the test I had an interview and Miss Johnson suggested that I go have lunch and return in an hour or two when the results of the interview would be complete. It doesn't take me long to have lunch, and it was snowing outside,so I just took an easy chair in front of the fireplace in the lobby of the Muehlbach hotel and day-dreamed about this paragon of femininity about to grace the airways. Times up, so I went back to TWA. This time to be ushered in to the interview room and told that I was too tall to be a hostess, (must have been the reason for the typing test) but that TWA really needed clerical help and that if I wanted it there was a wonderful job in the advertising department, starting in the morning. Well, why not? I might not like flying anyway, I had never been on an airplane.

"Two years later and a well rehearsed slouch with just a tiny knee bend, I got the dream job that for the next 40 some years I pinched myself everyday to see if it and I were real. Many wonderful experiences, but the most outstanding I must say was the six week round the world Ferguson *Great Air World Charter of 1970.* This was a group of 70 very experienced and very wealthy world travelers, who in essence had their own 707 with crew and a wonderful itinerary. Places like Morocco, Rabat, Carthage, Tunis, Athens, Addis Ababa, Nairobi, Teheran, Kabul, Delhi, Cambodia, Bangkok, Kuala Lumpur, Singapore, Bali, Hong Kong, Osaka and Tokyo. Did I miss any? The plane was fitted up in an all Royal Ambassador configuration, deeply reclining seats with the consul table between each, a lovely lounge, both forward and rear, complete with gorgeous flower arrangements from each country. Food was each country's finest: outbound from New York was a standing rib roast; Iran provided large individual crocks of their finest caviar for the appetizers followed by lamb entrees; India, it was curry; etc. We saw all the sights, the souks, mosques, cemeteries, palaces, ruins, beaches, gardens, fairs, etc. The same as our passengers. We did it all, and got paid. Financially and emotionally, what can compare to that?!

"On my Mom's wall hung a framed needlepoint with the caption *There are only two lasting things we can give our children . . . one is roots, the other wings.* Seems as though I got blessed, in a way, with both. My other interest is prairie restoration and wildflowers. Crews sometimes referred to me as Ona hayseed", I believed it referred to my interest in the tall grasses, the biomass of the mostly treeless meadows with the leaves, stems, flowers, fruits, seeds and roots of the many prairie forms, rather than a naive lady who undoubtedly had just fallen off the *turnip wagon.*

"During my 42 years with TWA I not only flew the line on both domestic and international routes, but I was also a supervisor and Director of Customer Service. I enjoyed flying the line so much, that in the 1970s I again flew international routes out of Chicago and St. Louis until I retired.

"During my career I worked on all the types of aircraft TWA had, including: the DC-3, DC-4, Martin 202 and 404, the beautiful Constellation, B-727, B-747, and other aircraft, as well as the L-1011 and B-767.

"On my last flight I was given a royal send off party. Decorations, posters, and pictures lined the walls of the

Ona Gieschen was presented a wild-flower corsage at her retirement after 42 years as a TWA flight attendant, 1988.

briefing rooms. The office management and staff were all there. To top it all off in recognition of my two interests - flying and wildflowers — a wildflower corsage was pinned on my uniform."

THE UNIQUE KC INTERNATIONAL AIRPORT

Since 1976, Ona Gieschen has been a member of the Kansas City-based Grassland Heritage Foundation, GAF. It was instrumental in creating and preserving a *man-made airport prairie* to make it unique among airports of the world in one of the prairie states. The airport is situated 25 miles north of Kansas City on 6,000 acres of working farmland. It integrates planting and cultivation of native grasses which have all but disappeared.

The organization was founded by Professor E. Raymond Hall, a noted prairie expert from Kansas State University, and a lawyer named Wagner with an interest in saving the prairie that once flourished. Wagner drew up the papers of incorporation for the Kansas City based Grassland Heritage Foundation.[31]

Ona Gieschen has seen the prairie from many angles, including from the air as a TWA hostess. Most vivid was her home in a farmhouse her great grandfather built in the 1850s. She owns 40 acres of prairie at this old homestead. It is kept as it was with tall grasses and wildflowers.[32]

Ona devotes a great deal of her time to prairie projects, including the planting of a large plot of land at the

Ona Gieschen is met by well-wishers on her last flight in 1988.

[31]*America West Airline Magazine*, May 1986

[32]Ibid.

Kansas City International Airport during the Bicentennial in 1976. The result was towering grasses that resulted in suggestions to *cut the weeds*. Since then signs help explain about the prairie grasses.[33]

Ona says, "It's hard to explain the appeal of prairies, it's so big and vast, the horizons on all sides and so much space. It must be like people who grew up by the ocean and feel a longing for the sea.[34] She continues a watchful eye for the GAF for the *amber waves of grain* as she did from the *spacious skies*.

TODAY'S DELTA PROFESSIONALS

Delta Air Lines

The training and requirements for Delta's flight attendants have come a long way since 1940. The FAA now requires flight attendants on all large scheduled aircraft. They must undergo four weeks of intensive training and constantly upgrade their knowledge and skills.

Delta's training program is equivalent to a semester of college. Most of the flight attendants are college graduates who meet the airline's requirements for a special, alert, caring person. Only one out of hundreds of applicants meets Delta's high standards and is accepted for training.

The classes held at Delta's flight attendant School in Atlanta include technical and operational instruction, makeup, grooming, speech and poise. Each trainee participates in role-playing sessions in order to learn to be a good listener and diplomat. An attendant never knows who will be on his or her flight and under what

[33]Ibid.

[34]Ibid.

circumstances.

School is in session five days a week from eight to five. Evenings are spent studying for tests. On Saturdays, trainees work at on-the-job training on Delta's regular flights. With the help of a supervisor, they apply classroom skills to actual situations. But this is not the end of their education.

Realistic emergency training takes place in a mock-up of an aircraft. With smoke billowing, fire lights flashing and crash noises blaring, evacuation training is practiced from doors, slides and wing and tail cone emergency exits. Every attendant is taught to expect the unexpected. On graduation day, a new flight attendant has really earned the coveted Delta wings.

New attendants continue on-the-job training while on reserve status. On designated reserve days, they fill in where they are needed. This means they work a variety of trips both long and short, with different types of equipment.

Delta flight attendant in serving smock, 1986. (Delta Air Lines Photo)

The Spirit of Delta aircraft, a gift to their airline from Delta employees. (Delta Air Lines Photo)

By working with experienced flight attendants, valuable experience is gained. Although junior flight attendants do not have a choice of bids, they can decide which days they will not fly and they know their working schedule as well as what cities they will fly to. Whenever new aircraft or modifications are introduced, training continues. Attendants are regularly tested on emergency equipment and the latest techniques.

No day is routine. People and personalities constantly change. Co-workers and passengers always vary. Weather and equipment is different, and each new flight offers its own choices and challenges to the more than 6,000 flight attendants, each individually trained to be part of Delta's professional team. The Delta slogan is *We like to fly and it shows.* Like the flight attendants of the other airlines, Delta's have formed a Clipped Wings Association which engages in philanthropic pursuits.

Delta flight attendants, 1986. (Delta Air Lines Photo)

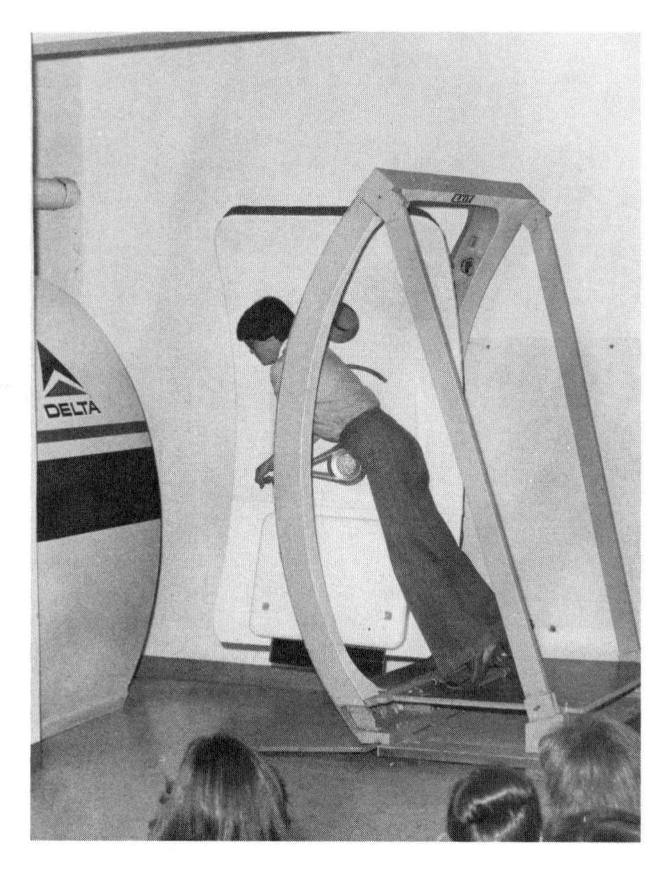

Delta Air Lines' training: how to open a pressurized door during evacuation. (Delta Air Lines Photo)

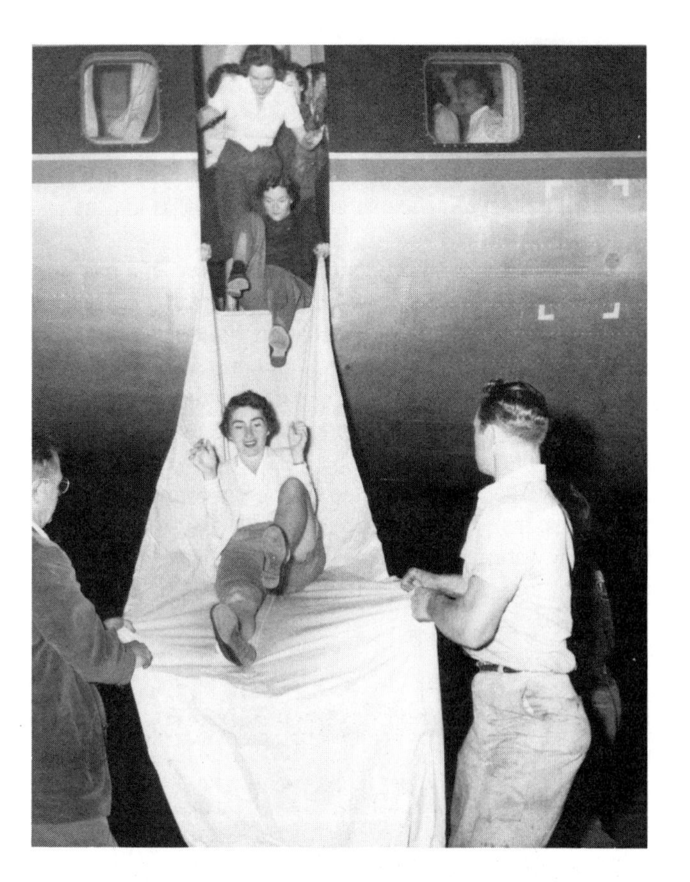

Evacuation slide. (Delta Air Lines Photo)

Make-up session for grooming. (Delta Air Lines Photo)

Water ditching procedures. (Delta Air Lines Photo)

Delta Air Lines' trainees study in mock-up fuselage, 1968. Today, Delta has new training facilities for procedures. (Delta Air Lines Photo)

BUSINESS AS USUAL FOR CONTINENTAL AIRLINES

In 1983 Continental Airlines filed for protection under Chapter 11 of the bankruptcy law after the company realized its labor contracts were so onerous that the company's survival was at stake. Under the protection of the bankruptcy law, Continental cancelled its labor contracts, including the flight attendant contract, and began reorganizing the company in the fall of 1983.

Reorganization has brought about major changes in Continental's management and labor relations. The company has instituted employee stock-ownership and profit sharing plans. These plans seem to be the way of the future for airlines to survive financial difficulties in hard economic times. In the meantime, Continental's bankruptcy was reviewed in Congress and the Supreme Court. In 1992 Continental came out of bankruptcy as a competitive major airline.

THE GOLDEN PENGUINS

AND THE DREAM OF THE 43RD REUNION

A special time to honor its early hostesses. Robert F. Six, former Continental President and Chairman of the Board, Emeritus, paid a tribute to not only Continental's hostesses, but to all flight attendants . . . .

A group of former Continental hostesses in Denver decided to organize an alumnae association in August 1961. They had the blessings and support of the airlines' officials for the project. The name *Golden Penguins* was chosen, *Golden* for Continental's Golden Jets, and *Penguin* for a bird that doesn't fly, representing the grounded hostesses.

Julie Borgman Looney was their first president, and Chris Carleton Inboden their vice president. Other officers included a secretary treasurer, program director and a publicity director. Their first undertaking was a membership drive.

Since 1961, Golden Penguins members have adopted various philanthropic goals and have raised money for the Colorado Boys Ranch, St. Anthony's Hospital Flight for Life, and the Ronald McDonald Halfway House.

In 1983, club members learned of Tommie Heck's dream through Clara Lou Casey Bascom. Clara Lou was a current member of Golden Penguins and had been in Continental Air Lines first hostess class with Tommie. The two had remained good friends, and she knew that Tommie

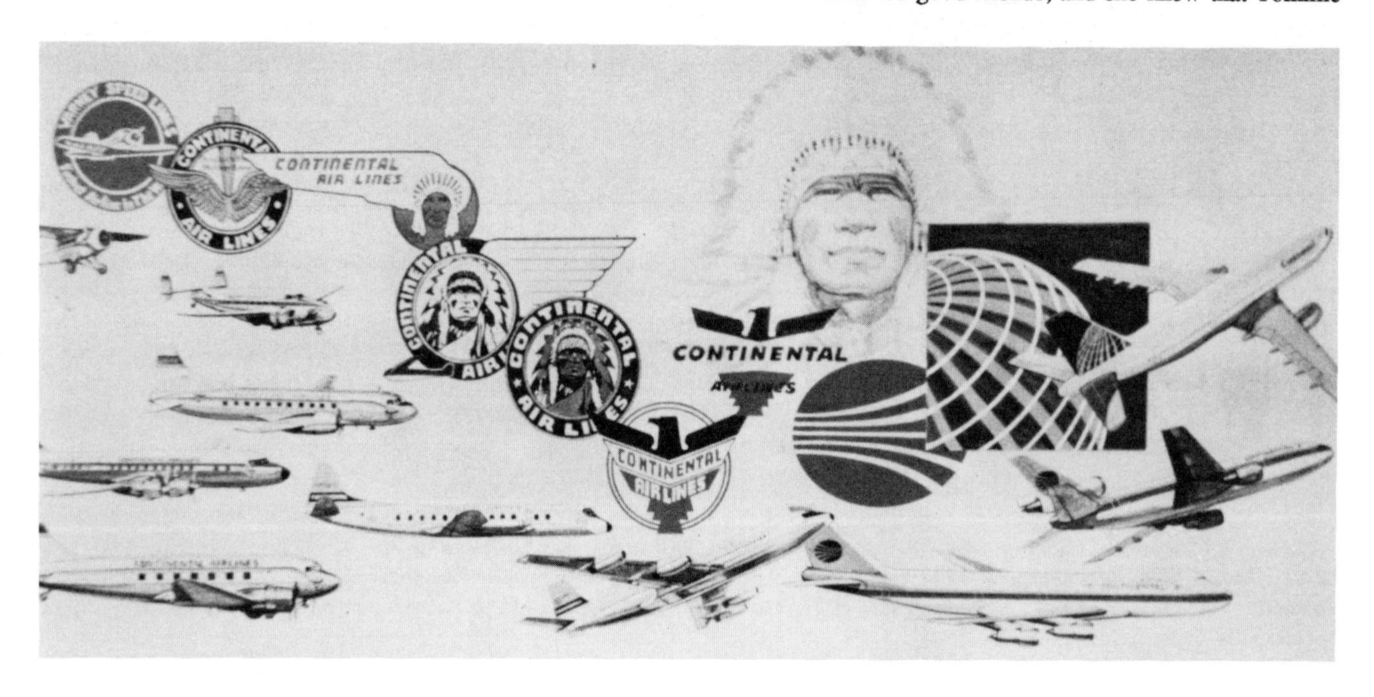

hoped to someday organize a reunion of the hostesses from the forties, some of whom she had helped to select and train.

Continental's fiftieth anniversary was scheduled for 1984, so Chris Inboden, President of Golden Penguins, helped to plan a 43rd hostess reunion to coincide with the celebration. Clara Lou and Tommie co-chaired a committee which contacted as many of the 1940s hostesses as possible. Robert F. Six, former President of Continental and Chairman of the Board Emeritus, was contacted to set a date for the reunion. August 25, 1984 was selected for a banquet at Heather Ridge Country club near Stapleton International Airport and Continental's early headquarters. Mr. Six agreed to be the guest speaker for the occasion.

Continental Airlines' former President and Chairman of the Board Emeritus, Robert Six (left); Mrs. Six (center) and Mildred Heck Carlisle (right) of the first hostess class, 1941, at the 43rd anniversary of hostess service, celebrated in 1984 in Denver, Colorado.

The word spread. Retired Continental Air Lines employees, pilots and officers wished to join in the celebration. Some two hundred of them, along with thirty former hostesses of the period 1941 through 1946 attended the reunion, along with Mr. and Mrs. Six.

Mr. Six highlighted the evening's festivities with his comments, saying, "Continental is half a hundred years old! There were times, and not a few times, when I thought that fifty days more might just round out our total corporate history." He added, "When you are running a tiny, tinker toy airline, meeting payroll with one hand and holding off creditors with the other, you don't look for miracles. You look for people. And we found them . . . skilled, dedicated, smart, loyal people. Tommie Heck started to select and train and monitor the newest thing in the sky — the flight attendants of Continental Airlines. She was intelligent, cheerful, helpful and darned pretty. Continental's Christmas present was when that first class of twelve climbed aboard those Lockheed Lodestars on Christmas Day, 1941. That marked the start of a tradition which has become a saga of service to the airline and to its passengers."

Mr. Six went on to comment that flight attendants as a group are rarely told how valuable their role in transportation is, and

Uniforms of Continental Airlines 1950-1990 at Continental's 50th anniversary celebration in Dallas, October 1992. Third from left: Marilyn Walker, Chairman of the Dallas Golden Penguins Committee. Fifth from right: Sherrill Dickey. Fourth from right: Tommie Heck Carlisle modeling the Hawaiian muumuu uniform.

he wished to substitute the word *hostess* for *flight attendant* in addressing the 1940s hostesses:

"I'm not a psychologist, but I've always thought that someone who brings me food and drink as a hostess is someone who has a dozen or twenty, or two hundred people in for a party. It's up to her whether it turns out to be a festival or a flop. She's there to comfort the apprehensive, cheer the saddened, guide and assist the aged, handicapped or bewildered, divert and watch over the minor traveling alone. She's the guardian of the sound sleeper and the friendly ear of the first flier, chattering his fears away. You hostesses had confidence, charm, authority. Yet you could be gentle with the innocent and stern with fools. Your wings were your badge, your manner your medals."

Hostesses made such an impact, Six stated, that in the seventies all males hired insisted on being called Hosts, and he said, "You not only did us proud, ladies; for small women, you left big footprints in the sky."

Tommie Heck Carlisle said of the reunion, "Everything starts with a dream." Her dream became a reality. The people she worked with, and for, honored her with their presence. Tommie commented, "Being one of twelve girls in the inaugural hostess class proved to be a special favor bestowed on me. As these forty-three years have elapsed, the most memorable characteristics of the personnel of Continental were the love and laughter. The Continental Air Lines reunion certainly exuded the love and respect each one had for the other."

Tommie Heck Carlisle represents today, as yesterday, the qualities Robert Six demanded for the Airline Pride Built.

A CHANGE FOR SHERRILL

Continental Airlines
American Airlines
Sherrill Dickey
1986 - Present

Flight attendants sometimes change airlines in their career. The retraining is always a blending of each airlines' service.

A petite young woman is enthusiastic for her career in the sky. She considers being a flight attendant the best job there is. Two airlines have been fortunate to know her charm — Continental and American Airlines. Here is her story.

THE INTERVIEW

"I had no reason for responding to Continental Airlines' open call for flight attendants (I was to learn later the girls called it a *cattle call*). I can't explain my sweaty palms or why I ate off my lipstick in the interview.

"Fact is, I was already in downtown Houston that day interviewing for a law clerk position, dressed in my best Italian suit and carrying my Cross briefcase. The interviewer at Baker and Botts had made me feel challenged and independent and upwardly mobile. I was between my third and fourth semesters in law school. What did I need a different career for? I'd been offered the clerkship.

"But Continental's recruiter, Debbie Watkins, made me feel challenged and independent and upwardly mobile, too. And she made me feel two more things. She made me feel proud to be a lady. And she made me feel beautiful. I'll never forget the last question she asked me: 'Do you have a problem wearing lipstick?'"

MERGER FEVER

"I began my career as a flight attendant in 1986, the year Continental emerged from its first bankruptcy and acquisitions and mergers in the industry were at an all-time

American Airlines flight attendant Sherrill Dickey with her husband, Continental Airlines captain James Minor.

high. Before my probationary year ended, CAL's parent company, Texas Air, had swallowed up New York Air, Peoples Express, Frontier, Eastern, Britt Airways, PBA/Bar Harbor, and Rocky Mountain Airways, in what was to make CAL, for a short time, the largest carrier in the industry.

"Growing pains brought operational problems, seniority integration wars, and even hostile passengers who had been loyal to *their* regional carrier. I heard so much of *Are you old Frontier?* in and out of Denver; *Are you old Texas International?* all over Texas; *Old People's Express?* on the east coast; and *Old New York Air?* out of Newark that I finally began responding to passengers by saying, 'Sir, I beg your pardon, I'm not even old!!'

"I feel that I represent a generation of professional women who have chosen flight service as a career. Many flight attendants my age have been flying fourteen years, but I've only flown half that because I have an undergraduate degree in English and graduate hours in Law and Humanities. I worked as a professional technical writer for four years, and still write and edit technical documents on a contract basis. Many women I work with say, *I only intended to do this for a few years. Now I've spent 10 (15, 20, etc.) years here and if the airline goes out of business, what will I do?* Some envy me my education and my having something to fall back on.

"So why do I pop Coke tabs at 37,000 feet? Because the sky is a wonderful place to find out who you really are. It's what we law scholars called an *inherently dangerous* work environment, thus the stringent safety regulations of which we must all be ever mindful. The camaraderie. The psychology. The opportunity for exposure to other cultures. The marvel that a couple of jet engines can really lift a massive tube off the ground; the trained awareness that a troubled mind might threaten to send this tube hurtling downward and that my effective response time, attention to detail and use of training techniques might calm the situation -- these are the reasons I fly."

A LADY FROM THE PAST

"I have had the unusual experience of serving as a flight attendant on a generation's worth of airliners: from the 1940s-era *round engine* prop Douglas DC-3 to the state-of-the-art MD-11, the French Airbus A-300 up through the biggest airliner flying today. Thus, my lifetime of memories has happened in a seven year hurricane. I know what it must be like to travel through time.

"My *back to the future* experience began when Mr. D. Joseph Corr, former CEO of TWA, became President and CEO of Continental in 1989. He brought with him a vision -- the hope and dream that *the airline that pride built* could reclaim part of her prestigious heritage with a flying billboard in the form of a restored Douglas DC-3. The

Continental flight attendant Sherrill Dickey (in the 1950 uniform) by the refurbished DC-3 of the 1950s.

DC-3 was the stuff legends are made of, the airplane that single-handedly brought the once-fledgling airline industry to profitability, an aircraft that was reliable, safe, comfortable, and in her day, Queen of the Skies. More than a few of her pilots called the DC-3 the *Grand Old Lady.*

"Mr. Corr was a lover and collector of antique aircraft, and he felt that by enlisting volunteer employees and retirees in this restoration they could rekindle the cohesiveness and kindred spirit that was once the airline industry. At the same time, the DC-3 program was created to celebrate a piece of history, a moment in time, before Airfones and Concordes and hijackings and frequent flyer miles, before deregulation changed the industry forever. In the DC-3s' day, air travel was still a little daring, but the most luxurious, the most expensive and by far the fastest way to travel.

"My husband, Captain James F. Minor, was chosen to head up the DC-3 restoration program at Continental, and various department heads comprised a Board of Directors for the Continental Historical Society. I was eventually named Vice President of Inflight Service for the Historical Society, and as the project grew, so did the Society's aspirations for the airplane, really, or was it the era that people had such a fondness for? Ask anyone who ever got behind the controls of a DC-3, or whoever served drinks to a group of movie stars.

"Though my parents were still in grade school in the 1940s, I was strangely connected to that decade as far back as I can remember. My Dad was a Glenn Miller fan, and strains of *A Sting of Pearls* and *Moonlight Serenade* were my lullabies. There's something about music that brings one back to a time and a place, and music was a big part of my entertainment of passengers on the Continental Historical Society's DC-3. Once the DC-3 was complete, inside and out, we began what was to be the busiest and most exciting three years of my airline career. I believe it was P.T. Barnum who said that everyone, in some way, is allotted ten minutes of fame in his lifetime.

"I felt famous every time I stepped out of the DC-3 at airports from El Paso to Portland, from Newark to Austin, from Washington to Wichita, from Bismarck to Oshkosh. I was given special permission by Continental to grant media interviews, and I appeared more than once on national news. I feel very honored to have been a part of the DC-3 program at Continental Airlines. When I interviewed for my flight attendant position at American, my recruiter asked, *What made you special at Continental — what set you apart form the rest of the flight attendants there?* I owe my future to the Grand Old Lady of aviation, a lady from the past."

"SOMETHING SPECIAL IN THE AIR"[1]
American Airlines
May 1992 - Present

Sherrill was assigned a two day trip on a 727 from Dallas with a layover in Oklahoma City for her first flight after graduation. She felt "squeaky clean" with her brand new uniform and luggage. A new experience was unfolding...

"Every person in an American uniform that I passed in the airport said hello to me. This may seem like a small thing to you, but the company I worked for before had a lot of labor problems and employees were generally unhappy. Today I felt that I was among a group of people who are truly proud of what they do. I flew with a girl who has 21 years seniority and you'd think she just stepped out of the Learning Center.

"Today reinforced something that I've known for a long time and couldn't quite put into words. This job is something you love with all your heart. At the end of the day, an Oriental man in a catering uniform was going out to his car at the same time I was. I had to go down the stairs. I must have said *thank you* about five times when he pointed to my wings, stopped me, smiled and said with a heavy accent, 'you work for American Airlines -- I work for you.' He made me feel like somebody really special."

FLIGHT ATTENDANT: A CAREER

Arrow Air
New York Air
Continental Airlines
Debbie Terrago
Manager of Inflight Training
1982 - Present

Careers in inflight service are built on practical knowledge. The opportunity to fly for several airlines made a new challenge possible for Debbie.

Continental flight attendant Debbie Terrago, Initial Training Curriculum Developer / Instructor, 1994. Debbie is wearing the classic 1994 uniform.

The DC-9 cabin trainer at Continental's training center in Houston. Main door cabin instructor: Debbie Terrago; evacuation slide instructor: DeAnna Bardsley; and overwing exit trainer: Bart "Chip" Astrup, 1994.

"I began my career as a flight attendant, June 24, 1982 for Arrow Air, Inc., an International charter airline headquartered in Miami, Florida with crew bases in New York, Los Angeles, and Chicago. Arrow Air's fleet consisted of B-727s, B-707s, DC-8s and DC-10s The Airline's operation consisted of Military and Civilian Charters. I grew up in a small town (Lowellville) in Ohio, just outside of Youngstown and was uncertain as to what my new career would entail. Within several days of receiving my wings and being assigned to the Chicago domicile, I worked my very first flight to Rome, Italy. Coming from a small town, my new career exposed me to a real culture shock. Upon experiencing a three day layover in Rome, I was headed back to Chicago with a good feeling about my newly found career. Back on familiar ground, I found out my next trip assignment — Malaga, Spain — with a five day layover. Life was GREAT!!!

"My trip assignments continued to keep me in awe. Tokyo, London, Ireland, Korea, Honolulu, Frankfurt, Munich, Diego Garcia (a Naval installation on an island in the middle of the Indian Ocean), Brazil, Suriname, Amsterdam, Netherlands, Keflavik, and I continued to explore numerous destinations and experience culture upon culture, time zone upon time zone. The friendships I shared were many, not to mention the collection of artifacts from all over the world. My career as a flight attendant, begun as a short-term, job suddenly transformed into a satisfying, long-term career. Throughout the years at Arrow Air, I transferred to Miami, Florida, where I assumed duties as a flight attendant instructor, flight attendant supervisor, and administrative assistant for the Inflight Department. I was also honored to represent Arrow Air, Inc., in the Interline Pageant and held the title of 'Miss Arrow Air, 1983-1984.' I also participated in a mini-evacuation on a DC-8-63 Aircraft as well as a proving flight on a DC-10 aircraft. Both demonstrations were observed by the FAA and certification was approved for both aircraft types.

"In February, 1986, Arrow Air, Inc. filed for bankruptcy and the airline which allowed me awesome opportunities, is now a heart felt memory. It was time once again to seek new employment. Although I had an option to choose another career, I knew within my heart, that I would once again travel the friendly skies. I was hired by New York Air, in April, 1986.

"Upon employment with New York Air and being assigned to the Washington Dulles domicile, I was ready for the transition from international flying to domestic destinations. I found my flight assignments to be quite refreshing, yet somewhat challenging. When flying international routes, I was afforded the luxury of delivering two or more meal services in accordance with a generous amount of scheduled flight time. I'll never forget my first shuttle between Washington's National and New York's LaGuardia airports. I never thought I'd accomplish a complete beverage service within fifty minutes of flight time (with a full load of customers on a MD-80 aircraft). I was in a great panic!! Upon completing several shuttle services that day, I found myself acclimated to the quick and efficient service. I was now ready for a new challenge.

"In 1987, New York Air was acquired by Continental Airlines (along with People's Express as well as former Frontier employees). In May, 1987, I assumed duties within the Inflight Training Department and currently hold a position as an inflight instructor. I have instructed Emergency Recurrent Training, Initial Training and also performed duties as an On-Line Instructor, an extension of Initial Training, given to flight attendants on board the aircraft. From time to time, I participate in special projects which pertain to Inflight Training functions.

"As Continental continues to grow, they provide their employees with personal growth as well. I am very fortunate to be part of the Inflight Instructor Group. Throughout my flight attendant career, I have learned that above my experiences, explorations, and tremendous opportunities as well as all of the practical knowledge I continue to gain, I always reflect upon my initial training programs as this era of time remains the gut of all other aspects of my career. I am proud to represent the Continental Inflight Training Department and look forward to the numerous possibilities of expanding our programs far beyond the horizons."

SAFETY
Continental's Inflight Training 1993

Continental's Manager of Inflight Training, Debbie Terrago, explains the scope of their professional training for their flight attendants:

"The first step for men and women recruited as Continental flight attendants is participation in a six weeks training program conducted at the Continental Training Facility in Houston, Texas. The program curriculum consists of a variety of topics such as Corporate Structure, Personnel Procedures, Food and Beverage Service. Customer Service, Appearance Standards, Federal Aviation Regulations and Specific Aircraft Training."

SAFETY DRILLS

"Additionally, the most intensive and demanding experience for the flight attendant candidates is their emergency training. This training combines lecture and drills pertaining to unplanned and planned emergencies for both land and water as well as the proper use of portable emergency equipment. The emergency training also includes the candidate's participation in a wet ditching drill, and several cabin evacuation drills. They will also demonstrate their knowledge of the use of portable emergency equipment through an oral competency check. They will also perform their proficiency by accomplishing the operation of each piece of portable emergency equipment through a *hands-on* drill.

"The cabin evacuation drills are conducted on board a DC-9-30 cabin trainer (acquired for use in 1982). The cabin trainer is elevated on struts and has the capability to tilt simulating a left gear collapse. Additionally, through a computerized system, the instructor can simulate a smoke-filled environment. During three consecutive days of cabin evacuation drills, the flight attendant candidates are divided into groups of three and encounter with various scenarios. The flight attendant candidates are evaluated on their overall performance to effectively react to various situations, brief able bodied assistants, evacuate the cabin trainer and effectively communicate as a crew. The first day is dedicated to practicing various scenarios. The second day is their drill (test) day. The third day is dedicated to those individuals who require an additional drill to successfully meet the standards of the above criteria.

"Similarly facilitated are three days of service

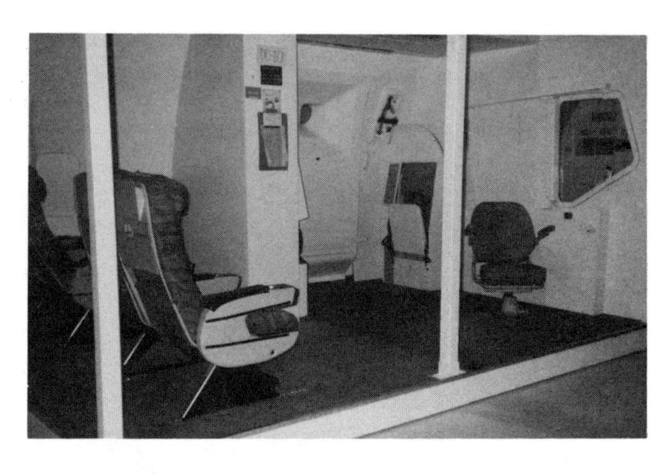

All aircraft doors have their own mock-ups and trainers: A-300: DeAnna Bardsley; DC-10: Chip Astrup; 747: Debbie Terrago; DC-9: Chip, DeAnna and Debbie. Tail cone exits and overwing exits are also their responsibility.

proficiency drills consisting of Continental's designated phases of inflight service. As in the safety proficiency drills, the candidates must also successfully demonstrate their proficiency in various service-related emergencies.

"During several weekends throughout the six weeks training program, the flight attendant candidates are assigned various flights on the DC-9, MD-80, B-727, B-737 and A-300 aircraft. These flight assignments allow the candidates to observe the various phases of flight. Additionally, they are given the opportunity to participate in many service related functions.

"The overall training is quite intense, but very effective in allowing the flight attendant candidates a wide variety of inflight topics.

"Upon successful completion of initial training, all flight attendants are required to maintain their inflight qualifications by annually attending a minimum of twelve hours of recurrent training (as prescribed by the Federal Aviation Administration). This annual event encompasses a variety of safety related topics. The flight attendants are also required to demonstrate (every other year) their proficiency of a *hands-on* drill for each type of aircraft exit and all portable emergency equipment. Additionally, they are evaluated on an annual basis on their overall competency of flight attendant safety related duties through a written examination.

"A portion of recurrent training is designated to allow the pilot and flight attendant groups to effectively interact through a combined session. This session is well received among all crew members as communication and coordination are continually enhanced and maintained.

"Once flight attendants complete their probationary period, they are eligible to apply for any existing flight service manager position. The flight service managers are interviewed by a group of inflight supervisors and carefully selected to represent Continental as a leader on board the aircraft. The flight service manager is responsible for delivering a consistent top quality, inflight product.

"Continental also offers contract training and cabin safety seminars to other airlines or business corporations.

"Continental is currently reviewing the possibility of incorporating a computer based training program into the various inflight training areas."

CHANGES IN SAFETY PAST TO PRESENT

An example of safety taken from the 1941-1945 *Continental Hostess Manual*:

ACCIDENTS[35]

In case of an accident involving the airplane when passengers are aboard, it is the duty of the hostess to see that all of the passengers are removed from the ship as quickly as possible. They should be advised to *move quickly to a point behind the tail of the ship, remain in a group and refrain from smoking. Since there may be a possibility of fire, the entire group of passengers should be removed as far as possible from the airplane.*

The hostess should at all times see that the aisle and the doorway of the plane remain clear of packages that might obstruct progress in deplaning. The hostess is also responsible to know thoroughly the operation of exit *doors.*

*Note from the author, former Continental hostess 1943-1945, who experienced a ground loop accident in 1943. The Lockheed Lodestar had *one* exit only. The hostess' fold up jump seat was located *across the exit door.* An elastic strap on the floor across from the exit held extra food trays that would not fit in the food compartment. In turbulence the food trays would come loose — in the case of an accident they were dumped in the rear of the aircraft.

TODAY'S VAST IMPROVEMENT IN SAFETY

New Regulatory Measures:[36]

1. Exit track lighting in airplane aisles
2. Smoking ban on domestic flights for better air quality.
3. Improved cabin interior fire retardation.
4. Flight attendants being seated during turbulence.
5. Flight attendant shoulder harnesses and PA systems
6. Smoke detectors in lavatories
7. Carry on baggage limits.
8. Foot brakes on service carts.
9. Cabin/galley redesign in some aircraft.
10. Protective breathing equipment for the cabin crew.
11. Prevention of removal of Boeing 747's overwing exit.

[35] *Continental Hostess Manual*, 1941-1943, "Accidents: Procedures Enroute" Section J, 18-214

[36] *Flight Log*, Vol. 3, No. 3, July-August 1993, pp 11-11.

PROFESSIONALS AT WORK
Continental's Inflight Training Staff
1993

I asked the Continental training staff to give their job titles, to tell about their most memorable flights, to give a quote about their jobs and any other comments and information. It is summed up as follows:

BERT "CHIP" ASTRUP

TITLE:	Inflight Regulatory Compliance Liaison (4 years) Inflight Curriculum Developer/Instructor (2 years) Flight Service Manager (5 1/2 years) Flight Attendant (6 1/2 years)
MOST MEMORABLE FLIGHT:	A 12 day trip to Tahiti..nothing but *sun* and *fun!!!!!*
QUOTE/PHRASE:	Due to my job, everyone always asks me, "where is it written in the manual?"
OTHER COMMENTS:	Best job in the world!
ADDITIONAL INFORMATION:	Born and raised in Portland, Oregon/Married/No children.

INITIAL TRAINING GROUP PHOTO

Front row: **Anne Johnson, Caroleanne Harrity, Sharron Graves, Mary Ann Megna**
Back row: **Ernie Dominguez, Ron Punneo, A. Wayne Wooden, DeAnna Bardsley, Millie Floyd, Jill Moynihan, Randy Wilson, Debbie Terrago, Susan Gwynn Stivala**

DEANNA BARDSLEY

TITLE: Initial Curriculum Developer/Instructor (1 year, 9 months)
Houston Astros Charter Coordinator (1 year)
Flight Attendant (3 1/2 years)

MOST MEMORABLE FLIGHT: Various charter flights...bringing the troops home from Saudi Arabia...the joy and excitement on their faces as we made our approach into Newark, New Jersey, past the Statue of Liberty, the tears in their eyes when they were met by supportive Americans waving flags and asking for autographs.

The 1993 baseball season while working as the Charter Coordinator for the Houston Astros...developing friendships with the local heros and superstars.

QUOTE/PHRASE: "Marry me, Fly free"

ADDITIONAL INFORMATION: Born and raised in Iowa (on a dairy farm)/Single/No children

DEBBIE TERRAGO

TITLE: Inflight Curriculum Developer/Instructor (2 1/2 years)
Cabin Safety Specialist (2 years)
Inflight Training Specialist (2 years)
Flight Service Manager (6 years)
Flight Attendant (11 1/2 years)

MOST MEMORABLE **FLIGHT:** **Being part of the Desert Storm Operation and flying Military Charters to Saudi Arabia.**

QUOTE/PHRASE: "You learn to build your roads on today, because tomorrow's ground is too uncertain for plans, and futures have a way of falling down in mid-flight."

ADDITIONAL INFORMATION: **Born and raised in Lowellville, Ohio/Single/No** children

PREVIOUS EXPERIENCE: **New York Air, Flight Attendant**
Arrow Air, Inc., Flight Attendant (4 1/2 years)

Left: Debbie Terrago; Right: DeAnna Bardsley; Front: Chip Astrup.

KATHERINE TEGGART

TITLE:	Inflight Curriculum Developer/Instructor (1 year) Supervisor, Leadership Training (4 years) Inflight Training Specialist (3 years) Flight Service Manager (8 years) Flight Attendant (12 1/2 years)
MOST MEMORABLE FLIGHT:	New Year's Eve, 1986
ADDITIONAL INFORMATION:	Born and raised in Ft. Worth, Texas/Single
PREVIOUS EXPERIENCE:	Jet Fleet Charter Airlines, Flight Attendant Dresser Industries, Flight Attendant People's Express, Customer Service Manager

RICK WEBB

TITLE:	Director, Inflight Service Training (1993 - present) Manager, Inflight Training Programs & Regulatory Compliance (1990 - 1992) Flight Attendant (14 1/2 years)
MOST MEMORABLE FLIGHT:	First flight
QUOTE/PHRASE:	"Birds of a feather, flock together"
ADDITIONAL INFORMATION:	Born and raised in Oceanside, CA/Married/2 boys

LEADERSHIP TRAINING GROUP PHOTO

Front row: **Jeffrey Schwind, Tim Reed**
Back row: **Randy Mullins, Victoria McGuffie, Doug Sparke**

LINE TRAINING GROUP PHOTO

Front row: **Susan Gwynn Stivala, Jamie L. Maier**
Back row: **Mary Jo Basso, Millie Floyd, Bert "Chip" Astrup, Elvia Pratt**

RANDY WILSON

TITLE:	Inflight Curriculum Developer/Instructor (2 years) Flight Service Manager (6 1/2 years Flight Attendant (7 1/2 years)
MOST MEMORABLE FLIGHT:	PDX-SEA...cloudy day...mountain peaks protruding through the clouds (Mt. Rainier; 3 sisters; Mt. Hood)...a spectacular sight
QUOTE/PHRASE:	"Telephone; Telegraph; Tell-a-Flight Attendant"
ADDITIONAL INFORMATION:	Born and raised in Brooklyn, New York/Single

A. WAYNE WOODEN

TITLE:	Supervisor, Initial Training (1 1/2 years)
MOTTO:	"Maturity is prolonging short term pleasures for long term goals"
ADDITIONAL INFORMATION:	Married/1 boy/Born and raised in Georgia
PREVIOUS EXPERIENCE:	People's Express, Customer Service Manager

DOUG SPARKE

TITLE:	Curriculum Developer/Instructor (1 year) Flight Service Manager (3 1/2 years) Flight Attendant (8 1/2 years)
MOST MEMORABLE FLIGHT:	Having a drunk customer ask 15 minutes after we rolled off the edge of an ice-slicked runway in Buffalo during the month of January when we would land. Having a Customer on a CLE-RSW Flight ask what those "white cottony things" were that we were flying over. He couldn't believe clouds could be below the airplane.
QUOTE/PHRASE:	"A vision can be very powerful, almost tangible. If you put you mind to it, you can accomplish anything."
ADDITIONAL INFORMATION:	Born in Los Angeles, California/Raised in Tustin (SNA), California/Single
PREVIOUS EXPERIENCE:	People's Express, Customer Service Representative/Manager (1 year)

SUSAN GWYNN STIVALA

TITLE: Inflight Curriculum Developer/Instructor (1 year, 10 months)
Flight Service Manager (6 years)
Flight Attendant (10 years)

MOST MEMORABLE FLIGHT: The aircraft I was flying on popped a door seal and it sounded like a decompression. Being on the line just a few months, my training kicked in . . . I sat on a customer's lap and grabbed an oxygen mask.

ADDITIONAL INFORMATION: Born in McAllen, Texas/Raised in Cherry Hill, New Jersey/Married

PREVIOUS EXPERIENCE: People's Express, Customer Service Manager, November, 1983 - January, 1987

ELVIA PRATT

TITLE: Administrative Assistant, Line Training (1 year, 4 months)
Flight Attendant (5 years)

ADDITIONAL INFORMATION: Born and raised in Mexico/Married

TIM REED

TITLE: Leadership Curriculum Developer/Instructor (4 1/2 years)
Flight Service Manager (6 years)
Flight Attendant (13 years)

MOST MEMORABLE FLIGHT: Cast and crew of Sesame Street was traveling to a location to film a show. Halfway through the flight, members of the cast went into the lavatory and changed into their costumes (Big Bird, Cookie Monster, etc.). They went through the cabin and played with all the children. It was not only enjoyable for the crew, but especially for the children.

ADDITIONAL INFORMATION: Single/No Children/Born in Sioux City, Iowa/Raised in Murfreesboro, Tennessee

PREVIOUS EXPERIENCE: Capital Air, Flight Attendant
Pan Am, Flight Attendant
New York Air, Flight Attendant

JEFFREY SCHWIND

TITLE: Leadership Curriculum Developer/Instructor (9 years)
Flight Service Manager (10 years)
Flight Attendant (10 years)

ADDITIONAL INFORMATION: Born and raised in Toledo, Ohio/Single/No Children

PREVIOUS EXPERIENCE: People's Express, Flight Attendant

SERVICE TRAINING GROUP PHOTO

Front row:	**Kim Zapalac, Leslie Gawlikowski**
Back row:	**Raymie Ollada, Hector J. Garcia, Mary Ann Megna**

KIM ZAPALAC

TITLE:	Inflight Curriculum Developer/Instructor (1 year) (Previous flight attendant experience from 1985-1987)
MOST MEMORABLE FLIGHT:	Bumpy flight during the service . . . I ended up on a man's lap . . . He said, "I have been flying for 25 years, and this is the best flight I've ever had"
ADDITIONAL INFORMATION:	Raised in Houston, Texas, 1973/Married/1 girl

MARY JO BASSO

TITLE:	Inflight Curriculum Developer/Instructor (2 years) Flight Service Manager (6 years) Flight Attendant (11 1/2 years)
QUOTE/PHRASE:	"Don't sweat the small stuff."
ADDITIONAL INFORMATION:	Born in St. Louis, Missouri/Raised in Hawthorne, New Jersey/Married/No Children
PREVIOUS EXPERIENCE:	People's Express Airlines, 1982-1987

ROB BENSON

TITLE: Senior Director, Training and Methods (2 1/2 years)
Captain, Boeing 727 (11 1/2 years)

MOST MEMORABLE FLIGHT: Havana - Great cigars and rum

QUOTE/PHRASE: "Know your stuff. Stand for something. Take care of your people."

OTHER COMMENTS: "Seize the moment."

ADDITIONAL INFORMATION: Born and raised in Madison, Wisconsin; Ohio, New Jersey; Delaware; Florida and Texas/Married/1 Yellow Lab, 1 German Shepherd, 4 Cats

PREVIOUS EXPERIENCE: Managing Officer, People's Express; Staff Vice President, Flying, Eastern

ERNIE DOMINGUEZ

TITLE: Training Specialist (2 1/2 years)
Inflight Regulatory Compliance Liaison (1 year)
Inflight Curriculum Developer/Instructor (2 1/2 years)
Flight Service Manager (7 years)
Flight Attendant (10 1/2 years)

QUOTE/PHASE: "Working together means winning together."

JILL MOYNIHAN

TITLE: Inflight Curriculum Developer/Instructor (1 year)
Flight Attendant (4 years, 1 month)

MOST MEMORABLE FLIGHT: Man from an adoption agency bringing a newborn baby girl from San Antonio to New York to meet her new parents and family. The whole family met the plane with video cameras, etc. I'm sure I'm in those pictures and will be part of that child's memoirs.

QUOTE/PHRASE: My favorite quote is from one of my Instructors when I went through Initial Training, that I continue to live by as a flight attendant . . . "A clean galley is a happy galley" . . . corny, but true!

OTHER COMMENTS: I have enjoyed this job more than any other job I've ever had . . . it has given me the chance to see the world, which is a precious gift.

ADDITIONAL INFORMATION: Born and raised in San Antonio, TX/Married

RANDY MULLINS

TITLE:	Leadership Curriculum Developer/Instructor Flight Service Manager Flight Attendant

RAYMIE OLLADA

TITLE:	Administrative Assistant, Service Training (1 year) Flight Attendant (5 1/2 years)

RONALD PUNNEO

TITLE:	Inflight Curriculum Developer/Instructor (2 years) Flight Service Manager (1 1/2 years) Flight Attendant (3 years)
MOST MEMORABLE FLIGHT:	Charter flight with Minni Pearl, Tammy Wynette and the rest of the Grand Ole Opry
ADDITIONAL INFORMATION:	Born and raised in Oklahoma/Single

A SECOND CHANCE
FOR FRONTIER AIRLINES
July 5, 1994

From excerpts form the Rocky Mountain News, July 6, 1994: Reborn Frontier takes off, by Lynn Bronikowski.

Flight #202 to Fargo, North Dakota and Gand Forks, North Dakota took off from Denver's Stapleton International Airport at 10:40 a.m. on Tuesday July 5, 1994. Frontier's 737-200 aircraft will fill a void in service to North Dakota and Montana serving these markets.

About 75% of Frontier's 200 employees worked for the original Frontier in 1986. The aircraft will feature extra leg room and food catered by Chelsea of Denver. Fine cheese and fruit plates and other quality snacks will be served.

CHANGES IN THE WORK FORCE[37]

Ada Brown
Edith Lauterbach

Ada Brown Greenfield, United Stewardess in 1940. She negotiated the first flight attendant contract in 1946. (Photo, courtesy of the Association of Flight Attendants, AFL-CIO.)

In the new air age, the job as an air hostess and stewardess in the 1930s and 1940s was considered adventurous and glamorous. Early stewardesses chosen by Ellen Church were all Registered Nurses and were known as "Sky Girls." They flew 100 hours for $125 a month.

During World War II in 1941 the Registered Nurses left the airlines to join the services in the war effort. Airlines then accepted applicants for stewardess with work experience with the public, but preferred a college degree.

It came to the attention of a United stewardess, Ada Brown, in the spring of 1946 that stewardesses had many discriminations: they had to be single, young, and follow strict rules of weight and height. They were selected by their physical attributes and personality. At times during an interview they were asked to lift their skirts so that the interviewer could observe their legs. It was not uncommon for girdle checks, and stocking seams had to be straight. These checks were not only done by stewardess supervisors, but also sometimes by playful crew members. Hemlines, nails, makeup and hair had to be perfect. Behavior was closely monitored and there were frequent line checks. Also meals were served at 14,000 feet in unpressurized cabins.

In 1945 the average seniority was 9 months with a high turnover for marriage. At the time of marriage a stewardess had to quit her job. The maximum age to fly was 32 years. In times of bad weather and mechanical delays the stewardess had to remain with passengers with no extra pay and with no rights. It was all part of being a stewardess.

Ada Brown, with the help of Edith Lauterbach, organized for better rights, and job changes slowly developed. They could not mention the word union; many fathers of stewardesses did not want their daughters to belong to a labor union. The organization that developed was called an association and became a part of the Pilot's Union.

In 1948 men joined United for heavy lifting on the Hawaiian route. They could be married and have children, but the stewardesses had to remain single. At this time most stewardesses flew an average of 18 months before they married. If by chance they secretly married and became pregnant, they had to obtain an illegal abortion.

By 1952 the Jet Age arrived. Suddenly there were twice the number of passengers and longer flights. The

Stewardesses of the 1930s taking the oath "not to marry." A requirement, in those days, for becoming an airline stewardess.

[37] *AFA Flight Log*, Association of flight attendants, (Washington DC, ALPA and AFLCIO, Winter, 1980)

work load more than doubled and safety became the primary factor.

In the 1960s the sex symbol of the stewardess was exploited. Short mini-skirts and hot-pants showed a lot of leg. National Airline adopted the sexiest slogan "I'm Sally, Fly Me." These slogans were on many huge bill boards advertising National Airlines. Continental Airlines had the slogan "We will move our tails for you."

1964 brought the Civil Rights Act that made big changes for all races. A stewardess by 1970 was now known as a flight attendant with the introduction of more men and a non-gender-specific name. Litigation followed and the rule of being single was changed. However, when a flight attendant had children she had to quit. Changes continued through various cases brought before the unions, such as new pregnancy rules with seven months the maximum to fly. Maternity uniforms were designed for the airlines. Maternity leaves were established, as well as for nursing mothers. A flight attendant can now work from ages 20 - 70 years.

Flight attendants are all ages, all races from all professions, hired to serve their airline as *safety professionals* as number one priority. Recurrent safety checks on all aircraft configurations are mandatory. Many a flight attendant has saved lives in emergency situations.

New improvements continue to be sought by the Association of Flight Attendants. They seek to standardize safety training through certification as well making the travelling public aware of their role as safety specialists on board aircraft. They work to improve cabin safety, pushing for FAA regulations mandating child restraint seats, dynamically tested passenger seats and improved fire protection in crashes.[38]

The early couriers, stewards, stewardesses and hostesses have become professionals with the help of the feminist movement and the clout of the Association of Flight Attendants, as well as other unions which represent their workforce.

Iris Peterson-Copin, United Airlines flight attendant, 1994.

SAFETY ON THE LINE

United Airlines
Iris Peterson-Copin

NUMBER TWO FLIGHT ATTENDANT

1994

Iris Peterson-Copin has been a United flight attendant for four decades. Her seniority ranks her number two. She has been actively involved with union activities since 1950 to make changes - both in discriminatory work practices and safety.

In 1965 she was asked to participate in suggestions for safety for the cabins of jumbo jets. She worked with aircraft engineers through 1968 and was instrumental in getting seventeen safety items accepted. The most important was conceiving the idea of an evacuation alarm on large aircraft, which has since become standard worldwide.

[38]*Flightlog*, Association of Flight Attendants, (Washington, DC, AFL-CIO), April/May, 1990.

Jo Humbert in her 1959 Capital uniform before the 1961 United merger.

FAMILIES IN THE AIR

About The Author

My stories flying for two airlines in the 1940s
The author's family continues in aviation

The Humbert Sisters

Cover Girl — Jo Humbert
Grace Humbert Benge

The Modeens – Marnae and Sally

The Maddens – Shanna and Skip

The Flying Cavanaghs

Aviation Careers Family Style

TWA's Ensley Sisters

Pauline Ensley Marshall
Ruth Ensley McFarland
Teresa Ensley Terrell

Daughters

Martha McFarland-Goetz
Ann Terrell Deery

TWA's Heck Sisters – Hilde and Gale

American's Three Generations

Marie Allen Sullivan
Jane Sullivan Warren
Lisa Warren

A Tribute To Courage

Uli Derickson

American's First In Flight

Juanita Carmichael

About the Author
Helen Elizabeth (Bailey) McLaughlin

My home was Denver, Colorado where I was born. I graduated from East Denver High School and Colorado College in 1942, with a B.A. in Sociology and credentials for teaching Elementary Education. I later, in 1970-1971, received further Elementary Education credits from Tampa University.

I was an air hostess for Continental Airlines 1943-1945 and a stewardess for United Air Lines 1946-1947. I married a United copilot, Burl McLaughlin, in 1947, at the time he returned to the United States Air Force. After a distinguished 30-year career, he retired as a Major General. He became a vice president for Eastern Airlines in 1971 and in January 1981, the president of a commuter airline, Mississippi Valley Airlines. At the 1985 merger with Air Wisconsin, he retired after 45 years in aviation.

The author as a Continental Hostess.

We have four children. Our oldest daughter, Becky, was a flight attendant for USAir Shuttle (all former Eastern crew members) until February 1994. She was a flight attendant for Eastern, 1977-1991 and for the Trump Shuttle. She is married to David Hobart. Our daughter, Patricia, assisted in developing my first book on inflight service, *Walking On Air*, and gave input into the development of this book. She will receive her Doctorate from the University of Oregon in 1994. Our daughter, Kathleen, a graduate of William Woods College in Missouri, has been of great assistance in developing *Footsteps In The Sky*. Our son, William, is a graduate of The Boston Conservatory and is a Premiere International flight attendant for American Airlines.

I will relate my experiences as author and having served as an air hostess and stewardess in the 1940s.

A ROOKIE'S SUMMER BLUES
Continental Air Lines
Betty Bailey (Helen Elizabeth) McLaughlin
1943

I was first a hostess with Continental Air Lines in 1943 during World War II. Some of my stories follow . . . .

I had the job of becoming an air hostess for Continental twice. First when I graduated from Colorado College in June 1942. Chief hostess Jean Wahlberg and President Robert Six hired me to train in June. I was so excited, but my father was not! I'd completed four years of college and had Colorado teacher's certification and a teacher I was to be! I declined the hostess job for Continental. I did teach second grade, but still I had my head in the clouds — wanting the job I'd yearned for since I'd first seen United stewardesses at the Denver Airport as a young girl.

By early spring, I interviewed again and was told I had a *strange history*. I'd had the job once (one very difficult to get, I might add) and turned it down! I was hired again to train at the Olin Hotel in Denver. The company was in an interim between Chief hostesses so Velma Brust, a senior hostess, was taken off the line to train me. I was needed on the line *yesterday* — as hostesses were getting married overnight with no notice when their service boyfriends came home on leave. It was World War II and the U.S. was involved both in Europe and the Pacific.

I was hard at work in a crash course learning in less than one week what other hostesses learned in five weeks. I studied Continental's routes, connecting routes for other airlines, Continental's history, Lockheed Lodestar's parts, the radio beam, weather and cloud formations, hostess regulations and duties, the treatment of airsickness and the use of seconal for extremely ill passengers, food service presentation; food service forms as well as hostess reports and irregularity reports. Ticketing was to be done by the hostess and the manifest that held tickets with passengers' names, addresses, their weights, and destinations. Hostesses were to address each person by name when giving a service and deplaning. Safety instruction was about seat belts, seats upright on landing, smoking regulations and ash trays, the use of the fire extinguisher, the location of the first aid kit. *In an emergency* - quickly get the passengers off the aircraft and group them back away from the tail section. I memorized airline and city codes. Security of cameras and questions asked at any military installations were to be reported to the captain and curtains drawn over windows. We had many war priority regulations.

Late on the first day, I was also sent to the tailor to get my measurements taken for the new navy blue faille summer uniform. A matching overseas-style military cap was to be worn with the Continental Thunderbird crest that I would receive with my wings on Friday. I was not to wear the beautifully-designed winter uniform of beige with red accents. I was to be the *first* hostess in the *new* summer style.

There was no special ceremony for me. I took my test, passed it, and Velma handed me my wings and Thunderbird crest. I was a *five day wonder!* I had already been issued my red shoulder bag, two white blouse slips, my crew luggage with my own name tag, and personal cards.

I had also been finger-printed and had my special pass for the airport wartime security, number 440, with my thumb print and photo on it. I thanked Velma for her week of instruction. At one o'clock I went to purchase navy and white spectator pumps and to pick up my uniform from the tailor. I could hardly wait to see my uniform and try it on. I was aghast! It hung on me! I complained, this is not my size - it is too big! The tailor assured me I'd *expand in the air!* To say I was disappointed was an understatement!

On the evening of the fifth day I had my *familiarization trip* at 5:00 p.m. to El Paso, Texas as a new Continental hostess — an evening dinner flight with stops at Colorado Springs and Pueblo, Colorado. Dinner was to be served between Pueblo and Albuquerque, New Mexico and on to El Paso at 9:15 p.m.

I was all right until we started over mountains and I smelled the coffee. I had wave after wave of nausea and I rushed to the blue room (lavatory) to use the sink. The cleaners would hate me and I couldn't let anyone use the lavatory in such a state! Even nauseated with airsickness, I cleaned it up after all the meals were served.

At Albuquerque a Mr. Burns was deplaning with a *burp cup* under his arm. I reached for it and felt its repulsive warmth and said I'd throw it away for him. Mr. Burns gummed words, "Oh no, it has my teeth in it!" I assured him his next flight would be better. Secretly, I hoped mine would be too! It was. I'd earned those wings! My summer navy blue uniform was baggy, not chic. I hadn't expanded in the air! Before my next flight my mother remade it. That day had been the *summer blues* for me, but with my mom's tailoring of my uniform, I felt good and I looked good and I loved my job and flying. I never was airsick again! Everyone called me the *Five Day Wonder* — ha, ha.

Later, my good friend, Jo Anne Hastings, was the only other hostess trained in five days. Other hostesses got the full treatment; ours was capsule style.

AROUND THE HORN

Continental Air Lines
Betty Bailey McLaughlin
1940s

I joined Continental Air Lines as an air hostess in early 1943. One of our routes, Trip One, was a long flight with eight intermediate legs. We left Denver, Colorado, our home base, in the morning at 8:30 a.m. for our destination of El Paso, Texas. The stops included Colorado Springs and Pueblo, Colorado; and Las Vegas, Santa Fe and Albuquerque, New Mexico. Albuquerque was a mid-point in our schedule. From here we went over mountains again, into Roswell, New Mexico, the beginning of the *horn*, to the flat-land oil fields of Hobbs and Carlsbad, New Mexico, terminating at 3:30 p.m. at El Paso, Texas. This was a long, rough ride, at best a *milk run*.

The Lockheed Lodestar's fourteen passenger aircraft never flew high enough to get above the turbulence and stench of the oil fields burning off the crude oil between Roswell, Hobbs and Carlsbad. Many of our passengers were airsick and burp cups were frequently used. This was a round quart-sized container. It was fastened to the floor by a clamp under each seat to grab when needed — usually too late! The hostess also broke ammonia capsules to give a nauseated passenger a whiff. Wet paper towels were placed on the forehead and the air vent directed to blow on the face. For a very ill passenger, Seconal, a sedative, was dispensed with care and usually only when the passenger was extremely airsick most of the flight.

At Hobbs, the agent kept a bucket and a scrub brush handy for these daily flights around the horn. The hostess did the cleanup of the aircraft and dispensed the Air-wick deodorizer...a smell I detest to this day!

Agents and crew members knew the regular passengers by name. These men were casually dressed, often with no hat or luggage. They boarded our flights like catching a bus. They were mostly ranchers or oil

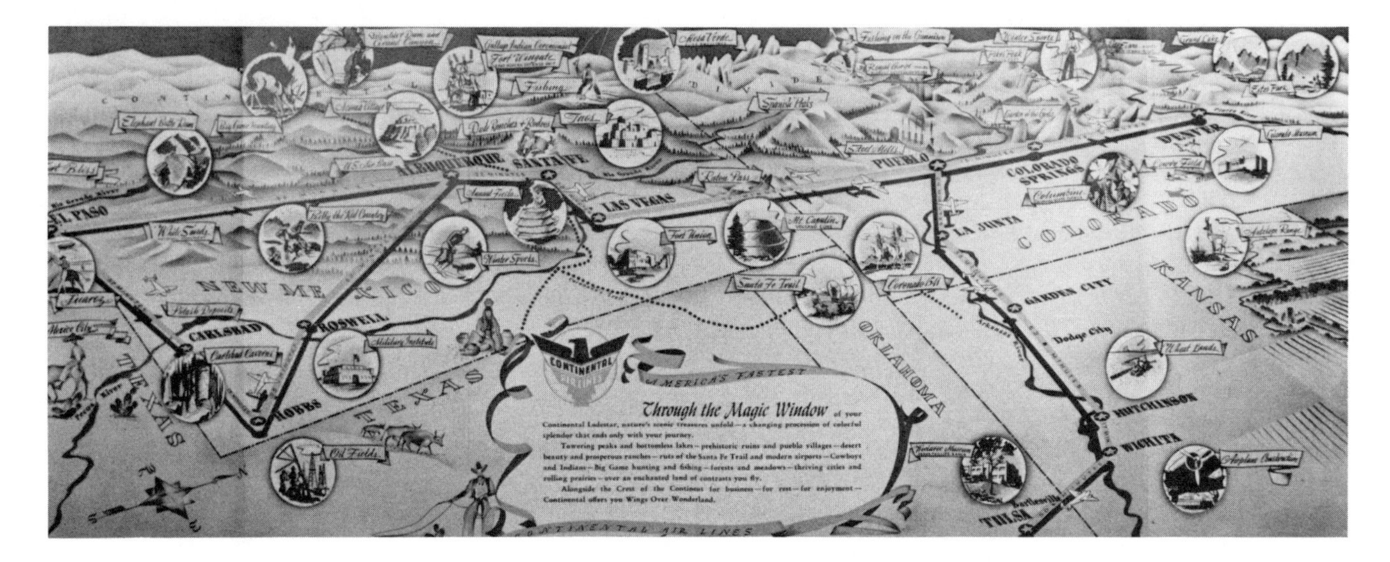

men going for pleasure to El Paso or across the border to Juarez, Mexico. Our flights weren't always on time, but they didn't seem to care, as long as the plane got there. Surface transportation in the area was poor and air transportation was the fastest means of getting people to their destination, and our casual and friendly *milk run* served this purpose.

WARNING TAKES ON A NEW MEANING

Continental Air Lines

Betty Bailey McLaughlin

I wondered when I was going to meet the two Romeo pilots that I had been warned about. Velma Brust, Continental's Senior hostess and my instructor, had given me *the warning* on the last day of my five-day crash hostess training course. Three months had passed and I was beginning to wonder if Velma had just been reminding me not to date pilots. It had me curious though, and their names stuck in my mind: Harry Tannyhill and Freddy Gray.

Early one morning as I checked in at the Denver dispatch office, I was all set for the long trip to El Paso with eight stops en route, but not for the surprise. I was to fly with none other than Captain Freddy Gray. So I was going to finally meet him!

Mulling over this development, I walked out to the parked aircraft to check supplies before the rest of the crew boarded to taxi the plane to the gate for passenger loading. While I was busy in the galley the crew came on board, each handing me his nameplate. I noted that Captain Gray had to stoop at the back of the Lodestar so as not to hit his head on the low cabin ceiling.

Wow, I exclaimed to myself as Gray made his way to the cockpit, *he must be at least six feet four inches tall.* He was very handsome, tall and dark. My heart skipped a beat, but why? After all, I was engaged to be married to a wonderful guy. My captain was an Army Air Corps officer. He was blond and very handsome too, and besides, he was twenty-three years old, not in his thirties as Captain Gray was reported to be.

I placed the name tags in the slots in the back of the cockpit door, set the temperature gauge for the cabin, and went to finish preliminary flight reports. I wonder what this day will bring, I mused. I could already feel a ripple of excitement as I thought about Velma Brust's warning to beware!

When we arrived at the gate a full load of fourteen passengers boarded. On the thirty-five minute flight to Colorado Springs, I served orange juice, sweet rolls, and coffee to the passengers and crew. As I handed Captain Gray his tray I noted that his eyes were sea green and they seemed to look straight through me.

During the short stop in Colorado Springs, Captain Gray did a very unusual thing. He got off the plane to get his own clearance from dispatch. The crew members rarely deplaned except at major stopovers. When he finally reappeared at the door, he paused a moment and seemed to size me up with those piercing green eyes. My heart did a flip-flop which infuriated me. I did not want to feel anything for this Casanova pilot, if that's what he was. He certainly had the reputation for it.

In the twenty minute flight from Colorado Springs to Pueblo, my passengers were either reading newspapers and magazines or otherwise occupied. Taking a few minutes to relax, I picked up a *Rocky Mountain News* and sat down on my jumpseat and flipped to the comics section. I was so engrossed in the newspaper that I didn't hear the cockpit door open, or the footsteps heading in my

Continental hostesses, 1943, in brown gabardine uniforms designed by Chief Hostess Tommie Heck. Left to right: Jo Anne Hastings, Janet Downy, Shirley French, Betty English, Tommie Heck, Peggy Kellerman, Carol Dunaway and Betty Bailey.

direction.

Suddenly a hand poked through the newspaper and grabbed my left hand. Startled, I let the paper fall, only to find Captain Gray crouching by my jumpseat.

"Where is it? Where's your ring?" he asked regarding the engagement ring he expected to find on my left hand. "I thought you were engaged."

"Wouldn't you like to know?!" I retorted, knowing full well that the ring was pinned to my bra. Don Raish, traffic manager and acting supervisor in the absence of a Chief Hostess, had told me when I was hired that he would prefer that I not wear my engagement ring while in uniform. With my remark, Captain Gray got to his feet and quickly returned to the cockpit.

Mr. Swanson, the passenger in the last seat in front of my jumpseat, had heard our exchange. "Miss Bailey," he said, turning around to speak to me, "that captain thinks you are really something. Just for fun, I'll bet you he'll ask you for a date before we ever get to Albuquerque, let alone El Paso. Want to bet?"

I smiled at him, embarrassed that he'd heard our conversation. "Yes," I replied, "I'll bet with you."

At Pueblo, Captain Gray got off the airplane again. On his return with the clearance he was also carrying a pink slip of paper that he pressed into my hand when he boarded the aircraft. Since we would be taking off in a matter of minutes I decided to look at the note later.

I prepared for takeoff and when I returned to my jumpseat, I took out the note Gray had handed me. I read the note that had been sent from Colorado Springs on the company teletype so that *everyone* at every station would read it too.

> Dear Betty,
>
> I'm getting awful jealous of all those Lieutenants and before you get all dated up for the eve I would like to file my priority if it is not already too late/ What I am trying to say is/ Would like very much to take you south of the border for dinner and a dance or two this gracious eve/ Does it sound like a deal? Promise to get you back early.
>
> Freddy the Freshman

I checked the passengers' seat belts before takeoff. As I came to Mr. Swanson in seat fourteen who had made the bet, I said, "You win," and showed him the pink teletype note.

"This has been more fun than any movie I've ever seen on boy meets girl," Mr. Swanson said, laughing heartily.

Our flight to El Paso arrived on time. I hadn't mentioned anything about the note from Captain Gray at any of the other stops. At El Paso, I deplaned with the big basket I had brought from Denver for my brother's friend, Roger Williams. I headed for Continental's dispatch office to meet the crew and take a taxi to the hotels. At that time, the hostesses stayed at the Paso Del Norte Hotel and the crews at the Cortez Hotel, probably a standard procedure to protect hostesses from Casanova pilots.

"What's in the basket, Little Red Riding Hood?" Captain Gray asked me in the dispatch office.

"A chocolate torte cake and some other goodies for Sergeant Roger Williams," I replied. Captain Gray promptly grabbed my basket and raced out of the room.

I ran after him, begging him to return it. The crew taxi was waiting and everyone was laughing as they watched the two of us play cat and mouse. Gray ducked back into the office and reappeared without the basket.

"Not unless you promise me a date," Freddy answered and grinned broadly.

"I already have a date with Roger for dinner tonight," I answered. "I always meet Roger and bring him things from his mother."

"Okay," Freddy conceded. "Be back at the hotel by ten and I'll take the second half of the evening. Don't eat much. I'm taking you to dinner." He went and retrieved the basket, but still kept it well beyond my reach, towering above me. "I'll carry this until I pick you up at the Del Norte Hotel. I'm not taking any chance that you'll change your mind between now and then."

I thought about the warning. What would it lead to? I felt uneasy. After all, I was engaged, but I really didn't see any harm in enjoying myself until I made the final walk down the aisle. Besides, I was thrilled about the prospect of going on a date with this bachelor pilot, and finding out what the talk was about. As it turned out, I had a wonderful time with Freddy, and we continued to see each other and became good friends. I didn't marry the Army Air Corps captain after all, but I didn't marry Freddy either.

Captain Fred Gray was killed in Continental's first

A 14-passenger Lockheed Lodestar of the 1940s. (Continental Airlines Photo)

fatal crash in Missouri in 1959. Investigation proved that a distraught passenger had purchased a large amount of flight insurance prior to boarding this Continental flight. When the plane was in flight, he went to the rear lavatory with a bomb in his briefcase. He ended his own life as well as those of all the plane's passengers and crew when he detonated the bomb. This was the first type of terrorism to plague the airlines. *Warning* takes on a new meaning: that no one is safe anywhere from terrorists.

Hijacking was next. TWA flight attendant Uli Derickson was on flight 847 with 147 passengers on board when two terrorists seized the aircraft at gunpoint and with grenades hijacked the plane to Beirut for a long siege of terror. Hijacking preparation training is now a part of inflight service curriculum.

THE WRONG ROOM

A regular room was reserved on the second floor of the Paso Del Norte Hotel in El Paso for Continental's overnight hostess layovers. At the same hotel, American Airlines reserved rooms on the third floor for their stewardess layovers.

I was to room with a new hostess, Jean Wagner, who was coming into El Paso on the night flight. I was looking forward to meeting her. She would be joining the sixteen of us who were all based in Denver. We all knew each other well and enjoyed each other's company, a new hostess was welcomed as a friend.

I arrived on my flight in El Paso at 3:00 pm. I had plans for my usual date with Army Sergeant Roger Williams, a family friend from Denver, now stationed at Fort Bliss. He had asked me to bring a swimming suit so we could go to the post's swimming pool for an early evening swim. I was to meet him in the hotel lobby at 5 pm.

After our refreshing swim at the Fort Bliss pool, Roger suggested that we take the bus back to town and walk across the bridge to Juarez, Mexico to eat dinner and browse in the shops. I liked the idea and heartily agreed. Going to Juarez was a fun experience all of the Continental hostesses enjoyed on our El Paso layovers. It also gave each of us the opportunity to purchase nylon stockings that were difficult to buy in the states because of a shortage of nylon; all the nylon was being used for parachutes for the war. We found that the Mexican stockings, even though they weren't of good quality, were preferable to using the Elizabeth Arden leg makeup that we all hated. I'd buy a pair of stockings and I had enough money to purchase a gallon of rum.

Walking across the bridge, we met my crew returning from Juarez. They looked angry, especially my Captain, Jack Weiler, who was also Continental's Chief Pilot and a former boxer. He looked fighting mad and had his fists clenched. As they approached Roger and me, I jokingly said, "You look mad enough to hit someone."

Captain Weiler hissed his reply through pursed lips. "You bet I'm mad! Some punk airmen just had the nerve to call us 4-Fs!" I knew this term meant *not eligible for wartime service.* It was a tag no he-man wanted, especially a pilot. Captain Weiler continued, "I wish we could wear our Continental uniforms, but we can't while off duty. I can't fight them or we'd get thrown in the Mexican jail or the army brig.

Roger and I left the crew still fuming and we crossed the check point into Juarez. After dinner, we went to buy my prized pair of nylon stockings. Then I looked at the rum list I always carried in my purse. It was a list of the Continental employees at the various stations who wanted my quota of one gallon of rum. Many of the other hostesses also had rum lists and we often compared them so we didn't all get rum for the same people. I laughed as I said to Roger, "Well, I guess I'll get my jug of rum. I feel like a rum runner."

Roger and I returned to the Del Norte Hotel close to midnight. I thanked him for a good time and entered the elevator. I had my hands full with my heavy jug of rum in one hand and my swimsuit rolled into my damp towel in the other, but I managed to press the button for the second floor, or so I thought...

As I got off the elevator, I turned right and went in the direction of my room. In my anticipation of meeting the new hostess Jean Wagner, and because it was late, I didn't notice the room number. My hands full, I decided to tap on the door with my foot instead of getting out my key. A sleepy-looking girl in a nightgown opened the door. I said, "Hi there!" as I entered the room, darkened except for light coming out of the bathroom. I went to the dresser, noting the uniform skirts hanging from the top drawers to hang out the wrinkles. I'd left my skirt caught by the drawer; Jean must have copied my example. I put my jug of rum on the dresser and thought, those overseas uniform caps somehow look different. It must be the poor light. "I'll hang my towel and swimsuit in the bathroom," I said. "How was your first flight, Jean? Welcome to Continental."

She just stood there glaring at me. I thought, *she doesn't seem very friendly, this Jean Wagner.* "You're drunk," she snapped, pointing at the rum on the dresser.

"I am not!" I blurted out. "I don't drink! That's for my list." I'm sure I didn't make much sense. I started toward where I thought I had left my suitcase to get my nightgown.

"My name is not Jean and this is an American Airlines room, and I think you got off on the wrong floor. My roommate is already here and in bed sound asleep."

In the darkened room I hadn't noticed the sleeping form in the second bed. "Oh," I said, "I'm so sorry. I had my hands full and I must have pressed the wrong button." I went and got my swimsuit and in my haste to get to the dresser for the jug of rum I tripped on a shoe and fell flat. As I rose to my feet I grabbed the rum and headed for the door. "Sorry, it won't happen again," I said as I made my exit.

In the hall, I looked at the room number: 307. She was right, it wasn't Continental's hostess room 207.

I made my way through the hall to the elevator and carefully pushed the button for the second floor. A sleepy and friendly Jean Wagner greeted me in hostess room 207. Even though it was late, we visited and Jean told me about her first flight as a CAL hostess. We laughed as I related my escapade of the mix-up of the rooms. I told her about our rum lists and that most of us didn't even drink.

As we turned out the light, we both knew the seventeenth hostess was glad she had chosen Continental.

BLOWOUTS!
Continental Air Lines
Betty Bailey McLaughlin
1943

The Tulsa trip was never my favorite. All hostesses were scheduled for at least one flight on this route each month. We were also scheduled for reserve each month. Some hostesses were lucky and got the days off...I never was one of them - I caught reserve *every* time...usually to Tulsa!

This was a long breakfast flight leaving Denver at 7:15 a.m. with many intermediate stops. It went to Colorado Springs and Pueblo, where it branched off to La Junta, Colorado. It then stopped at Garden City, Dodge City, and Wichita, Kansas. We arrived in Tulsa at 1:20 p.m. and then shuttled back to Wichita and terminated in Tulsa at 3:20 p.m. A total block-to-block flying time of just less than eight hours. I had two experiences on two flights, just hours apart - the frightening one was on this route.

1943 Continental hostess Vivian Lindsey with Captain Peter Brown in the doorway of a Lockheed Lodestar. Note the hostess jumpseat which folded out across the *exit* door.

NUMERO UNO

Our Lockheed Lodestar was landing in a downpour of rain at Albuquerque, New Mexico on the evening flight, trip 4 from El Paso, Texas to Denver. I had a full load of 14 passengers. Suddenly a bang! We swerved off the runway and plowed in the mud and jerked to a stop. I did not have any instructions from the cockpit and the hostess had no galley phone. I did what I had been instructed in my five day crash training...I quickly got my passengers off the aircraft and grouped them away from the tail section. An agent arrived in a station wagon and ordered me to get all the wet passengers with muddy shoes back on the aircraft. I felt reprimanded for the action I had taken.

The Station Manager took four passengers at a time in the station wagon to the terminal. Mechanics had arrived to change the blown tire. In several hours we were once again en route to Denver. I served passengers a late dinner out of Albuquerque. We arrived in Denver past our 9:30 p.m. arrival time - it was 11:00 p.m. At midnight I was on reserve status. At 5:00 a.m. I was called for a 7:15 a.m. trip to Tulsa...

THE *BIG* ONE!

I had a full load of 14 passengers out of Denver en route to Tulsa. I served breakfast juice, rolls and coffee out of Denver en route to Colorado Springs. We landed at our third stop after Pueblo at La Junta, Colorado. Since it was wartime (World War II) we shared the landing field with La Junta Army Air Base. It was 8:39 a.m. when we landed. All curtains were drawn in the aircraft. (This was done by all airlines on landings and takeoffs for security reasons where commercial planes landed at military installations.)

Three military men deplaned and a family of three boarded - a man, his wife and teenage daughter. They were returning to Wichita after a vacation in Colorado. The man had a camera that I had to take from him because of wartime security. He was very reluctant to give it to me. He said it contained all their vacation photos. I explained I would return it when he deplaned at Wichita.

All passengers were seated and seat belts checked, and the camera stowed for safe keeping. We started to taxi. I had my seat belt fastened, but I had not yet adjusted and tightened the buckle. Our jump seat was *across the exit door* in the rear of the aircraft. It had two clamps that held it in place, and these had to be pressed hard to release it to fold up after use.

Engines roared and we thundered down the runway for take off. We were rolling very fast ready for lift off when the plane lurched and then spun wildly! We were at an angle. Over head racks emptied with the wrenching and vibrations of the aircraft. I could hear the screams of the two women above the deafening roar and grinding of metal on concrete and the sound of windows shattering. Food trays dumped on me. My back hit the door handle, my seat belt being too loose to restrain me. The thermos rack by the door came out of its compartment and battered my head...I remembered last evening - but this was different! I was terrified and waiting for the plane to explode. All I could think of was — *I'm not good enough to die!*

It seemed an eternity until the deafening roar stopped. We lurched to a stop. Dust was settling, coats, hats, blankets, pillows, magazines, food and food trays were everywhere. I quickly released my jump seat and kicked objects away from the door. An Army captain in the last seat exclaimed, "Is this thing going to blow up?" I calmly answered, "no." I was straining, trying to open the door as the aircraft was on a decided tilt. About this time, our Captain, Dex Howe, opened the cockpit door and yelled, "Let's get the hell out of here!!"

I got all the passengers off the aircraft and away from the tail section. A young lieutenant remarked - "We thought you were goners when we saw the tire blow, the gear collapse and you spinning and sliding backwards in that ground loop!" It was then I noticed the aircraft was being foamed, its wing on the ground, propellers bent like hairpins, and shattered windows. We had ended up near parked fighters. I said a silent prayer of thanks that everyone was all right.

The passenger with the camera wanted it back to see if it was broken. I did get it, and other belongings out of the aircraft with the help of Guy Cox, the station manager. I also got the manifest with all passengers' tickets and also my purse. The La Junta passenger took a photo of the badly damaged Lodestar. A Lieutenant grabbed the camera from him and then explained, "*No* photographs may be taken on military installations!" This made the passenger very angry. I explained that in due time all developed photos would be returned with his camera after the photo he had just taken was removed. This seemed to satisfy him.

At the terminal, it was determined no one was injured - only badly frightened and shaken up. The La Junta woman had grabbed her blouse and popped all the buttons, which I fixed for her. I had retrieved the sewing kit from the hostess supply case from the plane. I had won a $25 War Bond for the suggestion to include it. I helped the station manager with passengers' belongings and baggage, I helped make train and bus connections for passengers and took some to lunch that had later connections. I kept a detailed account of *everything* that had happened, including each passenger's physical condition and behavior.

In the meantime, Captain Dex Howe, who was noted for his wit, called Denver Dispatch and said, "I have your airplane NC36 here at La Junta out in the weeds. I also have the *blowout kid*, hostess Betty Bailey, with me - she was just in a blowout last night at Albuquerque — this was the *big* one!"

At four o'clock after a long and exciting day the crew and myself boarded an Army C-47 aircraft flown from Lowry Army Air Base in Denver to get us. We sat in passenger seats taken from the Lodestar. They had been torn very loose from floor bolts in the mishap. It took over two months working night and day before Captain Fred Gray could test fly NC36 and it could be returned to commercial passenger operation.

As for me — I missed several flights with a very stiff back. I later learned my irregularity report had been used to verify the fact the family of three at La Junta were not seriously injured as the wife later claimed to be.

I was in *another* blowout and earned my name, *the blowout kid.* We had just started to roll for take-off at Denver — when it happened again — a blowout! We lurched to a stop, but not off the runway. Captain Wade Johnson came out of the cockpit and sat on the wing spar. He yelled as he pointed his finger at me, "You're a jinx!"

Our aircraft's blown tire was repaired. However, after the captain's remark, a gentleman refused to take the flight!

Three other Continental hostesses were in ground loops, including Ligea McCracken and JoAnne Hastings. In 1946, I had become a United stewardess when I learned that NC36 had ground-looped at Albuquerque and burned. All passengers and crew were safe. The hostess, after her *first* flight, said, "I quit!"

THE GOPHER HOLE

Continental Air Lines
Betty Bailey McLaughlin
1943

On the Tulsa route we landed at an intermediate stop at Garden City, Kansas. The airport was real country; it had cow pastures on either side of a dirt runway.

I had fourteen Ferry Command pilots on board. Military were frequent riders on all flights, as the U.S. was involved in World War II. They were all spiffed up in their uniforms and quite vocal about what a *rinky dink* airline it was to land in farm pastures. They were joking about the cows grazing just past the barbed wire fence as we taxied to the end of the runway for take-off. Suddenly — *Thump! Thud!* The aircraft jolted to a sudden stop!

The captain came out of the cockpit to go have a look at what caused this development. It proved to be that the tail wheel had fallen in a large gopher hole! He laughed, I laughed, we *all* laughed! The Ferry Command pilots really whooped it up with laughter and more jokes about our *cow poke* airline. Before too long we were off and flying again. On deplaning at Wichita all the pilot passengers thanked me for a ride on the *Gopher Express!* They said they'd had a *rip roarin'* good ride!

Continental Airlines' new logo on the tail of the aircraft. Many carriers are stressing *globalization* in their advertising and logos in 1994.

AN UNUSUAL TAKE OFF
United Air Lines
Betty Bailey McLaughlin
1946 - 1947

I became a stewardess for United Air Lines in 1946. My stories . . . .

Besides our regular schedule, United crews were sometimes asked to fly special charter flights. A charter I was asked to work, was to take the Brooklyn Dodgers to their rest camp in Redlands, California. On the DC-4 there were two stewardesses, an A and a B stewardess. Usually the A stewardess was an RN and also had more seniority. Our aircraft was luxurious and seated 44 passengers. We had a nice serving galley and special seats for the stewardesses. We also had two lavatories and a large coat compartment.

We served an elegant meal of steak catered from United's own kitchens. Food service had also supplied us with boxes of extra milk cartons, kept cold in insulated wrappings. The flight was fun, with a lot of joking among the teammates and us. On landing at Redlands, it was soon discovered the cargo compartment for all the Dodgers' luggage was jammed and could not be opened. It became evident that this situation was going to take some time.

Author Betty Bailey McLaughlin, United Airlines stewardess, 1946.

Large crowds at airports were the usual thing, especially on weekends or for special occasions, such as greeting the Brooklyn Dodgers team. Aviation was relatively new and exciting and people liked to watch aircraft land and take off. Our DC-4 was one of the largest aircraft used in commercial aviation at the time. It was a beautiful four-engine aircraft. The crowd that had assembled at the Redlands Airfield numbered two hundred or more people; they wanted to see the large DC-4 take off.

During the long wait to get the belly baggage compartment open, the captain had decided to have a generator hooked up to the DC-4 and to allow a tour through the aircraft. For the next several hours, the A stewardess and myself had over 200 individuals file through the cabin and also look in the cockpit. Everyone seemed thrilled to have the opportunity to talk to us and to view first hand the beautiful United DC-4.

It was getting dark when all the luggage had finally been removed. Since the Redlands airfield was not used by commercial aircraft, it did not have any landing lights. Over a loud speaker, our captain asked the crowd to help out the situation: please go to their cars, turn on their bright lights and aircraft personnel would direct them to park horizontally, side by side on both sides of the runway to light the way for our take off.

What a thrill, to see the cars' headlights lighting the way for our DC-4! Our captain had allowed two tired, but happy, stewardesses in the cockpit for take-off, to observe a moonlight flight down the coast, and to watch the sunrise over the San Francisco Bay. This city was always beautiful to approach by air, but this sunrise, so ethereal in the dawn over the glistening bay, the sleeping city, and majestic Golden Gate Bridge, was particularly spectacular this day.

MR. MOSS WENT TO TOWN
United Air Lines
Betty Bailey McLaughlin

In January 1947 Colorado was being hit hard by a very severe winter. My flight left Denver at 4 pm. It was a grey, cold, winter day. The weather got progressively worse and threatened to snow as our 21 passenger DC-3 landed at Salt Lake City.

I greeted a full load of passengers in Salt Lake City who would join me on the long flight over the mountains to Reno, Nevada, and then on to San Francisco. On take-off, however, the weather worsened, and I wondered if we were going to get that far.

I had just finished dinner service when the air became quite turbulent. It wasn't long before my call button glared red at the galley interphone, which indicated that the captain wanted to talk to me. Sure enough, the weather was closing in and we were going to terminate the flight and hold overnight in Reno, our next stop.

I then proceeded to ask all San Francisco passengers their addresses, and put them on their tickets in my passenger manifest. I notified each San Francisco passenger of our termination due to weather at Reno, Nevada. United would write each passenger a letter to apologize for the inconvenience. I only had one passenger deplaning at Reno. All of my 21 passengers were men, with the exception of Mrs. Brooks, a young Army wife. The passengers seemed elated over the prospect of a fun night at the gambling casinos in Reno, especially since the hotel accommodations and meals would be paid for by United Air Lines. They were ready for a night on the town, except for one passenger, Mr. Moss.

Mr. Moss had boarded at Salt Lake City. The passenger agent there had told me, "Miss Bailey, better keep an eye on Mr. Moss - his wife said this was his first ride on an airplane, and he is nervous about leaving her because they've never been apart in their twelve years of marriage. He is going to San Francisco to see his ill sister."

A United Airlines Mainliner DC-3 carried 21 passengers and 1 stewardess.

Mr. Moss was a small, frail man. He was a genuine Milquetoast and seemed like he needed someone to tell him what to do at every turn. His eyeglasses hung on the end of his nose. In his hands he clutched a Bible, which he read during most of the flight from Salt Lake City, except while dinner was being served. I noted that he only picked at his food and nervously sipped his tea.

After telling Mr. Moss about the termination of the flight, I took the precaution to reassure him that airplanes had certain safety minimums in storms, that United would provide hotel rooms and meals for passengers, and that we would all stay together until we could continue on to San Francisco. I also told him that United would send a wire to the people that were to meet him in San Francisco.

Mr. Moss wrung his hands and shook his head as he began to wail in a weak voice, "Oh my, oh my, what will my good wife say when she finds out I stayed in the sinful city of Reno? She will be so cross!" It seemed to ease his nervous twitching when I told him that I would stay with him. "Yes, Mr. Moss, I will be with all of you," I said. "We will stay together as a group until weather improves and we can continue our flight. I want you to stay right by me."

By the time my passengers had deplaned at Reno, the snow was blowing into drifts. Aircraft after aircraft was parked on the ramp. People seemed to be coming from all directions. I managed to keep my passengers together as they claimed their baggage. Arrangements were made for us to stay at a motel in downtown Reno. Transportation had also been arranged, but we had to go in five or six separate taxis. I made sure that I had the frightened Mr. Moss by the arm.

At the motel, a shortage of rooms necessitated that passengers double up. The men paired off and Mr. Moss was left without a room. At first the room clerk said he would put a cot in one of the rooms, but then remembered there was a tiny room off the room Mrs. Brooks and I were to share. "The only problem is," the clerk said, "the only door to this room is from your room." Mrs. Brooks and I agreed that this would be all right with us.

At the airport I had overheard the passengers talking about going to the casinos. They had also observed meek Mr. Moss. I could tell that they intended to take him along - like it or not. They seemed determined to spice up his seemingly dull hen-pecked life. They wanted Mrs. Brooks and me to go also. Mrs. Brooks declined. I told them that I was still on duty. I was anxious about Mr. Moss whom they had decided to drag along. "You be nice to him," I cautioned them, "and bring him back early." Early! It was already late.

Sometime during the night I awakened to loud pounding, scuffling noises, and much laughter. At first I could not remember where I was. I finally found the lamp switch, threw a blanket around my nightgown, and opened the door.

What a disheveled group they were! Mr. Moss, limp as a dishrag, was being carried by four men. Each of the men had a leg or an arm. It was Mr. Ross who spoke first. "Well, Miss Bailey, we have Moses here. I doubt, though, if he will ever be the same again. I'll bet his old lady skins him alive when she hears how much he drank. He really tied one on and then passed out; he sure went to town on the booze. We'll take him to his room." The foursome put Mr. Moss to bed and noisily left the room. On their way out they each added a sweet nothing message as they filed out the door. Their laughter echoed in the cold, still night air as I closed the door. As it grew quiet again I heard snoring come from the direction of the adjoining room.

The following day I had one sad-looking bunch of hungover passengers after I had finally managed to assemble everyone for lunch. But getting Mr. Moss out of bed was like waking the dead. He was a sight to behold. I think he felt so badly he wished he were dead. He kept holding his head in his hands and moaning, "What will my wife say?"

Mr. Moss was endeared as "Moses" by his fellow passengers with much joking. I think he secretly had enjoyed himself on this binge of his life - the first and probably the last. I even think he packed his Bible in his suitcase for the rest of the trip.

By this time the weather was clearing, and I had word from United at 3 pm that we would be departing for San Francisco at 4:30 pm. I arrived at the airport with my twenty bedraggled passengers. I kidded them that I would have to pass out the burp cups at the door, noting their assortment of hangovers from the night before. At the last moment, however, word came from Denver dispatch that our crew was to return to Denver so that we could keep our scheduled flights for the rest of the month.

I told my passengers that I would have to leave them. I gave Mr. Moss's hand a squeeze and a pat. He returned my silent gesture of goodbye with a weak grin and said, "Thank you, I had a good time." I thought to myself that he really did have fun, hangover and all. As I was leaving, my passengers surprised me with a loud "Hip, hip, hooray for Miss Bailey!"

I have often wondered what the unsuspecting stewardess thought when that group of twenty hungover passengers boarded her flight for San Francisco. I hoped they had smooth air for flying and Mr. Moss and the others wouldn't be airsick!

A United Airlines Mainliner DC-4 carried 44 passengers and 2 stewardesses.

THE "100" KEY

United Air Lines

Betty Bailey McLaughlin

Denver, my domicile, had been experiencing a severe winter. Our route over the Rocky Mountains into Salt Lake City, Utah; Reno, Nevada; into San Francisco had experienced many delays of flights, cancellations and holding of flights en route. Because of this, many crews had to be deadheaded back to their domiciles to take their other scheduled flights in time.

My good friend, Fay Steinsiefer, who also was based in Denver was put on my DC-3, 21-passenger flight to deadhead back to Denver on my return flight from San Francisco. It was amazing, Fay had been deadheading on three other recent flights of mine also. It was always fun as Fay had a great sense of humor. If something funny was going to happen it would happen when Fay was around.

She was the 21st person to board. She sat down in 7C in the back and said to me, "Betts, did you see that CUTE, blond co-pilot?" Well, we agreed that since she was in uniform we'd take turns serving the crew meals so she could look him over too.

The male passenger in 7B by the galley held up two quarters, laughed, and said to me, "I'll bet you each a quarter he saw both of you, too, and that he will be back here before we land in Denver." Obviously he had overheard our conversation.

Fay helped me serve my twenty passengers and we did take turns serving the crew. I served the Captain and Fay served the blond co-pilot. I was just cleaning up the galley when it happened...

The cockpit door opened and the tall, blond and handsome copilot swaggered down the aisle smiling at Fay and me. The man in 7B buzzed for service. He held up the two twenty-five cent coins and laughed heartily as he handed them to me. "What's up?" the co-pilot asked as we started to laugh. I took my 100-key from my pocket and opened the blueroom (lavatory) door for him, because usually the only reason a crew member came to the back of the airplane was to use the lavatory. The co-pilot's eyes bugged in surprise. Aghast, he exclaimed "Close it!" as he pointed to the lavatory, "There's a passenger in there!" I was mortified I'd done such a thing. I hadn't seen the passenger enter the lavatory since I'd been busy cleaning the galley. "I was just going to open the door for you," I said meekly.

"Instead of using the phone, I came back to tell you, we are diverting to Cheyenne," the co-pilot said, collecting himself. "It is starting to snow. Denver has a blizzard and is below minimums. You will need to get all passengers' addresses for the company to write a letter to them for the inconvenience. After you do, sit down. The air will be very turbulent."

"Too bad," said the passenger in 7B, "but you girls will no doubt get acquainted with that copilot in Cheyenne." I got the forms for my irregularity report. As I did so, I saw the "blue room" passenger hastily take his seat at 3C. Oh, how I hated to admit I had opened the lavatory door, and hated even more having to ask the passenger for his address.

According to the manifest, a Mr. Dawson was sitting in 3C. At I made my way down the aisle, I approached Mr. Dawson with embarrassment, avoiding all eye contact. "Mr. Dawson, we will terminate the flight at Cheyenne," I said as I reached his seat. "We're diverting there because of a blizzard in Denver. I'm going to need your address. By the way, I apologize for opening the door on you. I feel terrible."

"That's all right, Miss Bailey," he replied. "Shucks, I was just back there cleaning my glasses anyway," he said with a laugh as he patted my arm. "This flight has been a long one, but a fun one. But don't you worry, the copilot will get over it. You and your stewardess friend have given me something to talk about at cocktail parties."

Fay and I were with United crews working on a first-in, first-out basis out of Cheyenne during the big snow of 1947 that closed Denver's operations for two weeks.

Later, I met my own blond, handsome United copilot and married him on July 9, 1947 and became Mrs. Burl William McLaughlin.

Flight attendant Becky McLaughlin Barnes receiving her wings from her father, Burl W. McLaughlin, 1977.

SEQUENCE OF EVENTS

Eastern Airlines
Trump Shuttle
USAIR Shuttle
Becky McLaughlin Hobart
1977 - Present

Our family continues in aviation.

Her first flight as an Eastern Airlines flight attendant was, in Becky's words, "the hardest trip I ever worked. I left on Christmas eve on a three day flight, flying a second leg on Christmas day. I had departed from my assigned domicile, Boston, a city that was new to me. I had just arrived from Eastern's training in Miami and had moved into a tiny apartment with another flight attendant from my class. Our only bond being we both needed to find a place to live in two short days before our first flight assignments. On my first flight I found myself surrounded by strangers — my crew, the passengers — flying into strange airports, cities and hotels for layovers. I was a stranger in a crowd. I felt so alone. I am sure the fact it was Christmas helped to shroud me with the penetrating loneliness that overtook me. I realized that being a junior flight attendant meant giving up your family times, and special holidays were just another work day."

Becky joined Eastern in 1977, 28 years old and a single mother. She had four weeks of intensive, action-packed flight attendant training at Eastern's Miami Headquarters base in Florida. Her graduation and the day she got her wings proved to be a surprise. "My dad was there; Eastern's President, Frank Borman had asked him to

Eastern Airlines flight attendants, 1977. Becky McLaughlin Barnes is fifth from the left in the center of the first row.

pin on my wings! My dad was the Vice President of the New York Region for Eastern, and he had flown to Miami for my graduation. I was so thrilled and proud as he told me he was pinning on the wings I had earned for a job well done. I also knew that the cliché about Eastern's wings would prove true for me, I'd earn them every day.

"Boston was known to be a very senior base. Our class was the first time in years that new flight attendants were domiciled there. I soon learned that I could not bid for any of the great flight schedules and that I'd be on reserve status indefinitely; as a matter of fact, this was to continue for the next six years. One consolation: I purchased a beeper, so as not to be tied to a telephone when I was on standby awaiting a call for a flight. The beeper allowed me some semblance of a normal life schedule.

December 15, 1988

Ms. Becky B. Barnes
357 Commercial St. #310
Boston, Ma. 02109

Dear Becky,

I want to be the first to officially congratulate you and welcome you aboard the Trump Shuttle. Although we received many more applications than we were able to accommodate, you have been selected, based on your seniority, to join us as soon as the sale transaction is completed.

Your decision to be part of the most dynamic airline of the future will, I am quite certain, prove to be a very rewarding one. I very much look forward to meeting you in the near future.

Bruce R. Nobles, President of the Trump Shuttle, will be providing additional information to you as soon as it becomes available.

I wish you and your loved ones a very happy and healthy holiday season.

Sincerely,

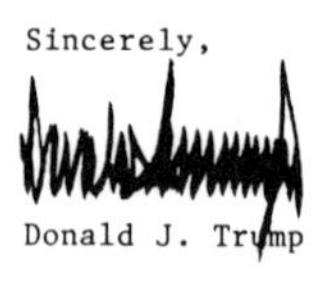

Donald J. Trump

Letter from Donald Trump.

"I had flown only six months when my status changed to a senior reserve flight attendant. Some flights were difficult, as I was very, very junior to have other flight attendants under my supervision. Some of them had flown for ten years or longer. I had to be very diplomatic on how I suggested any kind of service, ideas, or solved any inflight problems.

"However, this wasn't to last forever. The day came, six years later, when I could bid and hold a line. I would work three days and get four days off on DC-9 trips with six legs every day. I liked the responsibility to be a senior-first flight attendant that I was assigned for all flights. I began to really enjoy my job. Eastern gave me the responsibility to train all the Boston flight attendants in CPR. I was also sent to Miami to learn first-hand selling Eastern's service in public relations and relate what I had learned to the Boston flight attendants for the *Frequent Flyer Program* just coming on line, as well as the *Get Up and Go*, senior program. I was also called upon to take school children through the airport and our Eastern facilities, take them on an aircraft and serve them soft drinks to their delight. I especially enjoyed the opportunity to fly with my young son to Disney World. At that time Eastern was the airline to represent Walt Disney World.

"I survived the difficult days of the break-up of Eastern. All flights ceased on January 18, 1991. It was a sad day for a 60- year-old Eastern, called the *Wings of Pride*. I had earned my wings every day."

TRUMP CARD

"I was fortunate to be a part of the Eastern crews that joined Donald Trump's Shuttle. We flew Boston to New York and New York to Washington, and later charter flights. All aircraft were 727-200 with the classic paint scheme on the aircraft and elegant interiors.

"Trump had his own private jet aircraft. I have a friend who flew on it as flight attendant a lot. The 727 had Waterford crystal lamps in the main salon. Everything was 14K gold, including seat belt clasps and bathroom fixtures. The lavatories were marble; it also had a shower.

"Our uniforms were beautiful, we wore dark navy, with gold braid on the sleeves. Our skirts had a double kick pleat in back, lined in red. We wore white shawl collar blouses and all flight attendants wore the celebrated Trump pearls. We looked good and we felt good. Many passengers thought our pearls were real.

"Our service really began at the departure gate! A large beautiful bouquet of flowers was at every counter at the shuttle gates. At breakfast time, fresh rolls, fruit juices

Eastern planes now with Trump insignia.

and coffee was provided for passengers. All Washington, New York and Boston newspapers were available for shuttle passengers, and on board there was a selection of some 50 magazines, including *Town and Country*.

"On board we gave champagne splits and Trump chocolates. Our food service was cold, as we had no ovens. We had sour dough rolls, chicken breast sandwiches, Mexican corn salad and roast beef with horseradish relish. All service was coach, but everyone was treated like a first class passenger. On our flights we had elegant prizes; we gave one for each trip segment in a drawing. Service was always superb.

"Our interiors were plush, the cabin walls were in Tiger-eye maple. Seats were done in maroon and tan leather. The carpeting was tan and thick. Seat belts had a large red T on them for Trump. Our lavatories had beautiful marble sinks, with red Ts all around the bowl and mirrors with indirect makeup lighting. It was interesting to have crews from other airlines come to look at our aircraft. We enjoyed our jobs and were proud to have good always-on-time performance and friendly service. All employees believed that the customer was always right.

"The highlight of all my flights, was a Military Airlift Command charter carrying the last battalion of Marines home from Desert Storm in 1990. I had never seen an M16 gun before. The Marines came on board in full battle gear with their M16s. I said, 'ladies and gentlemen, please put your arms in the open overhead bins.' They all stood up and laughed and raised their arms up to the overhead bins! The Sergeant-at-Arms on duty said, 'Ma'am, these aren't arms,' holding up his gun, 'these are weapons!' Needless to say we all had a good laugh! Being from a military family, great pride in our armed forces overtook me.

"We flew into military bases for five days. The Marines had been picked up after being transported in a military C-141 aircraft at Dover Air Force Base, Delaware, next to San Antonio, Texas, then to San Bernadino, California and on to Tacoma, Washington. We had 24-hour layovers at San Antonio and at San Bernadino.

"My favorite flight was a Trump charter flight to

The short-lived Trump Shuttle (all former Eastern crews) inaugurated charter service to Barbados, 1991. Becky McLaughlin Barnes, second from left.

Nassau, showing off our airline to a group of travel agents.

We stayed at the Crystal Palace Hotel. There our first officer, David Hobart asked me to take a walk on the beach. Dave was also a single parent, a former Air Force pilot and an Eastern pilot. This ended up being a real Trump card in my life. The other crew members were so pleased, they took a picture of us by our aircraft before departure. We'd known each other before, and met on flights, but this was special for both of us.

"After the fall of the Trump empire, on occasion, the pilots had to fuel aircraft with their own credit cards where credit would not be extended. They were repaid. The pilot would also at other times on charters, carry blank checks to pay landing fees, hotels, cabs and meals for crew members, as well as fuel. The saying *Trump's Shuttle: The Diamond in the Sky* became *Trump's Shuttle: The Cubic Zirconia in the Sky*."

Trump Shuttle flight attendant Becky McLaughlin Barnes and second officer Dave Hobart before their marriage in October, 1992.

USAIR SHUTTLE

"Some Eastern pilots and flight attendants joined USAir Shuttle in the transaction of the bankruptcy sale and together with USAir management worked out the deal for the shuttle and Eastern's 727-200s. In-house flight attendants and pilots entered into supervisory rolls including catering.

"My romance with Dave Hobart was of interest to everyone. We had known each other for years from Eastern days to Trump and now USAir Shuttle. We were married at Cape Cod, October 24, 1992 at The Inn of the Mills. Some fifty close friends and family members joined in our celebration of happiness."

Becky is the proud grandmother of her son Brent's young son Zachary. She also gained two fine stepsons, Jason and Aaron Hobart — she played that Trump card right!

AN AMERICAN ON THE MOVE

American Airlines
William Bailey McLaughlin
1989 - Present

"Many moves as an Air Force brat gave me a wanderlust for life. I think it's in the genes. My mom and dad met while both flying for the airlines in the 1940s.

"Following World War II, my dad was first a copilot for TWA in New York. They hired too many pilots and he was furloughed after six months. He went into United's hangar at LaGuardia Airport in New York and was hired to go to Denver to train as a copilot. My mother was, at that time, a stewardess for United and Denver was her domicile as well as her home. She had first been an air hostess for Continental Airlines for two years before going with United. They were married in 1947 and my dad returned, as a permanent officer in the Air Force. Needless to say, the show went on the road and in the air.

Family flight attendants: Will McLaughlin, American international flight attendant with sister, Becky Barnes Hobart, Trump Shuttle, 1991.

"I am the youngest of four children. I have three sisters: Patricia, Kathleen and Becky. We have always been very close and good friends. We have lived in many states, as well as in Chatereaux, France and High Wycomb, England when my dad, as a Brigadier General, had airlift for Europe. We also traveled to Austria, Switzerland, Spain, Greece, Italy, and Germany. Even though I was very young, seeing foreign countries and their cultures, I knew that I would like to someday continue to travel to see the world. After a distinguished career in the Air Force, my dad retired and joined Eastern Airlines in management. We lived in Miami, Atlanta and then in Connecticut when my dad had offices for Eastern in New York City. At this time I had the opportunity to travel with my family to the Islands in the Caribbean and also Bermuda.

"In high school I studied French and German. I belonged to the Madrigal Choir. I received excellent training in the choir for my baritone voice. I also was involved in all the school theatrical productions. After graduation from New Canaan High School, I was a foreign exchange student in Hamburg, Germany for one year. While there, I became fluent in German. I used French also and learned some Spanish.

"On my return to the U.S. and home I attended The Boston Conservatory of Music where I studied dance, voice and theater. During this time, I worked at a French restaurant to help with school expenses. I was given a great deal of responsibility at the restaurant. Here I picked up skills in cooking and management. It was always in the back of my mind that I really wanted to travel and also use my language skills. I started looking into jobs with the airlines and that of a flight attendant. I was interviewed and accepted by several and I chose American Airlines. Training was to begin for me in early September. I quit my catering job in early June and went with the New Bedford Summer Theater. I was cast in three musicals: *Westside Story*, *Guys and Dolls*, and *Oklahoma* during this time.

"Training for American at their Learning Center was five and a half weeks in Dallas. I met great people, our instructors were very demanding, but caring individuals. For our class graduation, American Airlines provided space-available passes for our parents. My mom and dad came from Illinois. My oldest sister, Becky, flew from Boston to pin on my wings. She was a former Eastern flight attendant, and was at the time a flight attendant with the Trump Shuttle. I was also allowed to show my family around the Learning Center Facilities. My mom was especially interested as she is the author of *Walking on Air*, a book on inflight service.

"I had another week of international training and was sent to New York City as a German speaker for international flights. I found living very expensive in New York and really hard to get by. I think I lived on pasta and pop corn. When I worked trips, the American Airlines excellent food surely tasted good! We never ate until our service was finished. All B scale pay flight attendants found New York expensive. My entertainment consisted of: working out, walking, reading, video movies, airline people getting together, rollerblading down Manhattan's streets on weekends, museums, and, on rare occasions, to eat out. Sometimes I'd go to a walk-in-bar where they would let me sing. On some days off, my sister Becky would give me a Trump buddy pass to see her and friends in Boston.

"American has the best reserve system. While a B scale flight attendant everyone catches reserve every third month. It was a must to get a beeper. I had wonderful flights to Europe, but after four years I found that expenses kept going up, including my transportation to the airport. I caught the Carey Bus near Grand Central Station near my apartment. My sister Becky said of my apartment, "If Will doesn't answer in two rings, he isn't there, it is so small!"

"About this time I decided to apply for premium flight attendant training which I completed in the fall of 1992. Shortly thereafter, I managed a proffer bid to Chicago, O'Hare for international flights. I wanted to live near the water and be in the sunshine, so I moved to Los Angeles and commute to Chicago for my trips.

"When I'm on reserve, I catch American Eagle to my parents' home in Moline, Illinois. When I am on ready reserve of two hours notice, I sleep in the American Operations Quiet Room. This is a terrific facility. It has flight operations, our computer bidding center, mail boxes, banking for our credit union, a cafeteria, grooming room, three lounges (for TV, smoking, and non-smoking) and a baggage room. Our supervisors are there also and I have a great supervisor.

"My job as a premium or first flight attendant insures that cabin flight crews have smooth, coordinated service for our passengers. I am the link between the flight deck and the cabin. I also get better pay for my responsibilities, as well as being a German speaker. American gives beautiful service, I like being part of it. My flights take me to Zurich, London, Manchester, Frankfurt, Munich, Dusseldorf, Berlin, Glasgow, Stockholm and occasionally to my favorite city, Paris!"

American Airlines international flight attendants in the engine nacelle of a B-747 SP at Heathrow Airport, England. Will McLaughlin is standing on left.

COVER GIRL
UNITED'S NUMBER ONE
Pennsylvania Central, Capital, United Airlines
Margaret "Jo" Humbert
1945 - Present

United Airlines began the world's first stewardess service May 15, 1930. I selected Margaret Jo Humbert, Number One Flight Attendant for United Airlines, for the cover of Footsteps In The Sky.

"I can't believe I'm number one in Seniority of over 19,000 United flight attendants," says pretty, petite Jo Humbert. "It is hard to believe I've been around 49 years. I started flying when some of the people I fly with were born. I am not planning on quitting until I can't pass the physical. I love my job!"

Jo says of her desire to fly, "I wanted to be an airline stewardess since I was knee-high to a duck. My father took the family on Sunday drives to the Tri-Cities Airport near my home in Rogersville, Tennessee to watch the airplanes land and take off. I loved all this and I decided then that someday I too, was going to become a stewardess."

That desire became a reality for Jo Humbert. She had been a coed at the University of Tennessee and had one year to complete for a degree in Physical Education when the desire to fly overwhelmed her. "I'd just turned 21 and the age the airlines required to fly as an air hostess or stewardess. I decided I would apply for a job with Pennsylvania Central Airlines and if I was accepted I'd fly for a year or two and then return to school to get my degree. I began flying June 26, 1945 and flying was so much fun I never returned to school, and I still feel the same today."

Jo Humbert with sister, Grace Humbert Benge, as hostesses for Pennsylvania Central Air Lines in 1945.

Jo started flying on 21 passenger Pennsylvania Central DC-3s in 1945 and today flies on United's 747-400 with 438 passengers. She has checked out on 16 different aircraft in her wingspan of 49 years with Penn Central, Capital and the merger with United.

Capital was the first U.S. airline to fly jet-powered aircraft. Jo participated in the promotion of special courtesy press flights on the British Vickers Viscount which operated July 11, 1955 between Chicago, Washington, Norfolk and Washington. The Viscount aircraft joined Capital's fleet operating with jet service July 26, 1955.

Jo was publicized in 1959 in Capital's major advertising campaign as the first airline hostess to fly a million jet powered miles in the Viscount. Her photo was on the cover of the April 26, 1959 Capital Timetable. Also ads were in the magazine issues of: *Time*, *The New Yorker*, *Sports Illustrated* and *U.S. News and World Report.*

She has experienced other honors in her career and has flown with many celebrities including President Nixon, Henry Kissinger, Chief Justice Warren Berger, actor Robert Cummings and many senators and congressmen.

She was chosen as chief hostess on a five day Capital charter flight which carried General Douglas MacArthur, his wife and son on a trip through the South.

The Airline Pilots Association Council honored Jo at their annual party in Washington, DC on June 19, 1972. Some 600 United Airlines pilots paid special tribute to her "in recognition of her congeniality, cooperation and courtesy."

She was one of four stewardesses chosen in a United-Scandinavian Airlines exchange that lasted one month in April 1972. Jo says of the experience, "I wish all stewardesses could do this. We flew to Rome, New York, Lisbon, Madrid and Athens. We logged many exciting miles and had many prestigious passengers on our flights."

She was selected to be a crew member for United's inaugural flights to Hong Kong, Tokyo, and Shanghai and the list keeps growing.

Home for Jo is Rogersville, Tennessee but she commutes to San Francisco for her flight schedule and says, "I prefer Asian flights even though their duration is

Pennsylvania Central Hostesses after receiving their wings, 1945. Jo Humbert is 6th from left. (Capital Airlines Photo)

Jo's sister, Grace Humbert Benge (left), as an American Airlines trainee, 1948.

Jo Humbert, 1994 United Airlines Number One Flight Attendant, aboard a 747 SP before boarding passengers.

Smile Girl **contest among airline hostesses by *International Optimists*. Winner: Colonial Airlines. To her left and right: Delta Airlines sisters. Middle row: two Chicago and Southern finalists. Lower left: Jo Humbert, Capital Airlines, Colonial Airlines and TWA, 1946.**

Capital Airlines' MacArthur Charter. Left to right: Jo Humbert, MacArthur's son, Captain McQuiao, General MacArthur, Copilot Martin, Mrs. McArthur, hostess Shanna Madden Nicholson and a Capital representative. (Capital Airlines Photo)

United Airlines air hostess exchange with Scandinavian Airlines System in April, 1972. Jo Humbert is second from right. (United Airlines Photo)

Capital merged with United Airlines in 1961. Jo Humbert as a United flight attendant. (United Airlines Photo)

legs of four to six days. We fly in the daytime and this way body timing doesn't cause jet lag and I feel good. On trips to Europe leaving in the evening and flying all night disrupts sleep patterns and causes jet lag."

In 1992 James McLendon, President of United Airlines' Portland, Maine Mainliner Club, (UA employees) in conjunction with the United States Postal Service issued a special achievement cache in recognition of Jo Humbert's 47 years of service as a flight attendant and the first air hostess to fly a million jet miles on the Viscount. The cache is in a collector's envelope bearing a special cancellation honoring an individual or commemorating a special event.

Other features of the cache, are an autographed photo of Jo in her present uniform and the colorful 50 cent Harriet Quimby commemorative stamp. The proceeds will be donated to the Mid-Atlantic Air Museum in Reading, Pennsylvania for the restoration project of a Capital Viscount.

Today Jo says of her 49 years flying (celebrated June 26, 1994), "I've chosen the right career for me. It has enabled me to travel, to meet people and to learn about other cultures. I've been to places many people only dream of going."

Many airlines have established a trend toward more mature flight attendants. Jo Humbert is in every sense a beautiful and gracious lady. Her serene charm permeates in the courtesy, warmth and the congeniality she shows for all those she works with and serves. In every way she is a professional in a career she loves. Her beauty and charm have been compared by many to the former screen star, Grace Kelly, Princess Grace of Monaco.[1]

Collectors wishing to purchase the cache honoring Jo Humbert can write:

James McLendon
Portland, Maine Mainliner Club
P.O. Box 3729
Portland, ME 04104

[1]Information given to me in a personal interview with Jo Humbert, May 1993

FOLLOWING JO'S FOOTSTEPS

Capital Airlines
American Airlines
Grace Humbert Benge
1946 - 1947
1948 - 1953

Grace Humbert Benge was a Capital hostess at the same time as her sister "Cover Girl," Margaret Jo Humbert. Grace went on to fly for another airline.

Grace Humbert grew up in Rogersville, Tennessee and attended the University of Tennessee for three years. Her sister Jo had become an airline hostess for Capital Airlines. Grace was 21 years old at the time and left college as she wanted to follow in Jo's footsteps.

Grace trained at their hostess School in Washington, DC before starting on the line in 1946. Grace says of her experience as a Capital hostess: "I was based in Washington, DC and I made many short flights out of Washington. All Capital's flights originated out of their headquarters.

"With Capital I learned first hand of "the arrangement" that allowed you to take a vacation in exotic places...the airline pass! This was my downfall. Jo and I

Grace Humbert Benge in American's Link Trainer to learn aerodynamics. (American Airlines Photo)

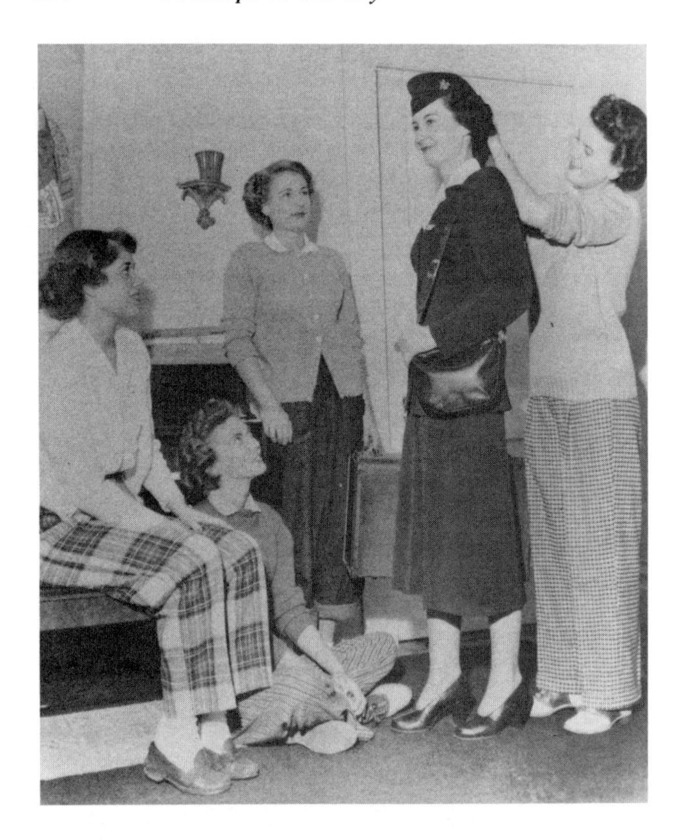

At the house on Hood Street, Grace in her American Airlines uniform, 1948.

both went to California for a vacation. We also stopped in San Diego to see our Navy boyfriends. We both could not get out of Los Angeles on our passes. We both missed our scheduled flights. I was automatically terminated when I reported late. Jo was given the option to stay or leave since she had a year's seniority over me. She stayed. I applied to American Airlines as a stewardess and was accepted."

Jo said of Grace's change from Capital to American, "Grace explained about the passes and that we couldn't get back to Washington for our scheduled flights. They were impressed with her and her honesty about the matter. They told her if her sister looked like her, they wanted her (me) too! I stayed with Capital and Grace went with American."

"I trained with American at their Ardmore, Oklahoma Flight Training Center for a month," said Grace, reflecting on her five years as an American stewardess. "There were six of us that lived in a boarding house on Hood Street at our home base of Dallas. We were known as the Hood Street Girls. We lived together and flew together. Our flights took us to a variety of places: Mexico City, New York, San Francisco, Los Angeles, and Chicago. During this time we had movie stars come to Hood Street for breakfast between flights, we were interviewed by *Look Magazine*, and the *Daily Times* Herald. The Hood Street Girls still get together once a year with our spouses for a reunion.

"The airlines taught me many things, but two I consider the most important. Capital taught me that my problems were not the airlines' problems. In other words, do not let your personal life interfere with how you perform your job. It has been an important lesson to me all my life.

"I learned from American Airlines the real meaning of service to a customer. To this day I practice the principles learned from American in my job as manager of a women's specialty shop, and it is still working!"

A SISTER ACT

Capital Airlines
Marnae Modeen
1949 -1954
Sally Modeen Mines
1951 - 1953

Other Capital Airlines sisters were employed at the same time like Jo and Grace Humbert.

Marnae Modeen, Capital Airlines hostess, 1949, as "Paul Revere" for a Capital Community Chest Drive promotion.

Marnae and Sally Modeen were both air hostesses with Capital Airlines before the United merger in 1961. Both were based in their home town of Minneapolis. Their flights took them to New York City, Washington DC and Virginia Beach.

Marnae was first accepted by American Air Lines to become a stewardess in 1948. She took her training at Ardmore, Oklahoma. She flew for a year and became so homesick she resigned her job as stewardess with American and returned to Minneapolis. She applied for a job with Capital and flew for five years before her marriage ended her flying career.

For the Minneapolis Fair, Muggs the Chimpanzee was flown in for the Dave Garaway TV show in connection with the Fair. Animals weren't allowed in the cabin, however Muggs got special TLC from Marnae on Capital's flight 419.

Marnae was selected in 1949 to represent Capital Airlines in a Community Chest fund drive. Henry Ford II was the Drive's Chairman. She took a letter from him to all the 75 cities that Capital serviced.

On one flight she was afraid she'd get fired when she had an entire pro-bowling team put off the airplane at Cleveland for drunken and disorderly behavior. She felt the other passengers did not need to put up with their loud, crude behavior. Capital's management applauded her dedication to good service in the thoughtfulness of her passengers. She had also felt it was safety too, as drunks can be dangerous.

Marnae married her Air Force fiance in 1954 and grounded herself. Sally was five years younger than Marnae. She began flying as a Capital hostess in 1951 and says of an unusual experience on one of her flights from Minneapolis to New York:

"An elderly passenger was boarded with a note pinned to his sweater that read:

> Dear stewardess:
>
> Would you please see that this man arrives at Pier 84 — Worth River, at the foot of West 44th Street in New York City after he leaves the plane.
>
> Thank you kindly

"This nice old man told me that he wanted to go home to die in his home of Genoa, Italy. I decided I was going to follow the instructions on the note pinned to his sweater.

"On landing I asked him to keep seated while I finished my duties before deplaning. I escorted him to our crew car and kept him by my side. I got some flack from the pilots, like 'we're not the Red Cross you know,' etc.

"After the crew was dropped off at their hotel I continued with my passenger to Pier 84. Because I was in uniform, the customs people were very kind and let me escort him to the head of the long line and onto the Andrea Doria (that was before the ship sank).

"This was just one of my wonderful experiences helping people as an air hostess. My sister Marnae and I have been so fortunate to have flown for a great airline, we have a lot of fun talking about our experiences."

A PROMISE: "I'D BE UP THERE"

Pennsylvania Central Capital United's Clipped Wings Shanna Madden Nicholson 1947 - 1951

Two sisters also flew for Capital Airlines and were known as the Madden sisters.

Shanna Madden Nicholson is a soft spoken lady with a southern accent. She was born in a small town in Eastern Kentucky. She had her primary and secondary education in Kentucky. She says of her education and work

Shanna Madden Nicholson, Capital Airlines hostess.

experience, "I earned my B.A. degree at Lincoln Memorial University in Tennessee. I worked as a postal clerk in our college post office and sales jobs in the summer. I had no other work experience, before becoming an air hostess." Shanna's story follows . . . .

"I became interested in aviation history and commercial aviation while in high school. At this time (World War II years), airlines required stewardesses to be nurses. During my years in college this requirement was dropped because nurses were needed in the war effort. I flooded airline personnel offices with letters and applications. On weekends I would haunt the airport at Knoxville and promised myself that one day I would be up there!

"I was accepted by both United Air Lines and Pennsylvania Central Airlines (later to become Capital). United's training class was already in session. Capital was in the process of forming their next class. I was to join this company and spent seven and a half years as a hostess, plus ten months as a receptionist in Hangar Three in Washington, DC.

"My training was four weeks at the Washington National Airport. Just as it is today, the primary focus was on safety, personal grooming, weather, interaction with passengers, knowledge of Capital's aircraft, and learning answers to future questions posed by nervous or curious passengers were other areas of study. The memory of graduation brings a smile as I remember my discomfort in trying to clutch a diploma in one hand and trying to hold up a too big skirt with the other. We graduated before our uniforms were ready and the ones we wore for graduation had been borrowed, mine was huge!

"In the beginning as 'low man on the totem pole,' my routes were on 'Tobacco Road' through the Carolinas and Georgia. Later when I had some seniority I bid all over the place. From Washington, DC to my home base to Chicago and also Missouri, flying for a month at a time with the same crew. I also bid on every charter that I could, resulting in some wonderful experiences. The best of these trips was the General MacArthur trip with his wife and son for five days in the South. I flew with Jo Humbert on this wonderful trip.

"Flying a charter from Baltimore to New Orleans, we had a DC-4 loaded with boisterous football boosters. With the exception of their loudness and off-key singing, all was going well. Until lunchtime. Crawling over legs in the aisles, we managed with dignity intact, to get everyone served. While my fellow flight attendant and I stood at the galley awaiting 'tray pick-up time,' we were startled to see a passenger running down the aisle. Not far behind him, but slightly off target, a small lemon tart was sailing along, seemingly in slow motion. Unable to duck, the missile hit me full force in the chest area, oozing filling down the front of my uniform.

"When order was restored, and the offender felt safe enough to return to his seat, he apologized and offered the explanation for his behavior: While eating his lunch, he kept looking at the tart and then at his seat-mate, picturing how it would fit over the nose and mouth area of his friend's face. He kept trying to push the image out of his mind, but to no avail. With one full sweep of his hand, he let his friend have the tart full in the face - ah, boys will be boys. He did pay for having my uniform cleaned, but for awhile, I was one sticky mess!!!

"I also enjoyed working trips with my sister Skip Madden Gumbert. Sharing the life of a flight attendant was a blessing and sometimes otherwise. Skip was younger than I and sometimes she strayed from the accepted rules and regulations of uniform conformity. On one occasion, I was called in to the office of the chief hostess to be severely reprimanded for being *out of uniform* when the local news hounds took a picture of me. The problem? My dear sister posed hatless, but *my* name was plastered under the news item!

"To preserve her somewhat shaky work ethic (my choice of words), I accepted a generous payment and a

Capital Airlines' University of Kentucky charter. Hostess Jo Humbert (lower right) worked the flight. (Capital Airlines Photo)

week's vacation at her expense (helping is what sisters are all about, right?). Over the years I have a nagging suspicion that she gave them my name — accidentally, you know. Everyone knew us at the Raleigh/Durham station, sooo the registered letter I received from the Chief hostess read:

> January 29, 1952
> Dear Shanna:
>
> Confirming our conversation of January 29, 1952, you are hereby suspended from schedule for one week from January 29 through February 4. The reason for this suspension is your failure to conform to uniform rules and regulations in regard to wearing your hat while being photographed for the *Hickory Daily Record* on September 11, 1951.
>
> You are expected to be at your base and available for schedule on February 5, 1952.
>
> Sincerely,
> Lee Neward, Chief Hostess
> Field Supervisor

"Another happening involving us pertained to charters we would fly. The famous basketball coach, Adolph Rupp, was known to be very superstitious. In addition to the brown suit he wore at each game, he insisted that either one or the other of the Madden sisters must be on the Capital charters. He felt that being Kentuckians, we brought him luck.

"When the Kentucky Wildcats were to meet Kansas for the National Championship in Minneapolis, Capital did not have a plane available for a charter. Coach Rupp brow-beat someone in the company, for both of us flew to Minneapolis. We were picked up at the airport and driven to our hotel. Awaiting us in the lobby were Coach Rupp and his assistant, Harry Lancaster, pacing the floor like caged animals. We left immediately for the game, where we were seated behind the Kentucky bench. Yep, victory was assured — Coach never thought otherwise. *Sigh . . . what can I say?*

"When I started my career flying, today's aircraft had not been built. The aircraft in Capital's fleet were DC-3s, DC-4s and the Constellations. When I worked as a receptionist later the Viscount jets made their appearance, but I never had the joy to work on them. The DC-3 is my favorite and its ability to weather any abuse man or nature could throw its way was remarkable. There was such an aura to it...it was like being wrapped in a security blanket.

"Capital Airlines was a family, and I have felt blessed to have been a part of it. I have *lived* my love of aviation, made life-long friends, and realized dreams never thought possible. United also holds a special part within me, as it has been very good to me and also holds my home airline within its system. Clipped Wings has allowed me to expand my circle of wonderful friends, and has allowed me to pursue my second love; that of working with the disadvantaged. I may have been born too early for some things and too late for others. But in between it has been a ball!"

Skip Madden Gumbert, Capital Airlines hostess.

THE NINETY-NINES, INC. AND THE INTERNATIONAL FOREST OF FRIENDSHIP, INC.

Skip Madden Gumbert

Shanna's sister, Skip Madden Gumbert, was a former Capital hostess and has been a pilot for about thirty-five years. She is a member of The International Ninety-Nines, Inc., a group of women pilots, which was founded in 1929 by 99 charter members. Amelia Earhart was its first President. Today there are more than 6,500 members in 40 countries.

The organization promotes friendship through flying and establishes lines of communication among women in all facets of aviation and aerospace. Currently the Ninety-

Niners has extensive aerospace programs, sponsors safety seminars, supports the regional and national meets for the National Intercollegiate Flying Association and sponsors competition to choose the U.S. precision flying team to compete in world-wide competition sponsored by the Powder Puff Derby.[2]

Other activities support the Forest of Friendship, Atchinson, Kansas, the birthplace of Amelia Earhart and the Amelia Earhart Scholarship awards. The Forest of Friendship is a living, growing memorial to the World History of Aviation and Aerospace.[3]

The forest is made up of trees from all 50 states and territories and 35 countries around the world where there are Ninety-Niners.[4] The trees' roots in Kansas soil are symbolic of *World Friendship Through Flying* — the motto of the Ninety Niners.

Eternally recognized flyers' names are engraved on a granite plaque. Amelia Earhart, Charles Lindbergh, General Hap Arnold, Jeana Yeager, Rajiv Gandi, the Wright Brothers, Sally Ride, Chuck Yeager, Beryl Markham, General "Jimmie" Doolittle and President George Bush. A bronze statue of Amelia Earhart graces the grounds' entrance to the International Forest of Friendship, Inc.[5]

Shanna has been honored at the International Forest of Trees for her promotion of aviation for youths and her involvement with women's history in aviation. To be honored one does not have to be a pilot; the park recognizes those who have promoted the growth and interest in aviation. Shanna has been working toward her private pilot's license too. She says of her honor of being enshrined in The International Forest of Trees. "Though I have pushed aviation for youths, with whom I have worked over the years, my special interest has been in women's involvement. I still think that what helped me slide by the Board, was that at my advanced age I would take up flying again." Shanna's dream is to be a Ninety-Niner like sister Skip. As she soars through the heavens, she is still up there! I'd call it on cloud 99!

1947 United Airlines stewardesses from Iowa. Left to right: Jane Colleen Fox, Ruby Guernsey, Nan Bowman Cavanaugh.

THE FLYING CAVANAGHS

United Air Lines
Nan Bowman Cavanagh
1947

Families share the airline experience from generation to generation.

Life has never stood still for petite, doll-like Nan Bowman Cavanagh. She grew up on a farm in Iowa where the United planes flew over their house. She dreamed of being a stewardess, but she also wanted to be a nurse.

Nan attended two years at the University of Iowa before entering Mercy Hospital's Nursing School in Iowa City. She earned her cap in August of 1946 and accepted a job at St. Anthony's Hospital in Denver. By December she applied for the job as a United stewardess and exchanged her nurse's cap for a stewardess uniform cap in January 1947 with Denver as her domicile.

Little did Nan know that a young United captain would romance her. Dale Cavanagh was visiting Denver for flight training and called a stewardess he had flown with, Kay Kahley for a date. She was busy but volunteered six names and telephone numbers of other stewardesses. Dale had a *Time* magazine with him available to write on and jotted down the names and numbers. Nan's name was number three on the list. After dating the first two on the list, Dale called Nan. Three was the charm; he stopped there, as he realized Nan was the girl he was looking for.

[2] *The International Forest of Friendship* (brochure), Lockwood Company, Inc., Atchinson, Kansas.

[3] Ibid.

[4] Ibid.

[5] Ibid.

Dale and Nan Cavanagh in their 1940 uniforms. Nan is seated in the engine nacelle of a DC-10.

A swift courtship followed. Nan and Dale were married in August of 1947. Nan was grounded, but says, "After forty-six years of marriage to Captain Dale Cavanagh, I am glad I made the cover of *Time* magazine."

In 1956, Nan won a system-wide "UAL All Sell" contest to generate additional ticket sales for United. She got together lists of Denver conventions and after making the initial contacts, made reservations on United, picked up the tickets and delivered them to the various companies and individuals. She averaged selling $3,000 worth of tickets a month with an average ticket price of $150. Each month for one year, she won a $25 savings bond. At the end of one year, she won the contest's trip for two to Hawaii all expenses paid, first class on a DC-7. The tour included spending money, inter-island tours, and husband Dale was paid his full salary during the two week vacation.

Nan had continued to be a booster for United through the years. In 1960 she represented United in a "Smile" contest, and at the same time recruited prospective stewardess candidates. She is an active member of the Denver chapter of Clipped Wings. Through the years she has given countless hours to their projects to raise money for handicapped children.

Retired United captain Dale Cavanagh helped me with editing. He provided me with aircraft configuration information.

Nan is sometimes known as "Lulu the Clown." She dresses in a clown disguise, complete with red wig, and entertains children. Wherever Nan is, there is action and compassion for people. She takes great pride in the fact that her son Michael has become a captain for Delta Air Lines. Michael follows the new trend of some modern crew members, living in one place and commuting for his flights. He makes his home in Pinedale, Wyoming and flies a Cessna 180 to Salt Lake City for his flights as a B-737 Captain. Michael carries on the tradition of the "Flying Cavanaghs."

Nan has been an active member of United's Clipped Wings Stewardess Alumnae Association in Denver since 1951. The chapter was first organized in 1948. Each year, Nan is involved in fund-raising drives to help mentally retarded children, which is the primary goal of Clipped Wings nationwide. When in Denver today she is still involved.

On September 15, 1972, Nan donned her 1947 United Air Lines stewardess uniform — which still fit perfectly after twenty-five years — to fly the route between Denver and Los Angeles. During the flight Nan described her duties as a stewardess in 1947 to interested passengers. The occasion was United's celebration of the Silver Anniversary of the Denver—Los Angeles route and in addition to being entertained by Nan's appearance, the passengers were treated to specially decorated terminals in the two cities.

In 1974, Nan was chairperson of the Clipped Wings extravaganza, *Remember When.* She and her committee rounded up antique automobiles, vintage airplanes, and stewardess uniforms from United's archives in Chicago. Uniform styles were modeled beginning with the 1930s, when Ellen Church designed the original stewardess apparel for Boeing Air Transport, and ending with the modern mix-and-match uniforms of the seventies. Nan was also involved in other community service activities. As a water safety instructor, she taught a children's swimming class, affectionately known as *Nan's Polliwogs,* in her backyard pool. She taught beginning tap dancing once a week to adult women, and she kept up her nursing credentials by attending workshops for nurses.

The Cavanaghs spend winter months in Naples,

Florida. Volunteer efforts abound for both Nan and Dale. In 1992 Nan obtained her Florida Nursing Certification so she could give nursing care for senior citizens at Naples' Senior Foundation. She also has a class for Water Aerobics and volunteers in a theater group. She is a lady with energy she extends with TLC to help others enjoy life as much as she does!

AVIATION CAREERS FAMILY STYLE

United Airlines
Marilyn "Dinny" Bartmess Henze
1959 - Present

Marilyn Bartmess Henze has been a flight attendant for United Airlines for 35 years and says of her job. "I love it! I get to fly with my sister, Marsha Bartmess Sanders two months every year. I've also had the opportunity to fly with my best friend, Phyllis Paladino for over 20 years almost every month! These happenings make Marilyn happy and it shows in her ready smile and attitude toward her job as a flight attendant.

Marilyn makes her home in Winneconne, Wisconsin and commutes to Chicago O'Hare Airport for her flights. She has always been involved in community service besides her job as a United flight attendant. In November 1992 she was asked to give a speech at Winneconne Middle Schools school assembly for their project for the Power of Positive Students Program. Marilyn related to the students. "The right attitude is more important than wealth, power, or whatever people think about you. Whatever you decide to do, like it and work hard at it. Be the best you can be and also keep a smile on your face." Marilyn believes that negative people pull you down. Her message was to build self esteem and in turn success and happiness are the result.

Marilyn says of her career as a United flight attendant: "I trained at United's Cheyenne Stewardess Center in 1959. After graduation I was sent to Chicago as my domicile and one year later transferred to Los Angeles. By January 1961 I was selected to be a trainer at the Stewardess Center in Cheyenne. In October 1961, when United opened up their new executive offices and training center in Chicago, I was there until I became a stewardess supervisor in June 1962. In January 1970, I returned to flying the line under the new name, flight attendant. I am still flying and I love my job!

"I have been married to Bud Henze, a United captain for 26 years. He retired as a DC-10 captain in 1985.

United Airlines flight attendants, August 1993. Janet Hensley (left) and Marilyn Bartmess Henze (wearing a dress style option summer uniform).

"My step-daughter, Cindy Henze Berkeley, made United history, November 8, 1989, as their first female captain. She first joined United as a flight officer in April 1978 at age 24, and comes from an aviation family. Her husband is the Manager of the Air Traffic Control Center in Aurora, Illinois. Cindy flies out of Chicago as her base.

"I have always been grateful for my career with United Airlines. I have met very few famous people on my flights and nothing unusual in experiences. I just like helping people. Our family is definitely an airline family and we all feel very fortunate to be involved in aviation."

United's first woman captain, Cindy Henze, November 8, 1989.

THE HECK SISTERS
TWA
Hilde and Gale

The Heck sisters, Hilde and Gale, looked like twins. They flew together on TWA's Stratocruisers. Passengers enjoyed them and crew members would jokingly say, "look who we have as hostesses today: Aw, Heck and What The Heck!"

Gale and Hilde were in the WACs (Women's Army Corps) during World War II. Their mother, Blanche, was also a WAC and they were the only mother and two daughters in any branch of the armed forces.

After army, the airlines appealed to the sisters. They attended Zell McConnell's school for eight weeks and then they were hired by TWA. They were first based in Kansas City and then New York.

Later, their mother, fearing an accident, wrote TWA requesting they not schedule her daughters on the same flight. TWA obliged her request much to the chagrin of Gale and Hilde.

TWA liked to feature *sister acts* among their hostesses. The sisters had worked well together and everyone had enjoyed them.

Crews and passengers all enjoyed the Heck sisters, Hilde and Gale.

Gale (left) and Hilde (center) being fitted for their TWA uniforms.

TWA'S ENSLEY SISTERS

Pauline, Ruth, Teresa

Three sisters represented TWA in the 1950s as a FAMILY IN THE AIR.

TWA hired three beautiful sisters from Oklahoma City to be air hostesses in a period between 1947 through 1958. Pauline, a redhead, was the first to be hired in 1947. She was flying as a hostess when brunette sister, Ruth, joined TWA's hostess staff in 1951. Blond Teresa followed their footsteps in 1952.

All three wore the same classic famous 1944 TWA cut-out uniform of light blue gabardine. The tailored jacket with covered buttons featured a triangular flap on the left shoulder with a TWA cut-out that showed through, over a navy round neck blouse slip. The uniform skirt lengthened as fashion had indicated in 1947. A matching blue hat with a red and blue cockade included silver TWA hostess wings. This uniform had followed the *Pretty Girl* uniform in 1944 and was worn for the longest period of time until 1955.

It was replaced by a uniform designed by Oleg Cassini and Briney Marlin of brown wool sharkskin. TWA was embroidered on the right side of the jacket which was worn over a blouse slip. A matching hat held hostess wings pinned to a red cockade. Ruth and Teresa also wore this uniform as they flew the skies as TWA hostesses. Pauline, Ruth and Teresa Ensley all have their stories to tell...

DANGER ON FLIGHT 96

TWA

Pauline Ensley Marshall

1947 - 1951

"After high school I attended Oklahoma City University and Oklahoma University both while working at Tinker Field. When I joined TWA in 1947 their hostesses were trained by McConnell Schools. Once on the line we were paid back our tuition. The course took eight weeks. My class was written up by *Life Magazine*, December 8, 1947.

"Upon completion of the training I was assigned Kansas City, Missouri as my base and first flew on DC-3 aircraft. Later I flew on the Constellations, called *Connies*. This was my favorite aircraft. They were so beautiful, besides it was a lot more fun flying with a partner. My partner was Maxine Power and I flew with her until 1950 when she married a TWA captain.

"The New York passengers were a breed of their own. One lady walked the aisle and not finding a seat, immediately flounced back to demand I find her a seat and informed me she wasn't going to stand up all the way!

"On a DC-3, the most frightened I ever got was when a passenger was thrown from her seat into the overhead rack during a sudden turbulence. She was badly shaken up, but not injured.

"The closest I came to danger was on a Constellation on flight 96 at the height of a storm while landing at Pittsburgh. Only our skilled pilot saved us.

"Captain Richardson had radioed ahead for an emergency landing as we had a ruptured gas tank. In the meantime, we learned later, there was a breakdown of Flight 419; an aircraft with a flat tire at the end of the same runway we were using. A TWA ground crew with three mechanics had been sent out with a spare tire. As our giant Constellation approached the runway a propeller blade struck the roof of this maintenance car and smashed the cart hauling the tire to splinters. The propeller broke off and two tires blew. Captain Richardson halted the aircraft midway down the runway.

"We immediately rushed our passengers off the *Connie* and into the storm as gasoline poured from the

Hostess Pauline Ensley Marshall (left) with hostess partner Maxine Power by the nose wheel of a TWA Constellation, 1950. (TWA Photo)

ruptured fuel tank. Fire equipment hurried to the ship. The three mechanics escaped serious injuries and death as the whirling propellers sheared through the roof of the maintenance car.

"I enjoyed my passengers and the opportunity to also have celebrities on my flights. The movie star I enjoyed the most was Zazu Pitts. She was a very gracious lady. She had been visiting in New Mexico and had purchased Indian jewelry for her daughter. She gave me one of these which I still wear and cherish.

"One of the captains Ruth and I both flew with became a dear friend of our families. When our family gets together we all remember good times. Two of my nieces are flying today for Continental and American. We've been a family in the sky."

TWA GAVE "ROYAL" SERVICE IN MORE WAYS THAN ONE

TWA
Ruth Ensley McFarland
1951-1958

"I was an X-ray Technician with a specialty in nuclear medicine and radiation therapy. My older sister Pauline was enjoying her life as a TWA hostess so much and her international flights to Europe, I too, became interested and I decided to apply to TWA for a hostess job. At my interview I was told that only two were accepted out of every 100 applicants. The requirements were very strict: either a Registered Nurse or at least two years of college; single; height 5'3" to 5'6½", absolutely no fat or overweight; reasonably attractive and very good health. I was thrilled to be accepted and anticipated life as a TWA hostess.

"Basic training was intense for six weeks. We had to learn aircraft types, emergency training, airline and city codes, great emphasis was given on the care and treatment of passengers. We were called hostesses, as we were to treat our passengers as we would guests in our home.

"I worked on DC-3s, DC-4s, Martin 404s and the Constellations. The Constellations were my favorite. Later for international flights on the *Connies* we had special training. We trained with the Coast Guard on ditching procedures getting into rubber rafts. We also had updates on this and also on other new procedures on aircraft and inflight service.

"Passengers were so nice to us, one passenger gave me tickets to Broadway plays. I had the Ambassador to France and his wife on board an international flight on the Constellation. She arranged for me to see the opening of Dior's Spring Collection. I tried on hats, dresses and a ball gown. I only weighed 103 and the model's dresses fit. This was in 1955 not too many years after World War II. I remember thinking that people in the audience did not look very fashionable as Europe was just beginning to recover from the war.

"We had a Count who worked for TWA as a purser. He was a real character. When we landed in Europe he went on his way to visit royalty. A story was told about a royal party in England by columnist Dorothy Kilgallon about the charming Count at the party. She couldn't believe that Counts have to work too.

"On one trip to Europe I took the Catholic Bishop of Kansas City on his way to Rome to see the Pope. On a return trip his casket was in the baggage compartment of the Constellation. He had suddenly died while in Europe. He had appeared to be in good health.

"I had my share of movie stars. Our passengers were an elite group of interesting people and included many celebrities who chose planes to travel. The job was glamorous in part because of this as well as the travel it afforded me.

"I always felt that TWA was first class in attitude toward passengers' care and comfort. I had the most exciting life, flying became one of the greatest adventures

TWA hostesses Ruth Ensley McFarland (left) and Betty Clingham celebrate TWA's inaugural flight into Oklahoma City, February 16, 1956. (TWA Photo)

TWA hostess with passengers aboard the Jetstream Constellation in the 1950s.

of my life. I met the most exciting and wonderful people doing fabulous things.

"I resigned TWA after six and a half years flying to marry and raise a wonderful family. After college, my daughter, Martha, became an American Airlines' flight attendant and is now in management. Our family continues in aviation today."

A FAMILY IN THE AIR

TWA

Teresa Ensley Terrell 1952

TWA hostess Teresa Ensley Terrell, 1952.

"I decided to apply with TWA for a hostess position for the excitement and change from hospital life as an X-ray technician. Last but not least, also because I had two sisters flying as hostesses for TWA and they loved it.

"I interviewed and was accepted by TWA in 1952 for hostess training four weeks in Kansas City. After graduation I was domiciled in Chicago and flew domestic routes both East and West and in between. I flew on DC-3s, DC-4s, the Martin-404s and the Constellations. My favorite aircraft was the Martin-404 because of closer contact with passengers.

"Some of my most thrilling and exciting experiences were brought about because of weather conditions. Horrible storms, including being struck by lightening. On one flight an engine went out and we had to make an emergency landing. I received a phone call from dispatch saying my mother had emergency surgery. I was devastated with no way to get home.

"I had the West Point football team on board a flight which was a lot of fun. I also had a flight with all military going to Korea. They were so appreciative of everything. The most fun was running into my sister Ruth at various airports, (Pauline had already married by that time). Ruth and I would compare notes and laugh. We were always laughing.

A new TWA hostess class graduating from the Kansas City training school. The hostesses are lined up before going on a training flight and final check before going on the line. Teresa Ensley Terrell is 4th to the right on the top steps. (TWA Photo)

"I, of course, left TWA when I married and became Mrs. Richard Terrell. I became the mother of six sons and one daughter, Ann. I was a very shy person and flying gave me more confidence in myself. I encouraged Ann to fly and *live a little* before settling down to marriage. She did both, she became a flight attendant for Continental Airlines and married David Deery. She is still flying and enjoys her job. She has always been so positive and never shy, a real natural for the job of a flight attendant.

"We have a son, Dick, flying as a Navy pilot. Our son, Tim, gave his Dad a gift of flying lessons. It had been his dream to fly since he was a child. My husband got his license at age 63 and is now taking acrobatic lessons — yeah! Beside my sisters, Pauline and Ruth, myself, my daughter, Ann, and my niece, Martha, with the airlines — Dick, a Navy pilot and my husband now a pilot — we are truly a *Family In The Air.*"

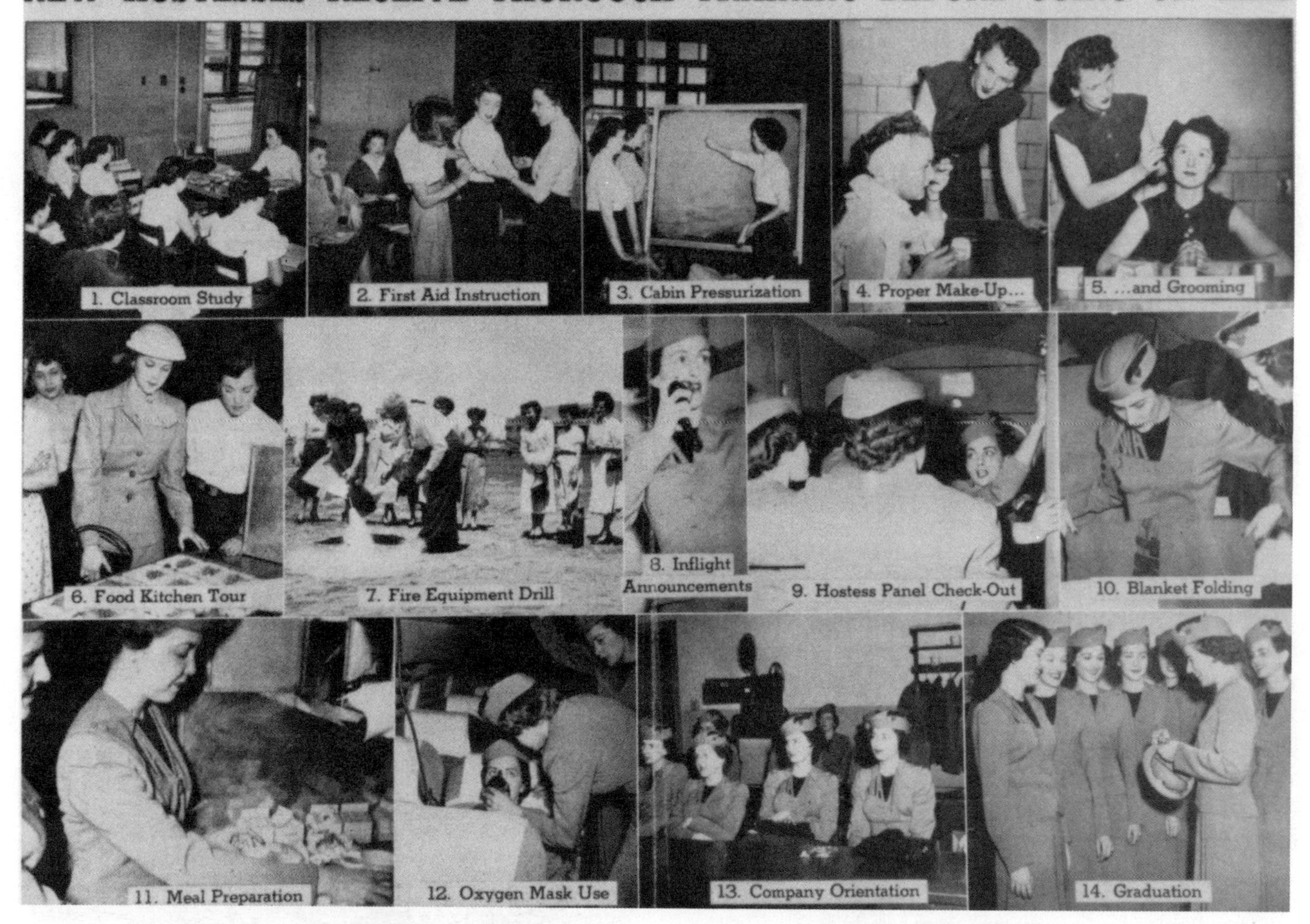

PROUD TO BE AN AMERICAN

American Airlines Martha McFarland-Goetz 1987 - Present

Martha McFarland-Goetz followed her mother's footsteps in inflight service.

"My career at American Airlines began in 1987 with a *dare* phone call. A friend and I were discussing future career goals after graduating from college, and a degree in Fine Arts hadn't exactly prepared me for entry into the big business world. I felt my options were limited, when suddenly I got an inspiring thought, and I said to my friend, 'I'll be an airline hostess like my mother.'

"My buddy challenged me to make good on the threat and dared me to call for an application. Opening up the Yellow Pages, the first airline under A was, of course, American Airlines. I called the local number at Will Rogers World Airport where an agent corrected my request for an *air hostess* application and informed me that the position I was seeking was that of *flight attendant*. She told me she didn't have any applications, but her friend, a recruiter, just happened to be at the airport waiting for a flight to Dallas (American's headquarters). After a brief discussion over the phone, the recruiter invited me for a formal interview in Dallas the next week. The rest is history.

"After six weeks of training, I shipped out to my first base of operations in San Francisco. While working as a domestic flight attendant I did everything from personal relations work at golf tournaments to giving emergency medical aid in flight. My proudest memory of those days was an event during an attempted hijacking and bomb threat when we successfully evacuated more than 180 passengers after an emergency landing. I learned a lot about my capabilities under pressure, looking down two stories with only cement and two helpful crew members waiting at the bottom of the slide. I came away from the experience feeling I could handle anything.

"After two years of flying, I joined the staff at Headquarters responsible for developing flight attendant procedures. I have worked on this staff to the present,

Martha McFarland-Goetz, American Airlines flight attendant and manager.

where I am editor of the flight attendant newsletter, *News AAloft*, and am responsible for writing all inflight announcements as well as producing the safety videos shown on board the aircraft.

"During my managerial career, I had the proud opportunity to serve my country by volunteering to fly CRAF missions during the Gulf War. Flying back-to-back trips between Saudi Arabia and Milan, Italy I met the men and women who participated in Desert Storm and gained first-hand knowledge of our operations there. Some nights we would fly into the desert practically blind to the runway due to heavy smoke from burning oil wells. Upon arrival we were greeted by hundreds of G.I.s, thankful American Airlines had come to take them home, and eager to photograph the crew as they wrapped us in their giant U.S. flags. It was the proudest moment in my career, and one that I will never forget.

"I'm proud to be an American Airlines employee and part of a family legacy of *Something Special in the Air*.

LIKE MOTHER, LIKE DAUGHTER: A FAMILY IN THE AIR

Continental Airlines
Ann Terrell Deery
1987 - Present

Ann Terrell Deery followed her mother's example to become a flight attendant.

"A nine to five job was not for me. I realized that after a year as an office manager, the job was not for me! My college roommate was flying for American Airlines, and suggested I give it a try. Since my mom had flown for TWA and had loved it, I figured I'd like it too. The old cliché, *like mother, like daughter* proved true for me. I interviewed with Continental Airlines and was hired. Shortly after being hired I was going through some of my keepsakes. I noticed that I had written in a 4th or 5th grade journal that the job I wanted was to become a stewardess. My dream came true.

"I was trained at

An American Airlines flight carried troops to Saudi Arabia during Desert Storm, 1991. Martha McFarland Goetz is standing in the center to the right of the captain. Photo was taken at night in front of the base PX.

Continental Airlines flight attendant Ann Terrell Deery, 1993.

Continental Headquarters Training Center in Houston, Texas for six weeks. I was first domiciled in Denver, Colorado. Then I moved to Houston in 1987 and I commute to Dallas to take my flights. I have worked the A-300, DC-101, 727, 737, MD-80 and the DC-9. The only aircraft in our fleet I haven't worked on is the 747. My favorite aircraft is the DC-9. I like the fact that it only holds 108 passengers and there are no ovens, but most of all because it flies into smaller cities. I have flown to Mexico, but not the international routes because of the long flight times and smoking is allowed. I try and bid lines that will keep me in the Midwest and the South. I try to stay away from both coasts. I love the people of the Midwest and South. They are nice and appreciative of you! I also like the long layovers in the smaller cities like: Boise, Idaho; Jackson Hole, Wyoming; Minot, South Dakota; Omaha, Nebraska; etc. It is really refreshing to meet the locals.

"Everyday brings new experience on the airplane, whether it is the crew you work with or the passengers. There is one experience that brings a smile every time I think about it. An elderly woman boarded the plane at Harlingen, Texas, and said to me, 'Make sure my husband gets on the plane.' I replied, 'What seat is he supposed to be in, and I'll make sure he gets on.' She told me he was dead and his coffin was being put on the plane. Talk about putting your foot in your mouth!

"I was working a flight from Denver to Fresno to Stockton, California when a passenger made several comments about hijacking to me and to my buddy bid partner, Lori. I told him that was nothing to joke about. Another flight attendant heard him and told the captain about him. The next thing this man said to me, 'I know you told the Captain about me, if I had a gun, I'd pull it out and blow you away!' After this remark I was frightened and told the captain again about this man's remarks. He had me sit in the cockpit for landing and to stay there until the Fresno police had the passenger in custody.

"Another incident that made me wonder about some people. We lost our third engine on take off out of Newark on a flight to Houston. We had to return to Newark. Many passengers were furious and were loudly remarking and yelling at us and the agents about missing their connecting flights in Houston. They were angry we didn't fly on two engines, never mind about their safety.

"Most times people are so nice, and as I said, I prefer people who fly out of the Midwest and South. I have gone to places and cities I would never have thought about, before this wonderful job. I have met so many interesting people. The best part is the fact I met my husband, David, while I was based in Denver. I have also met another flight attendant who is a very dear friend, Lori Sewell. I have buddy bid with her the past two years, what an adventure!"

AMERICAN'S THREE GENERATIONS

American Airlines
Lisa Warren
1984

These three flight attendant made a first in history for American Airlines.

American Airlines celebrated a special first in March 1984. Lisa Warren followed in her grandmothers' footsteps as a flight attendant for American. What made the occasion so special was that her grandmother, Marie Allen Sullivan, was one of the original four stewardesses hired by American Airways in 1933. Marie's daughter, Jane Sullivan Warren, had also been an American stewardess. Lisa had always wanted to be an airline stewardess like her mother and grandmother.

Marie was present at Jane's graduation in 1949 and

pinned on her daughter's wings. Like her mother, Jane had trained at American's Stewardess Center at Midway Airport in Chicago. Jane's flights from Chicago to California on 40-passenger Convairs took eight hours compared to her mother's long flights in Curtiss Condors. However, Jane had not had to be a Registered Nurse like her mother, because that requirement was dropped during World War II in 1942. Like her mother, Jane left the airline to marry.[6]

Lisa started her training June 1983 in Moline, Illinois at Mississippi Valley Airlines headquarters. MVA trained flight attendants for other commuter airlines under contract. There were 24 in her class: twelve trainees for MVA, three for Fisher Airlines, and nine for Imperial Airlines. Lisa earned her wings on July 11, 1983 and immediately left for California.

For the ensuing nine months she flew as a flight attendant for Imperial out of San Diego to Santa Barbara and Bakersfield. This experience proved to be a stepping stone for Lisa to join American Airlines, which had been her dream all along.

Lisa trained with American at their new Learning Center at the Dallas/Ft. Worth Airport in Texas. The center resembles a college campus in contrast to the Stewardess Center at Midway Airport attended by her grandmother and her mother.

Lisa's mother and grandmother were flown to Dallas in March 1984 for Lisa's graduation as the class of 84-7. At the graduation ceremonies both Marie and Jane reflected on their experiences and were presented red roses. Lisa became the third generation to wear American wings. National as well as local news featured this special happening in aviation inflight service.

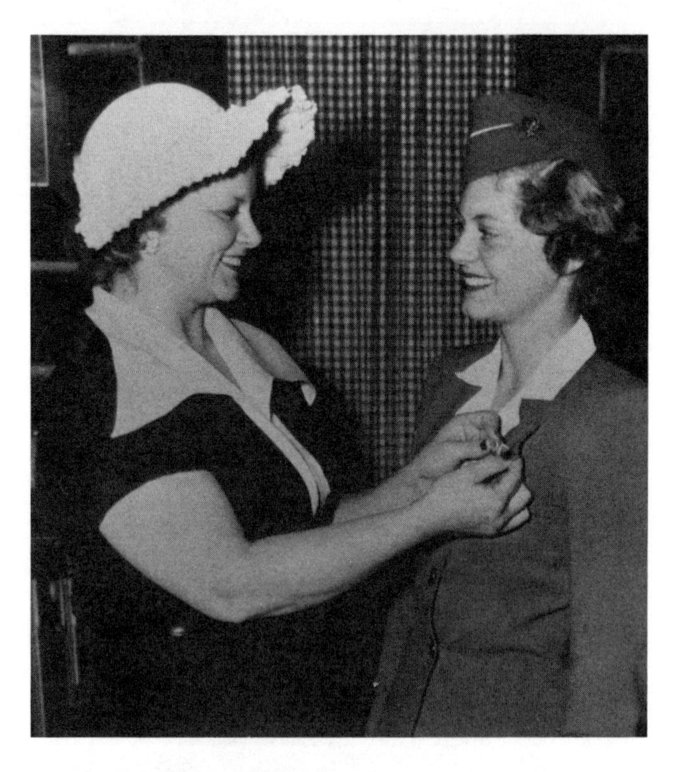

Marie Allen Sullivan pinning on her daughter's wings in 1949.

[6]*Flagship News*, excerpts from *They Were a Novelty*, Vol. 16, Number 5, 1983, p. 71.

Three generations of American Airlines flight attendants at a special graduation ceremony for Lisa Warren, class of 1984. On Lisa's right is her mother, Jane Sullivan Warren, class of 1949. On her left is her grandmother, Marie Allen Sullivan of American Airways first class, 1933. (American Airlines Photo)

A TRIBUTE TO COURAGE
TWA
Uli Derickson
1966 - 1988

The President of TWA Clipped Wings International, Jerri Costello Currigan, gave me a copy of Uli Derickson's speech given at the Clipped Wings Convention at the Holiday Inn Embarcadero in San Diego, California on October 7, 1989. She was the heroine of TWA's flight 847 that was hijacked on a flight from Athens to Rome and flew between Beirut and Algeria in June 1985. (Uli retired from TWA and is now flying for Delta.)

"Good evening. I am honored and happy to be a part of this year's Clipped Wings Convention here in San Diego. And so I wish to thank all members of your great organization for inviting me to attend.

Uli Derickson was a flight attendant for TWA for 22 years. She is now a flight attendant for Delta Air Lines.

"Last month, I retired from TWA after 22 years of service as a flight attendant. I am happy to be retired, although I enjoyed my career with what I consider to be a great airline. I think all of you ladies here tonight, as well as myself had the best of it serving as flight attendants during the early years, because of all the disturbances, bankruptcies etc., in the airline industry the past decade. I hope the future can be more enjoyable and productive for both employees and management than the past eight or ten years.

"President Pat Trussell asked me to talk to you at this convention and so I am coming to you tonight through the courtesy of faith, luck and the persistence of hope. Not to mention prayer, training, stubbornness, and the insistent belief that you *can* make a difference no matter what the moment or situation.

"I am going to mention a few beliefs tonight, and the first of them is my belief that any one of you flight attendants here tonight could just as easily have been handed the same surprise handed to me on June 14, 1985 -- a surprise, incidentally, I would rather *not* have been given.

"But I suppose we can't be choosy about what life decides to schedule for us. And mine was certainly an education in self determination.

"I have thought about it many times since, and I have come to the conclusion that perhaps, in some perverse way, I was fortunate to be thrust into a situation in which my own personal decision became important enough to mean the difference between surviving or not. Not only for me, but for others too.

"Because, making a difference is making a decision. And in order to make a responsible decision, we have to believe we can make it. And a belief is strongest when it is tested.

"As I said, I am going to mention a few of my beliefs this evening, and I am going to ask you to think about a few of yours. I imagine we will have a lot in common.

"I believe, for instance, that in order to make a difference, we have to make a difference to *ourselves*, and I also believe that deep down, unless there is something very badly damaged in us, we are really *all* survivors. If we *believe* we are.

"And because this high tech, depersonalized world we live in today seems to be complicated and violent enough to at least diminish us as individuals, I believe that our survival depends more than ever upon our *own belief* that we *matter*, and that we make a difference. You have a right to ask at this point, "What gives us the right to think that we matter? What *is* it in us that lets us survive? What is it that lets us make a *difference* in our lives and in the lives of others?

"I asked myself the same question, and I came up with a list, a very short list: Three words that I think stand for three qualities that each of us possesses, but that we sometimes forget to take out and dust off and practice until we absolutely have to:

Determination,
Imagination
Integrity.

"With them, we live.

"Without even *one* of them, I believe our survival is doubtful.

"Let us consider determination first. When the two hijackers on TWA flight 847 leaped from their seats and raised their weapons and began to scream, 'We have come to die!' I was terrified. I thought, that's what I have done, come here to die.

"That's a non-survival type thought if there ever was one. But it only lasted for a moment. Then, determination took over. And training, and, I suppose, experience. Because, after all, part of experience is what we do with our knowledge. And I *did* have some knowledge of the determination that is needed to survive.

"I was born in the Sudetenland, and at the end of World War II, my mother and father and I were forced to flee from Czechoslovakia to what is now East Germany. And then, my parents, determined that we were going to escape from *there* into *West* Germany. And we did it, by traveling for six nights and hiding for six days.

"My father watched for weeks before we left. Very carefully, he studied the changing of the guard. When the guards went for lunch, when they went for dinner, when there were dogs, and when there weren't. When, in other words, we could safely make it -- that is, unless we stepped on a mine.

"So we set out at night and we threaded our way to freedom. I was a five year old girl then, with a bad cough. And I remember my mother putting her hand over my mouth and throwing me to the ground when I began to cough, because she was determined that we would make it.

"And we did, finally.

"When we got there, we weren't really at the end of our journey. We were refugees. We were a minority. We weren't welcome because everybody was living in rubble, and even that was full to overflowing. There was hardly enough food to go around, and here we were, adding to the poverty, diminishing the living spaces. These were our own people, but they did not welcome us.

"Still, we knew by this time that there were no easy answers in life. We were *determined* to stay. And stay we did. And sooner or later, we found the freedom we were determined to find. That was *my* experience, and it was important to me in June 1985, but it is not unique.

"You had your own experiences, and each has been important, no matter how insignificant it seems at the time. Experiences that taught you something, which was very much like what I learned. All those days and nights in the fields taught me this, and taught it to me well — Don't give up, no matter how bad the situation is. No matter how impossible it seems, don't give up.

"And I am convinced that that experience helped me to make a difference. When those terrible first moments in the airplane arrived, I had one legacy given to me by the determination of my parents. I didn't know if I was brave or not. But I knew I wasn't helpless.

"So much for determination.

"Let's go on to imagination.

"Each of us has one. When we are very young, it runs riot. When we get older, it sometimes needs to be nudged. Certain leaders, certain ideas, certain people catch and fire our imaginations. When I was younger, President John F. Kennedy fired *my* imagination. In fact, he was the reason I came to America. I idolized him. He represented all that was hopeful and free to German youth, and that was why, when I came to America, I applied not for a visitor's visa, but an immigration visa. President Kennedy had so excited my imagination about what freedom was, I was ready to turn that imagination into tangible action, and begin a whole new way of life.

"That's an obvious example.

"There are *other* sources of imagination that are far more subtle and unexpected.

"How many of you, I wonder, have sat in a classroom and said to yourself, 'I can't *imagine* what good this course is ever going to be for me. How can it *possibly* help me? What am I *doing* here?'

"I am married to a TWA pilot. Two years after we were married, he was sent to Saudi Arabia to train Saudi Arabian pilots for their national airline. And, in a flash, I went from being a liberated American woman to being a woman in a Moslem society. And, in a Moslem society, as you probably know, a woman has very few rights -- about as many as a new copilot.

"After two weeks of this sort of life, I thought to myself, either I am going to go crazy, or I am going to do something productive. So, I went to school and I learned Arabic.

"Little did I know that ten years later, it would save my life, and possibly the lives of 147 others.

"Originally, there were three hijackers. The only one who could speak English had been bumped in Athens, because the plane was oversold.

"So, when that terrible moment came and these two men charged at us, yelling Arabic, all of a sudden *my* Arabic came rushing back to me, and I screamed back at the hijackers — in Arabic! I yelled out — and I can remember every word — 'Where are you from, I am from Germany, can I help you?'

"And I wish you could have seen the reaction. Here

was this western woman, shouting at them in Arabic. They probably thought they were dreaming. After the initial exchange in Arabic, I discovered that one of the hijackers was fluent in German.

"From that point on communications with him was in my native language which I translated to English for my crew members and passengers — however, I began to think in Arabic. I had to, because I knew that those three short sentences I had just spoken detached me from everyone else, forever, and gave me a terrible responsibility, besides. Before that moment I was just anybody; now I was a line of communication.

"So, my imagination — what was, I admit, fueled by desperation — began to work. I thought to myself in those first mad moments, I had started something. *Now* what? What do I *do*? What *can* I do?

"That's the problem with making decisions.

"First I had to put my knowledge to work. I remembered that, to Arabs, the Koran was important, that religion was important. That religion was, in fact, *central* in Arabic life. So I began to discuss religion with them. It was a beginning. I imagined that as long as we talked, we could stop the beating. Because that's the way *wars* end. When the fighting stops and the talking begins. So we talked. And kept on talking.

"I don't mean to simplify it. The talking wasn't continuous, by any means. The calm of that was matched by some terrible hysteria. Sometimes I thought we could keep on talking and reach some sort of peaceful solution, and then all of a sudden, without warning, the beating and the psychological terror they had been trained to inflict would begin again.

"But, it was not *all* madness. That's the point. Time was bought by talking.

"And imagination kept *on* playing a role in the decisions that were designed to make a difference.

"Between conversations, I tried to imagine what it was that consumed these young hijackers, and what might be done to at least *reach* that consuming passion. Because, if I could only reach it, there might be a chance of *diminishing* it. It stands to reason that you can't change what you can't touch.

"And finally, we both got there, when we concentrated on what *they* thought Americans thought about *them*. Because they are convinced that we are their worst enemy, that *everyone* in America is anti-Moslem and anti-Lebanon — and worse than that, *does not care*. 'Look at our children,' one of the hijackers said to me, 'they die in the streets daily. You scream when one American gets killed somewhere. In Lebanon, our people die every day, and nobody cares. Only *your* lives mean something to you.'

"Of course, *he* was thinking the same *way*, but then wasn't the time to debate that.

"What became necessary was to try to convince him that Americans were not as he portrayed them. And I had to imagine *his* feelings in order to try to change his imagined picture of all Americans.

"I spoke as earnestly as I could about the compassion of Americans and some of their sufferings, and the pilgrimages some of them have made to the Holy Land.

"I don't know if I succeeded in the long run. I know I did for the moment, Because there wasn't as much savagery after we talked as there was before we began.

"And if that was the case, then one person *did* make a difference — with help from two directions: From the past, and from above. I never prayed so hard in my life as I did during those two and a half days of captivity. They say that there are no atheists in foxholes. There aren't very many in the cabin of a hijacked airliner, either.

"And I am convinced that those prayers were answered. And I believe they pointed me toward the third quality that lets one person make a difference in this world: integrity.

"Integrity to me is believing in something, and being true to that belief, no matter how it is challenged.

"There are some other beliefs I have that dovetail with this general one and I suppose complement it:

"I believe that everyone has a heart and soul.

"I believe that, no matter how cruel and uncaring a person seems, if you search long and hard, you can hit that spot in every human being with which you can communicate.

"And I believe that everything is negotiable. You can negotiate anything. Of course, negotiation requires imagination, too. A bigot, for instance, has no imagination. He cannot imagine what it is like to be anyone else but himself.

"To do that, you have to have imagination, and compassion. And the integrity to allow that compassion to work, no matter what the odds are.

"Think of Anne Frank. What unimaginable suffering and isolation and cruelty to endure! And through it all to say, 'In spite of everything, I still believe that people are really good at heart!'

"As I said at the very beginning, I am sure I was lucky. But I am also sure that if I had not believed what Anne Frank did, and also believed in the *integrity* of that belief, I could not have done whatever I did. Because, I believed, first of all, what the hijackers said. I *believed* them when they shouted, 'We have come to die!'

"And I also believed they would kill us, because I was aware that they had been as well trained to do their jobs as we had been to do ours. They knew exactly how to demoralize people, with physical abuse, with fear, with psychological torture, with unexpected and unexplained violence. And that is the most demoralizing action of all, because you cannot reason with it. And they knew that.

"But, and this is most important — in the middle of the insanity, I still believed that there was something good at the heart of each of these hijackers, and it was up to me, if we were going to survive, to touch it.

"As I said, I could have been lucky. But I think my beliefs and the integrity of them helped the luck along.

"Let me illustrate this with one last story.

"At one point, one of the hijackers heard me humming — God knows why I was humming — one of those involuntary things you do when you are scared out of your wits, I suppose — and he asked me if I could sing. Did I know *backe' backe Kuchen* (*Patty Cake, Patty Cake* in English) — I asked him how he knew that song and it was then he told me that he had a German wife and baby in Germany. This struck something in me, and I thought, he is really sincere. And I sang *backe' backe Kuchen.* Then he said, 'sing me a hit song that I would hear if I was back in Germany.' 'I'll try,' I said, and I thought of a song I'd heard maybe 25 years ago, sung by a German singer named Freddie. It was his one hit, and it was called *People Without a Country*. The words were heartbreaking: 'I have no house, I have no friends, I have no place to go to . . . .'

"So I sang that song in German, and I looked right at this hijacker. And as I sang, his face began to soften, just a little bit.

"And then he stopped me. And he said, 'Sing it again, slower, I want to hear the words better.'

"And the second time I sang it, his eyes began to fill with tears. When I finished, he said, 'That is just like Lebanon.'

"And then I told him about my childhood, when I was hungry, too. When I had to pick apples from the ground, because if I picked them from the trees, I would be accused of stealing.

"And I knew at that moment, I had reached him. I'd reached whatever good there was that rested in him. And I am convinced to this day that it mattered, in the final outcome of that ordeal.

"So there it is. Making a difference, through determination and imagination and integrity — it can work for one or two individuals, or for the world.

"I have been asked if I am a changed person because of my experience aboard flight 847. And the answer is yes.

"For one thing, ever since I found I could charge $12,000 worth of jet fuel on my Shell credit card, I make sure I never leave home without it.

"For another thing, I believe more strongly in my religion than I ever did before.

"I appreciate freedom, too — more than I ever thought possible. Because, I tell you, you can't believe what it feels like to be held captive, under someone's total control -- until it happens to you. And to have your mind terrorized and held captive, too. When that happens, you realize how precious freedom is.

"And that doesn't mean freedom to ignore others. That's a kind of terrorism all in itself. No. Freedom implies a *responsibility* to others -- which is a *liberation* or *your* ability to make a difference. I know now, as a result of my experience, that when you are responsible for someone else other than yourself, it intensifies the fighting instinct in you. And the ability to act is the greatest freedom of all.

"So many people in America from all ethnic groups have made a difference in my life. I continue to thank them for being so supportive and for all their prayers during and following the ordeal, in June 1985. The outpouring was so overwhelming and so wonderful, and so indicative of all the gifts this country bestows on all of us -- not the least of which is making us feel we make a difference.

"It is one of the reasons I became an American Citizen in April 1987. I am grateful for that opportunity and for your having me here tonight.

"Thank you, and God bless you."

AMERICAN'S FIRST IN FLIGHT

By Martha McFarland-Goetz

American Airlines
Juanita Carmichael
1944 - present

The sky was the limit in 1968 when stewardesses were allowed to continue flying beyond 32 years of age. They could remain either in the air or in management on the ground. This one chose to stay in the air 50 years and has no plans to retire. She is a flight attendant for American Airlines, and the most senior flight attendant **in the world!** *Her story is reprinted here by permission from* AAIR MAIL.

Juanita Carmichael has filled more coffee cups, comforted more nervous passengers and logged more miles in the air than could ever be counted. At 73, Juanita is the most *senior* flight attendant in the skies, and with almost 50 years under her wings, she's one of the few who managed to stay there.

Juanita signed on with AA July 10, 1944. For a young woman fresh out of teaching college — who knew that a classroom was the last place she wanted to be — employment choices were few.

Juanita told a local newspaper, "when we were in grade school, we had career day," Juanita recalled. "There was a nurse, an airline stewardess and a model. Well, I grew up too short to be a model, and I could never be a nurse. Being a stewardess was something I always wanted to be, it was always a glamorous job and I loved to travel."

One day Juanita spotted a newspaper ad for American Airlines. At five-foot-even, she was only slightly discouraged by the height requirement of 5-foot-2. During the job interview, she was quizzed on current events and asked if she minded cutting her long hair. She walked out of the Gibson Hotel in Cincinnati an American Airlines stewardess-in-training.

During her half century of flying, Juanita has met many celebrities — among them, Cecil B. DeMille, Boris Karloff and Marilyn Monroe. On one flight, she helped Lauren Bacall dress and greet a horde of Hollywood photographers. On another, she and Bob Hope traded war stories about flying out of combat zones in Vietnam. She has strapped Lassie into his first-class seat, held the coats of the King and Queen of Tonga and stood by as Frank Sinatra stormed off a plane after a weather delay.

She's had memorable experiences with the ordinary traveller as well. An unusually bumpy flight once sent a passenger's false teeth sliding down the aisle.

Forty years of diaries, letters and photographs provide a recorded history of her career. She's also kept every uniform she's ever worn — from her first severe, blue serge suit, to the plaid mini skirts and go-go boots of the late 1960s and the floor length red, white and blue muumuu she now wears when she's flying Honolulu.

Juanita has been all over the world and collected many souvenirs in half a century of flying. "Each thing I look at reminds me of someplace I have been," Juanita said as she surveyed her keepsakes. And apparently she has every intention of collecting more, since she has no plans to stop flying.

"I wouldn't be happy grounded. Each trip is different, there aren't any trips you can compare. I like meeting new people. You really do have an opportunity to see wonderful things."

Juanita Carmichael, American Airlines' *Number One* and first in the world.

EPILOGUE

OVER SIXTY YEARS IN THE SKY

ONLY A MOMENT IN TIME

OVER SIXTY YEARS IN THE SKY ONLY A MOMENT IN TIME

Man has always been fascinated by flying machines and by the people who wore wings and walked the skies: from those *First Steps* of early couriers and pursers of the 1920s to when Boeing Air Transport (the predecessor of United Air Lines) put something new in the sky. On board two Boeing 80-A aircraft on May 15, 1930, were the world's first stewardesses. One flight left Oakland, California bound for Cheyenne, Wyoming while another flight left Chicago for Cheyenne. Steve Stimpson and Ellen Church's idea of Registered Nurses as the "Original Eight" stewardesses took flight. They were resented by macho pilots who tagged them *flying nursemaids*. Because these tiny women wore dark green uniforms, newspaper writers called them *The Little Green Swallows*. Airline officials had been skeptical and had given them a probationary time to prove themselves.

United's legacy to inflight service: (left to right) Mary O'Connor, Steve Stimpson, Ellen Church and Jackie Jos Ceaser (founder of United Airlines Clipped Wings).

It didn't take long for passengers to realize their worth and they liked being pampered. Travel started to build; some passengers were booking a flight to fly with a particular stewardess. The macho pilots decided the stewardesses were an improvement, as now they could direct all of their time to flying the airplane. A new era had begun. These "Original Eight" Registered Nurses had dared to try something different and with sheer grit had proved themselves by pioneering a new place for women in aviation.

By 1941 the profession widened its own horizons when it no longer required registered nurses, as nurses were needed in the World War II effort. This now gave opportunities to college and career-minded girls and later to men as well.

Women who had to remain single or leave the job, often married the airline and stayed with the job a lifetime. Gradually work rules changed along with "props" to jets. The airlines have grown from a handful of small companies to an industry of giants. The focus became passenger service and safety of the passenger as well as the crew. Everything was done to please the air traveler and to encourage him to fly again.

In the enlightened 1980s and 1990s the sexual connotations of the job disappeared. Today's flight attendants are well educated men and women of all ages and races, either single or married, with or without families. They are dedicated, highly trained safety specialists, in a job serving people and the airlines they work for. Inflight service has come a long way to a career in aviation.

In 1930, Ellen Church Marshall created this new and exciting profession as the world's first stewardess. To pay tribute to her and to her contribution to air transportation, in 1966 United had a bronze bust and a memorial plaque created of its *first* lady of the skies.

The bust is displayed in the lobby of United's Inflight Training Center in Chicago. A plaque was presented to 25 airlines and to the Union Hospital in Terre Haute, Indiana where she served as administrator until her death in August 1965.[1]

What changes will the future bring in inflight service? What can we anticipate in the year 2000 - into the next century?

From the alpha of the first footsteps in the sky, to the omega of present-day flight attendants is only a moment in time . . . for history also has wings.

[1]Letter to Jackie Jos Ceaser, United Airlines' WA Patterson, President, UAL September 12, 1966. Furnished by Vicy Morris, United Clipped Wings Historian.

United Airlines' "Original Eight" at the 35th anniversary of inflight service, 1965. All are in the same position as the first photo taken in 1930. Top: Ellen Church, the world's first stewardess. Left to right: Margaret Arnatt (the only survivor in 1994), Inez Kellerman, Cornelia Peterman, Harriet Fry, Jessie Carter.

Mildred "Sugar" Kane Connell, United stewardess, 1937, before a flight on the B-247. (United Airlines Photo)

APPENDIX

AIRLINE CLUBS AND ASSOCIATIONS

WHO TO WRITE TO BECOME A FLIGHT ATTENDANT

GLOSSARY OF TERMS

COMMON CITY AIRLINE CODES

BIBLIOGRAPHY

AIRLINE ASSOCIATIONS OF FORMER FLIGHT ATTENDANTS

First Stewardess	Airline	Flight Attendant Association
1933	American	Kiwis
mid 1940s	Alaska	
1937	Braniff	Clipped Bees
1940	Capital	United Clipped Wings (merger)
1941	Continental	Golden Penguins (Dallas has the only chapter at present)
1940	Delta	Clipped Wings
1931	Eastern	Silverliners International
1948	Frontier	Silent Flyers (merged with Continental)
1937	National	Alumnae Club
1939	Northwest	Ex-Stewardess Association
1950	Ozark	TWA's Clipped Wings (merger)
1944	Pan Am	World Wings International
1935	TWA	TWA Clipped Wings International
1930	United	United Clipped Wings
1935	Western	Stardusters

Write personnel or Inflight Service of the airline you worked for to obtain the association name and list of chapters. Many clubs have members at large or an *interline group* in larger cities. Example: Denver, Colorado. Continental's Golden Penguins now meet this way.

If the airline merged, you would join the association of the new airline. Example: Capital Airline merged with United in 1961, Penn Central and Capital former hostesses would join United Clipped Wings.

The Dallas chapter of Continental's Golden Penguins planned the 50th reunion of hostess service in Dallas, October 2-5, 1993. Marilyn Walker (third from left) was chairman.

UNITED'S CLIPPED WINGS

Stewardess Alumnae and Flight Attendants, Inc.[1]

United Clipped Wings, begun as Stewardess Alumnae, was formed in 1941 in Chicago by former Stewardess Jackie Jo Ceaser. The name *Clipped Wings* was used since a stewardess had her wings clipped when she married. Ex-stewardesses, however, did not want to sever ties with friends and United.

The name United Air Lines' Stewardess Alumnae, Inc. was first incorporated in 1948. This name applied until 1990 when an amendment changed it to the current United Airlines' Stewardess Alumnae and Flight Attendants, Inc. This was to reflect the change in membership. Clipped Wings' logo is clipped back wings with United's shield in the center.

In the beginning Clipped Wings was a social club, giving to poor families at Thanksgiving and Christmas. Also during World War II, working for the Red Cross and growing Victory Gardens. In the 1950's the mentally retarded were adopted as a nationwide philanthropy in addition to supporting local charities. Philanthropic funds went to research until 1987 when service-related projects also benefited.

Capital Hostesses were welcomed in 1966. By 1978 current flight attendants were granted full membership. Although wings no longer had to be *clipped* to join, the name was retained for sentimental reasons.

The first involvement with the International Special Olympics was in 1987. At the 1988 convention, Special Olympics was selected as the National Project.

Members participated at the International Games in Reno in 1989 and the Twin Cities Special Olympics in Minneapolis/St. Paul in 1991. In 1993 the Special Olympic World Games was held in Austria with overwhelming success. Over 120 members and guests joined the Clipped Wings delegation in Salzburg and Schladming. Volunteers assisted in sporting events as time keepers, huggers and coaches, as well as many other duties. They were great ambassadors for America and to those they served.

Plans are now being made in advance to prepare for the 1995 Summer Games in Hartford, CT.

Clipped Wings has 26 Chapters. Its charitable contributions have totaled over $2,813,153. Clipped Wings has a respected reputation in communities all over the world. Today it is the living legacy of Jackie Jo Ceaser, its founder.

If you are a former United stewardess, or Capital hostess or flight attendant and wish to join Clipped Wings, contact:

VP of Inflight Services
EXO
United Airlines, Inc.
PO Box 66100
Chicago, IL 60666

[1]*Clipped Wings Quarterly*, vol. 42, Issue No. 1, Fall Quarterly 1991, "How It All Began, Founded by Jackie Jos Ceaser," p 25.

AMERICAN'S KIWI CLUB

Former American Airline stewardesses and flight attendants started to get together in groups as early as the 1940s. In 1952 a nationwide organization was formed and given a national charter. It was named the Kiwi club, after the resourceful New Zealand bird that does not fly.

Membership since that time has increased to over 2,000 members. The organization has various groups in over 200 cities and towns in the United States. Its members and members-at-large have raised over a million dollars to support many charities in their communities. Some of their philanthropic projects have benefited the terminally ill, elderly people in need, mentally retarded and handicapped children, the needy people of other countries, homeless men, women and children, and the victims of multiple sclerosis and other diseases.

The Kiwi association has selected the U.S. Olympic Committee as their national project. Thousands of dollars were raised to train hundreds of athletes for the 1980 and 1984 Olympics. The Kiwi Club has chosen sports medicine and the training program at the Olympic Center in Colorado Springs to be the recipient of their donations.

In addition to their philanthropic endeavors, Kiwis are committed to American Airlines through their many services to their parent company. Kiwis volunteer time to act as guides at the American Airlines Learning Center and at American's headquarters at the Dallas/Ft. Worth Airport. Through the Kiwi Assistance Program, members are given a nominal fee to help American Airlines flight attendant recruitment interviewers. In addition, Kiwis receive job referrals, because of their background working with and serving people. The executive board of the Kiwis qualifies all employment opportunities before referring them to the membership.

The members are kept up to date on all happenings through the club's quarterly newsletter, *Kiwi Kaleidoscope*, as well as American's *Flagship News*.

The dedication of the Kiwis and respect for American

Airlines is returned in full measure. Robert L. Crandall, Chairman and CEO of American says of the Kiwis, "Over the years, the Kiwis have done outstanding work for their company and their organization. We are proud of their achievements and prouder still of the commitment to service that has been their trademark."

SILVERLINERS INTERNATIONAL

Silverliners is a non-profit international organization composed of former Eastern Air Lines flight attendants and companies with whom they merged. The first chapter, chartered in 1954, was named by Captain Edward V. Rickenbacker, the founder of Eastern. "Captain Eddie" liked to think that stewardesses were the silver lining of any dark cloud his passengers might encounter. There are now 22 Chapters throughout the United States and Mexico and, at-large members in Canada, Japan and France. The purpose then, and now, is to retain friendships made during flying days and help and support worthwhile charities within their local communities.

In December of 1982, Fantasy Flights to the North Pole, for children with special needs, were inaugurated and continue to be an important function. Though Silverliners no longer has the sponsorship of Eastern, other airlines (charter, military and scheduled) continue to assist. During the first two weeks of December this annual event continues throughout the United States.

Through the years, the organization has given thousands of hours raising money for various charities through bake sales, coupon sales, garage sales, flea markets, card parties, tennis and golf tournaments, raffles, luncheons, fashion shows, bazaars, dinners and balls and numerous other functions.

The charities helped by the Silverliners have been varied: mentally retarded young and old; American Cancer Society; Muscular Dystrophy; SIDS; Cystic Fibrosis; Juvenile Diabetes and Heart Foundation; blind, deaf and crippled children; battered children and mothers; troubled youth, orphanages, drug abusers and the list goes on.

Silverliners have escorted sick or dying children to Disneyland and Disney World. They have taken Foreign Exchange students into their homes, sent special children to camp and brightened their holidays with clothing and toys. The group has given hope and touched the lives of countless people by their sharing and caring.

Individually, several Silverliners support South Mountain Christian Camp in Bostic, North Carolina. This camp for disadvantaged children was founded by former Eastern Air Lines Captain O.A. Fish and his wife Charlotte.

The Silverliners worked on Eastern Airline projects at interline alumnae activities, new terminal dedications, businessmen luncheons, the 1981 Fiftieth Anniversary of Flight Attendants celebration and inflight fashion shows. Silverliners manned Eastern Air Lines booths at youth fairs, assisted with Eastern Air Lines travel agent tours and sales blitzes, and shuttle crowd control. They have served refreshments to military passengers at holiday travel times and always contributed to memorial funds for Eastern families.

In 1986, Silverliners International adopted Paul Newman's Hole In The Wall Gang Camp as their International charity and as of 1993 are within $20,000.00 of reaching their pledge of $75,000.00. The money contributed to the HITWGC is in addition to contributions made to individual chapter charities.

The members of Eastern's Silverliners feel that they have been enriched by reaching out to help others. They have grown too, in the friendships they have nurtured with their fellow members while pursuing their philanthropic activities.

In 1994, they will celebrate their fortieth birthday knowing Silverliners International charitable contributions now total over $2,000,000.00.

Former Eastern flight attendants interested in learning more about Silverliners International may contact:

Willie Podesta Young
Buck Grove Golf Course
Route 3, Box 283 A
Mattoon, IL 61938

TWA'S CLIPPED WINGS INTERNATIONAL INC.

Former TWA hostesses who met socially from time to time decided to organize, elect officers and establish dues at one of their lunches in Kansas City in October 1941. Thus was the beginning of TWA Clipped Wings International. The purpose of the organization is to bring together in civic, philanthropic, cultural and educational endeavors former hostesses and flight attendants.

The club has 875 active members in 38 cities including London, as well as an associate membership — members who do not live in cities with local chapters.

Clipped Wings International's acting president is Jerrlea Costello Currigan, a resident of Clever, Missouri and an associate member. She flew for TWA from 1963, upon graduation from Wichita State University to 1966. Carrying on a fifty-two year tradition of philanthropic and educational endeavors, Jerri directs the interests and fund-raising efforts of the organization.

Every two years, Clipped Wings International holds a convention involving all 38 chapters. The 1993 convention was held in Phoenix, Arizona. At the convention, a unified charity or the next two-year term is voted upon. Over the years, TWA Clipped Wings has donated over $300,000 to Project Hope, The Human Growth Foundation, Multiple Sclerosis and Alzheimers.

Clipped Wings is the only organization of former flight attendants that belongs to the *Federation Internationale des Hostesses et Convoyeuses de l'Air*.

Clipped wings has a museum in Kansas City which houses their extensive collection of uniforms and memorabilia. They also published a book covering the first 50 years of the TWA hostess - flight attendant. A video was recently produced which gives the history of the uniforms.

The club has volunteered hours working in several capacities for TWA in exchange for passes. They also publish a newsletter. For membership, contact:

TWA Clipped Wings International
728 Hidden Valley Road
Clever, Missouri 65631

PAN AM'S WORLD WINGS INTERNATIONAL INC.

Former Pan American flight attendants organized World Wings International in 1953, and it was chartered in 1959. Membership is composed of 1300 people in thirty chapters as well as members-at-large, throughout the world. Members of World Wings meet at annual conventions that span the globe from Hawaii to London.

Members are involved in projects that support their respective communities. World Wings has donated over $400,000 to various charities. Ninety percent of the funds raised are distributed in local chapters to philanthropic interests. The remaining ten percent remains in a charitable trust, to be presented at the annual convention to the international charity.

The first international charity was Sonoma State Hospital in California. It was chosen for the work of its Brain Behavior Research Center in the prevention of birth defects. Most recently, Gallaudet College in Washington, DC was the recipient of funds. Gallaudet is the only liberal

Pan American's Stewardesses of 1946. (Pan Am Photo)

arts college for deaf students in the world. This outstanding institution serves the deaf through education, research and public service here and abroad.

Each chapter of World Wings takes great pride in its international involvement, as well as its association with other chapters. Honorary members include Anne Morrow Lindbergh and Nanette Fabray. Since a great airline left the skies in 1991, World Wings International, Inc. members cherish the opportunity they had and the friendships they formed.

CONTINENTAL'S GOLDEN PENGUINS

Contact the Dallas chapter:
c/o M. Walker
2605 Westridge Drive
Plano, Texas 75075

new trail in commercial aviation

Eight graduate nurses hired in 1930 by Boeing Air Transport, a predecessor company of United Airlines, pioneered the flight attendant profession in Ford Trimotors. They loaded luggage, cleaned the planes, served meals and reassured passengers that flying was safe. Among early air travelers were celebrities like Will Rogers (bottom, left). In 1955, four of the original eight stewardesses (right) were reunited for the 25th anniversary of flight attendants. Cornelia Peterman Tyson (left), Inez Keller Fuite, Jessie Carter Bronson and Ellis Crawford Podola reminisced over a photo of themselves taken in 1930.

QUALIFICATIONS FOR FLIGHT ATTENDANTS - 1990s

Today's flight attendant applicant has a choice of many airlines, including commuters, regionals, national and major airlines. Restrictions of sex, race, marital status and motherhood no longer apply, and forced retirement at age 32 no longer exists. Longevity is now a matter of good health, and 65-70 is the current retirement age for some airlines.

Airlines still look for service oriented individuals who are poised, intelligent, good listeners, and who have the ability to project personal warmth. Thousands of applications are made to the airlines each year, and out of the hundreds who are interviewed, only one in 25 is chosen.

To apply for a flight attendant position, write to the airline and request information on their qualifications and application procedures. Enclose a self-addressed, stamped envelope with your request so that the airline can send you an application form. Be sure to fill in all the blanks on the application form with correct and current information. When you return it to the airline, enclose a current resume and anything else (such as photos) that is requested.

Many airlines will not accept applications unless they are actively seeking them. Check the yellow pages for the employment office or personnel office number of the airline and call for a recorded message that will tell you what positions the airline has open. This could save you time.

Inquires should be sent to:

Flight Attendant Recruitment
AMERICAN AIRLINES INC.
PO Box 650071
Dallas/Ft. Worth Airport, TX 75265-0071

Inflight Training
Continental Airlines, Inc.
4375 Wright Road
Houston, TX 77032

System Employment Manager
DELTA AIR LINES, INC.
GENERAL OFFICES
Hartsfield Atlanta International Airport
Atlanta, GA 30320

NORTHWEST AIRLINES
Flight Attendant Human Resources, MSF1470
5101 Northwest Drive
St. Paul, MN 55111-3034

TWA
Employment Office
PO Box 20126
Kansas City, MO 64195

Flight Service Recruitment — CHLPX
UNITED AIRLINES, INC.
PO Box 66100
Chicago, IL 60666

USAIR
Inflight Services
2345 Crystal Dr.
Crystal Park 4
Arlington, VA 22227

AIR WISCONSIN AIRLINE COMPANY
(UNITED EXPRESS)
Inflight Service
Outagamie Airport
Appleton, WI 54911

ALASKA AIRLINES, INC.
Human Resources
Box 68900
Seattle, WA 98168

ALOHA AIRLINES, INC.
Inflight Services
PO Box 30028
Honolulu, HI 96820

AMERICAN EAGLE (SIMMONS AIRLINES)
Inflight Services
Marquette County Airport
Neqaunee, MI 49866

AMERICA WEST AIRLINES, INC.
Inflight Service
4000 E. Sky Harbor Blvd.
Phoenix, AZ 85034

HAWAIIAN AIRLINES
Inflight Services
PO Box 30008
Honolulu, HI 96820

HORIZON AIR INDUSTRIES, INC.
Inflight Service
1952 Pacific Highway S.
Seattle, WA 98188

MESABA NORTHWEST AIRLINK
Inflight Service
7301 26th Ave. S.
Minneapolis, MN 55450

SOUTHWEST AIRLINES
Inflight Services
Box 36611
Love Field
Dallas, TX 75235

AIRLINE TERMS AND ABBREVIATIONS

Aft	Toward the tail section of the aircraft
Ailerons	Section of the aircraft used to bank or turn
Airspeed	Speed the aircraft passes through air (usually read in knots)
Alternate	A second airport used if aircraft cannot land at the scheduled airport
ATA	Actual Time of Arrival
ATC	Air Traffic Control
Base	The city a crew member is assigned (another term for domicile)
Bid	Request to fly a certain schedule or route. A bid is given on seniority basis
Blueroom	An aircraft's lavatory (other terms: Lav, Head)
Board	To get on an aircraft
Bulkhead	Dividing wall, usually between first class and coach section
Cabin	Section holding passengers
Checklist	List to be completed before moving aircraft
Cockpit	Section of aircraft for pilots
Commute	Go to another city to take a designated flight
Commuter	Airline member who lives someplace other than the base assigned for flights
Companionway	Section in an aircraft behind the cockpit door that leads to cockpit
Cycle	One take off and landing
Deadhead	Crew members in or out of uniform that sit in the cabin and ride as a non-revenue passenger; an aircraft flown empty to get it in position for its schedule
Decompression	Loss of pressurization
Delay	Behind schedule
Deplane	Leave the aircraft
Dispatch	Office of flight operations
Domicile	(see Base)
ETA	Estimated Time of Arrival
ETD	Estimated Time of Departure
F	Code used to designate a first class passenger
FAA	Federal Aviation Administration
F/A	Flight Attendant
FAR	Federal Aviation Regulation
Ferry	A flight with no revenue passengers
Flight plan	Detailed plan of a flight filed by the dispatcher with the air traffic control center
Forward	To front of aircraft
Fuselage	Main portion of an aircraft to which wings, tail and landing gear are attached
Furlough	Lay off
Galley	Buffet or aircraft kitchen
Ground speed	Airspeed at which aircraft travels over ground
Head wind	Wind blowing in opposite direction from which aircraft is moving (generally west to east in the United States). Head wind slows an aircraft's movement
Holding time	Extra time on the ground not allotted for in the schedule
Holding pattern	Assigned by ATC (see) for an airplane waiting to land for weather or a congested airport (used to be called stacking -- flying at a designated assigned altitude)
Inbound	Aircraft or crew arriving
Jetway	Covered walkway attached to the terminal to position at an aircraft door to board or deplane passengers
Knot	Speed; one nautical mile per hour; one knot = 1.15 statute miles
Landing	Bringing an aircraft to the ground
Landing gear	Portion of aircraft with wheels (Lowered for landing and retracted after take off)
Layover	Remain overnight
Leg	A segment of a flight
Log	A detailed record of the operation of an aircraft, crew, engine
Non-revenue	A passenger (normally an airline or travel industry employee) who flies without purchasing a ticket (also

	called a non-rev)
Outbound	Crew or aircraft leaving a station
PA	Passenger Address system used for announcements; Passenger Agent, an airline employee who deals with passengers on the ground before and after their flights
Pass	Issued by an airline under special conditions to fly non-revenue (see)
Pressurization	Quantities of air are pumped into a cabin to bring air pressure as close as possible to sea level, this is controlled from the cockpit
Prop	Aircraft propeller
Prop wash	Wind created by the whirling motion of the propellers
Ramp	The asphalt or concrete section of a terminal where an aircraft parks (Tarmac)
Revenue	Payment for a trip
RON	Remain Over Night
Rudder	Located in tail of aircraft, it controls forward direction of aircraft
Runway	Concrete strip used for takeoffs and landings of aircraft
Tail wind	Opposite of head wind. Wind blowing the same direction the aircraft is heading. A tail wind can aid an aircraft's progress
Taxi	Movement of an aircraft on the runway to position it for takeoff
Turbulence	Bumpy air caused by storms, mountains, air activity, heat or wind
Turn	Flight that departs and returns the same day to the same city
Unaccompanied Minor	Child under the age of twelve flying without an adult (a full-fare paying passenger over the age of twelve) traveling companion
VFR	Visual Flight Rules
WX	Weather
Y	Code used to indicate a coach class passenger

United's legacy of inflight service: 1933 United Air Line stewardesses (all registered nurses). Mary O'Connor, sixth from left; Marie Hess Conway, fifth from right. (United Airlines Photo)

COMMON CITY CODES

ABE Allentown/Bethlehem/Easton, PA
ABI Abilene, TX
ABQ Albuquerque, NM
ACA Acapulco, Mexico
ACT Waco, TX
AGS Augusta, GA
ALB Albany, NY
ALO Waterloo, IA
AMA Amarillo, TX
ANC Anchorage, AK
ANU Antigua, British VI
APF Naples, FL
ARN Stockholm, Sweden (Arlanda Airport)
ASU Asuncion, Paraguay
ATL Atlanta, GA
AUA Aruba, Netherland Antilles
AUS Austin, TX
AVL Asheville, NC
AXA Anguilla, Leeward Islands
AZO Kalamazoo, MI
BAQ Barranquilla, Columbia
BDA Bermuda
BDL Hartford/Springfield, CT
BFL Bakersfield, CA
BGI Barbados, West Indies
BHM Birmingham, AL
BMI Bloomington, IL
BNA Nashville, TN
BOG Bogota, Columbia
BOS Boston, MA
BPT Beaumont/Port Arthur, TX
BQK Brunswick, GA
BQN Aguadilla, PR
BRL Burlington, IA
BRU Brussels, Belgium
BTR Baton Rouge, LA
BUD Budapest, Hungary
BUF Buffalo, NY
BUR Burbank, CA
BWI Baltimore, MD
BZE Belize City, Belize (Goldson Airport)
CAE Columbia
ACK Akron/Canton, OH
CCS Caracas, Venezuela
CHA Chattanooga, TN
CHO Charlottesville, VA
CHS Charleston, SC
CID Cedar Rapids/Iowa City, IA
CLD Carlsbad, CA
CLE Cleveland, OH
CLL Bryan/College Station
CLO Cali, Colombia
CLT Charlotte, SC
CMH Columbus, OH
CMI Champaign/Urbana, IL
COS Colorado Springs, CO
CRP Corpus Christi, TX
CSG Columbus, GA
CUN Cancun, Mexico
CVG Cincinnati, OH
CWA Wausau/Stevens Point, WI
DAB Daytona Beach, FL
DAY Dayton, OH
DBQ Dubuque, IA
DCA Washington, DC (National Airport)
DEC Decatur, IL
DEN Denver, CO
DFW Dallas/Fort Worth, TX
DSM Des Moines, IA
DTW Detroit, MI (Metro Airport)
DUS Duesseldorf, Germany
EGE Vail, CO
EIS Tortolla, British VI
ELP El Paso, TX
ESF Alexandria, LA
EVV Evansville, IN
EWN New Bern, NC
EWR Newark, NJ
EYW Key West, FL
EZE Buenos Aires, Argentina
FAI Fairbanks, AK
FAR Fargo, ND
FAT Fresno, CA
FAY Fayetteville, NC
FDF Fort de France, Martinique
FLL Ft. Lauderdale, Hollywood, FL
FNT Flint, MI
FPO Freeport, Bahamas
FRA Frankfurt, Germany
FSD Sioux Falls, SD
FSM Fort Smith, AR
FWA Fort Wayne, IN
FYV Fayetteville, AR
GCM Grand Cayman Island
GDL Guadalajara, Mexico
GGG Longview/Kilgore, TX
GGT Georgetown, Exuma, Bahamas
GHB Governor's Harbour, Bahamas
GIG Rio De Janeiro, Brazil
GLA Glasgow, Scotland
GND Grenada, Windward Island
GPT Gulfport/Biloxi, MS
GRB Green Bay, WI
GRR Grand Rapids, MI
GRU Sao Paulo, Brazil
GSO Greensboro/Highpoint/Winston-Salem, NC
GSP Greenville/Spartanburg, SC
GTR Columbus/Starkville/West Point, MS
GUA Guatemala City, Guatemala
GUC Gunnison/Crested Butte, CO
GYE Guayaquil, Ecuador
HDN Steamboat Springs, CO
HHH Hilton Head Island, SC
HNL Honolulu, HI
HOU Houston, TX (Hobby Airport)
HPN White Plains/Westchester County, NY
HRL Harlingen/South Padre Island, TX
HSV Huntsville/Decatur, AL
IAD Washington, DC (Dulles Airport)
IAH Houston, TX (Intercontinental Airport)
ICT Wichita, KS
IDA Idaho Falls, ID
ILE Kileen/Ft. Hood, TX
ILM Wilmington, NC
IND Indianapolis, IN
ISP Islip, Long Island, NY (MacArthur Airport)
IYK Inyokem/Ridgecrest, CA
JAC Jackson Hole, WY
JAN Jackson, MS
JAX Jacksonville, FL
JFK New York, NY (Kennedy Airport)
JNB Johannesburg, South Africa
KIN Kingston, Jamaica (Manley)
LAF Lafayette, IN
LAN Lansing, MI
LAS Las Vegas, NV
LAW Lawton/Fort Sill, OK
LAX Los Angeles, CA
LBB Lubbock, TX
LCH Lake Charles, LA
LEX Lexington, LA
LFT Lafayette, LA
LGA New York, NY (LaGuardia Airport)
LGB Long Beach, CA
LGW London, England (Gatwick Airport)
LHR London, England (Heathrow Airport)

LIM	Lima, Peru
LIT	Little Rock, AR
LMT	Klamath Falls, OR
LPB	LaPaz, Bolivia
LRD	Laredo, TX
LRM	Casa de Campo/LaRomana, Dominican Republic
LSE	Lacrosse, WI
MAD	Madrid, Spain
MAF	Midland/Odessa
MAN	Manchester, England
MAZ	Mayaguez, PR
MCI	Kansas City, MO
MCO	Orlando, FL
MDT	Harrisburg, PA
MEM	Memphis, TN
MEX	Mexico City, Mexico
MFE	McAllen, TX
MGA	Managua, Nicaragua
MGM	Montgomery, AL
MHH	Marsh Harbour, Bahamas
MIA	Miami, FL
MKE	Milwaukee, WI
MKG	Muskegon, MI
MLB	Melbourne, FL
MLI	Moline, IL
MLU	Monroe, LA
MOB	Mobile/Pascagoula, AL
MQT	Marquette, MI
MRY	Monterey, CA
MSN	Madison, WI
MSP	Minneapolis, St. Paul, MN
MSY	New Orleans, LA
MTH	Marathon, FL
MTY	Monterrey, Mexico
MUC	Munich, Germany
MWX	Georgetown, Exuma, Bahamas
MXP	Milan, Italy (Malpensa Airport)
MYR	Myrtle Beach, SC
NAS	Nassau, Bahamas
NRT	Tokyo, Japan (Narita Airport)
OAJ	Jacksonville, NC
OAK	Oakland, CA
OGG	Kahului, Maui Island, HI
OKC	Oklahoma City, OK
OMA	Omaha, NE
ONT	Ontario, CA
ORD	Chicago, IL (O'Hare Airport)
ORF	Norfolk/Virginia Beach, VA
ORY	Paris, France (Orly Airport)
OWB	Owensboro, KY
OXR	Oxnard, CA
PAH	Paducah, KY
PAP	Port au Prince, Haiti
PBI	West Palm Beach, FL
PDX	Portland, OR
PFN	Panama City, FL
PGV	Greenville, NC
PHF	Newport News/Hampton, VA
PLS	Providenciales, Turks & Caicos Islands
POP	Puerto Plata, Dominican Republic
POS	Port of Spain, Tinidad & Tobago
PSP	Palm Springs, CA
PTP	Pointe-a-Pitre, Guadeloupe
PTY	Panama City, Panama
PUJ	Punta Cana, Dominican Republic
PVD	Providence, RI
PVR	Puerto Vallarta, Mexico
RDD	Redding, CA
RDU	Raleigh/Durham, NC
RFD	Rockford, IL
RIC	Richmond, VA
RNO	Reno, NV
ROA	Roanoke, VA
ROC	Rochester, NY
RST	Rochester, MN
RSW	Fort Myers, FL
SAL	San Salvador, El Salvador
SAN	San Diego, CA
SAP	San Pedro Sula, Honduras
SAT	San Antonio, TX
SAV	Savannah, GA
SBA	Santa Barbara, CA
SBN	South Bend, IN
SBP	San Luis Obispo, CA
SCL	Santiago, Chile
SDF	Louisville, KY
SDQ	Santo Domingo, Dominican Republic
SEA	Seattle/Tacoma, WA
SFO	San Francisco, CA
SGF	Springfield, MO
SHV	Shreveport, LA
SJC	San Jose, CA
SJO	San Jose, Costa Rica
SJT	San Angelo, TX
SJU	San Juan, Puerto Rico
SKB	St. Kitts/Nevis, Leeward Islands
SLC	Salt Lake City, UT
SLU	St. Lucia, Windward Island VI
SMF	Sacramento, CA
SMX	Santa Maria, CA
SNA	Orange County, CA
SPI	Springfield, IL
SPS	Wichita Falls, TX
SRQ	Sarasota/Brandenton, FL
STL	St. Louis, MO
STN	London, England (Stansted Airport)
STS	Santa Rosa, CA
STT	St. Thomas, VI
STX	St. Croix, VI
SWF	Newburgh, NY (Stewart Airport)
SXM	St. Maarten, Netherland Antilles
SYR	Syracuse, NY
TCB	Treasure Cay, Bahamas
TCL	Tuscaloosa, AL
TGU	Tegucigalpa, Honduras
PHL	Philadelphia, PA
PHX	Phoenix/Scottsdale, AZ
PIA	Peoria, IL
PIT	Pittsburgh, PA
PNS	Pensacola, FL
TLH	Tallahassee, FL
TOL	Toledo, OH
TPA	Tampa/St. Petersburg, FL
TRI	Tri City Airport, TN
TUL	Tulsa, OK
TUP	Tupelo, MS
TUS	Tucson, AZ
TVC	Traverse City, MI
TXK	Texarkana, AR
TXL	Berlin, Germany
TYR	Tyler, TX
TYS	Knoxville, TN
UIO	Quito, Ecuador
UVF	St. Lucia, Windward Islands (Hewanorra International Airport)
VIS	Visalia, CA
VPS	Ft. Walton, Beach/Destin, FL
VVI	Santa Cruz, Bolivia
YEG	Edmonton, Alberta, Canada
YOW	Ottowa, Ontario, Canada
YUL	Montreal, Quebec, Canada (Dorval Airport)
YWG	Winnipeg, Manitoba, Canada
YVR	Vancouver, British Columbia, Canada
YYC	Calgary, Alberta, Canada
YYZ	Toronto, Ontario, Canada
ZRH	Zurich, Switzerland

BIBLIOGRAPHY

Aerorama, "50th Anniversary of Quad City Airport", Moline, Illinois, 1972.

AFA Flightlog, Association of Flight Attendants (Washington, DC, ALPA and AFL-CIO, winter 1980).

AFA Flightlog, Association of Flight Attendants (Washington, DC, ALPA and AFL-CIO, May 1990).

"A Grass Roots Rooting Section," *OAG Frequent Flyer*, March 1984.

Airliners, A Special Salute to Eastern, World Transport Press, Inc., v. 4 n. 2, Summer 1991.

Airline Stewardess Handbook, Careers Research, Inc., Miami, Florida, 1968.

Allen, C.B., "The Airline Attendant's Job," *Aviation*, April, 1931.

Allen, Oliver E., *The Airline Builders*, TIme-Life Books, Alexandria, VA 1981

American Airlines, *Corporate Communications*, Dallas/Ft.Worth Airport, Texas, n.d.

American Airlines, "They Were A Novelty," *Flagship News*, V 16 n. 5 1983.

Arend, Geoffrey, "Great Airports-Miami," *Air Cargo News*, New York, 1978.

Association of Flight Attendants, "Fifty Years of Flight Attendants," *AFA Flight Log*, Washington, D.C. 1980.

BackChannels, Publication of Army Officers' Wives, Washington, D.C., December 1990.

Bean, Barbara, *Of Magic Sails*, Graphic Alliance, Chicago, Illinois, 1975.

Becker, Ken, "Honored Here: Ellen Church Started It All 50 Years Ago," *Times Plains Dealer*, Cresco, Iowa, 28 May 1980.

Borman, Frank, letter to EAL employees, 19 February 1984.

Bronikowski, Lynn, "Reborn Frontier Takes Off, *Rocky Mountain News,* 6 July 1994.

"A Brief History Of United's Growth From Biplane to Widebody Jets," *United News*

Chatanooga News Sentinal, 20 July 1975.

Collectables Illustrated, January/February 1984.

"Continental's Big Horn Route is Real *Milk Run* Writer Finds," *American Aviation*, 15 November 1943.

"Continental's New Look," *Daily Breeze*, San Francisco, 1 December 1963.

Continental Airlines, *Hostess Traffic Manual*, 1941.

Continental Airlines, "America's Fastest," *The Eagle*, Denver, May 1943.

Cosley, Jerry, "Oldest Stewardess Retires: Ida Staggers Feted by TWA," *TWA Today*, v. 35 n. 15, 1972.

Daily Courier, The, Forest City, North Carolina, 15 April 1984.

Daley, Robert, *An American Saga, Juan Trippe and His Pan American Empire*, Random House, New York, 1980.

Daien, April, "Retired Stewardess Talks About 36 Years of Flying," *Arizona Republic*, 2 August 1972.

Davies, R.E.G., *Delta, An Airline and It's Aircraft*,
Paladwar Press, Miami, Florida 1990.

Delta Air Lines, "Inflight Service," *Delta Digest*, 8 March 1980.

Delta Air Lines, "Mother Mary," *Delta Digest*, April 1972.

Delta Air Lines, "Today's Delta Professional," *Delta Digest*, October 1977.

Eastern Airlines, "Classic Quality," *Eastern Falcon*, n. 5, 1980.

Greer, William, *An Illustrated Guide To The Worlds Airlines*, Arco Publishing, New York, 1982.

Howe, Glenn, *Dinner In The Clouds*, Zeta Publishers, Corona del Mar, California, 1985.

Humbert, Margaret Jo, interview, May 1993.

Imperial Airways, "Channel Crossing Safety Regulations," Amended instructions to Stewards, February, 1930.

"In Flight Reunion,"*TWA, On The Line*, 1988.

"In Flight Service," *TWA, On The Line*, 1989.

Johnson, Robert E., *Airway One, United Airlines*, R.R. Donnelly and Sons, Chicago, 1974.

Klemesrush, Judy, "Stewardess, 1930 Style" *New York Times*, 15 May 1970.

Knoxville News Sentinal, 31 December 1973.

Lubus, Catherine, *Careers As A Flight Attendant*, Rosen Publishing Group, Inc., New York, 1991.

"Mary O'Connor," *United Wilted Wings*, October, 1955, Convention Issue.

Martin, Dick, "Cresco Woman Was World's First Stewardess," *The Telegraph Herald*, Dubuque, Iowa, 24 February 1963.

McFarland, Ruth, TWA, letters to the author, 1993-1994.

Merzer, Martin, "Flight Attendant to V.P.," *Miami Herald*, n.d.

Meyer, Dee, "TWA: 1926-1984," slide show script.

Morton, Alexander Clark, *The 1977-78 Airline Guide To Stewardess and Steward Careers*, Arco Publishing Co. Inc., New York.

Morton, Alexander Clark, *Passenger and Inflight Service, 50th Anniversary of Flight Attendants 1930-1980*,
Miami Springs, Florida.

Nielsen, Georgia Panter, *From Sky Girl to Flight*
Attendant, ILR Press, Cornell University, Ithaca, New

York, 1982.

O'Connor, Mary, personal letters, 1992-1993.

Olderman, Murray, "The Friendly Skies Weren't Always So Friendly," *Rocky Mountain News*, 23 SEptember 1974.

Pan American Empire, Random House, New York, 1980

Pan American World Airways, *The First Fifty Years of Pan American Airways, Inc.*, 1977.

Pan American World Airways, "Where Are They Now," *The Clipper*, November 1982.

Pan American World Airways, "Clipper Fleet-Stewardesses Join Clipper Fleet Flight Crews," *The Clipper*, n.d.

Passenger And Inflight Service, "Pan Am Pioneer Recalls 50 Years," January/February, 1978.

Rogersville Review, Tennessee, 29 October 1992.

Serling, Robert J., *Howard Hughes' Airline*, St. Martins/Marek, New York, 1983.

Six, Robert, speech delivered at CAL 43rd Hostess Reunion, 25 August 1984.

"Spirit of Aloha," *Aloha Airlines Magazine*, July/August 1986.

Staggers, Ida (TWA), letters to author, 1984 & 1992.

Steele, Donna, *Wings of Pride*, Walsworth Publishing, Maceline, Missouri, 1985.

Tanner, Izola Readle, personal interview 20 April 1985, Interview, April 1993.

Taylor, Frank J., *High Horizons*, McGraw-Hill, New York, 1964.*Texas Week, Inc.*, Austin, Texas

Timnick, Lois, "Stewardess Hangs Up Wings at 65," *Los Angeles Times*, 9 September 1983.

Trans World Airlines, "On the Line," *Newsletter of Inflight Services*, v. 1, Janaury 1984.*TWA/St.Louis Weekly*, 26 October 1986.

TWA Today, v.35, 1972.

United Airlines, "Mary O'Connor," *United Airlines News*, n.d.

United Airlines, *The Mainline, The Story of United Airlines*, United States.

United Airlines, *The Friendly Skies*, United States, 1980.

United Airlines' Stewardess Manual, 1946.

United Clipped Wings Quarterly, v. 38 n. 3, Spring 1988.

United Clipped Wings Quarterly, v. 43 n. 3, Spring 1993.

United Times, v. 2 n. 17, December 1989.

United Times, v. 6 n. 6, July 1993.

United Times, v. 6 n. 7, August 1993.

Wall, Robert, *Airliners*, Prentice-Hall, Englewood Cliffs, New Jersey, 1980.

Walters, Brian, *The Illustrated History of Air Travel*, Crescent Books, New York, 1978.

Warren, Jane Sullivan (American Airlines), telephone interview, April 1984.

Wolfe, Vicky Cole, letters to the author, 1984 & 1993.

Young, Vicy Morris, *United Airlines 1930s Manual*, United Clipped Wings Archives.

United honored its "Original Eight" stewardesses in 1975 by naming a B-747 after them. The remaining five stewardesses are shown chritening the aircraft with champagne. (United Airlines Photo)

HISTORY TAKES FLIGHT

Continental Airlines Celebrated 60 Years On July 15, 1994 At El Paso, Texas

On July 15, 1934, Jesse Hart was the pilot on a Lockheed Vega aircraft that flew its first flight for Varney Speed Lines' Southwest Division. The four passenger Vega carried mostly mail for El Paso, Texas, with stops at Albuquerque, Santa Fe and Las Vegas, New Mexico to Pueblo, Colorado. Don Davis, now a retired Continental employee was the only passenger on a short leg of that first flight.

Varney Speed Lines founded in 1934 by Walter T. Varney transported nine passengers and mail during its first two weeks of operation. In 1937, Robert F. Six became the President of the airline and renamed it Continental because the route paralleled the Continental Divide.

Continental's Director of Communications, Ray Scippa, and Marketing Director, George Igo, planned and hosted the 60th Celebration party at the El Paso International Airport held on Friday, July 15, 1994. The open house was festive. The public was welcome and entire families were there, as well as Continental's retired and present employees, press photographers, and El Paso's Shriners and civic dignitaries.

Cakes colorfully decorated with Continental's different logos of the decades were displayed and later served with soft drinks by Continental employees to everyone present. Balloons, confetti and clowns entertained both adults and children at the festivities.

Continental's refurbished historical 24 passenger DC-3 had been flown from Dallas on July 14 and was on display on the nearby ramp. During the day rides were given on the DC-3 for a contribution of $10 per person which went to the Shriners' Medical Transport Unit, (which provides transportation to burn centers for critically burned children). El Paso's Shriners monitored the rides.

The Continental Historical DC-3 travels with a crew of three of Continental's current Captains. A thirty-five year veteran, James Minor, is the chief pilot; Timothy Ruhl is the co-pilot; and Joe Bowyer acts as both a pilot and as a licensed mechanic for the DC-3.

Recently retired American Airline flight attendant, Sherrill Dickey, is the Historical DC-3 Inflight Manager and is in charge of the DC-3's hostess service. She wore a vintage 1958 summer beige Continental uniform and baret style cap. She was assisted by two of Continental's international flight attendants who are currently based in Houston and were specially selected for the commemorative flight celebration. Jennifer Dement, a pretty, petite blond and tall, elegant Valerie Vologna both wore authentic medium blue 1952 uniforms furnished by former hostesses of Continental's Dallas Golden Penguins. White gloves, navy and white spectator pumps and authentic Thunderbird hat crests and wings of the 1940-1950 decades complimented each uniform.

Speeches were given by Continental's corporate hosts and El Paso dignitaries before Captain James Minor cut the ribbon for the commemorative flight. The first flight would duplicate Varney Speed Lines' route to Pueblo, Colorado with stops and receptions at Albuquerque, Santa Fe and Pueblo. The stop at Las Vegas was to drop off a mail bag.

Passengers on board the DC-3 included Director of Communication, Ray Scippa, and other invited retired and current Continental employees, the media, photographers, (including *Time-Life*) and editors of travel publications. Former Continental hostess Marilyn Muncy Walker who was based in El Paso from 1956 to 1958 was a guest. It was her original 1958 uniform that was worn by Sherrill Dickey. Marilyn is an active member and a former President of the Dallas chapter of Continental's Golden Penguins. She has worked previous flights on the historical DC-3 and also is a tour guide at the Dallas Pioneer Museum of Flight. She was chairman for the 50th anniversary of Continental's inflight service held in Dallas October 2-5, 1992. Continental also helped with the anniversary celebration.

I was honored as an aviation author, aviation historian of inflight service, and former (early 1940s) Continental hostess. What a thrill for me, as well as the many other people who not only saw the DC-3 but also had the opportunity to take a ride for a donation of $10 for a worthy cause, to take a step in a time capsule of flight.

Continental flight attendants in rear of the DC-3 on the July 15th, 1994 Commemorative flight El Paso to Pueblo.

Jennifer Dement, Sherrill Dickey and Valerie Vologna model vintage Continental Airlines hostess uniforms, circa 1952-58, on the ramp in Albuquerque, N.M. with Continental's restored DC-3. On July 15, 1994, these three hostesses helped re-create a moment in time to mark the 60th anniversary of Varney Speed Lines' (re-named Continental Airlines in 1937) original mail route from El Paso, Texas to Pueblo, Colorado on the same date in 1934. Dement and Vologna are currently Houston-based international flight attendants for Continental. Dickey worked as a flight attendant for eight years and now manages the Inflight portion of Continental's DC-3 program. (photo by Jim Thompson for *The Albuquerque Journal*)

Sherrill Dickey recently retired as an American Airlines' flight attendant 1992-1994. She was first a flight attendant for Continental 1984-1992. She is the Manager of DC-3 Inflight for Continental's Historical Society. This is a position she had previously held along with a regular flying schedule with Continental before joining American.

Sherrill has kept her maiden name although married to Continental Captain James Minor.

Captain Minor was selected by Continental to locate a DC-3 to refurbish for Continental's Historical Society. The DC-3 was first NC25673 and delivered to American Airlines on May 8, 1940. It became Fleet #73: "Flagship Big Springs." It was later sold to: Trans-Texas Airlines, Provincetown-Boston Airlines and now is Continentals Historical DC-3. (The Stapleton Innerline-Lance Ross)

Capt. James F. Minor, whose 35-year career as a pilot began with flying this very DC-3(N25673) in 1959, was honored to fly as Pilot in Command for Continental Airlines' historic re-enactment flight July 15, 1994. Minor manages the fully restored DC-3, which Continental uses for historic events, company promotions, charity fund-raisers and inauguration of Continental service to new markets. (photo by Debra Shore of The Portrait Studio, Dallas)

Nostalgia

The legacy of commercial aviation growth has always been of interest to the American public. As we approach the year 2,000, Americans are becoming more aware of the aviation history of the past century thanks to the efforts of: our nation's space program; our air and space museums; books; aviation historians and collectors; the media's special programs honoring the 50th anniversary of the DC-3; as well as the airlines celebrating their own anniversaries of their first inflight service.

The traveling public is being treated to the presence on flights of many flight attendants that have flown over forty years.

Airlines' retired employees have also become interested in preserving the aircraft of the past, such as the Boeing-247; DC-3; Lockheed-Constellation; Martin-404; and the Vicker's Viscount.

The Capital Airlines' Association boasts over 2,000 active members. It has an annual September picnic held in Washington, DC. They are involved in funding the restoration of a Vicker's-Viscount.

TWA's SAVE A CONNIE's organization has it's headquarters and museum in Kansas City. The organization has restored both a Lockheed-Constellation and a Martin-404. These beautiful aircraft are flown to airshows and displayed for the public to see. Retired TWA crew members explain about the operation and service to TWA of each of the aircraft.

Continental Airlines Historical Society has restored a DC-3. The aircraft is used for promotional flights and is frequently on display at airshows throughout the U.SA.

Boeing Aircraft's Museum of Flight in Seattle, Washington displays a restored Boeing-247. The aircraft was located in a dump where it had been junked. It has been restored to all of its original 1930s splendor as a member of the United Air Transport fleet (that became United Airlines).

The recently formed United Airline Historical Society has as it's President, former Captain Don Toeppen. Their organiza-

TWA's Martin-404

TWA's Ona Gieschen is shown in the center (in a serving smock). Ona retired in 1988 after 42 years as a flight attendant for TWA. She is a curator at TWA's SAVE A CONNIE MUSEUM in Kansas City.

Dorothy Crowley Bledsoe, SEA past Nat. Pres., lends a helping hand to Edward Carlson, C.W. Honorary Member and Chrm. of Board of UAL, Inc. Standing by are current UAL flight attendants, Toosje Maaskant, Peggy Verger and Marilyn Chishold. The airplane is a 80-A, one of the "Original Eight" flew on, found in the city dump in Anchorage, Alaska by Bob Reeves, Pres. of Reeves Aleutian Airlines. A friend of Reeves, UAL Captain Jack Leffler was instrumental in getting the plane donated to the Pacific Museum of Flight in SEA. Completely restored by the Boeing Management Assoc., it was on display in SEA for the week of activities celebrating the 50th Anniversary of Inflight Service 1980.

WEARING ANGEL'S WINGS

IN MEMORY OF:

PAN AMs'
Elaine Sweiner Lee
(1991)

TWAs'
Ida Staggers
January 11, 1993

United and Americans'
Harriett Heffron Gleeson -
September 12, 1993

Uniteds'
Mary O'Connor
April 12, 1994

The omega — but only for a moment — history has wings.